CORTINA METHOD

CONVERSATIONAL
GERMAN
IN 20 LESSONS

Other Cortina Language Books

Spanish in 20 Lessons
French in 20 Lessons
German in 20 Lessons
Italian in 20 Lessons
Russian in 20 Lessons
Modern Greek in 20 Lessons
Inglés en 20 Lecciones
Francés en 20 Lecciones
Inglês em 20 Lições
American English in 20 Lessons
Conversational Brazilian Portuguese
Brazilian-Portuguese Conversation Course
Conversational Japanese
Spanish Conversational Guide
Spanish in Spanish
Français en Français
English in English
Deutsch auf Deutsch
Italiano in Italiano

CORTINA METHOD

CONVERSATIONAL
GERMAN
IN 20 LESSONS

ILLUSTRATED

Intended for self-study and for use in schools

With a Simplified System of Phonetic Pronunciation

Based on the Method of

R. DIEZ DE LA CORTINA

UNIVERSITIES OF MADRID AND BORDEAUX
AUTHOR OF THE CORTINA METHOD
ORIGINATOR OF THE PHONOGRAPHIC METHOD OF
TEACHING LANGUAGES.

By

EVA C. LANGE, Ph.D.

ASSISTANT PROFESSOR,
ST. JOSEPH'S COLLEGE FOR WOMEN, BROOKLYN
LECTURER, HUNTER COLLEGE OF
THE CITY OF NEW YORK

An Owl Book

HENRY HOLT AND COMPANY
New York

CORTINA LEARNING INTERNATIONAL, INC.
Publishers • WESTPORT, CT 06880

Cataloging Information

Cortina Method German in 20 Lessons, intended for self-study and for use in
 schools; with a simplified system of phonetic pronunciation, by Eva C.
 Lange, based on the method of R. Diez de la Cortina. New York, R. D.
 Cortina Co., 1977.
 360 p. illus. 21 cm.

 1. German language—Conversation and phrase books. 2. German
language—Grammar. I. Title.
PF3111.L24 1977   438.242   54-14375
ISBN 0-8327-0004-5 (hardbound)
ISBN 0-8327-0012-6 (paperback)

Printed in the United States of America
HH Editions 9 8 7 6 5   9702-5M

Introduction

How a Knowledge of German Can Help You

ALERT AMERICANS and other English-speaking people are once again learning German and are rapidly restoring it to its former position as one of the most studied of foreign languages. There are many reasons for the revival of interest in this useful and expressive tongue.

Germany, Austria, and the other German-speaking countries of Central Europe offer many tempting rewards for the traveler. The great cities—Berlin, Munich, Vienna—with their historical buildings, fascinating history, taste-tempting restaurants, and the enchanting country of the Rhine, the Black Forest, the Alps make a visit to these lands a cherished memory. And when you visit them, you will find your knowledge of the native tongue a source of unending satisfaction and pleasure. You will be able to become more intimate with the German-speaking people and you will be welcomed as a cultured friend, not merely as a tourist. You will be invited into their homes. And, on the practical side, you will find also that your knowledge of German will save you money when you deal with tradespeople, hotel keepers, ticket sellers, etc.

German has always been a language of art and culture—of poetry, of fiction, of philosophy, and opera. Many of the masterpieces of world literature were written in German—Goethe's *Faust,* Schiller's dramas, Heine's lyric poems, the philosophical works of Kant, Schopenhauer, Hegel, and Nietzsche, to mention only a few. In addition to these classics, modern writers have produced many works in German which make fascinating reading—Thomas Mann, Stefan and Arnold Zweig, Gerhart Hauptmann, Arthur Schnitzler, Jakob Wassermann, Franz Kafka, and others. With a knowledge of German many hours of pleasure will be in store for you as you read these great writings, old and new, 'in the full flavor of their original language.

German opera too boasts many fine masterpieces, and an understanding of the language in which they were composed and are performed will add a new dimension of pleasure when you hear such works as Richard Wagner's *Die Walküre, Götterdämmerung, Tristan und Isolde, Lohengrin, Die Meistersinger;* Mozart's *Magic Flute (Die Zauberflöte);* Beethoven's *Fidelio;* Johann Strauss' *Die Fledermaus.* And in the concert hall too knowing the meaning of the lyrics of the great German *lieder* will broaden your appreciation of the music.

One should not forget also that Germany is quickly resuming its former importance as a commercial country. More and more people in the English-speaking world are having business dealings with Germany. German products—machines, automobiles, toys, scientific instruments—are finding their way into other countries, and Germany in turn is buying goods for import. Knowing how to deal with Germans in their native language is a decided advantage for businessmen and others who have commercial relations with Germany.

And if you work in industry or science, you will know how important German is as a technical language. Workers in these fields as well as in medicine, biology and related fields are constantly confronted with scientific and technical developments in Germany, Switzerland and Austria. It goes without saying that an ability to read the original papers and journals will be of infinitely greater benefit than the brief and incomplete abstracts which are sometimes available in English.

In short, your study of German will bring you many hours of pleasure in your cultural pursuits and will also have numerous practical advantages.

Preface

IN 1882, THE CORTINA ACADEMY OF LANGUAGES was founded in the United States by Count Cortina. Besides engaging professors for all the modern languages (French, Spanish, German, Italian, Portuguese and English) Count Cortina himself gave language instruction for many years. From this actual teaching experience, Professor Cortina developed a new simplified method that became an instant success. It has never been surpassed since. For more than 90 years the method has been constantly refined and improved from the Academy's long experience in teaching languages, and in terms of the changing needs of the present-day language student. It is now known all over the world as THE CORTINA METHOD.

Because of the success of and the demand for Cortina instruction from students who could not attend classes, the Academy was forced to publish Cortina lessons in book form. Well over two million Cortina language books have been sold, and they are a clear testimonial to the ease with which students have learned a new language through THE CORTINA METHOD.

Many thousands of students have learned a new language by this method at home, in their spare time. Many others have used THE CORTINA METHOD in schools and colleges throughout the United States and South America.

You may ask: "What is the secret of THE CORTINA METHOD's success? How is it different from other ways to learn a language?" One of the main reasons is that the lessons are devoted to everyday topics which encourage the student to learn. The lessons begin with subjects that we all used as children when we learned our native tongue. For instance, right from the start, the first lessons teach you the same words that a child first speaks: *Mother, father, brother, sister,* as well as everyday words relating to meals, drinks, clothing, and so on. These words are easily put to use at once and are much more interesting than the abstract and academic words a student is usually asked to learn. Knowing that he can put these words to immediate use adds color and excitement to language study and keeps the interest of the student at a high level throughout his language-learning experience.

Two Useful Features

The Editors have included two new features in this edition which will also be found of great help to the student:

First, the format of the lessons has been arranged to allow for the inclusion of carefully chosen illustrations. The drawings have been arranged to highlight the subject matter of the lessons and thus will greatly aid the student in memorizing the foreign words through the graphic representation.

Second, a complete REFERENCE GRAMMAR has been appended at the back of the book so that the student may refer to any part of speech he wishes as he advances in his studies. The necessary grammar for the lessons is included in the footnotes, lesson by lesson, for the student's convenience.

In addition, practical bi-lingual dictionaries have been included which contain not only all of the words of the twenty lessons but also many other useful words as well.

How To Study

Language is habit. We are constantly expressing thoughts and ideas in speech, from habit, without paying any particular attention to the words, phrases, or idioms we use. When we say *"How do you do," "It's fine today," "I've had a wonderful trip,"* we do so spontaneously. We are merely repeating a speech pattern we have used so many times before that it has become automatic—a habit. Repetition, therefore, is the basis of language learning; and consequently it is extremely important that the student acquire the correct German pronunciation at the very beginning so that he learns the right speech habits.

For this purpose a basic feature of the CORTINA METHOD is the emphasis on *speaking* the language. At the outset we provide a GUIDE TO GERMAN PRONUNCIATION. It explains how to pronounce German sounds, words, and phrases through simple phonetic symbols based on English spelling, with special explanations of how to articulate those sounds which occur only in the German language. In Lessons 1-16 the entire German vocabularies and conversations are transcribed in these symbols. Using them as a guide, the student will be able to read each entire lesson aloud, and he should do so as many times as necessary to be able to read the German text aloud easily and correctly. Through this practice, not only will the student attain fluency, but he will eventually be able to express his ideas in German just as easily and effortlessly as he does in English.

LESSON ARRANGEMENT. The lessons are arranged so that the student can follow them easily. For each of the first sixteen lessons there is (a) a vocabulary of important words of a general character, (b) a specific vocabulary covering the topic of the lesson, and (c) dialogues showing how these vocabularies are used in everyday conversation. To the right of each word or sentence is given the phonetic spelling so that the student can pronounce them correctly, and in the next column is given the English translation of the German text.

The student should start each lesson by memorizing as much of the general vocabulary as possible. Then, in turning to the conversation that follows, he will complete his mastery of these words by actually using them *to express ideas.* The conversational sentences should be read, making general reference to the translation of each sentence. *Learn* the thoughts that the German sentence conveys

5

rather than a word-for-word translation. The lesson has been mastered when the student can read the lesson aloud without reference to either the PRONUNCIATION or TRANSLATION columns.

The best way to express your thoughts in your new language is to try to use the basic speech patterns illustrated by the sentences of the lessons with a few variations as, for example, substituting one verbal form for another, and one noun for another, etc. Try also to imagine true-to-life situations and the way you would react to them conversationally, but don't try to learn too many basic speech patterns at once. Try to digest and master a few at a time.

Don't be afraid of making mistakes! It is only natural to make errors in spelling and grammar when you write down your translations. Your mistakes are really of great value to you, because they reveal your weak spots. Then you can eliminate them by consulting the grammar section and, of course, the spelling in the book. In this way, you see that when you are in doubt, it is actually of greater benefit to you to *guess wrong* than to *guess right*—because in the latter case you may not know *why* your solution is correct.

As you proceed from lesson to lesson, don't neglect to review, review, *and review again* the material of the previous lessons. Constant review and repetition will not only help you to retain what you have learned, but will also give you an ever firmer grasp of the language, enabling you at the end to use it spontaneously.

The last four lessons differ in form. On the assumption that the student has mastered the basic elements of German, they consist of dialogues (with footnotes) centering around topics of cultural, historical, and practical interest. All the words used are given in the GERMAN-ENGLISH DICTIONARY in the back of the book.

The grammatical explanations in the FOOTNOTES are of great importance to the student and close attention should be paid to them. They also clear up many of the idiomatic difficulties and are very helpful because they give other illustrations of the language in actual use. For more elaborate grammatical explanation of any particular lesson the student can refer to the PLAN FOR STUDY which precedes the complete REFERENCE GRAMMAR.

Remember that there is no better way to learn a language than the way children learn—by speaking it. The CORTINA METHOD is based upon this principle with necessary modifications to adjust this natural method to the adult mind. With a little application you will have a lot of fun learning this way. What a satisfaction it will be to have *this important second language* at your command!

Table of
Contents

Vocabularies and Conversations

7

Dialogues

REFERENCE
GRAMMAR

THE ARTICLE

THE NOUN

---

* § is the symbol for paragraph.

THE PRONOUN

THE PREPOSITION

THE ADJECTIVE

THE ADVERB

THE CONJUNCTION

THE VERB

Dictionaries

GUIDE TO

German Pronunciation

Part I

GERMAN IS A highly phonetic language; that is, every word is usually pronounced as it is spelled. With a few exceptions, there are no mute letters in German. Every sound has its fixed symbol and there are just a few simple basic rules which will help you to pronounce the vowels correctly as clear sounds.

In indicating the pronunciation of German words in this book, we use a simplified scheme based, insofar as possible, on common English sounds. Syllable divisions are indicated by a hyphen (-) and accented syllables are followed by an apostrophe ('); thus, in the word *lesen,* meaning "to read," the accent would fall on the first syllable, as indicated in lay'-zĕn. This phonetic transcription of sounds should be carefully studied and the formation of each sound should be practiced until it is thoroughly mastered.

VOWELS

All German vowels are pure, single vowels; for example, the *a* in *Vater* (fah'-tĕr) father, is like the *a* in the English "father" and not like the *a* in the English word "made," which, in English, is pronounced like a diphthong. Similarly, the *o* in *Globus* (gloh'-bus) is a pure *o*, without the following *u* sound as in English.

Be careful in speaking German to avoid pronouncing single vowels like diphthongs. Make long vowels much longer and short vowels shorter than in English.

15

German Spelling	German Example	Sound	Phonetic Symbol
a (short)[1]	Mann (man) man	Like the a in sofa, but make sound shorter and fuller than in English.	a
a (long), written also aa, ah	Vater (fah'-tĕr) father Saal (zahl) hall mahnen (mah'-nĕn) to warn	Like the a in father. Open mouth wide when saying.	ah
e (short)	Bett (bet) bed	Like the e in met.	e
e (long), written also ee, eh	lesen (lay'-zĕn) to read See (zay) sea geht (gayt) goes	Like the ay in day, but draw corners of lips farther back than in English, without making sound a diphthong.	ay[2]
e (unaccented)[3]	Vater (fah'-tĕr) father beginnen (bĕ-gi'-nĕn) to begin	Like the e in father. Short, weak, and slurred. Appears only in unaccented syllables.	ĕ
i (short)[4]	bitte (bi'-tĕ) please	Like the i in fit.	i
i (long), written also ie,[5] ih, ieh	Maschine (ma-shee'-nĕ) machine sie (zee) she ihre (ee'-rĕ) her zieht (tseet) pulls	Like the ee in tree, but draw corners of mouth farther back than in English; clear ee sound.	ee
o (short)	oft (oft) often	Like the o in obey. Round lips; produce a quick, short, clear o.	o

---

[1] Do not confuse this sound with the short a in English as in "man," which is not a pure a sound but intermediate between a and e. Simply shorten the vowel a in "father," but open your mouth less widely.

[2] Be very careful in making this sound. The ay is just an approximate sound. Pronounce only the first part; avoid the slide as in English to ee sound.

[3] This rather weak and slurred German e sound appears only in unaccented syllables, in the endings el, em, en, er, etc. and in the prefixes be and ge. No other German vowel loses its clear, definite sound value in an unaccented syllable.

[4] This sound is to be pronounced distinctly even in unaccented syllables: wenig (vay'-nich) little.

[5] In foreign words derived from Latin, however, each vowel in the combination ie is pronounced separately: Familie (fa-mee'-liĕ) family; italienisch (ee-tah-liay'-nish) Italian.

GERMAN SPELLING	GERMAN EXAMPLE	SOUND	PHONETIC SYMBOL
o (long), written also *oo, oh*	**Rose** (roh'-zĕ) rose **Boot** (boht) boat **hohl** (hohl) hollow	Like the *o* in *rose,* but round lips farther; produce a long, pure sound; don't drawl it to *o*ᵘ.	**oh**
u (short)	**Mutter** (mu'-tĕr) mother	Like the *u* in *put.* Protrude and round lips; make it a pure *u* in German.	**u**
u (long), written also *uh*	**du** (doo) thou, you **Uhr** (oor) clock	Like the *oo* in *food,* but lips more protruded and rounded; clear sound.	**oo**
y	**Typistin** (ti-pee'-stin) typist **Typus** (ti'-pus) type	Usually like the German short *i;* see p. 16.	**i**

MODIFIED VOWELS (UMLAUT)

The umlaut (¨) may be placed over the letters ä, ö, ü, and when used changes the pronunciation of these vowels.

GERMAN SPELLING	GERMAN EXAMPLE	SOUND	PHONETIC SYMBOL
ä (short)	**Lämmer** (le'-mĕr) lambs	No difference between short German *e* and *ä.*	**e**
ä (long), written also *äh*	**Däne** (day'-nĕ) Dane **mähen** (may'-ĕn) to mow	Like the *a* in *fare.* No difference between long *e* and long *ä,* but without *ee* slide at the end.	**ay**
short *ö*	**Hölle** (hö'-lĕ) hell	No English equivalent. Round lips as for *o,* then try to pronounce *ee.*	**ö**
ö (long,) written also *öh*	**Römer** (röh'-mĕr) Roman **Höhle** (höh'-lĕ) hollow	Same as above but longer; protrude lips much more. Like French *eu.*	**öh**
ü (short)	**Mütter** (mü'-tĕr) mothers	No English equivalent; like French *u.* Round the lips as for *o,* then try to pronounce short *i.*	**ü**
ü (long), written also *üh*	**über** (üh'-bĕr) above **Mühe** (müh'-ĕ) effort	Same as above but longer	**üh**

DIPHTHONGS

A diphthong is a combination of vowel sounds pronounced as one
unit. A diphthong in German always has two vowels (written in
two letters); for example, *Wein* (vīn) wine; *Haus* (hows) house; *Leute*
(loi'-tĕ) people. All German diphthongs are sounded slightly shorter
than English diphthongs.

GERMAN SPELLING	GERMAN EXAMPLE	SOUND	PHONETIC SYMBOL
ei,⁶ written also *ey*,⁷	ein (īn) a Meyer (mī'-ĕr) proper name	Like the *i* in *mine*.	ī
ai, ay	Mai (mī) May Bayern (bī'-ĕrn) Bavaria		
au	Haus (hows) house	Like the *ow* in *cow*, but less drawled.	ow
eu, written also *äu*	heute (hoi'-tĕ) today Häuser (hoi'-zĕr) houses	Like the *oi* in *oil*.	oi

CONSONANTS

Most German consonants are similar to their English equivalents.
They are, however, more explosive and aspirated. The German *p*,
t, *k*, especially, are much more explosive and aspirated than the
English *p*, *t*, *k*.

Double consonants are pronounced like the corresponding single
consonants. They only indicate that the preceding vowel is short:
Mutter (mu'-tĕr) mother.

Except between two vowels, *b, d, g* at the end of a word or syllable
are pronounced as *p, t, k,* but the original spelling is retained:
Tag (tahk) day; *Kind* (kint) child; *lobten* (lohp'-ten) praised.

GERMAN SPELLING	GERMAN EXAMPLE	SOUND	PHONETIC SYMBOL
b (initial)	beten (bay'-tĕn) to pray	At the beginning of a syllable, like English *b*.	b

---

⁶Remember and learn to distinguish from the start: the combination *ei* is a
diphthong: *ein* (in) a. *ie* is *never* a diphthong, but a long *ee*: *Sie* (zee) you; *viel*
(feel) many.

⁷*ey* is used only in proper names.

GERMAN SPELLING	GERMAN EXAMPLE	SOUND	PHONETIC SYMBOL
b (final)	**gab** (gahp) gave	At the end of a word and before *st* and *t*, pronounce like English *p*.	**p**
c[8]	**Caesar** (tsay'-zahr) Caesar	Like *ts* in *bits*. Press tongue against teeth; produce sharp hissing sound.	**ts**
	Cassius (ka'-sius) Cassius	Like *k* as in *king*.	**k**
ch[9]	**ich** (ich) I	No English equivalent; nearest approximation the *h* in *hue, humor*, but more strongly aspirated.	***ch***
ch[9]	**ach** (akh) Ah!	No English equivalent; the same as *ch* in Scotch "lo*ch*". Peculiar guttural sound made by humping the tongue at the back of the mouth, as if to say *k*, but not quite closing the opening, so that a throat-clearing sound is made.	**kh**
ch	**charmant** (shar-mant') charming	Pronounced like the *sh* in *push* in some foreign words.	**sh**
d (initial)	**da** (dah) there	At the beginning of a syllable like English *d*, but touch the back of upper teeth with tongue.	**d**
d (final)	**Kind** (kint) child	At the end of a word or of a syllable, like English *t*.[10]	**t**

---

[8]*c* is found only in foreign words or names and in combinations, such as *ch, ck*, forming new consonants. Pronounce *c* as *ts* before *ä, e, i* and *y*. Pronounce *c* as *k* before other sounds.

[9]There are two pronunciations of the *ch* consonant combination: 1. as *kh* following *a, o, u, au;* that is, after vowels formed in the back of the mouth. 2.

German Spelling	German Example	Sound	Phonetic Symbol
f	finden (fin'-děn) to find	Like English f.	f
g (initial)	gehen (gay'-ěn) to go	At the beginning of a word or syllable, like the English g of go.	g
g (final)[11]	Tag (tahk) day	At the end of a word or syllable, like k, but more aspirated than in English.	k
h	haben (hah'-běn) to have Schönheit (shöhn'-hīt) beauty	As in English, but pronounced only at the beginning of a word or a syllable.	h
h	geht (gayt) goes	Silent when in the middle of a word.	—
j[12]	ja (yah) yes	Like English y in yes.	y
k (written also ck[13])	Kind (kint) child Ecke (e'-kě) corner	As in English.	k
l	lang (lang) long	Approximately like English l. Tip of tongue pressed against upper teeth; back of tongue flat; not arched as in English; never silent as in English calm.	l
m	mein (mīn) my	As in English.	m
n	nein (nīn) no die Bank (bangk) bench	As in English. As in English, before k.	n ng

---

as ch following i, e, ä, ö, ü, ei, äu, eu, and r, l, m, n; that is, after vowels and consonants formed in the front of the mouth; kh is a guttural or harsh sound; ch is a softer sound, formed in the front part of the mouth.

[10]A similar development is seen in English in the past tense of some verbs; for example, "dreamed" is now "dreamt". The d in pronunciation has hardened to t, but unlike German, the spelling has also changed.

[11]Suffix ig in final position is pronounced as ch: König (köh'-nich) king. However, ig in medial position is pronounced g: Königin (köh'-ni-geen) queen.

[12]In foreign words, j is pronounced like the s in "pleasure": ex. Journalist (zhur-na-list') journalist.

[13]This ck stands for double k (kk) and, therefore, shortens the preceding vowel.

GERMAN SPELLING	GERMAN EXAMPLE	SOUND	PHONETIC SYMBOL
p	Pass (pas) passport	More aspirated than in English.	p
qu	Qual (kvahl) torture	No exact equivalent; similar to *qu* in *quiver*. Merging *k* + *v*, not *k* + *w* as in English; *v* must be heard. *k* + *v* = *kv*.	kv
r[14]	Rose (roh'-zĕ) rose	No exact equivalent in English. 1. Trilled *r*: raise the tip of the tongue against the top of the mouth, vibrate it rapidly (tongue-tip *r*). 2. Uvular or guttural *r*, similar to the sound uttered when gargling. *r* is never slurred as in English, but is less conspicuous in the suffix *er*.	r
s, in initial position and before vowels	sagen (zah'-gĕn) to say Rose (roh'-zĕ) rose Else (el'-zĕ) Elsie	Like English *z*.	z
s (final); *s* (double)	Glas (glahs) glass Gasse (ga'-sĕ) street Fuss (foos) foot	Like *s* in *sit*.	s
t	tun (toon) to do	Like English *t*.	t
v[15]	Vater (fah'-tĕr) father	Like English *f*.	f
w	Wein (vīn) wine	Like English *v*.	v
x	Hexe (he'-ksĕ) witch	English *ks* sound.	ks

---

[14]Both the trilled *r* and the uvular or guttural *r* are found in Germany. The trilled *r* is less common but is the accepted pronunciation for the stage and for singing.

[15]In many foreign words, however, *v* is pronounced like the English *v* (German *w*): *November* (noh-vem'-ber) November.

GERMAN SPELLING	GERMAN EXAMPLE	SOUND	PHONETIC SYMBOL
z	Zimmer (tsi'-měr) room	Sharp explosive sound in German; exaggerate rather than make it too soft.	ts
	BUT: Salz (sals) salt ganz (gans) entirely	The nature of the preceding liquid consonants, *l* and *n*, cause the *z* in these combinations to be pronounced *s* as in *sit*.	s

Consonant Combinations

GERMAN SPELLING	GERMAN EXAMPLE	SOUND	PHONETIC SYMBOL
chs	sechs (zeks) six	Like *x* in *six*.	ks
dt	Stadt (shtat) city	Like English *t*.	t
ng	Singer (zing'-ěr) singer	The *g* is not sounded separately.	ng
pf	Pferd (pfayrt) horse	Like *pf* in *helpful*, but more like one sound than in English. Both consonants must be heard.	pf
ph[16]	Philosophie (fee-loh-zoh-fee') philosophy	Like English *f*.	f
ps[16]	Psalm (psalm) psalm	Like *ps* in *rhapsody*. *ps* in German is also pronounced at the beginning of words.	ps
sch	Schiff (shif) ship	Like English *sh*.	sh
sp	sprechen (shpre'-chěn) to speak	At the beginning of a word, pronounce as *shp*.	shp
sp	Knospe (kno'-spě) bud	Pronounced like English *sp* within or at the end of a word.	sp

[16]These special consonant combinations are used only in foreign words, derived from the Greek.

GERMAN SPELLING	GERMAN EXAMPLE	SOUND	PHONETIC SYMBOL
st[17]	Stein (shtīn) stone	At the beginning of a word, pronounce as *sht*.	sht
st	Laster (la'-stĕr) vice erst (ayrst) first	Pronounced like English *st* within or at the end of a word.	st
th	Thron (trohn) throne	Never like the English *th* as in *thing* or *this*, but like *t* as in *top*.	t
tion[18]	Nation (nah-tsion') nation	Sharp *ts*, not *sh*.	tsion
tz	Hitze (hi'-tsĕ) heat	Always like *ts* as in *cats*.	ts

THE GERMAN ALPHABET

The symbols for the German alphabet most commonly used today are the same as those used in English. However, until quite recently, a somewhat different letter style, called Gothic, was the standard for German. Although there has been a tendency for Gothic to give way to the Latin alphabet, we reproduce both here for reference purposes.

LATIN ALPHABET		NAME OF LETTER	GOTHIC ALPHABET	
A	a	*ah*	𝔄	𝔞
B	b	*bay*	𝔅	𝔟
C	c	*tsay*	ℭ	𝔠
D	d	*day*	𝔇	𝔡
E	e	*ay*	𝔈	𝔢
F	f	*ef*	𝔉	𝔣
G	g	*gay*	𝔊	𝔤
H	h	*hah*	ℌ	𝔥
I	i	*ee*	ℑ	𝔦

[17]In a few words which have not become Germanized, *st* at the beginning of a word is pronounced *st* just as it is in English, as in *Stenographie* (stay-noh-grah-fee') stenography.

[18]This special consonant combination is used only in foreign words derived from the French.

LATIN ALPHABET		NAME OF LETTER	GOTHIC ALPHABET	
J	j	*yot*	ℑ	i
K	k	*kah*	ℜ	ℓ
L	l	*el*	ℒ	l
M	m	*em*	𝔐	m
N	n	*en*	𝔑	n
O	o	*oh*	𝔒	o
P	p	*pay*	𝔓	p
Q	q	*koo*	𝔔	q
R	r	*er*	ℜ	r
S	s	*es*	𝔖	s
T	t	*tay*	𝔗	t
U	u	*oo*	𝔘	u
V	v	*fow*	𝔙	v
W	w	*vay*	𝔚	w
X	x	*iks*	𝔛	x
Y	y	*ipsilon*	𝔜	y
Z	z	*tset*	ℨ	z

In addition to these letters, there are a few special letters and letter combinations:

s	ſ
ss	ſſ
ss	ß
ck	ck
ch	ch
tz	tz

GERMAN IN 20 LESSONS

Vocabularies and
Conversations

Erste Lektion

Neue Wörter für diese Lektion

NEW WORDS FOR THIS LESSON   (noi'-ĕ vör'-tĕr führ dee'-zĕ lek-tsiohn')

sprechen[1] (shpre'-*ch*ĕn)	to speak	bitte (bi'-tĕ)	please
er spricht (ayr shpri*ch*t)	he speaks	müssen (mü'-sĕn)	must
ich spreche (*ich* shpre'-*ch*ĕ)	I speak	nicht wahr? (ni*ch*t vahr)	isn't it so?

ich möchte (*ich* mö*ch*'-tĕ)	I should like
der Herr (dayr her)	the master, gentleman, Mister
der[2] Dampfer (dayr dam'-pfĕr)	the steamer
die[2] Eisenbahn (dee ī'-zĕn-bahn)	the railroad
das Flugzeug[2] (das flook'-tsoik)	the airplane
auf Wiedersehen (owf vee'-dĕr-zayn)	good-bye

ernst (ernst)	serious	jetzt (yetst)	now	nach (nahkh)	to, after
heute (hoi'-tĕ)	today	dann (dan)	then	oder (oh'-dĕr)	or
nicht (ni*ch*t)	not	ja (yah)	yes	wie (vee)	as, how
nur (noor)	only	nein (nīn)	no	schon (shohn)	already
sehr (zayr)	very	auch (owkh)	also	schnell (shnel)	fast, quick
spät (shpayt)	late	oft (oft)	often	bald (balt)	soon

der Lehrer (dayr lay'-rĕr)	the teacher	gut (goot)	good, well
haben (hah'-bĕn)	to have	schlecht (shle*ch*t)	bad, badly
er hat (ayr hat)	he has	immer (i'-mĕr)	always
wo (voh)	where	danke (dang'-kĕ)	thank you
wohnen (voh'-nĕn)	to live, reside	gern (gern)	like, gladly
		wenig (vay'-ni*ch*)	little
er wohnt (ayr vohnt)	he lives	kommen (ko'-mĕn)	to come
gehen (gay'-ĕn)	to go	er kommt (ayr komt)	he comes
er geht (ayr gayt)	he goes	Sie sind (zee zint)	you are
fahren (fah'-rĕn)	to ride, travel	er ist (ayr ist)	he is
		der Tag (dayr tahk)	the day
er fährt (ayr fayrt)	he rides	warum (vah-rum')	why

26

DIE· FAMILIE

THE FAMILY   (dee fa-mee'-lĭĕ)

der **Mann** (dayr man)   the man, husband
die **Frau** (dee frow)   the woman, wife, Mrs.
der **Junge** (dayr yung'-e),   the boy
   der **Knabe** (dayr knah'-bĕ)
das **Mädchen**[3] (das mayt'-*ch*ĕn) the girl

der **Vater** (dayr fah'-tĕr) father
die **Mutter** (dee mu'-tĕr) mother
die **Eltern** (dee ĕl'-tĕrn) parents
das **Kind** (das kint) child

der **Sohn** (dayr zohn)   son
der **Gatte** (dayr ga'-tĕ)   husband
der **Onkel** (dayr ong'-kĕl)   uncle
die **Tante** (dee tan'-tĕ)   aunt

die **Tochter** (dee tokh'-tĕr)   daughter
der **Bruder** (dayr broo'-dĕr)   brother
die **Schwester** (dee shve'-stĕr)   sister
der **Vetter** (dayr fe'-tĕr)   cousin (*masc.*)
die **Kusine** (dee koo-zee'-nĕ)   cousin (*fem.*)
der **Grossvater** (dayr grohs'-fah-tĕr)   grandfather
die **Grossmutter** (dee grohs'-mu-tĕr)   grandmother
der **Verwandte** (fĕr-van'-tĕ)   relative

Die Nationalitäten[4] und die Sprachen[4]
(dee nah-tsioh-nah-lee-tay'-tĕn unt dee shprah'-khĕn)

DIE NATIONALITäT (Nationality)
der **Deutsche**[5] (dayr doit'-shĕ)
  the German
Amerikaner (a-may-ree-kah'-nĕr)
  the American
Spanier (shpah'-niĕr)
  the Spaniard
Italiener (ee-tah-liay'-nĕr)
  the Italian
Franzose (fran-tsoh'-zĕ)
  the Frenchman

DIE SPRACHE (Language)
Deutsch (doitsh)
  German
Englisch (eng'-lish)
  English
Spanisch (shpah'-nish)
  Spanish
Italienisch (ee-tah-liay'-nish)
  Italian
Französisch (fran-tsöh'-zish)
  French

Die Länder (len'-dĕr) Countries

Deutschland (doitsh'-lant)
  Germany
Amerika (a-may'-ree-ka)
  America

Spanien (shpah'-niĕn)
  Spain
Italien (ee-tah'-liĕn)
  Italy

Frankreich (frangk'-rīch)
  France
England (eng'-lant)
  England

CONVERSATION

1 Guten Tag, Herr Miller.

2 Guten Tag, Herr Smith.

3 Warum sind[6] Sie[7] so ernst?

4 Ich spreche nicht gut[8] Deutsch.[9]

5 Sie sprechen sehr gut Deutsch.

6 Danke sehr. Die deutsche Sprache[9] ist nicht so schwer.

7 Wir sprechen jetzt nur Deutsch. Ich bin Ihr Lehrer.

8 Sehr gut. Sprechen Sie viel Deutsch zu Hause?[10]

9 Wir sprechen oft zu Hause Deutsch.[11]

10 Ihre[12] Mutter kommt aus[13] Deutschland, nicht wahr?

11 Nein, meine[12] Mutter kommt aus[13] New Jersey.

12 Und ihre[12] Eltern?

13 Ihre Eltern, mein[12] Grossvater und meine[12] Grossmutter, kommen aus[13] Berlin.

14 Sprechen Ihre Schwester und Ihr Bruder so gut Deutsch wie Sie?

15 Mein Bruder spricht gut. Meine Schwester spricht nicht[14] so gut.

FOOTNOTES: *1.* This is the infinitive of the verb "to speak." The personal endings of the present tense of most verbs, attached to the infinitive stem, are the same in German; namely, *ich* (I)—*e; du* (you—familiar sing.)—*st; er* (he), *sie* (she), *es (it)—t; wir* (we)—*en; ihr* (you—familiar pl.)—*t; sie* (they)—*en; Sie* (you —polite sing. and pl.)—*en* [§61]. However, some verbs change their infinitive stem vowel in the second and third persons singular: *ich spreche,* I speak; *du sprichst,* you (thou) speak; *er, sie, es spricht,* he, she, it speaks; *wir sprechen,* we speak; *ihr sprecht* (plural of *du*), you speak; *sie sprechen,* they speak; *Sie*

PRONUNCIATION	TRANSLATION
1 goo'-tĕn tahk, her *Miller.*	Good day (Hello, How do you do), Mr. Miller.
2 goo'-tĕn tahk, her *Smith.*	Hello, Mr. Smith.
3 vah-rum' zint zee zoh ernst?	Why are you so serious?
4 ich shpre'-*chĕ* ni*ch*t goot doitsh.	I do not speak German well (*lit.,* I speak not well German).
5 zee shpre'-*chĕn* zayr goot doitsh.	You speak German very well (*lit.,* very well German).
6 dang'-kĕ zayr. dee doit'-shĕ shprah'-khĕ ist ni*ch*t zoh shvayr.	Thanks very much. The German language is not so difficult.
7 veer shpre'-*chĕn* yetst noor doitsh. i*ch* bin eer lay'-rĕr.	Now we shall speak only German (*lit.,* we speak now only German). I am your teacher.
8 zayr goot. shpre'-*chĕn* zee feel doitsh tsoo how'-zĕ?	Very good. Do you speak (*lit.,* speak you) much German at home?
9 veer shpre'- *chĕn* oft tsoo how'-zĕ doitsh.	We often speak German at home (*lit.,* we speak often at home German).
10 ee'-rĕ mu'-tĕr komt ows doitsh'-lant, ni*ch*t vahr?	Your mother comes from Germany, doesn't she (*lit.,* not true)?
11 nīn, mī'-nĕ mu'-tĕr komt ows *New Jersey.*	No, my mother comes from New Jersey.
12 unt ee'-rĕ el'-tĕrn?	And her parents?
13 ee'-rĕ el'-tĕrn, mīn grohs'-fah-tĕr unt mī'-nĕ grohs'-mu-tĕr, ko'-mĕn ows ber-leen'.	Her parents, my grandfather and grandmother, come from Berlin.
14 shpre'-*chĕn* ee'-rĕ shve'-stĕr unt eer broo'-dĕr zoh goot doitsh vee zee?	Do your sister and brother speak German as well as you (*lit.,* speak your sister and brother so well German as you)?
15 mīn broo'-dĕr shpri*ch*t goot. mī'-nĕ shve'-stĕr shpri*ch*t ni*ch*t zoh goot.	My brother speaks well. My sister does not speak (*lit.,* speaks not) so well.

sprechen (formal address), you speak. Whenever there is such a vowel change, the third person singular will be given in the vocabulary.   2. There are three genders in German, not only of the pronouns, *er* (he), *sie* (she), *es* (it), as in English, but also of nouns. The gender of nouns is indicated by the definite article, *der*, masculine; *die*, feminine; *das*, neuter; as shown by the nouns given. When a pronoun is used instead of a noun, the pronoun must be of the same grammatical gender as the noun: *der Dampfer*, the steamer: *er* (he); *die Eisenbahn*, the railroad: *sie* (she); *das Flugzeug*, the airplane: *es* (it).   3. The gender

16 Sprechen Sie auch Französisch?

17 Nein, ich[15] spreche nicht Französisch; und Sie?

18 Ich spreche Französisch, Italienisch und ein wenig Spanisch.

19 Gut. Sie sind[16] dann mein Lehrer in Frankreich.

20 Ich bin gern Ihr Lehrer.

21 Mein Vater ist jetzt in Berlin.

22 Ist Ihr Vater nicht Deutscher[17]?

23 Mein Vater war Deutscher.[17] Er ist jetzt Amerikaner.[17]

24 Haben Sie noch Verwandte in Deutschland?

25 Ja, ich habe einen[18] Onkel und eine[18] Tante in Hamburg.

26 Haben sie Kinder?

27 Ja, sie haben einen[18] Sohn und eine[18] Tochter.

28 Wo wohnen sie?

29 Mein Onkel, meine Tante und meine Kusine wohnen in Hamburg.

30 Wo wohnt[19] der Sohn?

31 Mein Vetter wohnt in Berlin.

32 Wir fahren[20] nun bald mit dem[21] Dampfer nach Hamburg.

---

of nouns does not always correspond to the natural gender of the substantive. *4.* The plurals of nouns in German are variously formed. The feminine nouns *die Nationalität* and *die Sprache* add *-en* and *-n* respectively to form the plural. *5.* The feminine forms of the nationalities given are as follows: *die Deutsche; die Amerikanerin; die Spanierin; die Italienerin; die Französin.* *6. sind* (are) is one of the plural forms of the irregular verb *sein* (to be). The complete present tense of *sein:* SINGULAR: *ich bin,* I am; *du bist,* you are (familiar form); *er, sie, es ist,* he, she, it is; PLURAL: *wir sind,* we are; *ihr seid,* you are (familiar form); *sie sind,* they are; *Sie sind,* you are (sing. and pl., polite form). The familiar forms *du* (you—sing.) and *ihr* (you—pl.) are used in addressing the Deity, relatives, children, close friends, a pet. The polite form *Sie* (you—sing. and pl.) is used in speaking

16 shpre'-*ch*ĕn zee owkh fran-tsöh'-zish?

Do you also speak (*lit.*, speak you also) French?

17 nīn, ich* shpre'-*chĕ* ni*ch*t fran-tsöh'-zish; unt zee?

No, I do not speak (*lit.*, speak not) French; and you?

18 ich shpre'-*chĕ* fran-tsöh'-zish, ee-tah-liay'-nish unt īn vay'-ni*ch* shpah'-nish.

I speak French, Italian, and a little Spanish.

19 goot.zee zint dan mīn lay'-rĕr in frangk'-rīch.

Fine! Then you will be (*lit.*, you are then) my teacher in France.

20 ich bin gern eer lay'-rĕr.

I'll gladly be (*lit.*, I am gladly) your teacher.

21 mīn fah'-tĕr ist yetst in ber-leen'.

My father is now in Berlin.

22 ist eer fah'-tĕr ni*ch*t doit'-shĕr?

Isn't your father German?

23 mīn fah'-tĕr vahr doit'-shĕr. ayr ist yetst a-may-ree-kah'-nĕr.

My father was a German. He is now an American.

24 hah'-bĕn zee nokh fĕr-van'-tĕ in doitsh'-lant?

Do you still have relatives in Germany?

25 yah, ich hah'-bĕ ī'-nĕn ong'-kĕl unt ī'-nĕ tan'-tĕ in ham'-burk.

Yes, I have an uncle and an aunt in Hamburg.

26 hah'-bĕn zee kin'-dĕr?

Have they any children?

27 yah, zee hah'-bĕn ī'-nĕn zohn unt ī'-nĕ tokh'-tĕr.

Yes, they have a son and a daughter.

28 voh voh'-nĕn zee?

Where do they live (*lit.*, where live they)?

29 mīn ong'-kĕl, mī'-nĕ tan'tĕ unt mī'-nĕ koo-zee'-nĕ voh'-nĕn in ham'-burk.

My uncle, my aunt, and [girl] cousin live in Hamburg.

30 voh vohnt dayr zohn?

Where does the son live?

31 mīn fe'-tĕr vohnt in ber-leen'.

My [boy] cousin lives in Berlin.

32 veer fah'-rĕn noon balt mit daym dam'-pfĕr nakh ham'-burk.

We will soon be going to Hamburg by steamer (*lit.*, we ride now soon with the steamer to Hamburg).

---

to acquaintances, strangers, etc. [§25].   7. The personal pronoun *Sie*, "you," in direct address is always written with a capital letter to distinguish it from *sie*, "they." The possessive adjective of direct address in the polite form is also written with a capital letter: *Ihre Mutter*, "your mother"; *Ihr Lehrer*, "your teacher"; but, *ihre Eltern*, "her (their) parents."   8. Almost any adjective can be used as an adverb without any change in form or ending; e.g., *gut* means "good" as well as "well"; *schlecht*, "bad" or "badly"; *leicht*, "easy" or "easily". *Gern* is one of the few real adverbs and can be used only as such.   9. *Ich spreche Deutsch*. Here the word *Deutsch* is used as a noun, meaning the language. In *die deutsche Sprache* (the German language), however *deutsche* is an adjective modifying the noun *Sprache*, and is, therefore, written with a small letter like all other adjectives.

33 Mein Onkel, meine Tante und meine Kusine warten schon auf[22] uns.

34 Hamburg ist sehr interessant.

35 Meine Kusine will[23] uns[24] Hamburg zeigen.

36 Fahren wir von Hamburg nach Berlin mit dem[21] Flugzeug oder mit der Eisenbahn?

37 Wie Sie wollen,[23] mit dem Schnellzug oder dem Flugzeug.

38 Es ist auch mit dem Automobil sehr interessant.

39 Gut, wir fahren mit dem Auto. Es ist spät. Ich muss gehen.

40 Kommen Sie[25] bitte Sonntag zu Kaffee und Kuchen!

41 Ach! Zum[26] Kaffeeklatsch! Ich komme gern.

42 Auf Wiedersehen, Herr Smith!

43 Auf Wiedersehen, Herr Miller!

Adjectives referring to nationality are not capitalized in German.   10. *zu Hause* (at home), referring to one's own home. There are expressions in every language which cannot be translated literally, that is word by word, and if thus translated would make no sense. These expressions are called *idioms,* and will be referred to in the footnotes by the abbreviation "ID." They should be learned by heart. *11.* The word order in German differs in several respects from English. Note the difference in the translation. In German, the adverb or any other part of speech does not come between the subject and the verb in a declarative sentence. The adverb of time precedes all other adverbs or adverbial phrases: *Wir sprechen oft zu Hause Deutsch. Mein Vater ist jetzt in Berlin.* [§79].   *12.* The possessive adjectives refer in stem to the possessor (*mein,* my; *sein,* his; *ihr,* her; etc.), but must agree in gender, case, and number with the noun they modify: *meine* (my) *Mutter; ihre* (her, their) *Eltern; mein Bruder; meine Schwester;* etc. [§8, a, 1-3; b, c]. Since *Grossvater* is masculine and *Grossmutter* is feminine, the possessive adjective must be repeated before each.   *13. aus Deutschland.* ID., a native of Germany, *lit.* "out of Germany."   *14.* The negative in German is expressed by *nicht* (not), which follows the verb.   *15.* The personal pronoun of the first person, *ich* (I), is always written with a small letter, except at the beginning of a sentence. *16.* The *present tense* is often used to express the *future,* especially in conversational German.   *17.* Nouns referring to nationality are used without the indefinite article, except when preceded by an adjective. *Er ist Amerikaner,* "He

33 mīn ong'-kĕl, mī'-nĕ tan'-tĕ, unt mī'-nĕ koo-zee'-nĕ vahr'-tĕn shohn owf uns.

My uncle, aunt, and cousin are already waiting for us.

34 ham'-burk ist zayr in-tĕ-re-sant'.

Hamburg is very interesting.

35 mī'-nĕ koo-zee'-nĕ vil uns ham'-burk tsī'-gĕn.

My cousin wants to show us (*lit.*, wants to us show) Hamburg.

36 fah'-rĕn veer fon ham'-burk nahkh ber-leen' mit daym flook'-tsoik oh'-dĕr mit dayr ī'-zĕn-bahn?

Will we travel from Hamburg to Berlin by (*lit.*, with the) airplane or (the) railroad?

37 vee zee vo'-lĕn, mit daym shnel'-tsook oh'-dĕr daym flook'-tsoik.

As you wish; by express train, or airplane.

38 es ist owkh mit daym ow-toh-moh-beel' zayr in-tĕ-re-sant'.

It is also very interesting by automobile.

39 goot, veer fah'-rĕn mit daym ow'-toh. es ist shpayt. *ich* mus gay'-ĕn.

All right (*lit.*, good), we'll go by auto. It is late. I must go.

40 ko'-mĕn zee bi'-tĕ zon'-tahk tsoo ka'-fay unt koo'-khĕn.

Please come for coffee and cake on Sunday (*lit.*, Come you please Sunday to coffee and cake).

41 akh. tsum ka'-fay-klatsh. *ich* ko'-mĕ gern.

Ah! For a (*lit.*, to) "Kaffee-klatsch" (*lit.*, coffee gossip)! I'll gladly come.

42 owf vee'-dĕr-zayn, her *Smith*.

Good-bye, Mr. Smith!

43 owf vee'-dĕr-zayn, her *Miller*.

Good-bye, Mr. Miller!

---

is an American." *Er ist ein guter Amerikaner,* "He is a good American."   *18.* The definite article *ein* (a), the negative *kein* (no), also take endings, as do the possessive adjectives: *einen Onkel* is in the masculine accusative case because it is the direct object of the verb; *eine Tante* is the feminine accusative case.   *19.* There is only *one* form for the present and past tenses in German; for example, *er wohnt,* "he lives," also means "he is living," "he does live." Also, the formation of questions and negatives differs in German from English. The "do" or "does" of the question in English ("Where does the son live?" *Wo wohnt der Sohn?*) and of the negative ("I do not speak German." *Ich spreche nicht Deutsch.*) is never translated in German.   *20.* Distinguish between *fahren* (to travel, ride) and *gehen* (to walk).   *21. dem* is the dative case of *der*, the masculine article, and also the dative of the neuter article *das.*   *22. warten auf.* Id: "to wait for," *lit.*, "to wait on."   *23. sie will,* "she wants, wishes;" *Sie wollen,* "you want, you wish." *Wollen* is a verb like "will," "can," "must" in English. Such verbs require an infinitive to complete the thought: *Sie will uns zeigen.* "She will show us." These verbs belong to the small group whose present singular endings do not follow the general pattern of German verbs [§71, a-d].   *24. uns* (us) dative case of *wir* (we) ("show *to* us"). The forms of the dative and accusative cases of *wir* are the same in German—*uns.*   *25. Kommen Sie! lit.,* "Come you," is an imperative form of formal address.   *26. zum,* "to the," is a contraction of *zu + dem.*

Zweite Lektion

SECOND LESSON   (tsvī'-tĕ lek-tsiohn')

Neue Wörter für diese Lektion

NEW WORDS FOR THIS LESSON   (noi'-ĕ vör'-tĕr führ dee'-zĕ lek-tsiohn')

fühlen (füh'-lĕn)	to feel	**geben** (gay'-bĕn)	to give
wohl (vohl)	well	er gibt[1] (ayr gipt)	he gives
aber (ah'-bĕr)	but	**wünschen** (vün'-shĕn)	to wish
allein (a-lin')	alone	**trinken** (tring'-kĕn)	to drink
setzen (ze'-tsĕn)	to set, put	**schwarz** (shvarts)	black
neben (nay'-bĕn)	next to, near	**weiss** (vīs)	white
		süss (zühs)	sweet
essen (e'-sĕn)	to eat	**bitter** (bi'-tĕr)	bitter
er isst[1] (ayr ist)	he eats	**wann** (van)	when

natürlich (na-tühr'-li*ch*)	naturally
die Reise (rī'-zĕ)	trip, voyage
verlassen (fĕr-la'-sĕn)	to leave
er verlässt (ayr fĕr-lest')	he leaves
erzählen (ĕr-tsay'-lĕn)	to tell, relate
das Vergnügen (fĕr-gnüh'-gĕn)	pleasure
der Nachmittag (nahkh'-mi-tahk)	the afternoon
der Vormittag (fohr'-mi-tahk)	the forenoon
ganz (gans)	entirely, complete(ly)

hier (heer)	here	**von** (fon)	from, of
dort (dort)	there	**noch ein(e)** (nokh īn)	another one
reisen (rī'-zĕn)	to travel	**das Stück** (shtük)	piece
der Monat (moh'-nat)	month	**kaufen** (kow'-fĕn)	to buy
lieber (lee'-bĕr)	rather	**alles** (a'-lĕs)	everything
nehmen (nay'-mĕn) ·	to take	**fragen** (frah'-gĕn)	to ask
er nimmt (ayr nimt)	he takes	**nett** (net)	lovely
vielleicht (fee-lī*ch*t')	perhaps	**danken** (dang'-kĕn)	to thank
bis (bis)	until, to	**die Seite** (zī'-tĕ)	side

34

SPEISEN UND GETRÄNKE

<small>MEALS AND DRINKS</small>   (shpī'-zěn unt gě-treng'-kě)

das Frühstück	breakfast	das Mittagessen	dinner
(früh'-shtük)		(mi'-tahk-e-sěn)	
das zweite Frühstück	lunch	das Abendessen	supper
(tsvī'-tě . . .)		(ah'-běnt- . . .)	

das Tischtuch (tish'-tookh)	tablecloth
die Tasse (ta'-sě)	cup
die Untertasse (un'-těr-ta-sě)	saucer
der Löffel (lö'-fěl)	spoon
der Teelöffel (tay'-lö-fěl)	teaspoon
die Gabel (gah'-běl)	fork
das Messer (me'-sěr)	knife
der Teller (te'-lěr)	plate
das Glas (glahs)	glass

das Fleisch (flīsh)	meat	der Schinken	ham
das Rindfleisch (rint- . . .)	beef	(shing'-kěn)	
das Kalbfleisch	veal	der Speck (shpek)	bacon
(kalp'- . . .)		der Braten (brah'-těn)	roast
das Lammfleisch	lamb	gebraten (gě-brah'-těn)	roasted
(lam'- . . .)		gekocht (gě-kokht')	boiled
das Schweinefleisch	pork	das Gemüse (ge-müh'-zě)	vegetables
(shvī'-ně . . .)		der Fisch (fish)	fish

roh (roh)	rare	der Zucker (tsu'-kěr)	sugar
durchgebraten (durch'-	well done	die Kekse (kayk'-zě)	cookies
gě-brah-těn)		die Schokolade	chocolate
der Kuchen (koo'-khěn)	cake	(sho-koh-lah'-dě)	
der Kaffee (ka'-fay)	coffee	das Wasser (va'-sěr)	water
der Tee (tay)	tea	der Wein (vīn)	wine
die Sahne (zah'-ně)	cream	die Flasche (fla'-shě)	bottle
die Milch (milch)	milk	der Krug (krook)	pitcher

CONVERSATION

1 Guten Tag, Herr Smith, wie geht es Ihnen?[2]

2 Danke, es geht mir[2] gut; und Ihnen, Frau Miller?

3 Ich fühle mich[3] sehr wohl, danke.

4 Wie geht es Ihrem[2] Gatten?

5 Nicht so gut. Er fühlt sich[3] so allein in Berlin.

6 Das ist sehr natürlich.

7 Setzen Sie sich[4] bitte, Herr Smith! Hans, setze dich[4] neben Herrn Smith!

8 Darf[5] ich Ihnen[6] Tee oder Kaffee geben?

9 Eine Tasse Kaffee, bitte.

10 Nehmen Sie Zucker und Sahne, oder Milch?

11 Ich nehme nur einen[7] Teelöffel Zucker, aber keine[7] Sahne. Ich trinke Kaffee schwarz, aber süss.

12 Hier ist der Zucker, Herr Smith. Und Hans, was wünschst du?

13 Ich trinke eine[7] Tasse Tee mit Zitrone und Zucker.

14 Hier ist ein[7] Teller[8] mit Kuchen und Keksen. Dort ist die Schlagsahne.

15 Bald reisen Sie[8] mit meinem[7] Sohn nach Deutschland, nicht wahr?

FOOTNOTES: *1. essen* (to eat) and *geben* (to give) are two verbs that change their stem vowels from *e* to *i* in the present tense: *er isst* (he eats) ; *er gibt* (he gives) [§65, a, 2 (a).   *2. Wie geht es Ihnen?* ID: How are you? lit., How goes it to you? *Ihnen* is the dative case of *Sie*. *es* is the subject of the sentence. *Es geht mir gut,* "I am fine." *mir,* "to me," is the dative of *ich,* I. *Wie geht es Ihrem Gatten?* "How is your husband?" *Ihrem,* "to your," dative of *Ihr,* "your."   *3. sich fühlen,* lit., to feel oneself, a verb with a reflexive pronoun referring back to the subject.

PRONUNCIATION	TRANSLATION

1 goo'-tĕn tahk, her *Smith*, vee gayt es ee'-nĕn?

Hello, Mr. Smith, how are you (*lit.*, how goes it to you)?

2 dang'-kĕ, es gayt meer goot, unt ee'-nĕn, frow *Miller?*

Thank you, I am fine; and you (*lit.*, it goes well to me, and to you), Mrs Miller?

3 ich füh'-lĕ mi*ch* zayr vohl, dang'-kĕ.

I am feeling very well, thank you.

4 vee gayt es ee'-rĕm ga'-tĕn?

How is your husband?

5 nicht zoh goot. ayr fühlt zi*ch* zoh a-līn' in ber-leen'.

Not so well. He feels so lonely in Berlin.

6 das ist zayr na-tühr'-li*ch*.

That is very natural.

7 ze'-tsĕn zee zi*ch* bi'-tĕ, her *Smith*. hans, ze'-tsĕ di*ch* nay'-bĕn hern *Smith*.

Please, sit down (*lit.*, Seat yourself please), Mr. Smith. Hans, sit down (*lit.*, seat yourself) next to Mr. Smith.

8 darf i*ch* ee'-nĕn tay oh'-dĕr ka'-fay gay'-bĕn?

May I give you tea or coffee?

9 ī'-nĕ ta'-sĕ ka'-fay, bi'-tĕ.

A cup of coffee, please.

10 nay'-mĕn zee tsu'-kĕr unt zah'-nĕ, oh'-dĕr mil*ch*?

Do you take sugar and cream, **or** milk?

11 i*ch* nay'-mĕ noor ī'-nĕn tay'-lö-fĕl tsu'-kĕr ah'-bĕr kī'-nĕ zah'-nĕ. i*ch* tring'-kĕ ka'-fay shvarts ah'-bĕr zühs.

I take only a teaspoonful of sugar (*lit.*, a teaspoon sugar), but **no** cream. I drink coffee black, but sweet.

12 heer ist dayr tsu'-kĕr, her *Smith*. unt hans vas vünshst doo?

Here is the sugar, Mr. Smith. **And** Hans, what do you want?

13 i*ch* tring'-kĕ ī'-nĕ ta'-sĕ tay mit tsee-troh'-nĕ unt tsu'-kĕr.

I'll drink (*lit.*, I drink) a cup of tea with lemon and sugar.

14 heer ist īn te'-lĕr mit koo'-khĕn unt kayk'-zĕn. dort ist dee shlak'-zah-nĕ.

Here is a plate with cake and cookies. There is the whipped cream.

15 balt rī'-zĕn zee mit mī'-nĕm zohn nahkh doitsh'-lant, ni*ch*t vahr?

Soon you will travel to Germany with my son, won't you?

The pronoun is really part of the verb. *Fühlen* takes the accusative: *ich fühle mich,* "I feel, I am feeling (myself);" *du fühlst dich,* "you feel, you are feeling (yourself);" *er, sie, es fühlt sich,* "he, she, it feels (himself, herself, itself)"; *wir fühlen uns,* "we feel (ourselves)"; *ihr fühlt euch,* "you feel (yourselves)"; *Sie fühlen sich,* "you feel (yourself, yourselves)." Only the third persons singular and plural and the polite form have a special reflexive form; namely, *sich.* 4. *Setzen Sie sich!* is the imperative of the reflexive verb in the polite form; *setze dich!*

16 Der Dampfer verlässt New York in einem Monat.

17 Das Schiff fährt nur bis Cuxhaven. Wir nehmen von dort die Eisenbahn nach Hamburg.

18 Mein Schwager, meine Schwägerin und meine Nichte wohnen dort. Mein Neffe wohnt in Berlin.

19 Ja, Ihr Sohn erzählte mir das.

20 Noch eine Tasse Kaffee, Herr Smith? Oder trinken Sie lieber ein Glas[9] Wein oder vielleicht ein Gläschen[9] Likör?

21 Nein, danke. Darf ich um ein Glas[9] Wasser bitten?[10]

22 Gern. Hier ist ein Krug mit Eiswasser und dort stehen die Wassergläser.[11]

23 Mich fragst du nicht, Mutter? Gib[12] mir bitte ein Glas Wein!

24 Na, du bist hier zu Hause. Nimm,[12] was du willst!

25 Ach, diese Mütter![13] Ich esse noch ein Stück von[9] deinem[14] Kuchen.

26 Haben Sie schon alles für[15] die Reise?

27 Nein, ich muss noch viel kaufen.

---

is in the familiar form, since mother is speaking to son.   *5. darf* (may), verb like "will." It does not conform to the rule for personal endings in the present tense [§61].   6. *Ihnen,* "to you," is dative of *Sie.* The dative often expresses *to* (you), *for* (you).   7. The indefinite article *ein* usually takes the same case endings as the definite articles, with three exceptions; namely, the nominative masculine and neuter singular and the neuter accusative singular. *Kein,* "no," and all possessive adjectives follow the same scheme: *mein Vater* (masc. nom.); *meine Mutter* (fem. nom.); *einen Amerikaner* and *einen Teelöffel* (masc. acc.); *keine Sahne* (fem. acc.); *meinem Sohn* (masc. dat.); *meiner Seite* (fem. dat.); etc. [§7].   8. In addition to normal word order (subject followed by verb), there

16 dayr dam'-pfĕr fĕr-lest' *New York* in ī'-nĕm moh'-nat.	The steamer will leave (*lit.*, leaves) New York in a month.
17 das shif fayrt noor bis cuks-hah'-fĕn. veer nay'-mĕn fon dort dee ī'-zĕn-bahn nahkh ham'-burk.	The ship goes only to Cuxhaven. We shall take (*lit.*, we take) the railroad from there to Hamburg.
18 mīn shvah'-gĕr, mī-nĕ shvay'-gĕrin unt mī'-nĕ nich'-tĕ voh'-nĕn dort. mīn ne'-fĕ vohnt in berleen'.	My brother-in-law, my sister-in-law, and my niece live there. My nephew lives in Berlin.
19 yah, eer zohn ĕr-tsayl'-tĕ meer das.	Yes, your son told me that.
20 nokh ī'-nĕ ta'-sĕ ka'-fay, her *Smith?* oh'-dĕr tring'-kĕn zee lee'-bĕr īn glahs vīn oh'-dĕr fee-licht' īn glays'-chĕn lee-köhr'?	Another cup of coffee, Mr. Smith? Or would you prefer (*lit.*, drink you rather) a glass of wine, or perhaps a cordial (*lit.*, a little glass liqueur)?
21 nīn dang'-kĕ. darf *ich* um īn glahs va'-sĕr bi'-tĕn?	No, thank you. May I ask you for a glass of water?
22 gern. heer ist īn krook mit īs'-va-sĕr unt dort shtay'-ĕn dee va'-sĕr-glay-zĕr.	Gladly. Here is a jug of ice water and there are (*lit.*, stand) the water glasses.
23 *mich* frahkst doo nicht, mu'-tĕr. gip meer bi'-tĕ īn glahs vīn.	Me, you don't ask, Mother! Please give me a glass of wine.
24 nah, doo bist heer tsoo how'-zĕ. nim vas doo vilst.	Well, you are at home here. Take what you want.
25 akh, dee'-zĕ mü'-tĕr. ich e'-sĕ nokh īn shtük fon dī'-nĕm koo'-khĕn.	Ah, these mothers! I am going to eat another piece of your cake.
26 hah'-bĕn zee shohn a'-lĕs führ dee rī'-zĕ?	Do you already have everything (*lit.*, all) for the trip?
27 nīn, ich mus nokh feel kow'-fĕn.	No, I still have to buy a lot (*lit.*, much).

is also the inverted word order (verb followed by subject), which is used in both English and German in questions. In English this word order may also be used for emphasis: "Here is the plate." In German, however, the inverted word order *must* be used, not only in questions, but also whenever anything precedes the subject of the main clause: *Bald reisen Sie mit meinem Sohn* . . . *Ja, nein, gut,* etc. are exceptions which are explained in the Reference Grammar [§53, e; 79, a]. *9.* After nouns expressing quantity, the English "of" is not expressed in German: *ein Glas Wein,* a glass of wine; *eine Tasse Kaffee,* a cup of coffee; *ein Flasche Bier,* a bottle of beer; *zwei Liter Milch,* two quarts of milk; etc. However, when an adjective precedes the noun, "of" is expressed: *ein Stück von deinem Kuchen.* *10.*

28 Ich auch. Ich gehe gern mit Ihnen mit. Wann gehen Sie?

29 Ich gehe Mittwoch vormittag.

30 Sehr schön! Wir sehen uns im Warenhaus wieder.[16]

31 Ich danke[17] Ihnen, Frau Miller, für[15] einen netten Nach-mittag.

32 Das Vergnügen war ganz auf meiner Seite.

33 Auf Wiedersehen, Frau Miller und Herr Miller.

34 Auf Mittwoch!

---

bitten um, ID., to ask for; *lit.,* "to beg about or around."   *11. Die Wassergläser,* plural of *das Wasserglas.*   *12. Gib!* "give," imperative singular familiar form of *geben,* "to give," and *Nimm!* "take," imperative singular familiar form of *nehmen,* "to take." Both imperatives are irregular.   *13. Die Mütter,* "the mothers," plural of *die Mutter,* "the mother." The formation of the plural is rather complicated in German and will be taken up in detail in the Reference Grammar of this book. Sometimes no change takes place in the plural, or only an umlaut is added, as in *Mütter;* or an *e* and umlaut, as in *die Söhne,* "the sons" (sing. *der Sohn*); or *er* and umlaut as in *die Gläser,* "the glasses" (sing. *das Glas*); or *en* and no umlaut

28 *ich* owkh. *ich* gay'-ĕ gern mit ee'-nĕn mit. van gay'-ĕn zee?

I, too. I'll gladly go with you. When are you going?

29 *ich* gay'-ĕ mit'-vokh fohr'-mi-tahk.

I'll go Wednesday morning.

30 zayr shöhn. veer zay'-ĕn uns im vah'-rĕn-hows vee'-dĕr.

Very good. We'll see each other again in the department store (*lit.*, us in the department store again).

31 *ich* dang'-kĕ ee'-nĕn, frow *Miller*, führ ī-nĕn ne'-tĕn nahkh'-mi-tahk.

I thank you, Mrs. Miller, for a lovely afternoon.

32 das fĕr-gnüh-gĕn var gans owf mī'-nĕr zī'-tĕ.

The pleasure was all mine (*lit.*, completely on my side).

33 owf vee'-dĕr-zay n, frow *Miller* unt her *Miller*.

Good-bye, Mrs. Miller and Mr. Miller!

34 owf mit'-vokh.

Until Wednesday!

---

as in *die Frauen*, "the women" (sing. *die Frau*).   *14. deinem*, dative case, masculine, of the familiar of the possessive adjective "thine." The preposition *von* requires the dative case of the noun or pronoun.   *15. für*, "for," takes the accusative case: *für die Reise* (acc. fem.); *für einen Nachmittag* (acc. masc.).   *16. wiedersehen* (to see again) is a verb with a separable prefix; i.e., the prefix detaches itself and follows the verb: *Ich stehe auf*, "I get up" (infinitive *aufstehen*, "to get up"); but, in an expanded phrase or sentence, the prefix is at the end: *Wir sehen uns im Warenhaus wieder*; *uns*, "us," is the accusative of *wir*.   *17. danken*, "to thank," always requires an object noun or pronoun in the dative case.

Dritte Lektion

THIRD LESSON   (dri'-tĕ lek-tsiohn')

Neue Wörter für diese Lektion

schön (shöhn)	beautiful	brauchen (brow'-khĕn)	to need
hässlich (hes'-li*ch*)	ugly	die Treppe (tre'-pĕ)	stairs
der Fahrer (fah'-rĕr)	driver	oben (oh'-bĕn)	upstairs
warten (var'-tĕn)	to wait	unten (un'-tĕn)	downstairs
er wartet (var'-tĕt)	he waits	von oben (fon oh'-bĕn)	from the top
wollen (vo'-lĕn)	to want, wish	von unten (fon un'-tĕn)	from the bottom
er will (vil)	he wants		
machen (ma'-khĕn)	to make, to do	kurz (kurts)	short
		lang (lang)	long
braun (brown)	brown	suchen (zoo'-khĕn)	to look for
das Paar (pahr)	pair, couple	passen (pa'-sĕn)	to fit, suit

einsteigen (īn'-shtī-gĕn)	to get in (a car)	
er steigt ein[1] (ayr shtīkt īn)	he gets into	
aussteigen (ows'-shtī-gĕn)	to get out (a car)	
er steigt aus[1] (ayr shtīkt ows)	he gets out	
etwas (et'-vas)	a little, some, something	
bequem (bĕ-kvaym')	comfortable	

die Qualität (kva-lee-tayt')	quality
gefallen (gĕ-fa'-lĕn)	to like, to be pleased
rechts (re*ch*ts)	right, on the right
links (lingks)	left, on the left
bitten (bi'-tĕn)	to ask for, to beg
das Warenhaus (vah'-rĕn-hows)	department store
die Rolltreppe (rol'-tre-pĕ)	escalator
der Fahrstuhl (fahr'-shtool)	elevator

das Stockwerk (shtok'-verk), der Stock (shtok)   story, floor, flat
aussehen (ows'-zay-ĕn), er sieht aus[1] (ayr zeet ows) to look, appear
aufsetzen (owf'-ze-tsĕn), er setzt auf[1] (zetst owf)   to put on, wear, set upon

42

KLEIDUNG UND SCHUHWERK

CLOTHING AND FOOTWEAR   (kli'-dung unt shoo'-verk)

der Anzug (an'-tsook)	suit	der Stoff (shtof)	cloth
die Tasche (ta'-shĕ)	pocket	die Kunstseide	rayon
die Weste (ve'-stĕ)	vest	(koonst'-zī-dĕ)	
der Ärmel (er'-mĕl)	sleeve	das Nylon (nee'-lohn)	nylon
der Kragen (krah'-gĕn)	collar	das Leder (lay'-dĕr)	leather
der Mantel (man'-tĕl)	overcoat	die Grösse (gröh'-sĕ)	size
der Hut (hoot)	hat	die Farbe (fahr'-bĕ)	color

der Handschuh (hant'-shoo),   glove, gloves
  die Handschuhe (hant'-shoo-ĕ)
die Hose *(sing.)* (hoh'-zĕ),   trousers, pants
  die Hosen *(pl.)* (hoh'-zĕn)
die Jacke (ya'-kĕ), das Jacket (zha-ket')   jacket
der Knopf (knopf),   button, buttons
  die Knöpfe (knö'-pfĕ)
das Oberhemd (oh'-bĕr-hemt)   shirt
das Unterhemd (un'-tĕr-hemt)   undershirt
die Unterhosen *(pl.)* (un'-tĕr-hoh-zĕn)   underpants

der Schlips (shlips), die Krawatte (krah-va'-tĕ)   necktie
die Manschette (man-she'-tĕ),   cuff, cuffs
  die Manschetten (man-she'-tĕn)
die Socke (zo'-kĕ), die Socken (zo'-kĕn)   sock, socks
der Schuh (shoo), die Schuhe (shoo'-ĕ)   shoe, shoes
die Gummischuhe (gu'-mi-shoo-ĕ)   rubbers, galoshes
die Hausschuhe (hows'-shoo-ĕ)   slippers
die Wäsche (ve'-shĕ)   wash
das Taschentuch (ta'-shĕn-tookh),   handkerchief,
  die Taschentücher (. . . tü-*ch*ĕr)   handkerchiefs
drücken (drü'-kĕn)   to pinch, press

wieviel (vee-feel')	how much	breit (brīt)	broad, wide
wie viele (vee fee'-lĕ)	how many	weit (vīt)	wide
kosten (ko'-stĕn)	to cost	eng (eng)	narrow,
teuer (toi'-ĕr)	expensive		tight
billig (bi'-li*ch*)	cheap	hoch (hohkh)	high
billiger[2] (bi'-li-gĕr)	cheaper	niedrig (nee'-dri*ch*)	low
neu (noi)	new	besser (be'-sĕr)	better
weich (vī*ch*)	soft	genug (gĕ-nook')	enough
hart (hart)	stiff, hard	gleich (glī*ch*)	immediately
der Kopf (kopf)	head	der Eingang (īn'-gang)	entrance
steif (shtīf)	stiff	der Ausgang	exit
grüssen (grüh'-sĕn)	to greet	(ows'-gang)	

CONVERSATION

1 Guten Tag, Herr Smith, wie geht's?[3]

2 An solchem[4] schönen Tag, sehr gut.

3 Fahren wir mit der[5] Untergrundbahn, dem Omnibus oder der Autodroschke?

4 Nehmen wir ein Taxi! Es geht schneller und ist bequemer.

5 Sie haben recht.[6] Steigen Sie bitte ein![7]

6 Fahren Sie uns[8] zum Warenhaus!

7 Hier ist das Warenhaus. Steigen Sie nur aus![7] Ich bezahle den Fahrer. Wieviel zeigt der Taxameter?

8 Zwei Dollar und dreissig Cent.

9 Kommen Sie, bitte! Dies ist der Eingang.

10 Wollen[9] Sie die Rolltreppe oder den Fahrstuhl nehmen?

11 Oh! Ich fahre lieber mit dem Fahrstuhl. Die Rolltreppe macht mich nervös.

12 Warten Sie einen Moment! Welches Stockwerk?

13 Ich brauche ein Paar Schuhe und einen Hut.

14 Und ich möchte[10] Oberhemden, Unterhemden, Unterhosen und Socken kaufen.

FOOTNOTES: *1.* When a verb has a separable prefix, the third person singular of the present tense will be given in addition to the infinitive.   *2.* The regular comparative in German is formed by adding –*er* to the adjective: *billig* (cheap), *billig*er (cheaper); *weit* (wide), *weiter* (wider) [§49, 50].   *3. Lit.,* how goes it?. Less formal than *Wie geht es Ihnen?,*   *4. solchem,* the dative masculine. *solch* "such a," belongs to the *der*-word group [§5, a, b].   *5. der* "the," dative case singular of the feminine article *die,* after *mit.* Certain prepositions—*aus* (out), *ausser* (besides), *bei* (near, at), *mit* (with), *nach* (after), *seit* (since), *von* (of, from),

PRONUNCIATION	TRANSLATION
1 goo'-tĕn tahk, her *Smith,* vee gayts?	Good day, Mr. Smith. How are you?
2 an sol'-*ch*ĕm shöh'-nĕn tahk, zayr goot.	On such a beautiful day, very well.
3 fah'-rĕn veer mit dayr un'-tĕr-grunt-bahn, daym om'-ni-bus oh'-dĕr dayr ow'-toh-drosh-kĕ?	Shall we go (*lit.,* go we) by subway, by bus, or by cab?
4 nay'mĕn veer īn tak'-si. es gayt shne'-lĕr unt ist bĕ-kvay'-mĕr.	Let us take a taxi. It goes faster and is more comfortable.
5 zee hah'-bĕn *rech*t. shtī'-gĕn zee bi'-tĕ īn.	You are right. Please, get in.
6 fah'-rĕn zee uns tsum vah'-rĕn-hows.	Drive us to the department store.
7 heer ist das vah'- rĕn-hows. shtī'-gĕn zee noor ows. *ich* bĕ-tsah'-lĕ dayn fah'rĕr. vee'-feel' tsīkt dayr tak-sa-may'-tĕr?	Here is the department store. Go ahead! I'll pay the driver. How much does the meter show?
8 tsvī do'-lar unt drī'-si*ch* tsent.	Two dollars and thirty cents.
9 ko'-mĕn zee bi'-tĕ. dees ist dayr īn'-gang.	Come on, please. This is the entrance.
10 vo'-lĕn zee dee rol'-tre-pĕ oh'-dĕr dayn fahr'- shtool nay'-mĕn?	Do you want to take the escalator or the elevator?
11 oh, *ich* fah'-rĕ lee'-bĕr mit daym fahr'-shtool. dee rol'-tre-pĕ makht mi*ch* ner'-vöhs'.	Oh, I'd rather take (*lit.,* ride with) the elevator. The escalator makes me nervous.
12 var'-tĕn zee ī'-nĕn moh-mĕnt'. vel'-*ch*ĕs shtok'-verk?	Wait a moment. Which floor?
13 ich brow'-kh*ĕ īn pahr shoo'-ĕ unt ī'-nĕn hoot.	I need a pair of shoes and a hat.
14 unt i*ch* möc*h*'-tĕ oh'-bĕr-hem-dĕn, un'-tĕr-hem-dĕn, un'-tĕr-hoh-zĕn unt zo'-kĕn kow'-fĕn.	And I would like to buy shirts, undershirts, shorts, and socks.

zu (to)—must take the dative case [§37]. *6. recht haben* (to be right), *lit.*, to have right. *7. einsteigen* (to get in); *aussteigen* (to get out). Both of these verbs have separable prefixes. In the simple tenses the prefix is separated from the verb and follows the main clause or sentence: *Steigen Sie nur aus!* *8. Steigen Sie ein! Fahren Sie uns! Kommen Sie, bitte!* are imperatives. In the imperative mood of the polite form, the pronoun must be expressed, and the word order is inverted; i.e., the verb precedes the subject. An exclamation mark must be used after a command or request. *9.* A "will" verb. There are six such verbs in German: *wollen*

15 Hier ist eine Übersicht: Herrenschuhe, Gummischuhe, Handschuhe im[11] sechsten Stock; Hüte und Schlipse im[11] dritten Stock.

16 Herrenwäsche gibt[12] es im Erdgeschoss.

17 Wir beginnen von oben und gehen die Treppe hinunter.

18 Sechsten Stock, bitte!

19 Ich möchte[10] ein Paar Schuhe haben. Grösse 12[13] (zwölf), Weite C.

20 Welche Farbe wünschen Sie? Schwarz, braun oder weiss?

21 Ich suche ein Paar braune Schuhe.

22 Nein, diese Schuhe passen nicht. Sie drücken. Sie sind zu eng; auch etwas zu kurz.

23 Wie passen diese, mein Herr?

24 Die passen gut. Wieviel kosten sie?

25 Sie kosten 20[13] (zwanzig) Dollar und 50[13] (fünfzig) Cent.

26 Das ist sehr teuer. Haben Sie nicht billigere Schuhe?

27 Nicht in dieser Qualität und diesem Stil.

28 Wie gefallen Ihnen diese Schuhe,[14] Herr Miller?

29 Sie gefallen mir sehr.[14]

30 Gut; ich nehme sie. Wo ist die Hutabteilung?

31 Hier rechts ist die Treppe. Und da links ist die Hutabteilung.

(to want, to wish); *sollen* (ought to, shall); *können* (to be able, can); *mögen* (to like, may); *müssen* (must, have to); *dürfen* (to be permitted, may). These verbs have an irregular present tense and require the infinitive of another verb without *zu* (to), as in English: "He must go." This infinitive is placed at the end of a clause or sentence. Note the vowel change in the singular [§71, a].   *10. Ich*

15 heer ist ī'-nĕ üh'-bĕr-*zicht*: he'-rĕn-shoo-ĕ, gu'-mi-shoo-ĕ, hant'-shoo-ĕ im zek'-stĕn shtok; hüh'-tĕ unt shlip'-zĕ im dri'-tĕn shtok.

Here is a directory: men's shoes, rubbers, and gloves (in the), sixth floor; hats and ties (in the) third floor.

16 he'-rĕn-ve-shĕ gipt es im ayrt'-gĕ-shos.

Men's underwear is on the ground floor.

17 veer bĕ-gi'-nĕn fon oh'-bĕn unt gay'-ĕn dee tre'-pĕ hi-nun'-tĕr.

We'll start at the top and walk down the stairs.

18 zek'-stĕn shtok, bi'-tĕ.

Sixth floor, please.

19 ich möch'-tĕ īn pahr shoo'-ĕ hah'-bĕn. gröh'-sĕ tsvölf, vī'-tĕ tsay.

I should like to have a pair of shoes. Size 12, width C.

20 vel'-chĕ far'-bĕ vün'-shĕn zee, shvarts, brown oh'-dĕr vīs?

Which color do you want, black, brown, or white?

21 ich zoo'-khĕ īn pahr brow'-nĕ shoo'-ĕ.

I'm looking for a pair of brown shoes.

22 nīn, dee'-zĕ shoo'-ĕ pa'-sĕn ni*ch*t. zee drü'-kĕn. zee zint tsoo eng; owkh et'vas tsoo kurts.

No, these shoes do not fit. They pinch. They are too narrow; also a little too short.

23 vee pa'-sĕn dee'-zĕ, mīn her?

How do these fit, sir?

24 dee pa'sĕn goot. vee-feel' ko'-stĕn zee?

They fit well. How much do they cost?

25 zee ko'-stĕn tsvan'-tsi*ch* do'-lar unt fünf'-tsi*ch* tsent.

They cost $20.50.

26 das ist zayr toi'-ĕr. hah'-bĕn zee ni*ch*t bi'-li-gĕ-rĕ shoo'ĕ?

That is very expensive. Don't you have cheaper shoes?

27 ni*ch*t in dee'-zĕr kva-lee-tayt' unt dee'sĕm shteel.

Not in this quality and this style.

28 vee gĕ-fa'-lĕn ee'-nĕn dee'-zĕ shoo'-ĕ, her *Miller?*

How do you like these shoes, Mr. Miller?

29 zee gĕ-fa'-lĕn meer zayr.

I like them very much.

30 goot, ich nay'-mĕ zee. voh ist dee hoot'-ap-tī-lung?

All right, I'll take them. Where is the hat department?

31 heer re*ch*ts ist dee tre'-pĕ. unt dah ist lingks dee hoot'-ap-tī-lung.

Here on the right are the stairs. And on the left is the hat department.

---

möchte (I should like to.) *11. im*, dative case, contracted from *in dem.* *12. es gibt.* ID., there is, there are, *lit.*, it gives, third person sing. present of *geben* (to give), a so-called strong verb; the infinitive stem vowel *e* changes to *i (ie)* in second and third persons singular: *ich gebe, du gibst, er, sie, es gibt, wir geben, ihr gebt, sie geben, Sie geben.* *13.* Numbers over ten are usually not written out in Ger-

32 Was wünschen Sie, meine Herren? Wünschen Sie einen steifen oder weichen Hut?

33 Nur keinen steifen Hut! Ich möchte einen weichen Filzhut.

34 Dieser[15] hier ist das Neuste.

35 Nein, die Krempe ist zu breit und der Kopf zu hoch. Er ist auch ein bisschen zu eng. Dieser Hut[16] ist besser.

36 Er[17] steht Ihnen sehr gut.[17] Sie sehen sehr elegant aus und doch sehr solide. Die Farbe gefällt mir[14] auch.

37 Der Hut ist auch sehr preiswert. Er[17] kostet nur sechs Dollar.

38 Ich nehme ihn und setze ihn gleich auf.

39 So, das ist genug für heute.

40 Grüssen Sie bitte Ihre Frau Mutter[18] von mir.

41 Danke; sie lässt natürlich auch grüssen.

---

man.   *14. Wie gefallen Ihnen diese Schuhe?* ID., *lit.,* "How please to you these shoes?" *Sie gefallen mir gut.* "They please to me well." *Er gefällt mir.* "He (it) pleases to me." Whatever pleases or is liked is the subject of the sentence and whom it pleases or who likes it is in the dative case.   *15. Dieser* (this one). *Any* adjective can be used in German to replace a noun without the translation of "one."   *16. dieser Hut* (this hat). *Dieser* is a demonstrative adjective here, modifying the noun "hat." It requires the ending of the definite article. These demonstrative adjectives are classified as *der*-words in the Reference Grammar [§5, a-c].   *17. Er steht Ihnen sehr gut* (It is very becoming to you). ID., *lit.,* He

32 vas vün-shĕn zee, mī'-nĕ he'-rĕn?
vün'-shĕn zee ī-nĕn shtī'-fĕn oh'-
dĕr vī'-*ch*ĕn hoot?

What do you wish, sirs? Do you wish a derby (*lit.*, stiff hat) or a felt (*lit.*, soft) hat.

33 noor kī'-nĕn shtī'-fĕn hoot. *ich* möc*h*'-tĕ ī'-nen vī-*ch*ĕn fils'-hoot.

By no means (*lit.*, only no) a derby! I would like to have a soft felt hat.

34 dee'-zĕr heer ist das noi'-stĕ.

This one over here is the latest fashion (*lit.*, the newest).

35 nīn, dee krem'-pĕ ist tsoo brīt unt dayr kopf tsoo hohkh. ayr ist owkh īn bis'-*ch*ĕn tsoo eng. dee'-zĕr hoot ist be'-sĕr.

No, the brim is too wide and the crown (*lit.*, the head) too high. It is also a little too tight. This hat is better.

36 ayr shtayt ee'-nĕn zayr goot. zee zay'-ĕn zayr ay-lĕ-gant' ows unt dokh zayr zoh-lee'-dĕ. dee far'-bĕ gĕ-felt' meer owkh.

It is very becoming. You look very elegant and yet very conservative. I also like the color.

37 dayr hoot ist owkh zayr prīs'-vayrt. ayr ko'-stĕt noor zeks do'-lahr.

The hat is also very reasonable. It costs only six dollars.

38 *ich* nay'-mĕ een unt ze'-tsĕ een glī*ch* owf.

I'll take it and put it on immediately.

39 zoh das ist gĕ-nook' führ hoi'-tĕ.

Well, that's enough for today.

40 grüh'-sĕn zee bi'-tĕ ee'-rĕ frow mu'-tĕr fon meer.

My best regards to your mother (*lit.*, Greet you please your Mrs. mother from me).

41 dang'-kĕ, zee lest na-tühr'-li*ch* owkh grüh'-sĕn.

Thank you; she naturally sends her regards, too.

---

stands to you very well. *Er* (he, it) is masculine because it refers to *der Hut*. 18. The Germans are much more formal in their relationship to acquaintances or even to friends than Americans. *Ein Freund* (a friend) is a term which is used very sparingly. Therefore, the rather formal discourse of the two young men is very natural in German. When you inquire about a grown-up member of the family, the correct forms are: *Wie geht es Ihrer Frau Mutter?* (How is your "Mrs." mother?), *Ihrem Herrn Vater* ("Mr." father), *Ihrem Fräulein Tochter* ("Miss" daughter), *Ihrem Herrn Sohn* ("Mr." son), etc., unless you know the family very well.

Vierte Lektion

FOURTH LESSON (feer'-tĕ lek-tsiohn')

Neue Wörter für diese Lektion

die Zeit (tsīt), die Zeiten[1] (tsī'-tĕn)	time,-s
der Name (nah'-mĕ), die Namen (nah'-mĕn)	name,-s
darum (dah'-rum)	therefore, because of
der Augenblick (ow'-gĕn-blik), die Augenblicke (ow'-gĕn-bli-kĕ)	moment. -s

ohne (oh'-nĕ)	without	klein (klīn)	little
versuchen (fĕr-zoo'-khĕn)	to try	hell (hel)	light
als (als)	than, as, when	dunkel (dung'-kĕl)	dark
über (üh'-bĕr)	over, above	leider (lī'-dĕr)	unfortunately
sogar (soh-gahr')	even		
sitzen (zi'-tsĕn)	to sit	glücklich (glük'-lich)	happy
ruhig (roo'-ich)	calm, quiet	spielen (shpee'-lĕn)	to play
unruhig (un'-roo-ich)	restless	winken (ving'-kĕn)	to wave
schlafen (shlah'-fĕn)	to sleep	das Heimweh (hīm'-vay)	homesickness
er schläft (shlayft)	he sleeps	die Heimat (hī'-mat)	native country
leben (lay'-bĕn)	to live		
gross (grohs)	big, great	da (dah)	there

nach oben (nahkh oh'-bĕn)	(to go) upstairs	
nach unten (nahkh un'-tĕn)	(to go) downstairs	
laufen (low'-fĕn)	to run	
er läuft (loift)	he runs	
führen (füh'-rĕn)	to lead	
sondern (zon'-dĕrn)	but (on the contrary)	

kaum (kowm)	hardly	hören (höh'-rĕn)	to hear
atmen (aht'-mĕn)	to breathe	ansehen (an'-zay-ĕn)	to look at
beinah (bī-nah')	almost	er sieht an (zeet an)	he looks at
lassen (la'-sĕn)	to let	fürchten (fürch'-tĕn)	to fear
er lässt (lest)	he lets	er fürchtet (fürch'-tĕt)	he fears

50

DIE TRANSPORTMITTEL

MEANS OF TRANSPORTATION   (trans-port'-mit-tĕl)

das Flugzeug (flook'-tsoik)	airplane
das Auto, Automobil (ow'-toh-moh-beel),	automobile
der Kraftwagen (kraft'-vah-gĕn)	
die Fahrkarte (fahr'-kahr-tĕ)	ticket
die Hin- und Rückfahrkarte (hin unt rük-...)	round-trip ticket
der Fahrkartenschalter (...shal-tĕr)	ticket window
der Flughafen, Flugplatz (flook'-hah-fĕn, flook'-platz)	airport
das Reisebüro (rī'-zĕ-bü-roh)	travel agency

das Gepäck (gĕ-pek')	luggage
das Handgepäck (hant'-gĕ-pek)	hand baggage
der Koffer (ko'-fĕr)	trunk
der Handkoffer (hant'-ko-fĕr)	suitcase
der Gepäckträger (gĕ-pek'-tray-gĕr)	porter
die Aktentasche (ak'-tĕn-ta-shĕ)	brief case
das Gepäck aufgeben	to check
(gĕ-pek' owf'-gay-bĕn)	baggage

die Seefahrt (zay'-fahrt)	sea voyage
erster Klasse, zweiter Klasse, dritter Klasse	first class, second class,
(ayr'-stĕr kla'-sĕ, tsvī'-tĕr..., dri'-tĕr...)	third class
die Kabine (ka-bee'-nĕ)	cabin, stateroom
die Touristenklasse (too-ri'-stĕn-kla-sĕ)	tourist class
der Zahlmeister (tsahl'-mī-stĕr)	purser, paymaster
der Herrensalon (he'-rĕn-za-long)	smoking room
der Damensalon (dah'-mĕn-za-long)	ladies' lounge

die Tafel (tah'-fĕl)	dining table	die Fahrt (fahrt)	trip
das Deck (dek)	deck	der Hafen (hah'-fĕn)	harbor
der Saal (zahl)	hall, large room	der Pier (peer)	pier

der Raum (rowm), die Räume (roi'-mĕ)	space, room,-s
der Tisch (tish), die Tische (ti'-shĕ)	table,-s
ausruhen (ows'-roo-ĕn)	to rest
die Abfahrt (ap'-fahrt), die Abfahrten (ap'-fahr-tĕn)	departure,-s
der Pass (pas), die Pässe (pe'-sĕ)	passport,-s
die Einreiseerlaubnis (īn'-rī-zĕ-ĕr-lowp-nis)	entry permit
der Reisescheck, die Reiseschecks (rī'-zĕ-sheks)	travelers' check,-s
gemütlich (gĕ-müht'-lich)	cozy, comfortable
ungemütlich² (un'-gĕ-müht-lich)	uncomfortable
das Bett (bet), die Betten (be'-tĕn)	bed,-s

CONVERSATION

1 Sieh, da kommt Smith!

2 Er läuft[3] so schnell mit seinem Gepäck.

3 Guten Morgen, Frau Miller. Ich kann kaum atmen. Komme ich zu spät?[4]

4 Oh, nein, wir haben noch[5] Zeit. Warum geben Sie Ihr Gepäck nicht[6] auf?

5 Mein Koffer ist schon auf dem Schiff.[7] Dies ist nur mein Handgepäck.

6 Sie haben Ihren Namen und die Kabinennummer gleich auf dem Handkoffer und dem Kabinenkoffer. Das ist sehr praktisch.

7 Darum kam ich beinah zu spät;[4] die Gepäckzettel wollten nicht kleben.

8 Hören Sie die Schiffspfeife? Lassen Sie uns an Bord gehen!

9 Ich komme noch[5] mit aufs[7] Schiff und sehe mir[8] die Kabine an.

10 Wartet[9] einen Augenblick! Wo sind meine Papiere?

11 Vielleicht in der Aktentasche unter Ihrem[7] Arm?

12 Aber natürlich! Hier sind mein Pass, die Einreiseerlaubnis,[10] die Schiffsfahrkarte und meine Reiseschecks.

13 Hans, du bist so vergesslich. Gib deine Papiere und Wertsachen dem Zahlmeister zum Aufbewahren!

FOOTNOTES: *1.* From this lesson on, the nominative plural for each noun will be given in the vocabulary. All other cases of the plural can be formed if the nominative plural is known, since the article declension in the plural is the same for all genders (nom. *die;* gen. *der;* dat. *den;* acc. *die*), and since only an *–n* is added to the nominative plural in the dative case (*die Männer—den Männern;*

PRONUNCIATION

1 zee, dah komt *Smith.*

2 ayr loift zoh shnel mit zī'-nĕm gĕ-pek'.

3 goo'-tĕn mor'-gĕn, frow *Miller.* ich kan kowm aht'- mĕn. ko'-mĕ ich tsoo shpayt?

4 oh, nīn, veer hah'-bĕn nokh tsīt. vah-rum' gay'-bĕn zee eer gĕ-pek' nicht owf?

5 mīn ko'-fĕr ist shohn owf daym shif. dees ist noor mīn hant'-gĕ-pek.

6 zee hah'-bĕn ee'-rĕn nah'-mĕn unt dee ka-bee'-nĕn-nu-mĕr glīch owf daym hant'-ko-fĕr unt daym ka-bee'-nĕn-ko-fĕr. das ist zayr prak'-tish.

7 dah-rum' kahm ich bī-nah' tsoo shpayt; dee gĕ-pek'-tse-tĕl vol'-tĕn nicht klay'-bĕn.

8 höh'-rĕn zee dee shifs'-pfī-fĕ? la'-sĕn zee uns an bort gay'-ĕn.

9 ich ko'-mĕ nokh mit owfs shif unt zay'-ĕ meer dee ka-bee'-nĕ an.

10 var'-tĕt ī'-nĕn ow'-gĕn-blik. voh zint mī'-nĕ pa-pee'-rĕ?

11 fee-līcht' in dayr ak'-tĕn-ta-shĕ un'-tĕr ee'-rĕm arm?

12 ah'-bĕr na-tühr'-lich. heer zint mīn pas, dee īn'-rī-zĕ-ĕr-lowp-nis, dee shifs'-fahr-kar-tĕ unt mī'-nĕ rī'-zĕ-sheks.

13 hans, doo bist zoh fĕr-ges'-lich. gip dī'-nĕ pa-pee'-rĕ unt vayrt'-za-khĕn daym tsahl'-mī-stĕr tsoom owf'-bĕ-vah-rĕn.

TRANSLATION

Look, there comes Smith.

He is running so fast with his baggage.

Good morning, Mrs. Miller. I can hardly breathe. Am I late?

Oh, no, we still have time. Why don't you check your baggage?

My trunk is already on the ship. This is only my hand luggage.

You have your name and cabin number right (*lit.,* immediately) on your suitcase and trunk. That is very practical.

Because of it, I was almost late; the baggage labels wouldn't (*lit.,* wanted not) stick. Do you hear the steamer whistle? Let us go on board.

I'll come on shipboard with you and look at your cabin.

Wait a moment! Where are my identification papers?

Perhaps in your brief case under your arm?

But of course! Here are my passport, the entry permit, the steamer ticket, and my travelers' checks.

Hans, you are so absent-minded (*lit.,* forgetful). Give your papers and valuables to the ship's purser for safekeeping.

---

die *Pässe*—den *Pässen;* die *Söhne*—den *Söhnen*). If, however, the plural nominative ends in *–en,* a dative *–n* is not added (die *Frauen*—den *Frauen;* die *Französinnen*—den *Französinnen*).   2. To change an adjective from a positive to a negative, the prefix *un–* is often added and then the prefix is stressed.   3. er *läuft,* "he runs;" infinitive *laufen,* "to run." German verbs are divided into two groups.

14 Mutter, du hast wie immer recht!

15 Nun müssen wir unsere Kabine suchen.

16 Wir haben eine Aussenkabine auf dem⁷ B-Deck. Steward, wo ist die zweite Klasse?

17 Diese Treppe führt hinunter in die⁷ zweite Klasse, Deck B.

18 Diese Kabine ist sehr gemütlich. Sie hat sogar fliessendes Wasser.

19 In der⁷ Touristenklasse stehen die Betten nicht frei. Da hat man ein Bett über dem⁷ andern.

20 Du bist nun zufrieden, Mutter, und kannst ruhig schlafen, nicht wahr?

21 Komm, nun zeigen wir dir¹² noch die anderen¹¹ Räume.

22 Dies ist der Speisesaal.

23 Wir sitzen nicht an einer⁷ langen Tafel, sondern an kleinen¹¹ Tischen zu vier.

24 Wie gross¹¹ und hell¹¹ der Saal ist!

25 Hier ist der Rauchsalon und dort der Damensalon; beinah wie zu Hause.¹³

26 Na, Mutter, willst du nicht mitkommen?

27 Nein, ich muss mich von dir ausruhen.

---

strong and weak verbs. The outstanding characteristic of the strong verbs is the change of the stem vowel in the different tenses. Most strong verbs with the infinitive stem vowels *a, e, au* change these vowels to *ä, i (ie), äu,* respectively, in the second and third persons singular of the present tense: *fahren* (to ride), *du fährst. er fährt; sehen* (to see), *du siehst, er sieht; geben* (to give), *du gibst, er gibt; laufen* (to run), *du läufst, er läuft.* In the weak verbs the stem vowel never changes. *4. zu spät kommen,* "to be late." ID., *lit.,* to come too late. The *zu* may not be omitted, since it means *too* late.   *5. noch,* "still, yet." Often not translatable,

14 mu'-tĕr, doo hast vee i'-mĕr recht.

Mother, you are right, as always (*lit.*, you have as always right).

15 noon mü'-sĕn veer un'-zĕ-rĕ ka-bee'-nĕ zoo'-khĕn.

Now we have to look for our cabin.

16 veer hah'-bĕn ĭ'-nĕ ow'-sĕn-ka-bee-nĕ owf daym bay'-dek. stoo'-art voh ist dee tsvĭ'-tĕ kla'-sĕ?

We have an outside cabin on B deck. Steward, where is the second class?

17 dee'-zĕ tre'-pĕ führt hi-nun'-tĕr in dee tsvĭ'-tĕ kla'-sĕ, dek bay.

This staircase leads down to the second class, deck B.

18 dee-zĕ ka-bee'-nĕ ist zayr gĕ-müht'-lich. zee hat zoh-gahr' flee-sĕn-dĕs va'-sĕr.

This cabin is very cozy. It even has running water.

19 in dayr too-ri'-stĕn-kla-sĕ shtay'-ĕn dee be'-tĕn nicht frī, dah hat man īn bet üh'-bĕr daym an'-dĕrn.

In tourist class the beds don't stand free. There (*lit.*, one has) one bed is above the other.

20 doo bist nun tsoo-free'-dĕn, mu'-tĕr, unt kanst roo'-ich shlah'-fĕn, nicht vahr?

Now, you are satisfied, Mother, and will be able to sleep peacefully, won't you?

21 kom. nun tsī-gĕn veer deer nokh dee an'-dĕ-rĕn roi'-mĕ.

Come, now we'll show you the other rooms.

22 dees ist dayr shpĭ'-sĕ-zahl.

This is the dining hall.

23 veer zi'-tsĕn nicht an ĭ'-nĕr lang'-en tah'-fĕl, zon'-dĕrn an klī'-nĕn ti'-shĕn tsoo feer.

We do not sit at a long table, but at small tables for four.

24 vee grohs unt hel dayr zahl ist!

How large and light this hall is!

25 heer ist dayr rowkh'-za-lohng unt dort dayr dah'-mĕn-za-lohng; bĭ'-nah vee tsoo how'-zĕ.

Here is the men's smoking lounge and there is the ladies lounge; almost like at home.

26 nah, mu'-tĕr, vilst doo nicht mit'-ko-mĕn?

Well, Mother, don't you want to come with us?

27 nīn, ich mus mich fon deer ows'-roo-ĕn.

No, I have to take a rest from you.

---

like *schon*, "already," and *ja*, "yes." German conversation is full of these little words which take different shades of meaning, and each has to be learned.   6. Note the position of *nicht*. Usually *nicht* has the tendency to precede the very word it actually negates. In this case, the prefix *auf* gives the verb *geben* a different meaning, which explains the position of *nicht*.   7. *auf*, "on, on top of," is one of the prepositions that takes either the dative or the accusative case. "Place where" requires the dative: *Mein Koffer ist auf dem Schiff.*—"My trunk is on the ship." "Place where to" requires the accusative: *Ich komme aufs* (contraction—*auf das*)

28 Frau Miller, ich höre das erste Signal zur[14] Abfahrt. Sie müssen leider das Schiff verlassen.

29 Nun aber schnell nach oben!

30 Auf Wiedersehen, Herr Smith, glückliche[11] Reise und viel Vergnügen!

31 Leben Sie wohl, Frau Miller, und sorgen Sie sich nicht um[15] Ihren Sohn!

32 Lass es dir gut gehen, mein Junge! Grüsse[16] Vater, Tante und Onkel und alle Verwandten von mir! Glückliche Reise![17]

33 Das Schiff setzt sich in Bewegung und die Kapelle spielt "Auld Lang Syne".

34 Ich bekomme schon jetzt Heimweh.

35 Mir ist auch komisch zumute,[18] die Heimat zu verlassen.

Schiff.—"I'll come on the ship." The prepositions which follow the same rule are: *an* (at, on); *auf* (on, on top of); *hinter* (behind); *in* (in, into); *neben* (next to); *über* (over, above); *unter* (under, among); *vor* (in front of); *zwischen* (between). *8. sich ansehen* is used reflexively and requires the dative form of reflexive pronoun. *an*, "at," is a separable prefix, i.e. the prefix follows the verb when used in the simple tenses [§68]. *9.* All verbs whose infinitive stems end in a *t* insert an *e* before an ending starting with *t* or *st*: *ich warte* (I wait), *du wartest, er wartet, wir warten, ihr wartet, sie warten, Sie warten. 10.* Notice the glottal stop after *Einreise—(erlaubnis)* in the pronunciation. *11.* Notice the difference in endings of the adjectives. *12. dir zeigen,* "show to you." *Dir* is the dative case of *du*.

28 frow *Miller,* ich höh'-re das ayr'-stĕ zig'-nahl tsoor ap'-fahrt. zee mü'-sĕn lī'-dĕr das shif fĕr-la'-sĕn.
29 noon ah'-bĕr shnel nahkh oh'-bĕn.
30 owf vee'-dĕr-zayn, her *Smith,* glük'-li-*ch*ĕ rī'-zĕ unt feel fĕr-gnüh'-gĕn.

31 lay'-bĕn zee vohl, frow *Miller,* unt zor'-gĕn zee *zi*ch ni*ch*t um ee'-rĕn zohn.
32 las es deer goot gay'-ĕn, mīn yung'-ĕ. grüh'sĕ fah'-tĕr, tan'-tĕ unt ong'-kĕl unt a'-lĕ fĕr-van'-tĕn fon meer. glük'-li-*ch*ĕ rī'-zĕ.

33 das shif zetst *zi*ch in bĕ-vay'-gung unt dee ka-pe'-lĕ shpeelt *Auld Lang Syne.*
34 ich bĕ-ko'-mĕ shohn yetst hīm'-vay.
35 meer ist owkh koh'-mish tsoo-moo'-tĕ, dee hī'-mat tsoo fĕr-la'-sĕn.

Mrs. Miller, I hear the first signal for departure. Unfortunately, you have to leave the boat.
But now let's hurry upstairs (*lit.,* now but quick upstairs)!
Good-bye, Mr. Smith, bon voyage and lots of fun.

Good-bye (*lit.,* live you well), Mrs. Miller, and don't worry about your son.
Good luck (*lit.,* let it to you go well), my boy. Give my love to Father, Aunt and Uncle and all our relatives (*lit.,* all relatives from me). Bon Voyage!
The ship is moving (*lit.,* sets itself in motion) and the band is playing *Auld Lang Syne.*
I'm getting homesick already.

I also feel strange about leaving my native country.

Zeigen is an intransitive verb that requires the dative.   *13. zu Hause,* "at home." ID. It is used only when referring to one's own home.   *14. zur,* contraction of *zu der.*   15. *sich sorgen um,* ID., "to worry about." *Lit.,* "to oneself worry about"; *um,* "about, around," is a preposition that takes the accusative case.   16. *grüsse!* (familiar form), *grüsst! grüsen Sie!* (polite form), can have many meanings, depending on to whom one speaks: "best regards," "remember me to," "give my love to," etc.   17. *Glückliche Reise,* "bon voyage." *Lit.,* Happy trip.   *18. Mir ist komisch zumute,* "I am feeling funny." *Lit.,* to me is funny to mood. The dative case is required, as in most idiomatic expressions referring to one's well-being or emotions.

Fünfte Lektion

Neue Wörter für diese Lektion

weniger (vay'-ni-gĕr)	less	zuerst (tsoo-ayrst')	first, at first
mehr als (mayr als)	more than	tun (toon)	to do, make
sollen (zo'-lĕn)	supposed to	die Zahl,-en* (tsahl)	number
er soll (ayr zol)	he ought to	wer (vayr)	who
zusammen (tsoo-za'-mĕn)	together	das Spiel,-e (shpeel)	game, play
rechnen (rech'-nĕn)	to figure	gewinnen (gĕ-vi'-nĕn)	to win, gain
verlieren (fĕr-lee'-rĕn)	to lose	der Punkt,-e (pungkt)	point, dot
können (kö'-nĕn)	to be able	mieten (mee'-tĕn)	to rent
er kann (kan)	he can	bleiben (blī'-bĕn)	to remain

das Wetter (ve'-tĕr)	weather
die Sonne,-"e (zo'-nĕ)	sun
bewölkt sein (bĕ-völkt' zīn)	to be cloudy
es ist bewölkt (es ist . . .)	it is cloudy

der Regen (ray'-gĕn)	rain	der Donner (do'-nĕr)	thunder
regnen (rayg'-nĕn)	to rain	der Blitz,-e (blits)	lightning
das Gewitter,- (gĕ-vi'-tĕr)	thunderstorm	der Sturm,-"e (shturm)	storm
		die Wolke,-n (vol'-kĕ)	cloud

soviel wie (zoh-feel' vee)	as much as
das Glück (glük)	luck, happiness
das Unglück (un'-glük)	misfortune, bad luck
der Liegestuhl,-"e (lee'-gĕ-shtool)	deck chair
recht haben (recht hah'-bĕn)	to be right

FRACTIONS	**BRÜCHE**	(brü'-chĕ)

ein Drittel (dri'-tĕl)	a third	ein Achtel (akh'-tĕl)	an eighth
ein Viertel (feer'-tĕl)	a fourth	die Hälfte (helf'-tĕ)	the half
ein Sechstel (zeks'-tĕl)	a sixth		

halb, ein Halbes (halp, hal'-bĕs)	half, a half
ein Siebentel (zee'-bĕn-tĕl)	a seventh
ein Zwanzigstel (tsvan'-tsik-stĕl)	a twentieth
ein Hundertstel (hun'-dĕrt-stĕl)	a hundredth

GRUNDZAHLEN

(grunt'-tsah-lĕn)

0. die Null,-en (nul)
1. ein, eins (īn) (īns)
2. zwei (tsvī)
3. drei (drī)
4. vier (feer)

5. fünf (fünf)
6. sechs (zeks)
7. sieben (zee'-bĕn)
8. acht (akht)

9. neun (noin)
10. zehn (tsayn)
11. elf (elf)
12. zwölf (tsvölf)

13. dreizehn (drī'-tsayn)
14. vierzehn (feer'-tsayn)
15. fünfzehn (fünf'-tsayn)
16. sechzehn (zech'-tsayn)

17. siebzehn (zeep'-tsayn)
18. achtzehn (akht'-tsayn)
19. neunzehn (noin'-tsayn)
20. zwanzig (tsvan'-tsich)

21. einundzwanzig (īn'-unt- . . .)
22. zweiundzwanzig (tsvī'-unt- . . .)
23. dreiundzwanzig (drī'-unt- . . .)

30. dreissig (drī'-sich)
31. einunddreissig (īn'-unt- . . .)
32. zweiunddreissig (tsvī'-unt- . . .)

40. vierzig (feer'-tsich)
50. fünfzig (fünf'-tsich)
60. sechzig (zech'-tsich)

70. siebzig (zeep'-tsich)
80. achtzig (akh'-tsich)
90. neunzig (noin'-tsich)

100. hundert (hun'-dĕrt)
101. hunderteins (hun'-dĕrt-īns')
102. hundertzwei (. . . -tsvī')
200. zweihundert (tsvī'-hun-dĕrt)
202. zweihundertzwei

300. dreihundert
1000. tausend (tow'-zĕnt)
2000. zweitausend (tsvī'-tow-zĕnt)
100,000. hunderttausend
1,000,000. eine Million (mil-iohn')

ORDNUNGSZAHLEN

(ord'-nungs-tsah-lĕn)

erste (ayr'-stĕ)	first	siebente (zee'-bĕn-tĕ)	seventh
zweite (tsvī'-tĕ)	second	achte (akh'-tĕ)	eighth
dritte (dri'-tĕ)	third	neunte (noin'-tĕ)	ninth
vierte (feer'-tĕ)	fourth	zehnte (tsayn'-tĕ)	tenth
fünfte (fünf'-tĕ)	fifth	elfte (elf'-tĕ)	eleventh
sechste (zek'-stĕ)	sixth	zwölfte (tsvölf'-tĕ)	twelfth

zwanzigste (tsvan'-tsik-stĕ)	twentieth
dreissigste (drī'-sik-stĕ)	thirtieth
hundertste (hun'-dĕrt-stĕ)	hundredth
hunderterste (hun-dĕrt-ayr'-stĕ)	hundred first
tausendste (tow'-zĕnt-stĕ)	thousandth

---

*From this point on plurals will be indicated in condensed form; that is, endings only will be given and vowel changes where they occur.

Conversation

1 Dort kommen unsere neuen Bekannten. Guten Morgen, meine Damen! Setzen wir uns auf unsere Liegestühle, Nummer sechzehn, achtzehn und zweiunddreissig. Wo ist Ihr Stuhl, Herr Smith?

2 Ich habe noch keinen gemietet.[1] Wieviel kostet ein Liegestuhl?

3 Fünfzig Cent[2] den Tag und zwei Dollar[2] für die Reise. Aber heute können wir kaum an Deck bleiben.

4 Sie haben recht. Es ist nach dem Regen und Gewitter kalt geworden.[3]

5 Jetzt kann ich es ja sagen. Ich fürchtete[4] mich vor[5] dem Gewitter. Das Blitzen war[6] nicht so schlimm, aber das Donnern...

6 Ich weiss, Fräulein Barnett. Ich werde[7] auch nervös, wenn es donnert. Darum ging[8] ich in die Kabine.

7 Oh, diese Frauen! Der Himmel ist nur leicht bewölkt, aber die Sonne scheint durch die Wolken. Wir hatten[9] soweit Glück. Das Wetter ist nicht schlecht; es ist nur kalt.

8 Ich habe eine Idee. Wir gehen in den Rauchsalon und spielen bis zum Mittagessen Karten.

9 So können wir uns die Zeit vertreiben.[10] Vielleicht wird es später dann schön und warm werden.

FOOTNOTES: *1. Ich habe . . . gemietet* (have . . . rented), the present perfect tense of *mieten* (to rent), a weak verb [§64, d].   2. Monetary units do not take a plural ending in German. Therefore, *ein Cent* (one cent), but also *fünfzig Cent* (fifty cents), *zwei Dollar* (two dollars).   *3. ist geworden* (has become) is the present perfect tense of *werden*. Most verbs are conjugated with *haben* (to have), as in

PRONUNCIATION

1 dort ko'-měn un'-zě-rě noi'-ěn bě-kan'-těn. goo'-těn mor'-gěn, mī'-ně dah'-měn. ze' tsěn veer uns owf un'-zěrě lee'-gě-shtüh-lě, nu'-měr zech'-tsayn, akh'-tsayn unt tsvī -unt-drī-si*ch*. voh ist eer shtool, her *Smith?*

2 i*ch* hah'-bě nokh kī'-něn gě-mee'-tět. vee'-feel ko'-stět īn lee'-gě-shtool?

3 fünf'-tsi*ch* tsent dayn tahk unt tsvī do'-lar führ dee rī'-zě. ah'-běr hoi'-tě kö'-něn veer kowm an dek blī'-běn.

4 zee hah'-běn re*ch*t. es ist nahkh daym ray'-gěn unt gě-vi' těr kalt gě-vor'-děn.

5 yetst kan i*ch* es yah zah'-gěn. i*ch* für*ch*'-tě-tě mi*ch* fohr daym ge-vi'-těr. das blī'-tsěn vahr ni*ch*t zoh shlim ah'-běr das do'-něrn . . .

6 i*ch* vīs . . . i*ch* vayr'-dě owkh ner-vöhs' ven es do'-něrt. dah'-rum ging i*ch* in dee ka-bee'-ně.

7 oh dee'-zě frow'-ěn! dayr hi'-měl ist noor li*ch*t bě-völkt' ah'-běr dee zo'-ně shīnt dur*ch* dee vol'-kěn. veer ha'-těn zoh-wīt' glük. das ve'-těr ist ni*ch*t shle*ch*t; es ist noor kalt.

8 i*ch* hah'-bě ī'-ně ee-day'. veer gay'-ěn in dayn rowkh'-za-long unt shpee'-lěn bis tsum mi'-tahk-e-sěn kar'-těn.

9 zoh kö'-něn veer uns dee tsīt fěr-trī'-běn. fee-li*ch*t' virt es shpay'-těr dan shöhn unt varm vayr'-děn.

TRANSLATION

There come our new acquaintances. Good morning, ladies. Let us sit down on our deck chairs; numbers 16, 18, and 32. Where is your chair, Mr. Smith?

I still have not rented one. How much does a deck chair cost?

Fifty cents a day and two dollars for the trip. But today we can hardly stay on deck.

You are right. It got cold after the rain and thunderstorm.

Now I can say it. I was afraid of the storm. The lightning was not so bad, but the thunder . . .

I know, Miss Barnett. I get nervous, too, when it thunders. Therefore, I went to the cabin.

Oh, these women! The sky is only slightly cloudy, but the sun is shining through the clouds. We have been lucky so far. The weather is not bad; it is only cold.

I have an idea. Let's go into the smoking room and play cards until dinner.

Thus we can pass the time (*lit.,* drive the time away). Perhaps it will become fair and warm later.

English, but some verbs are conjugated with *sein* (to be) [§59]. *4. ich fürchtete* (I was afraid) is the past tense of the weak verb *fürchten* (to fear). Since the infinitive stem of *fürchten* ends in t (*fürcht*), an *e* is inserted between the verb stem and the endings of the past tense. All tenses of the weak verb are based on the infinitive stem. The personal endings of the past are: *ich— te, du— -test, er— -te,*

10 Bitte, geben Sie zuerst, Herr Smith! Mischen Sie die Karten gut! Wer schreibt auf?

11 Das möchte ich gern tun. Die Zahlen auf deutsch[11] machen mir noch Schwierigkeiten!

12 Bis zwanzig ist das System wie im Englischen, aber nach zwanzig muss[12] man im Deutschen addieren: ein-und-zwanzig, dass heisst,[13] man zählt[12] von hinten nach vorne.[14]

13 Ich habe schon lange nicht gespielt.[15] Wir brauchen zweiundfünfzig Karten und spielen bis eintausend. Wer zuerst tausend hat, gewinnt das Spiel, nicht wahr?

14 Ja! Sie spielen bitte aus. Das war ein guter[16] Stich. Nun kommen Sie heran, Herr Miller.

15 Wieviel ist das? Drei mal zwölf ist sechsunddreissig.[17]

16 Achtundvierzig[17] hatten[9] Sie schon; das ist zusammen vierundachtzig.

17 Fräulein Kruger gab[18] eben. Jetzt geben Sie und ich mische die Karten. Sie können nicht immer alle Trümpfe haben.

---

wir— -ten, ihr— tet, ste— -ten, Sie— -ten [§61, b].   *5. sich fürchten vor.* ID., to be afraid of. *sich fürchten* is a reflexive verb [§27]. *vor* (before, in front of) takes either accusative or dative. In this expression, however, it takes the dative case [§38, b]. *6. war* (was), past tense of *sein* (to be), an irregular verb which, however, takes the regular strong endings of the past tense: *ich war* (I was), *du warst* (you were), *er war* (he was), *wir waren* (we were), *ihr wart* (you were), *sie waren* (they were), *Sie waren* (you were) [§59, 2].   *7. Ich werde* (I become). *Werden* (to become, get) is a verb in its own right and is also used as an auxiliary verb (helping verb) in German to form the future tenses: *es wird werden* (it will become). *Werden* is an irregular verb. The present tense is: *ich werde, du wirst, er wird, wir werden, ihr werdet, sie werden, Sie werden* [§59]. *8. Ging ich* (I went). The personal endings of the past tense are the same for all strong verbs. The first and third persons singular have no endings: *ich—, du— -st, er—, wir— -en, ihr— -t, sie— -en, Sie— -en.* These endings are added to the so-called past stem of the verb. The stem corres-

10 bi'-tĕ gay'-bĕn zee tsoo-ayrst' her
Smith! mi'-shĕn zee dee kar'-tĕn
goot. vayr shrīpt owf?

Please, Mr. Smith, you deal first.
Shuffle the cards well. Who will
keep score (*lit.*, write down)?

11 das möch'-tĕ *ich* gern toon. dee
tsah'-lĕn owf doitsh ma'-khĕn
meer nokh shvee'-rik-kī-tĕn'.

I would like to do that. The numbers in German still cause me
difficulty.

12 bis tsvan'-tsi*ch* ist das zi-staym'
vee im eng'-li-shĕn ah'-bĕr nahkh
tsvan'-tsi*ch* mus man im doit'-
shĕn a-dee'-rĕn: īn-unt-tsvan'-
tsi*ch*, das hīst, man tsaylt fon
hin'-tĕn nahkh for'-nĕ.

Up to twenty the system is the
same as in English, but after
twenty one must add in German: one-and-twenty, that is,
one counts from back to front.

13 ich hah'-bĕ shohn lang'-e ni*ch*t
gĕ-shpeelt'. veer brow'khĕn tsvī-
unt-fünf'-tsi*ch* kar'-tĕn unt
shpee'-lĕn bis īn-tow' zĕnt. vayr
tsoo-ayrst' tow'-zĕnt hat, gĕ-vint'
das shpeel, ni*ch*t vahr?

I have not played for a long time.
We'll need fifty-two cards and
we'll play to one thousand.
Whoever has a thousand first
wins the game, right?

14 yah; zee shpee'-lĕn bi'-tĕ ows. das
vahr īn goo'-tĕr shti*ch*. noon ko'-
mĕn zee he-ran', her *Miller.*

Yes. Please, you lead. That was
a good trick. Now it's your
turn, Mr. Miller.

15 vee-feel' ist das? drī mahl tsvölf
ist seks'-unt-drī-si*ch*.

How much is that? Three times
twelve is thirty-six.

16 akht'-unt-feer'-tsi*ch* ha'-tĕn zee
shohn; das ist tsoo-za'-mĕn feer'-
unt-akh'-tsi*ch*.

You had forty-eight already; together that makes eighty-four.

17 froi'-līn Kruger gap ay'-bĕn. yetst
gay'-bĕn zee unt *ich* mi'-shĕ dee
kar'-tĕn. zee kö'-nĕn ni*ch*t i'-mĕr
a'-lĕ trüm'-pfĕ hah'-bĕn.

Miss Kruger just dealt. Now you
deal and I will mix the cards.
You can't always have all the
trumps.

---

ponds to the first person singular and must be learned for each strong verb
[§65, b; §67, b]. *9. wir hatten . . . Glück* (we were lucky), past tense of *Glück
haben.* ID., to be lucky. *hatten* (had), past tense of *haben* (to have), which is conjugated almost like a weak verb, although slightly irregular in its stem: *ich hatte*
(I had), *du hattest* (you had), *er hatte* (he had), *wir hatten* (we had), *ihr hattet*
(you had), *sie hatten* (they had), *Sie hatten* (you had). *10. sich die
Zeit vertreiben mit.* ID., to pass the time with or to while away one's time with.
11. auf deutsch. ID., in German, *lit.*, on German. *12. man muss* ("one" must);
man zählt ("one" counts). The indefinite pronoun *man* is frequently used in
German when referring to people in general. *13. dass heisst* (abbr. *d.h.*). ID., that
is, *lit.*, that is called. *14. von hinten nach vorne.* ID., backward, *lit.*, from back
to front. *15. ich habe gespielt* (I have played), the present perfect tense of
spielen (to play). The past tense is a simple tense, the present perfect is a compound tense of the past: *ich habe gespielt* (I have played), *du hast gespielt* (you

18 Sehen Sie wie hoch Herr Smith steht! Er hat schon fünf-
hundertzweiundneunzig;[17] ich habe über zweihundert-
zehn Punkte weniger.[19]

19 Und Fräulein Barnett hat hundertfünfundsiebzig[17]
Punkte mehr als[20] ich.

20 Was soll *ich* sagen? Ich habe, alles zusammengerechnet,[21]
nur hundertsiebenundsiebzig.[17] Herr Smith hat also
über drei mal soviel wie[22] ich.

21 Ja, ja, "Glück im Spiel, Unglück in der Liebe." Dann
verliere ich schon lieber[23] im Kartenspiel.

22 Herr Smith hat tausendeinhundertzweiundvierzig.[17] Ich
gratuliere.

23 Nun haben wir noch fünfundzwanzig Minuten bis zum
Essen. Wir ziehen uns erst um[24] und treffen uns[25] bei
Tisch.[26]

24 Wir haben uns sehr gut amüsiert.[27]

---

have played), *er hat gespielt* (he has played), *wir haben gespielt* (we have played),
ihr habt gespielt (you have played), *sie haben gespielt* (they have played), *Sie haben
gespielt* (you have played). The present perfect is formed with the present tense
of *haben* (to have) or *sein* (to be) and the past participle of the main verb. The past
participle of weak verbs is derived from the infinitive stem to which the prefix
ge- and the suffix *-t* are added: *gespielt* (played) [§60, b; 64, c]. Note the position
of the past participle at the end of the sentence [§79]. *16. ein guter Stich* (a good
trick). Adjectives preceding nouns take definite endings, depending on whether
or not they are preceded by an article. Predicate adjectives, however, that is,
adjectives that follow *sein* (to be), remain unchanged: *Das Wetter ist nicht schlecht.
Es ist gut.* The weather is not bad. It is good [§42, a; §42, b; §43]. *17.* Numbers
are written in one word, except *Million, Billion*, etc., since these numbers are
nouns. The construction of numbers and their uses are explained in detail in §51

18 zay'-ĕn zee vee hohkh her *Smith*
shtayt! ayr hat shohn fünf'-hun-
dĕrt-tsvī'-unt-noin'-tsi*ch*, unt *ich*
hah'-bĕ üh'-bĕr tsvī'-hun-dĕrt-
tsayhn pungk'-tĕ vay'-ni-gĕr.

19 unt froi'-līn *Barnett* hat hun'-
dĕrt-fünf-unt-zeep'-tsi*ch* pungk'-
tĕ mayr als i*ch*.

20 vas zol *ich* zah'-gĕn? *ich* hah'-bĕ
a'-lĕs tsoo-za'-mĕn-gĕ-re*ch*-nĕt
noor hun'-dĕrt-zee-bĕn-unt-zeep'-
tsi*ch*. her *Smith* hat al'-*zoh* üh'-
bĕr feer mahl zoh-feel' vee i*ch*.

21 yah, yah, glük im shpeel. un'-
glük in dayr lee'-bĕ. dan fĕr-
leer'-ĕ *ich* shohn lee'bĕr im kahr'-
tĕn-shpeel.

22 her *Smith* hat tow'-zĕnt-īn-hun-
dĕrt'-tsvī'-unt-feer'-tsi*ch*. *ich* gra'-
too-lee'-rĕ!

23 noon hah'-bĕn veer nokh fünf'-
unt-tsvan'-tsi*ch* mee-noo'-tĕn bis
tsum e'-sĕn. veer tsee'-ĕn uns
ayrst um unt tre'-fĕn uns bī tish.

24 veer hah'-bĕn uns zayr goot a-
müh-zeert'.

Look how much Mr. Smith has
scored. He has five hundred
ninety-two already, and I have
over two hundred ten points
less.

And Miss Barnett has a hundred
seventy-five points more than I.

What should *I* say? I have only
one hundred seventy-seven all
told (*lit.*, all counted together).
Mr. Smith has therefore more
than three times as much as I.

Yes, yes. "Lucky at cards, unlucky
at love." In that case, (*lit.*,
then) I would rather lose at
card playing.

Mr. Smith has eleven hundred
forty-two. Congratulations!
(*lit.*, I congratulate).

Now we still have twenty-five
minutes till dinner. We will
change (our clothes) first and
then meet at dinner.

We had a very good time.

---

of the Reference Grammar.   *18. gab* (gave), past tense of *geben* (to give), strong
verb. *Ich gab* (I gave), *du gabst* (you gave), *er gab* (he gave), *wir gaben* (we gave),
ihr gabt (you gave), *sie gaben* (they gave), *Sie gaben* (you gave).   *19 weniger* (less),
comparative of *wenig* (little).   *20. mehr als* (more than). *Mehr* (more) is the comparative of *viel* (much).   *21. ich habe zusammengerechnet* (I have added up),
present perfect of *zusammenrechnen* (to add up), from *rechnen*, to figure, and
separable prefix *zusammen* (together).   *22. soviel wie* (as much as). Notice the use
of *wie* (as), and *als* (than), in the comparative.   *23. lieber* (rather), comparative
of *gern* (like).   *24. sich umziehen* (to change one's clothes), reflexive verb with
separable prefix [§27; §68, b, 1].   *25. sich treffen* (to meet), reflexive verb.
26. bei Tisch. I*D.*, at dinner, *lit.*, at table.   *27. sich amüsieren.* I*D.*, to have a good
time. *Lit.*, to amuse oneself, reflexive weak verb. *Wir haben uns amüsiert* (we
have had a good time), present perfect tense.

6 Sechste Lektion

Neue Wörter für diese Lektion

der Tag,-e (tahk)	day	morgen (mor'-gĕn)	tomorrow
die Woche,-n (vo'-khĕ)	week	morgen früh (. . . früh)	tomorrow morning
der Monat,-e (moh'-nat)	month		
das Jahr,-e (yahr)	year	gestern (ges'-tĕrn)	yesterday
heute (hoi'-tĕ)	today		

der[1] Morgen,- (mor'-gĕn)	morning	
der Vormittag,-e (fohr'-mi-tahk)	forenoon	
der Mittag,-e (mi'-tahk)	noon, midday	
der Nachmittag,-e (nahkh'-mi-tahk)	afternoon	
der Abend,-e (ah'-bĕnt)	evening	
die Nacht,-"e[1] (nakht)	night	
die Mitternacht,-"e (mi'-tĕr-nakht)	midnight	

zusammen (tsoo-za'-mĕn)	together	erkennen (ĕr-ke'-nĕn)	to recognize
hinten (hin'-tĕn)	at the back	das Volk,-"er (folk)	people, nation
vorn(e) (forn)	in front		
schlimm (shlim)	bad	das Lied,-er (leet)	song
stellen (shte'-lĕn)	to put, place (upright)	folgen (fol'-gĕn)	to follow
		bedeuten (bĕ-doi'-tĕn)	to mean
helfen (hel'-fĕn)	to help	die Schule,-n (shoo'-lĕ)	school
er hilft (hilft)	he helps	singen (zing'-ĕn)	to sing

die Welt,-en (velt)	world	das Datum (dah'-tum),	the date
drüben (drüh'-bĕn)	over there	Daten (dah'-tĕn)	
letzt (letst)	last	gerade (gĕ-rah'-dĕ)	just now, exactly
aufgeregt (owf'-gĕ-raykt)	excited		
ebenso (ay'-bĕn-zoh)	just the same	beide (bī'-dĕ)	both
		die Lust (lust)	desire
durch (dur*ch*)	through	besonders (bĕ-zon'-dĕrs)	especially
wissen (vi'-sĕn)	to know	frei (frī)	free, open
er weiss (vīs)	he knows	wieso (vee-zoh')	how, why

66

DER TAG • DAS JAHR • DIE JAHRESZEITEN
THE DAY, THE YEAR, THE SEASONS   (tahk, yahr, yah'-rĕs-tsī-tĕn)

DIE SIEBEN TAGE DER WOCHE
THE SEVEN DAYS OF THE WEEK   (dee zee'-bĕn tah'-gĕ dayr vo'-khĕ)

der¹ Sonntag (zon'-tahk)	Sunday	Freitag (frī'-tahk)	Friday
Montag (mohn'-tahk)	Monday	Sonnabend	Saturday
Dienstag (deens'-tahk)	Tuesday	(zon'ah-bĕnt)	
Mittwoch (mit'-vokh)	Wednesday	Samstag (zams'-tahk)	Saturday
Donnerstag	Thursday		
(do'-nĕrs-tahk)			

DIE ZWÖLF MONATE
THE TWELVE MONTHS   (dee tsvölf moh'-na-tĕ)

der¹ Januar (ya'-noo-ar)	January	August (ow-gust')	August
Februar (fay'-broo-ar)	February	September (zep-tem'-bĕr)	September
März (merts)	March	Oktober (ok-toh'-bĕr)	October
April (a-pril')	April	November	November
Mai (mī)	May	(noh-vem'-bĕr)	
Juni (yoo'-ni)	June	Dezember	December
Juli (yoo'-li)	July	(day-tsem'-bĕr)	

DIE VIER JAHRESZEITEN
THE FOUR SEASONS   (dee feer yah'-rĕs-tsī-tĕn)

der¹ Frühling	spring
(früh'-ling)	
der Sommer (zo'-mer)	summer
der Herbst (herpst)	fall
der Winter (vin'-tĕr)	winter

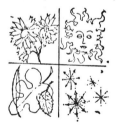

am Morgen² (am mor'-gĕn), morgens² (mor'-gĕns)	in the morning
heute morgen (hoi'-tĕ mor'-gĕn)	this morning
gestern abend (. . . ah'-bĕnt)	last night
übermorgen (üh'-ber-mor-gĕn)	day after tomorrow
vorgestern (fohr'-ge-stĕrn)	day before yesterday
vor einer Woche³ (fohr ī'-nĕr vo'-khĕ)	a week ago
vor einem Monat (. . . moh'-nat)	a month ago
vor einem Jahr (. . . yahr)	a year ago
in acht Tagen (. . . akht tah'-gĕn)	within a week
in einem Monat³ (. . . moh'-nat)	within a month
heute über³ acht Tage (hoi'-tĕ üh'bĕr akht tah'gĕ)	a week from today

Conversation

1 Wie herrlich blau der Himmel ist!

2 Das war gestern ein gemütlicher Abend. Die Zeit vergeht auf dem Schiff sehr schnell.

3 Der wievielte ist heute?⁴ Man vergisst hier das Datum.

4 Heute ist Mittwoch, der 10. (zehnte) Juli. Am Montag,⁵ den 8. (achten) Juli,⁵ fuhren wir ab.

5 Montag landen wir in Hamburg. So haben wir noch Donnerstag, Freitag, Sonnabend und Sonntag auf dem Schiff.

6 Wie schön! Noch beinah eine Woche!

7 Eine Seereise ist wirklich das Schönste auf der Welt.

8 Fahren Sie zum ersten Mal nach Europa, Fräulein Kruger?

9 Oh, nein, dies ist schon meine dritte Reise nach drüben. Letzten Winter waren wir im Februar⁶ in Österreich und im März⁶ in Deutschland; und dann fuhren wir über Frankreich nach England.

10 Es ist sehr schön im Winter⁶ und im Frühling⁶ in den Alpen.

11 Dies ist meine erste Europareise. Ich bin natürlich ganz aufgeregt.

FOOTNOTES: *1.* All parts of the day, days of the week, months, seasons are masculine with the exception of *die Nacht* (the night) and compounds with *die Nacht.* *2. am Morgen* (in the morning). *der Morgen* (the morning). *Morgen* is a noun and is written with a capital letter, but *morgens,* etc., are adverbs and, therefore, are written with a small letter. *3.* The expressions of time formed with the doubtful prepositions take the dative, with the exception of *über: am Morgen, in der Nacht, vor einer Woche, in einem Monat;* but, *über eine Woche,* etc. [§38, b]. *4. Der wievielte ist heute?* or *Den wievielten haben wir heute?* "What is today's date?" ID., *lit.,* The how many is today? *or* The how many do we have today? The verb *sein* (to be) takes the nominative [§21, b]. *haben* (to have) takes the accusative

PRONUNCIATION

1 vee her'-li*ch* blow dayr hi'-měl ist.

2 das vahr ge'-stĕrn in gĕ-müht'-li-*ch*ĕr ah'-bĕnt. dee tsit fĕr-gayt' owf daym shif zayr shnell.

3 dayr vee'-feel-tĕ ist hoi'-tĕ? man fĕr-gist heer das dah'-tum.

4 hoi'-tĕ ist mit'vokh, dayr tsayn'-tĕ yoo'-li. am mohn'-tahk, dayn akh'-tĕn yoo'-li, foo'-rĕn veer ap.

5 mohn'-tahk lan'-dĕn veer in ham'-burk. zoh hah'-bĕn veer nokh do'nĕrs-tahk, frī'-tahk, zon'-ah-bĕnt unt zon'-tahk . . .

6 vee shöhn. nokh bī'-nah ī'-nĕ vo'-khĕ!

7 ī'-nĕ zay'-rī-zĕ ist virk'-li*ch* das shöhn'-stĕ owf dayr velt.

8 fah'-rĕn zee tsum ayr'-stĕn mahl nahkh oi-roh'-pah . . .

9 oh, nīn, dees ist shohn mī'-nĕ dri'-tĕ rī'-zĕ nahkh drüh'-bĕn. lets'-tĕn vin'-tĕr vah'-rĕn veer im fay'-broo-ar in öh'-stĕr-rī*ch* unt im merts in doitsh'-lant; unt dan foo-rĕn veer üh'-bĕr frangk'-rī*ch* nahkh eng'-lant.

10 es ist zayr shöhn im vin'-tĕr . . . früh'-ling in dayn al'-pĕn.

11 dees ist mī'-nĕ ayr'-stĕ oi-roh'-pah-rī-zĕ. i*ch* bin na-tühr'-li*ch* gans owf'-gĕ-raykt.

TRANSLATION

How magnificently blue the sky is.

That was a very congenial evening yesterday. Time passes very quickly on the ship.

What is today's date? One forgets the date here.

Today is Wednesday, July 10. We sailed on Monday, July 8.

We'll land in Hamburg Monday. So we still have Thursday, Friday, Saturday, and Sunday on board.

How beautiful! Still almost a week!

An ocean voyage really is the most beautiful thing in the world.

Are you going to Europe for the first time, Miss Kruger?

Oh, no, this is (already) my third trip abroad. Last winter we were in Austria in February and in Germany in March; and then we journeyed to England by way of France (*lit.,* over France to England).

In the winter and in the spring it is very beautiful in the Alps.

This is my first trip to Europe. Naturally I am very excited.

case [§24, a].   *5. am Montag.* ID., *lit.,* on the Monday. *den 8. Juli.* ID., *lit.,* the 8th July. The date is expressed by the article in the accusative; the day precedes the month, and the period after the number indicates the ordinal number.   *6. im Februar, im März, im Winter, im Frühling,* etc. The months are usually used with the article in German; the seasons always. *Im* is a contraction of *in dem.*   *7. ich habe besucht,* present perfect of *besuchen* (to visit), weak verb [§64, d].   *8. ich bin gereist* (I have traveled), present perfect of *reisen* (to travel), weak verb. Most verbs are conjugated with *haben* (to have) in German, but some are conjugated with *sein* (to be) [§63, b].   *9.* There are three translations of the English verb "to know" in German: 1. *wissen*—to know one single fact; 2. *kennen*—to know a person

12 Mir geht es ebenso, Fräulein Barnett. Ich habe nur letzten Herbst Verwandte in Kanada besucht.[7] Ich war dort zwei Monate.

13 Ich bin vor fünf Jahren durch Mexiko gereist,[8] aber Europa kenne[9] ich noch nicht.

14 Da beginnt die Musik. Erkennen Sie, was sie spielen?

15 Das ist ein Potpourri deutscher Volkslieder.

16 Jetzt höre ich es. Das ist: "Ich weiss[10] nicht, was soll es bedeuten."[11]

17 Nun folgt: "Du, du liegst mir im Herzen."[12]

18 Wie oft haben wir diese Lieder in der[13] Schule gesungen.[14] "Lang, lang, ist's (es) her."[15]

19 So schlimm ist es doch nicht, Herr Miller.

20 Warten Sie einmal! Ich habe die Schule vor elf Jahren verlassen.[8] Ich bin schon 27 (siebenundzwanzig).

21 Ich werde auch schon 25 (fünfundzwanzig).

22 Vergessen wir unser Alter, Herr Smith! Fräulein Barnett, darf ich bitten?

23 Gern! Das ist gerade ein Walzer von Strauss.

24 Wie ist es mit uns beiden? Haben Sie Lust, Fräulein Kruger?

25 Zum Tanzen, immer! Besonders im Sommer[6] unter freiem Himmel.

---

or place, to be acquainted with; 3. *können*—to know how. *10. ich weiss* (infinitive: *wissen*, to know) is very similar to the conjugation of the "will" verbs. The present tense is: *ich weiss, du weisst, er weiss, wir wissen, ihr wisst, sie wissen.* *11.* A very well-known German folksong; the text is by Heinrich Heine (1797-1856), the music is by Friedrich Silcher (1789-1860). *12.* Two old folksongs, authors unknown. *13.* "to school, in school, to church, in church" always take the article

12 meer gayt es ay'-bĕn-zoh, froi'-lĭn *Barnett.* i*ch* hạh'-bĕ noor lets'- tĕn herpst fĕr-van'-tĕ in ka'-na- dah bĕ-zukht'. i*ch* vahr dort tsvī moh'-na-tĕ.

13 i*ch* bin fohr fünf yah'-rĕn dur*ch* mek'-si-koh gĕ-rīst', ah'-bĕr oi- roh'-pah ke'-nĕ i*ch* nokh ni*ch*t.

14 dah bĕ-gint' dee moo-zeek'. ĕr- ke'-nĕn zee vas zee shpee'-lĕn?

15 das ist īn pot'-poo-ri doit'-shĕr folks'-lee-dĕr.

16 yetst höh'-rĕ i*ch* es. das ist "i*ch* vīs ni*ch*t vas zol es bĕ-doi'-tĕn".

17 nun folkt "doo doo leekst meer im her'-tsĕn."

18 vee oft hah'-bĕn veer dee'-zĕ lee'- dĕr in dayr shoo'-lĕ gĕ-zung'-ĕn. lang, lang, ists hayr.

19 zoh shlim ist es dokh ni*ch*t .˙. .

20 var'-tĕn zee in'-mahl. i*ch* hah'-bĕ dee shoo'-lĕ fohr elf yah'-rĕn fĕr- la'sĕn. i*ch* bin shohn zee'-bĕn- unt-tsvan'-tsi*ch*.

21 i*ch* vayr'-dĕ owkh shohn fünf'- unt-tsvan'-tsi*ch*.

22 fĕr-ge'-sĕn veer un'-zĕr al'-tĕr, . . . darf i*ch* bi'-tĕn?

23 gern. das ist gĕ-rah'-dĕ īn val'- tsĕr fon shtrows.

24 vee ist es mit uns bī'-dĕn? hah'- bĕn zee lust, froi'-lĭn *Kruger?*

25 tsum tan'-tsĕn, i'-mĕr! bĕ-zon'- dĕrs im zo'-mĕr un'-tĕr frī'-ĕm hi'-mĕl.

I feel the same way (*lit.*, to me it goes the same), Miss Barnett. I only visited relatives in Canada last fall. I was there for two months.

Five years ago I traveled through Mexico, but Europe I don't know as yet.

(There) the music is starting. Do you recognize what they are playing?

That is a potpourri of German folksongs.

Now I hear it. That is, "I do not know what it means . . ."

Now following, "Thou, thou art in my heart . . ."

How often did we sing these songs in school. "Long, long ago . . ."

It isn't that bad, Mr. Miller!

Wait a moment! I left school eleven years ago. I am already twenty-seven.

I'll be twenty five.

Let us forget our age, Mr. Smith. Miss Barnett, may I have the pleasure?

Gladly. Now that is a waltz by Strauss.

How about us (*lit.*, How is it with the two of us?)? Do you feel like dancing, (*lit.*, have you the desire) , Miss Kruger?

To dance? Always! Especially under the sky in the summer.

ⁱin German, in addition to the proper preposition: *in die (zur, zu der) Schule,* "to school;" *in der Schule,* "in school;" *in die Kirche (zur Kirche)* "to church;" *in der Kirche* "in church [§9, a, 6].   *14. haben gesungen* (have sung), present perfect of *singen* (to sing), strong verb. The past participle of strong verbs is formed with the prefix *ge* + stem *(sung)* and the suffix *-en: gesungen.*

Siebente Lektion

Neue Wörter für diese Lektion

die Ankunft,-e (an'-kunft)	arrival
anlangen (an'-lang-ĕn),	to arrive
langt an¹ (langkt an')	
sich trennen (zich tre'-nĕn)	to part, separate
vorläufig (fohr'-loi-fich)	for the present, for the time being
bei (bī)	by, with, at
aufsuchen (owf'-zoo-khĕn),	to look up
sucht auf (zookht owf')	

trotz (trots)	in spite of	davon (dah-fon')	from it, of it
sobald (soh-balt')	as soon as	passieren (pa-see'-rĕn)	to pass, go on
recht (recht)	very, right		
baldig (bal'-dich)	soon	ehe (ay'-ĕ)	before
geboren (gĕ-boh'-rĕn)	born	küssen (kü'-sĕn)	to kiss
soviel (zoh-feel')	that much	jung (yung)	young
tragen (trah'-gĕn)	to wear, carry	mehr (mayr)	more
		solange (zoh-lang'-ĕ)	as long as
er trägt (traykt')	he wears	einige (ī'-ni-gĕ)	few, a few

gnädige Frau (gnay'-di-gĕ frow)	madam
liebenswürdig (lee'-bĕns-vür-dich)	charming
nennen (ne'-nĕn)	to call, to name
gemeinsam (gĕ-mīn'-zahm)	jointly, in common, together
unternehmen (un-tĕr-nay'-mĕn)	to undertake
heissen (hī'-sĕn)	to be called, named
ausser (ow'-sĕr)	beside(s), except

die Sache,-n (za'-chĕ)	thing	böse sein (böh'-zĕ zīn)	to be angry
der Gang,-"e (gang)	passageway	erwachsen (ĕr-vak'-sĕn)	grown-up
der Gast,-"e (gast)	guest	förmlich (förm'-lich)	formal
die Nähe (näh'-ĕ)	nearness	all, alle (al, a'-lĕ)	all

72

DIE ZOLLREVISION

The Customs Examination   (tsol'-ray-vee-ziohn)

der Zoll,-ᵉe (tsol)	custom
zollfrei (tsol'-frī)	free of duty
verzollen (fĕr-tso'-lĕn)	to pay duty
der Zollbeamte,-n (tsol'-bĕ-am-tĕ)	customs officer
die Zollrevision,-en (tsol'-ray-vee-ziohn)	customs examination
zollpflichtig (tsol'-pflich-tich)	subject to duty

die¹ Zollerklärung,-en (tsol'-ĕr-klay-rung),	custom declaration
die Zolldeklaration (tsol'-day-klah-ra-tsiohn)	
die Zollstelle,-n (tsol'-shte-lĕ), das	custom-house
Zollamt,-ᵉer (tsol'-amt)	
die Passkontrolle (pas'-kon-tro-lĕ)	passport inspection
die Ausweispapiere (ows'-vīs-pah-pee-rĕ)	identification papers

die Geschäftsreise,-n (gĕ-shefts'-rī-zĕ)	business trip
die Vergnügungsreise,-n (fĕr-gnüh-gungs- . . .)	pleasure trip

einführen (īn'-füh-rĕn), führt ein (führt īn)	to import, to introduce
der Tabak,-e (tah'-bak)	tobacco
der Karton Zigaretten (kar'-tong tsee-ga-re'-tĕn)	carton of cigarettes
die Zigarre,-n (tsee-ga'-rĕ)	cigar
alkoholische Getränke (al-koh-hoh'-li-shĕ)	alcoholic beverages
gĕ-treng'-kĕ)	

der Staat,-en (shtaht)	state
der Staatsbürger,- (. . . bür-gĕr)	citizen
persönlich (per-zöhn'-lich)	personal
aufschliessen (owf'-shlee-sĕn)	to unlock
die Ordnung,-en (ord'-nung)	order
in Ordnung sein (. . . zīn)	to be in order

annehmen (an'-nay-mĕn), nimmt an (nimt an)	to accept, assume
der Gebrauch (gĕ-browkh'),	use
die Gebräuche (pl.) (gĕ-broi'-chĕ)	customs
willkommen (vil-ko'-mĕn)	welcome
anfangen (an'-fang-ĕn), fängt an (fengkt an')	to begin
einfallen (īn'-fa-lĕn), fällt ein (felt īn')	to occur, what is the idea
entschuldigen (ĕnt-shul'-di-gĕn)	to excuse
vorstellen (fohr'-shte-lĕn), stellt vor (shtelt fohr)	to introduce
kennenlernen (ke'-nĕn-ler-nĕn),	to get acquainted, to meet
lernt kennen (lernt ke'-nĕn)	

CONVERSATION

1 Hier sind wir[2] gut in Cuxhaven trotz[3] des Sturms und der Seekrankheit angelangt.[4]

2 Nun müssen wir uns leider trennen.[5]

3 Fräulein Barnett und ich fahren direkt nach[6] Frankfurt am Main, wo[7] wir zwei bis drei Wochen bleiben werden.[8]

4 Und[9] Herr Smith und ich bleiben vorläufig bei[6] meinen Verwandten in Hamburg. Sobald wir nach[6] Frankfurt kommen, werden[8] wir Sie im Hotel aufsuchen.

5 Das wird uns sehr freuen.

6 Vielleicht können[10] wir etwas Gemeinsames[11] unternehmen?

7 Ja,[12] es gibt[13] viel Interessantes[11] in Frankfurt zu sehen.

8 Da sehe ich schon die Passkontrolle und die Zollbeamten.

9 Glückliche Reise und auf Wiedersehen!

10 Darf[10] ich bitte Ihren Pass und Ihre Ausweispapiere sehen? Wie heissen Sie,[14] und wo und wann sind[15] Sie geboren?

FOOTNOTES: *1.* From this point on, the personal pronoun *er* (he), will no longer be given in German, nor will this verb form be translated. It is to be understood that it designates the third person singular of the present tense.   *2.* Notice again the inverted word order, because the main clause does not begin with the subject [§79, b].   *3. trotz* (in spite of) is one of the prepositions that always requires the genitive case [§39, a].   *4. sind angelangt* (have arrived), the present perfect of *anlangen* (to arrive), which is an intransitive verb, indicating a change of place. Therefore, it is conjugated with *sein* (to be) [§63, b]. The *ge* of the past participle is inserted between separable prefix and verb.   *5. sich trennen* (to separate). The infinitive is always the last word in a main clause [§79, f].   *6. nach*

PRONUNCIATION	TRANSLATION
1 heer zint veer goot in cuks-hah'-fĕn trots des shturms unt dayr zay'-krangk-hīt an'-gĕ-langkt.	Here we are safely (*lit.*, are we good ... arrived) in Cuxhaven in spite of the storm and the seasickness.
2 noon mü'-sĕn veer uns lī'-dĕr tre'-nĕn.	Now, alas, we must part.
3 froi'-līn *Barnett* unt *ich* fah'-rĕn dee-rekt' nahkh frangk'-furt am mīn, voh veer tsvī bis drī vo'-khĕn blī'-bĕn vayr'-dĕn.	Miss Barnett and I are going directly to Frankfort-on-the-Main where we will stay for two or three weeks.
4 unt her *Smith* unt *ich* blī'-bĕn fohr'-loi-fich bī mī'-nĕn fĕr-van'-tĕn in ham'-burk. zoh-balt' veer nahkh frangk'furt ko'mĕn, vayr'-dĕn veer zee im hoh-tel' owf'-zoo-khĕn.	And Mr. Smith and I will remain for the time being with my relatives in Hamburg. As soon as we come to Frankfort we will look you up at the hotel.
5 das virt uns zayr froi'-ĕn.	That will please us very much.
6 fee-līcht' kö'-nĕn veer et'-vas gĕ-mīn'-zah-mĕs un-tĕr-nay'-mĕn.	Perhaps we will be able to do something together.
7 yah es gipt feel in-tĕ-re-san' tĕs in frangk'-furt tsoo zay'ĕn.	Yes, there are many interesting things to be seen in Frankfort.
8 dah zay'-ĕ *ich* shohn dee pas'-kon-tro-lĕ unt dee tsol'-bĕ-am-tĕn.	(There) I see the immigration and customs officials already.
9 glük'-li-chĕ rī'-zĕ unt owf vee'-dĕr-zayn.	Bon voyage and good-bye.
10 darf *ich* bi'-tĕ ee'-rĕn pas unt ee'-rĕ ows'-vīs-pa-pee-rĕ zay'-ĕn? vee hī'-sĕn zee, unt voh unt van zint zee gĕ-boh'-rĕn?	May I please see your passport and your identification papers? What is your name and where and when were you born?

Frankfurt (to Frankfort). Prepositions are used very idiomatically and should be learned in the various expressions as they occur in the text. *Nach* is used for "to" a city or country: *nach Berlin* (to Berlin); *nach Deutschland* (to Germany). *Zu,* "to" (a person), "to the house of." *Sie geht zu ihrer Freundin.* "She is going to her friend's house." *Er geht zum Doktor.* "He is going to the doctor's." *Bei* "at the house of": *bei meinen Verwandten bleiben,* "to stay at my relative's house." **7.** *wo* (where), a subordinating conjunction, introduces a dependent clause in which the helping word *werden* is the last word. Contrast with word order after coordinating conjunction [§55, §56]. **8.** *wir werden bleiben* (we shall remain), is the future tense which is formed in German with the present tense of *werden*

11 Ich heisse[14] Robert Smith. Ich bin[15] am 19. (neunzehnten) September 19 . . . [16] (neunzehnhundert . . .) in New York geboren. Also bin ich amerikanischer[17] Staatsbürger.

12 Sind Sie auf einer Geschäftsreise oder fahren Sie nur zum Vergnügen?

13 Ich bin auf einer Vergnügungsreise.

14 Ihre Papiere sind in Ordnung. Gehen Sie durch diesen Gang zur Zollrevision!

15 Da drüben steht unser Gepäck. Der Zollbeamte wartet schon auf uns.

16 Haben Sie etwas zu verzollen?

17 Ich glaube[18] nicht. Ich habe einen Karton Zigaretten und ungefähr zwanzig Zigarren.

18 So viel können[10] Sie zollfrei einführen. Wie ist es mit neuer[17] Kleidung?

19 Ich habe nur getragene[17] Sachen ausser einem Paar Schuhen und einigen Wäschestücken zum persönlichen Gebrauch.

20 Schliessen Sie bitte die beiden[17] Koffer, den Handkoffer und die Aktentasche auf! Hier ist eine Flasche Kognak. Alkoholische[17] Getränke müssen verzollt werden.[8]

(to become), and the infinitive of the main verb. The infinitive is placed at the end of the main clause [§63, c; 64, f]. German word order differs very much from English word order, but it is covered by definite rules. The infinitive, the past participle, or the separable prefix is placed at the end of a main clause [§79]. *9. und* (and), co-ordinating conjunction, i.e., it introduces a clause equal in value to the main clause. The word order is normal after the five coordinating conjunctions: *aber* (but), *denn* (because, for), *oder* (or), *sondern* (but [on the contrary]), *und* (and). The verb follows the subject [§79]. *10.* For complete conjugation

11 ich hī'-sĕ . . . ich bin am noin'-tsayn-tĕn zep-tem'-bĕr noin'-tsayn hun'-dĕrt . . . in *New York* gĕ-boh'-rĕn. al'-zoh bin *ich* a-may-ree-kah'-ni-shĕr shtahts'-bür-gĕr.

12 zint zee owf ī'-nĕr gĕ-shefts'-rī-zĕ oh'-dĕr fah'-rĕn zee noor tsum fĕr-gnüh'-gĕn?

13 ich bin owf ī'-nĕr fĕr-gnüh'-gungs-rī-zĕ.

14 ee'-rĕ pa-pee'-rĕ zint in ord'-nung. gay'-ĕn zee dur*ch* dee'-zĕn gang tsoor tsol'-ray-vee-ziohn.

15 dah drüh'-bĕn shtayt un'-zĕr gĕ-pek'. dayr tsol'-bĕ-am-tĕ var'-tĕt shohn owf uns.

16 hah'-bĕn zee et'-vas tsoo fĕr-tso'-lĕn?

17 ich glow'-bĕ ni*cht*, ich hah'-bĕ ī'-nĕn kar-tong' tsee-ga-re'-tĕn unt un'-gĕ-fayr tsvan'-tsi*ch* tsee-ga'-rĕn.

18 zoh feel kö'-nĕn zee tsol'-frī īn'-füh-rĕn. vee ist es mit noi'-ĕr klī'-dung?

19 ich hah'-bĕ noor gĕ-trah'-gĕ-nĕ za'-khĕn ow'-sĕr ī'-nĕm pahr shoo'-ĕn unt ī'-ni-gĕn ve'-shĕ-shtü-kĕn tsum pĕr-zöhn'-li-*ch*ĕn gĕ-browkh'.

20 shlee'-sĕn zee bi'-tĕ dee bī-dĕn ko'-fĕr, dayn hant'-ko-fĕr unt dee ak'tĕn-ta-shĕ owf. heer ist īn'-ĕ fla'-shĕ ko'niak. al -koh-hoh-li -shĕ gĕ-treng'-kĕ mü'-sĕn fĕr-tsolt' vayr'-dĕn.

My name is Robert Smith. I was born September 19, 19— in New York. Therefore I'm an American citizen.

Are you on a business trip or are you traveling for pleasure only?

I am on a pleasure trip.

Your papers are in order. Go through this passageway to the customs inspection.

Our luggage is (*lit.*, stands) over there. The customs official is already waiting for us.

Do you have anything to declare?

I don't think so. I have a carton of cigarettes and about twenty cigars.

You may import that amount (*lit.*, so much) free of duty. How about (*lit.*, how is it with) new clothes?

I have only used things except for a pair of shoes and several shirts and underwear (*lit.*, pieces of wash) for personal use.

Please unlock both trunks, your suitcase, and the briefcase. Here is a bottle of cognac. Duty must be paid on alcoholic beverages.

---

of *können* (to be able, can), *dürfen* (to be permitted, may) *müssen* (to have to, must), *mögen* (to like), *sollen* (ought to, shall), *wollen* (to wish, will), see §71, *11. etwas Gemeinsames* (something jointly). *viel Interessantes* (many) ["much"] interesting things). Adjectives following *etwas* and *viel* are used as neuter nouns, but take strong adjective endings. *12.* After *ja* (yes), *nein* (no), *gut* (all right) and exclamations, (*ach, oh,* etc.), normal word order is followed and these particles are set off by commas [§79]. *13. es gibt*—"there are" (*lit.*, it gives).

21 Die Flasche ist angebrochen. Wir haben auf dem Schiff davon[19] getrunken.

22 Dann ist die Flasche zollfrei. Sie können[10] passieren.

23 Das[20] ging wirklich schnell. Dort sehe ich auch meinen Onkel, meine Tante und Kusine. Sie winken.

24 Willkommen in Deutschland, mein Junge! Wie[21] geht es Mutter?

25 Ihr geht es sehr gut. Ehe[22] ich es vergesse, ich sollte alle grüssen und küssen. Ich fange mit Kristine an!

26 Was fällt dir ein! Ich bin jetzt eine junge Dame; kein Kind mehr.

27 Darf ich euch meinen Freund vorstellen? Herr Smith: Herr, Frau und Fräulein Miller.

28 Sehr angenehm. Wir freuen uns, Sie kennenzulernen.[8] Wir hoffen, dass[23] Ihnen Deutschland gefallen wird,[23] und Sie sich gut amüsieren werden.[23]

29 Vielen Dank, gnädige Frau.

30 Solange Sie in Hamburg bleiben, sind Sie natürlich unser Gast.

---

14. Wie heissen Sie? ID.: "What is your name?" *Ich heisse . . .* ID. "My name is . . ." *15. Ich bin geboren* (I was born). The present tense is used in German for a living person. *16. am 19 September*—"September 19th" (*lit.,* on 19th September). For expressions of dates, etc. see §51. c, 1-3. *17. amerikanischer Staatsbürger* (American citizen). Not only *der-* and *ein-*words are inflected in German, but also descriptive adjectives take endings indicating gender, number,

21 dee fla'-shĕ ist an'-gĕ-bro-khĕn. veer hah'-bĕn owf daym shif dah-fon' gĕ-trung'-kĕn.

The bottle is started. We drank from it on the steamer.

22 dan ist dee fla'-shĕ tsol'-frī. zee kö'-nĕn pa-see'-rĕn.

Then the bottle is duty-free. You may pass.

23 das ging virk'-lich shnel. dort zay'-ĕ ich owkh mī'-nĕn ong'-kĕl, mī'-nĕ tan'-tĕ unt koo-zee'-nĕ. zee ving'-kĕn.

That really went fast. (There) I (also) see my uncle, my aunt, and my cousin. They are waving.

24 vil-ko'-mĕn in doitsh'-lant, mīn yung'-ĕ! vee gayt es mu'-tĕr?

Welcome to Germany, my boy. How is your mother?

25 eer gayt es zayr goot. ay'-ĕ ich es fĕr-ge'-sĕ ich zol'-tĕ a'lĕ grüh'sĕn unt kü'-sĕn. ich fang'-ĕ mit kris-tee'-nĕ an!

She is fine (*lit.*, it goes very well with her). Before I forget, I am supposed to greet and kiss everyone. I'll begin with Christine.

26 vas felt deer īn? ich bin yetst ī'-nĕ yung'-ĕ dah'-mĕ; kīn kint mayr.

What is the matter with you (*lit.*, occurred to you)? I am now a young lady; no longer a child (*lit.*, no child more).

27 darf ich oich mī'-nĕn froint fohr'-shte-lĕn? her *Smith:* her, frow unt froi'-līn *Miller.*

May I introduce my friend to you? Mr. Smith: Mr., Mrs., and Miss Miller.

28 zayr an'-gĕ-naym. veer froi'-ĕn uns, zee ke'-nĕn-tsoo-ler-nĕn. veer ho'-fĕn, das ee'-nĕn doitsh'-lant gĕ-fa'-lĕn virt, unt zee zich goot a-müh-zee'-rĕn vayr'-dĕn.

Pleased to meet you. We are glad to make your acquaintance (*lit.*, to learn to know). We hope that you will like Germany, and that you will have a good time (*lit.*, will amuse yourself well).

29 fee'-lĕn dangk, gnay'-di-gĕ frow.

Many thanks, madam (*lit.*, gracious lady).

30 zoh-lang'-e zee in ham'-burk blī'-bĕn, zint zee na-tühr'-lich un'-zĕr gast.

As long as you remain in Hamburg, naturally you will be our guest.

---

and case of the noun they modify. Whenever an adjective is not preceded by a *der*-word or an inflected *ein*-word, the adjective ending must indicate the gender, number, and case of the noun it modifies. This is called the strong declension of the adjective. After *der*-words or inflected *ein*-words, the adjective ending is weak; the ending –*en* predominates [§5, §8, §43]. *18. ich glaube*—I think, Id. (*lit.*, I believe). *19. davon* (from it). Whenever the pronoun "it" is used in English

31 Sie sind sehr liebenswürdig, Frau Miller. Wie kann ich das nur annehmen?

32 Machen Sie sich keine Sorgen! Wir haben ein Landhaus in der Nähe von Hamburg.

33 Machen Sie sich bitte keine Umstände!

34 Aber, nein; meine Tochter kann[10] mir helfen.[24]

35 Dort steht unser Wagen. Steigen wir alle ein!

---

with a preposition, it is translated in German by *da* (there), with the preposition: *damit* (with it), *dahinter* (behind it), etc. [§26, a-c].   *20. das* (that), a demonstrative pronoun at the beginning of the sentence, is not inflected.   *21.* Note the various translations of *wie: Wie geht es Mutter?* (How is Mother?). *Wie heissen Sie?* (What's your name?). *Soviel wie ich* (As much as I).   *22. ehe* (before), is a

31 zee zint zayr lee'-bĕns-vür-di*ch*, frow *Miller!* vee kan i*ch* das noor an'-nay-mĕn?

You are very kind, Mrs. Miller. How can I accept?

32 ma'-khĕn zee zi*ch* kī'-nĕ zor'-gĕn. veer hah'-bĕn īn lant'-hows in dayr nay'-ĕ fon ham'-burk.

Don't worry (*lit.,* make yourself no worries). We have a country house near (*lit.,* in the near of) Hamburg.

33 ma'-khĕn zee zi*ch* bi'-tĕ kī'-nĕ um'-shten-dĕ!

Please don't go to any trouble (*lit.,* make yourself please no extra work).

34 ah'-bĕr, nīn! mī'-nĕ tokh'-tĕr kan meer hel'-fĕn.

Of course not. My daughter can help me.

35 dort shtayt un'-zĕr vah'-gĕn. shtī'-gĕn veer a'-lĕ īn.

There is our car. Let us all get in.

---

subordinating conjunction, after which the verb is at the end of the clause [§79]. *23. dass* (that) is another subordinating conjunction and, therefore, the verb is at the end of the clause. In compound tenses, the helping verb is last; the past participle precedes it. *24. helfen* (to help) is an intransitive verb that requires the dative case as sole object in German [§62, b, c].

Achte Lektion

Neue Wörter für diese Lektion

aus (ows)	out of, from	bekannt (bĕ-kant')	familiar, known
grün (grühn)	green		
rot (roht)	red	früher (früh'-ĕr)	formerly
hübsch (hüpsh)	pretty, nice	riesig (ree'-zich)	enormous
bemerken (bĕ-mer'-kĕn)	to notice	schelten (shel'-tĕn)	to scold

das Fenster,- (fen'-stĕr)	window
der Vorort,-e[1] (fohr'-ort)	suburb
ungefähr (un-gĕ-fayr')	about, nearly
die Minute,-n[1] (mee-noo'-tĕ)	minute
der Bahnhof,-¨e[2] (bahn'-hohf)	station

geradeaus (gĕ-rah-dĕ-ows')	straight ahead
darüber (da-rüh'-bĕr)	over it, above it
die Pfeife,-n (pfī'-fĕ)	pipe
sich fühlen (zich füh'-lĕn)	to feel
während (vay'-rĕnt)	while (conj.); during (prep.)

das Nötige (nöh'-ti-gĕ)	necessary things
eintreten (īn'-tray-tĕn), tritt ein (trit īn')	to enter
aufhängen (owf'-heng-ĕn), hängt auf (hengkt owf)	to hang up
vorkommen (fohr'-ko-mĕn), kommt vor (komt fohr')	to seem to, to be found
einschalten (īn'-shal-tĕn), schaltet ein (shal'-tĕt īn)	to switch on
ausschalten (ows'-shal-tĕn), schaltet aus (shal'-tĕt ows)	to switch off

scheinen (shī'-nĕn)	to seem, appear	schmutzig (shmu'-tsich)	dirty, soiled
nochmals (nokh'-mahls)	once again	damals (dah'-mahls)	at that time
bereits (bĕ-rīts')	already	anstatt (an-shtat')	instead of

82

DAS HAUS UND HEIM

House and Home   (hows unt hĭm)

das **Zimmer,-** (tsi'-mĕr)	room
das **Esszimmer** (es'-tsi-mĕr),	dining room
das **Speisezimmer** (shpī'-zĕ-tsi-mĕr)	
das **Wohnzimmer** (vohn'-tsi-mĕr)	living room
das **Herrenzimmer** (he'-rĕn-tsi-mĕr)	den
das **Schlafzimmer** (shlahf'-tsi-mĕr)	bedroom
das **Badezimmer** (bah'-dĕ-tsi-mĕr)	bathroom
das **Mädchenzimmer,-** (mayt'-chĕn-tsi-mĕr)	servant's room
die **Küche,-n** (kü-chĕ)	kitchen
der **Korridor,-e** (ko'-ree-dohr)	hall, floor
die **Garderobe,-n** (gar-droh'-bĕ)	clothesrack
die **Schublade,-n** (shoop'-lah-dĕ)	drawer
das **Handtuch,-"er** (hant'-tookh)	towel
das **Badetuch,-"er** (bah'-dĕ-tookh)	bath towel
die **Seife,-n** (zī'-fĕ)	soap

das **Mietshaus,-"er** (meets'-hows),	apartment house
das **Wohnhaus,-"er** (vohn'-hows)	
das **Einfamilienhaus** (īn-fa-mee'-liĕn-hows)	one-family house
die **Wohnung,-en** (voh'-nung)	apartment
der **Schornstein,-e** (shorn'-shtīn)	chimney
der **Ziegel,-** (tsee'-gĕl)	brick
das **Klavier,-e** (khah-veer'),	piano
das **Piano,-s** (pee-ah'-noh)	
die **Kommode,-n** (ko-moh'-dĕ)	dresser
der **Kleiderschrank,-"e** (klī'-dĕr-shrangk)	wardrobe
die **Gardine,-n** (gar-dee'-nĕ)	curtain
der **Vorhang,-"e** (fohr'-hang)	drape

das **Dach,-"er** (dakh)	roof	das **Bild,-er** (bilt)	picture
der **Balkon,-s** (bal-kong')	balcony	die **Lampe,-n** (lam'-pĕ)	lamp
der **Schalter,-** (shal'-tĕr)	switch	der **Sessel,-** (ze'-sĕl)	easy chair
das **Licht,-e** (licht)	light	der **Teppich,-e** (te'-pich)	rug
der **Schrank,-"e** (shrangk)	closet	der **Spiegel,-** (shpee'-gĕl)	mirror
die **Möbel** (möh'-bĕl)	furniture		

CONVERSATION

1 Wir wohnen in einem Vorort von Hamburg, ungefähr zwanzig Minuten vom Bahnhof mit dem Wagen.[1]

2 Von diesem Fenster aus kön-nen Sie den Schornstein[2] und das Dach[2] mit den roten[3] Zie-geln[2] sehen.

3 Wie hübsch sehen die weissen[3] Mauern mit den grünen[3] Fen-sterläden[1] aus! Jetzt bemerke[4] ich auch den Balkon.[5]

4 In Deutschland haben viele Häuser[1] Balkons.[5] Der Balkon ist wie ein extra Zimmer.

5 Das Haus scheint sehr gross zu sein.

6 Wir haben sieben Zimmer[2] ausser der Küche und dem Mädchenzimmer.

7 Hier sind wir. Nun geht es durch den Garten[2] ins Haus.

8 Treten Sie bitte ein! Nochmals willkommen! Kristine, du zeigst Herrn Smith und Hans das Haus und ihre Zimmer.

9 Also, dies ist der Korridor. Hier an der Garderobe hängen Sie Ihren Hut und Mantel auf.

10 Habt ihr noch keine eingebauten[6] Schränke?

FOOTNOTES: *1.* Nouns are classified according to their plural endings into *strong, weak,* or *mixed* declension. The strong declension, which has a variety of endings, is subdivided into three different classes: *Class I* adds no ending but takes umlaut whenever possible in the plural. *Class II* adds *–e* and usually takes umlaut in the plural. *Class III* adds *–er* and always takes umlaut in the plural. All mas-culine and neuter *strong* nouns take *–(e)s* in the genitive case singular. Feminine nouns never take an ending in any declension in the singular [§10, §11,

PRONUNCIATION	TRANSLATION
1 veer voh'-nĕn in ī'-nĕm fohr'-ort fon ham'-burk, un-gĕ-fayr' tsvan'-tsi*ch* mee-noo'-tĕn fom bahn'-hohf mit daym vah'-gĕn.	We live in a suburb of Hamburg about twenty minutes from the station by car.
2 fon dee'-zĕm fen'-stĕr ows kö'-nĕn zee dayn shorn'-shtīn unt das dakh mit dayn roh-tĕn tsee'-gĕln zay'-ĕn.	From this window you can see the chimney and the roof with its red bricks.
3 vee hüpsh zay'-ĕn dee vī'-sĕn mow'-ĕrn mit dayn grüh'-nĕn fen'-stĕr-lay-dĕn ows! yetst bĕmer'-kĕ *ich* owkh dayn bal-kong'.	How pretty the white walls look with the green shutters. Now I also notice the balcony.
4 in doitsh'-lant hah'-bĕn fee'-lĕ, hoi'-zĕr bal-kongs. dayr bal-kong' ist vee īn eks'-trah tsi'-mĕr.	In Germany, many houses have balconies. The balcony is like an extra room.
5 das hows shīnt zayr grohs tsoo zīn.	The house seems to be very large.
6 veer hah'-bĕn zee'-bĕn tsi'-mĕr ow'-sĕr dayr kü'-*ch*ĕ unt daym mayt'-*ch*ĕn-tsi-mĕr.	We have seven rooms besides the kitchen and the servant's room.
7 heer zint veer. noon gayt es dur*ch* dayn gar'-tĕn ins hows.	Here we are. Now we go through the garden into the house.
8 tray'-tĕn zee bi'-tĕ īn! nokh'-mahls vil-ko'-mĕn! kri-stee'-nĕ, doo tsīkst hern *Smith* unt *Hans* das hows unt ee'-rĕ tsi-mĕr.	Please enter. Welcome again. Christine, show Mr. Smith and Hans the house and their rooms.
9 al'-zoh, dees ist dayr ko'-ree-dohr. heer an dayr gar-droh'-bĕ heng'-en zee ee'-rĕn hoot unt man'-tĕl owf.	Now, this is the corridor. You hang up your hat and coat here at the clothes rack.
10 hahpt eer nokh kī'-nĕ īn'-ge-bow-tĕn shreng'-kĕ?	Don't you have built-in closets yet?

§12, §13]. *2.* These are nouns belonging to the *strong* declension. The plurals indicated in the vocabulary show to which class they belong. *3.* Whenever a descriptive adjective modifying a noun is preceded by a *der*-word or an inflected *ein*-word, the adjective ending is weak. In the declension of the weak adjective, the predominant ending added to the adjective stem is –*en*. Only in the nominative case singular, masculine, feminine, and neuter, and in the accusative case singular, feminine, and neuter, is the *weak adjective* ending –*e* [§44, a, b]. *4.*

11 Nein, die[7] gibt es nur in ganz neuen, modernen[8] Häusern. Links ist das Esszimmer. Es führt in die Küche.

12 Warte, Kristine! Die Möbel im Wohnzimmer scheinen neu zu sein, während[9] die Bilder und Lampen mir bekannt vorkommen.

13 Du hast recht, Hans. Das Sofa hatten wir bereits, aber[10] Vater hat die Sessel, die Stühle und den Teppich letztes Jahr gekauft.

14 Ist der Flügel nicht auch neu? Hattet ihr früher nicht ein Klavier?

15 Das stimmt. Hinter dem Wohnzimmer ist noch das Herrenzimmer.

16 Diese Treppe führt nach oben zu den Schlafzimmern.

17 Geradeaus ist das Badezimmer, mit fliessendem heiss- und kaltem[11] Wasser, Waschbecken, Brausebad usw[12] (und so weiter).

18 Rechts liegt das Schlafzimmer der Eltern, mit zwei Betten und Nachttischen zu beiden Seiten, so wie eine Kommode mit Spiegel darüber.

19 Und der Frisiertisch mit dem grösseren Spiegel ist für die Frau Mama. Der Kleiderschrank ist ja riesig.

---

bemerken (to notice) is a verb with an inseparable prefix. There are seven inseparable prefixes: *be—, ent— (emp—), er—, ge—, miss—, ver—, zer* [§68, a, 1-5]. All other prefixes are separable prefixes; a few of the latter, however, are either separable or inseparable. In the past participle, these verbs with inseparable prefixes do not take the prefix *ge-*; e.g., **bemerken—bemerkt:** *er hat bemerkt* (he has noticed) [§68, b]. *5. der Balkon* (the balcony), *die Balkons* (the balconies)—one of the foreign words which take *–s* in the plural. *6. eingebauten* (built-in), past participle derived from *einbauen* (to build in). When past par-

11 nĭn, dee gipt es noor in gans noi'-ĕn, moh-der'-nĕn hoi'-zĕrn. lingks ist das es'-tsi-mĕr. es führt in dee kü'-*che*.

No. They are only found in very new, modern houses. To the left is the dining room. It leads into the kitchen.

12 var'-tĕ, kri-stee'-nĕl dee möh'-bĕl im vohn'-tsi-mĕr shī'-nĕn noi tsoo zīn, vay'-rĕnt dee bil'-dĕr unt lam'-pĕn meer bĕ-kant' fohr'-ko-mĕn.

Wait, Christine! The furniture in the living room seems to be new, while the pictures and the lamps look familiar to me.

13 doo hast re*ch*t, Hans. das zoh'-fah ha'-tĕn veer bĕ-rīts', ah'-bĕr fah'-tĕr hat dee ze'-sĕl, dee shtüh'-lĕ unt dayn te'-pi*ch* lets'-tĕs yahr gĕ-kowft'.

You are right, Hans. We already had the sofa but father bought the easy chair, the chairs, and the rug last year.

14 ist dayr flüh'-gĕl ni*ch*t owkh noi? ha'-tĕt eer früh'-ĕr ni*ch*t īn kla-veer'?

Isn't the grand piano also new? Didn't you used to have a small piano?

15 das shtimt. hin'-tĕr daym vohn'-tsi-mĕr ist nokh das he'-rĕn-tsi-mĕr.

That's right. In back of the living room is the den.

16 dee'-zĕ tre'-pĕ führt nahkh oh'-bĕn tsoo dayn shlahf'-tsi-mĕrn.

These stairs lead up to the bedrooms.

17 gĕ-rah-dĕ-ows' ist das bah'-dĕ-tsi-mĕr, mit flee'-sĕn-dĕm hīs-unt kal'-tĕm va'-sĕr, vash'-be-kĕn, brow'-zĕ-bat unt zoh vī'-tĕr.

Straight ahead is the bathroom, with hot and cold running water, washbasin, shower, etc.

18 re*ch*ts leekt das shlahf'-tsi-mĕr dayr el'-tĕrn, mit tsvī be'-tĕn unt nakh'-ti-shĕn tsoo bī'-dĕn zī'-tĕn, zo vee ī'-nĕ ko-moh'-dĕ mit shpee'-gĕl da-rüh'-bĕr.

To the right is my parents' bedroom, with two beds and night tables on both sides, as well as a dresser with a mirror above it.

19 unt dayr free-zeer'-tish mit daym gröh'-sĕ-rĕn shpee'-gĕl ist führ dee frow ma-mah'. dayr klī'-dĕr-shrangk ist yah ree'-zi*ch*.

And the dressing table with the larger mirror is for mother (*lit.,* Mrs. Mama). The wardrobe is enormous.

---

ticiples are used as adjectives, they follow the rules for adjective declension [§69, c]. Here the ending is weak after an inflected *ein*-word [§45, a-b].   7. *die* (they), "the." Articles are used as demonstrative pronouns [§31, c].   8. *neuen modernen Häusern* (new modern houses). The adjective endings are strong since the preceding word does not have any inflectional ending. Where there is a succession of descriptive adjectives, they all take the same ending as the first adjective.   9. *während* (while) is a subordinating conjunction, and, therefore, the verb is at the end of this dependent clause. This word order will be referred to as "dependent

20 Hier, Herr Smith, ist das Fremdenzimmer. Wie oft hat meine Tante gescholten, weil[13] die Gardinen und Vorhänge vom Rauchen[14] so schnell schmutzig wurden.[13]

21 Damals rauchte mein Vetter nur Pfeife anstatt Zigarren und Zigaretten. Er fühlte sich sehr erwachsen.

22 Dies ist das Zimmer meines Vetters, der jetzt in Berlin wohnt.[15] Hier werden Sie wahrscheinlich hausen, Herr Smith. Nicht wahr, Kristine?

23 Du hast recht. Der Schalter für das elektrische Licht ist rechts von der Tür. Schalten Sie bitte das Licht ein. Handtücher, ein Badetuch, Seife und alles Nötige[16] finden Sie in der Kommodenschublade.

24 Recht herzlichen Dank!

25 Machen Sie sich's (es) bequem und schlafen Sie gut! Gute[17] Nacht, Herr Smith. Gute Nacht, Hans!

26 Schlafen Sie wohl, Fräulein Kristine!

---

word order" [§56].   *10.* *aber* (but) is a coordinating conjunction that introduces a clause of equal value to the main sentence and, therefore, the word order is normal, i.e., the verb follows the subject. In compound tenses, the past participle or the infinitive is at the end of the sentence.   *11. heiss– und kaltem* (hot and cold). Since the word is hyphenated, only the second adjective requires an inflectional ending, but it applies to both adjectives. The adjective ending is strong [§43].   *12. usw., und so weiter* (and so forth), is usually abbreviated in German, just as "etc." is abbreviated in English.   *13. weil* (because) and *während* (while) are subordinating conjunctions and require dependent word

20 heer, her *Smith*, ist das frem'-děn-tsi-měr. vee oft hat mī'-ně tan'-tě gě-shol'-ten, vil dee gar-dee'-něn unt fohr'-heng-ě fom row'-khěn zoh shnel shmu'-tsi*ch* vur'-děn.

Here, Mr. Smith, is the guest room. How often my aunt scolded me because the curtains and the drapes became dirty so quickly from my smoking.

21 dah'-mahls rowkh'-tě mīn fe'-těr noor pfī'-fě an-shtat' tsee-ga'-rěn unt tsee-ga-re'-těn. ayr fühl'-tě zi*ch* zayr ěr-vak'-sěn.

At that time, my cousin smoked only a pipe instead of cigars and cigarettes. He felt very grown up.

22 dees ist das tsi'-měr mī'-něs fe'-těrs, dayr yetst in ber-leen' vohnt. heer vayr'-děn zee vahr-shīn'-li*ch* how'-zěn, her *Smith*. ni*ch*t vahr, kri-stee'-ně?

This is the room of my cousin who now lives in Berlin. You will probably stay here, Mr. Smith. Isn't that true, Christine?

23 doo hast re*ch*t. dayr shal'-těr führ das ay-lek'-tri-shě li*ch*t ist re*ch*ts fon dayr tühr. shal'-těn zee bi'-tě das li*ch*t īn. hant'tü-*ch*ěr, īn bah'-dě-tookh, zī'-fě unt a'-lěs nöh'-ti-gě fin'-děn zee in dayr ko-moh-děn-shoop-lah-dě.

You are right. The electric light switch is to the right of the door. Please switch on the light! You'll find hand towels, a bath towel, soap, and everything necessary in the drawer of the dresser.

24 re*ch*t herts'-li-*ch*ěn dangk!

Many thanks.

25 ma'-khěn zee zi*ch*s (es) bě-kvaym' unt shlah'-fěn zee goot. goo'-tě nakht, her *Smith*. goo'-tě nakht *Hans*.

Make yourself comfortable and sleep well. Good night, Mr. Smith. Good night, Hans.

26 shlah'-fěn zee vohl, froi'-līn kri-stee'-ně!

Sleep well, Miss Christine.

order. See Note 9.   *14. vom Raucnen* (from smoking). Infinitives can be used as nouns; they are neuter and capitalized.   *15. der jetzt in Berlin wohnt* (who now lives in Berlin) is a relative clause which requires dependent word order.   *16. alles Nötige* (all necessary things) is derived from the adjective *nötig* (necessary). Adjectives can be used as nouns in all three genders. They then follow the adjective declension and are capitalized like any other noun. Here *Nötige* is used as a neuter noun preceded by the inflected *alles;* therefore, it takes the weak adjective ending.   *17. gute,* adjective with strong ending modifying *die Nacht.*

Neunte Lektion

Neue Wörter für diese Lektion

sowie (zoh-vee')	as well as	wichtig (vich'-tich)	important
es gibt (gipt)	there are	lehrreich (layr'-rīch)	instructive
nächst (naychst)	next	bilden (bil'-děn)	to form

herumlaufen (he-rum'-low-fěn),
läuft herum (loift he-rum') — to run around
ungefährlich (un'-gě-fayr-lich) — harmless
graben (grah'-běn), gräbt (graypt) — to dig
anstrengend (an'-shtreng-ěnt) — strenuous

entlang (ěnt-lang')	along	füllen (fü'-lěn)	to fill
ausserhalb (ow'-sěr-halp)	outside of	um . . . zu (um . . . tsoo)	in order to
berühmt (bě-rühmt')	famous	verlieren (věr-lee'-rěn)	to lose
die Art,-en (art)	type, kind	ein paar (īn pahr)	a few,
die Angst,-"e (angkst)	fear		a couple

der Laden,-" (lah'-děn),
der Kaufladen,-" (kowf'-lah-děn) — store
der Preis,-e (prīs) — price
der Einkauf,-"e (īn'-kowf) — purchase
Einkäufe machen (īn'-koi-fě ma'-khěn) — go shopping
der Händler,- (hen'-dlěr) — dealer

mitbringen (mit'-bring-ěn)	to bring (with one)
bedeutend (bě-doi'-těnt)	significant
der Durchgang,-"e (durch'-gang)	way through, passage
Europa (oi-roh'-pah)	Europe
die Vereinigten Staaten (fěr-ī'-nik-těn shtah'-těn)	**United States**

IN DER STADT

IN THE CITY   (in dayr shtat)

die Stadt,-"e (shtat)	city	die Ecke,-n (e'-kĕ)	corner
die Strasse,-n (shtrah'-sĕ)	street	die Allee,-n (a-lay')	avenue
die Sehenswürdigkeiten	the sights	die Kirche,-n (kir'-chĕ)	church
(zay'-ĕns-vür-dich-kī-tĕn)		der Park,-e (pahrk)	park

das Theater,- (tay-ah'-tĕr)   theater
der Film,-e (film)   motion
                                 picture
das Kino,-s (kee'-noh)   cinema
das Gebäude,-   building
  (gĕ-boi'dĕ)
das Postamt,-"er   post office
  (post'-amt)

die Hauptstadt,-"e (howpt'-shtat)   capital
die Hafenstadt,-"e (hah'-fĕn-shtat)   seaport
das Krankenhaus,-"er (krang'-kĕn-hows)   hospital
das Rathaus,-"er (raht'-hows)   city hall
der Schutzmann (shuts'-man), Schutzleute (... loi-tĕ)   policeman
die Polizeistation,-en (po-lee-tsī'-shta-tsiohn)   police station

die Strassenbahn,-en (shtrah'-sĕn-bahn)   streetcar
der Omnibus,-se (om'-nee-bus)   bus
die Hochbahn,-en (hohkh'-bahn)   elevated train
die Untergrundbahn,-en (un'-tĕr-grunt-bahn)   subway

die Strecke,-n (shtre'-kĕ)   distance
das Leben,- (lay'-bĕn)   life
beobachten (bĕ-oh'-bakh-tĕn)   to watch, observe
besagen (bĕ-zah'-gĕn)   to say, indicate
gewöhnlich (gĕ-vöhn'-lich)   customary, usual

der Käfig,-e (kay'-fich)	cage	der Tiger,- (tee'-gĕr)	tiger
das Tier,-e (teer)	animal	der Affe,-n (a'-fĕ)	monkey,
der Löwe,-n (löh'-vĕ)	lion		ape
der Elefant,-en	elephant	der Seehund,-e	seal
(ay-le-fant')		(zay'-hunt)	
der Bär,-s,-en (bayr)	bear		

der Radioapparat,-e (ra'-dioh-ah-pah-raht)   radio set
der Fernsehapparat,-e (fern'-say-a-pah-raht)   television set
die Rundfunkstation,-en (runt'-fungk-shta-tsiohn) broadcasting station
die Fracht (frakht)   freight
das Frachtschiff,-e (frakht'-shif)   freighter

CONVERSATION

1 Vielleicht sehen wir uns heute einige[1] Sehenswürdig-keiten an?

2 Das[2] ist eine gute Idee. Wir wollten nicht zu lange in Hamburg bleiben.

3 Hamburg ist vor allem[3] eine grosse Handels- und Hafenstadt. Sehen wir uns zuerst den Hafen an.

4 Wie kommt man[4] zum Hafen?

5 Mit der Strassenbahn, dem Omnibus oder der Untergrundbahn. Wir nehmen alle drei; dann können wir mehr[5] von der Stadt sehen.

6 Hier müssen wir aussteigen. Dort ist schon der Hafen, mit leichten und schweren Dampfern, Frachtschiffen und Vergnügungsdampfern aus aller Welt.

7 Hamburg ist einer[6] der bedeutendsten[7] Häfen des Kon-tinents, nicht wahr?

8 Ja, es ist als Durchgangshafen für die Ausfuhr und Ein-fuhr von Waren aus vielen[8] Ländern wichtig.

9 Sind nicht viele[8] Auswanderer von hier nach den Verei-nigten[9] Staaten gefahren?

10 Ja, und nicht nur Deutsche, sondern auch Polen, Russen und Italiener haben hier Europa verlassen,[10] um nach Amerika einzuwandern.[11]

FOOTNOTES: *1.* einige (several, a few). An indefinite adjective which is conju-gated like the *der*-words [§5].   2. das (that) is a demonsrative pronoun here and so is not inflected [§31, c].   *3.* vor allem (primarily, *lit.,* before all). *All* is an indefinite pronoun and is inflected as such [§35, c, 5].   *4. man* is an indefinite

PRONUNCIATION

1 fee-*lich*t' zay'-ĕn veer uns hoi'-tĕ ī'-ni-gĕ zay'-ĕns-vür-di*ch*-kī-tĕn an?

2 das ist ī'-nĕ goo'-tĕ ee-day'' veer vol'-tĕn ni*ch*t tsoo lang'-ĕ in ham'-burk blī'-bĕn.

3 ham'-burk ist fohr a'-lĕm ī'-nĕ groh'-sĕ han'-dĕls- unt hah'-fĕn-shtat. zay'-ĕn veer uns tsoo-ayrst' dayn hah'-fĕn an.

4 vee komt man tsum hah'-fĕn?

5 mit dayr shtrah'-sĕn-bahn, daym om'-nee-bus oh'-dĕr dayr un'-tĕr-grunt-bahn. veer nay'-mĕn a'-lĕ drī; dan kö'-nĕn veer mayr fon dayr shtat zay'-ĕn.

6 heer mü-'sĕn veer ows'-shtī-gĕn. dort ist shohn dayr hah'-fĕn, mit lī*ch*'-tĕn un*t* shvay'-rĕn dam-'pfĕrn frakht'-shi-fĕn unt fĕr-gnüh'-gungs-dam-pfĕrn ows a-'lĕr velt.

7 ham'-burk ist ī-nĕr dayr bĕ-doi'-tĕnt-stĕn hay'-fĕn des kon-tee-nents', ni*ch*t vahr?

8 yah es ist als dur*ch*'-gangs-hah-fĕn führ dee ows'-foor unt īn-' foor fon vah'-rĕn ows fee'-lĕn len'-dĕrn vi*ch*'-ti*ch*.

9 zint ni*ch*t fee'-lĕ ows'-van-dĕ-rĕr fon heer nahkh dayn fĕr-ī'-nik-tĕn shtah'-tĕn gĕ-fah'-ren?

10 yah, unt ni*ch*t noor doit'-shĕ, zon-dĕrn owkh' poh'-lĕn ru'sĕn unt ee-ta-liay'-nĕr hah'-bĕn heer oi-roh'-pah fĕr-la'-sĕn um nahkh a-may'-ree-ka īn'-tsoo-van-dĕrn.

TRANSLATION

Perhaps today we can do some sightseeing.

That is a good idea. We do not intend to stay too long in Hamburg.

Hamburg is primarily a large commercial city and a harbor (*lit.*, commercial and harbor-city). Let's look at the harbor first.

How do we get (*lit.*, how comes one) to the harbor?

With the streetcar, the bus, or subway. We will take all three; then we can see more of the city.

We have to get out here. There is the harbor (already), with light and heavy steamers, freighters, and excursion boats from all over the world.

Hamburg is one of the most important harbors of the continent, isn't it?

Yes, it is important as a gateway (*lit.*, going through harbor) for exports and imports from many lands.

Didn't many emigrants leave from here for the United States?

Yes, not only Germans but also Poles, Russians, and Italians left Europe from here to immigrate to America.

pronoun followed by a verb in the third person. This is a very common construction in German and is translated in various ways: "one," "people," "we," "they," and often by the passive in English [§35, a and §75, g]. *5. mehr* (more) is the comparative of *viel* (much), which is irregular. *6. einer* (one) is the nomina-

11 Das war alles sehr interessant und lehrreich. Wohin gehen wir von hier?

12 Wir fahren eine Strecke und gehen dann zu Fuss[12] zum Alsterbecken.

13 Von der Alster, einem Nebenfluss der Elbe,[13] habe ich schon gehört.

14 Die Alster bildet Seen! Es wimmelt hier von Segelbooten, Motorbooten und Ruderbooten. Ganz Hamburg scheint auf dem Wasser zu sein.

15 Kommen Sie diese schöne Promenade entlang! Wir können von hier das Leben zu Wasser und zu Lande beobachten.

16 Jetzt fahren wir zu Hagenbecks Tierpark. Er liegt ausserhalb[14] der Stadt.

17 Den Namen Hagenbeck habe ich schon oft in den Staaten[15] gehört; als berühmten Händler mit wilden Tieren und Gründer einer neuen Art von Zoologischem Garten.

18 Der Name "Tierpark" besagt, dass es nicht ein gewöhnlicher[16] Zoologischer Garten ist.

---

tive masculine of the indefinite singular pronoun *ein,* referring to *der Hafen.* When an *ein*-word is used instead of a noun, even the three uninflected cases (nominative masculine singular and nominative and accusative neuter singular) take case endings [§35, c, 1].   *7. bedeutendsten* (most significant) is a present participle used as an adjective in the superlative. It follows the rule for adjective declensions. The present participle is formed by adding *d* to the infinitive: *bedeuten* (to signify), *bedeutend* (significant) [§69, b].   *8. vielen* (many) is declined like an adjective.   *9. Vereinigten* (united) is the participle of *vereinigen* (to unite) and is here used as an adjective and declined accordingly.   *10. verlassen* (to leave), is a strong verb with an inseparable prefix.   *11. um . . . einzuwandern* (in order to immigrate). *um* plus *zu* is always used in German when a definite purpose is expressed. It is followed by an infinitive [§40, b]. Notice the position of *zu*

11 das vahr a'-lĕs zayr in-tĕ-re-sant' unt layr'-rĭch. voh-hin' gay'-ĕn veer ſon heer?

That was all very interesting and instructive. Where do we go from here?

12 veer fah'-rĕn ī'-nĕ shtre'-kĕ unt gay'-ĕn dan tsoo ſoos tsum al'-stĕr-be-kĕn.

We ride a distance and then we'll walk to the Alster basin.

13 ſon dayr al'-stĕr ī-nĕm nay'-bĕn-flus dayr el'-bĕ, hah'-bĕ *ich* shohn gĕ-höhrt'.

I have already heard about the Alster, a tributary of the Elbe.

14 dee al'-stĕr bil'-dĕt zay'-ĕn! es vi'-mĕlt heer ſon zay'gĕl-boh-tĕn, moh-tohr'-boh-tĕn unt ruh'-dĕr-boh-tĕn. gans ham'-burk shīnt owf daym va'-sĕr tsoo zīn.

The Alster forms lakes. It is teeming here with sailboats, motorboats, and rowboats. All of Hamburg seems to be on the water.

15 ko'-mĕn zee dee'-zĕ shöh'-nĕ proh-mĕ-nah'-dĕ ent-lang'! veer kö'-nĕn ſon heer das lay'-bĕn tzoo wa'-sĕr unt tsoo lan'-dĕ bĕ-oh'-bakh-tĕn.

Come along this beautiful promenade. From here we can observe life on the water and on the land.

16 yetst fah'-rĕn veer tsoo hah'-gĕn-beks teer'-park. ayr leekt ow'-sĕr-halp dayr shtat.

Now we are going to Hagenbeck animal park. It lies outside the city.

17 dayn nah'-mĕn hah'-gĕn-bek hah'-bĕ *ich* shohn oft in dayn shtah'-tĕn gĕ-höhrt'; als bĕ-rühm'-tĕn hend'-lĕr mit vil'-dĕn tee'-rĕn unt grün'-dĕr ī'-nĕr noi'-ĕn art ſon tsoh-oh-loh'-gi-shĕm gar'-tĕn.

I have often heard the name "Hagenbeck" in the States—as a famous dealer in wild animals and the founder of a new type of zoological garden.

18 dayr nah'-mĕ teer'-park' bĕ-zahkt' das es ni*cht* īn gevöhn'-li-*ch*ĕr tsoh-oh-loh'-gi-shĕr gar'-tĕn ist.

The name "animal park" indicates that it is not the usual zoological garden.

inserted between the separable prefix and the verb. *12. zu Fuss* (on foot). ID., *lit.,* to foot. *13. die Elbe* is an important river which has its source in the mountains of Czechoslovakia, traverses Germany, and empties into the North Sea. *14. ausserhalb* (outside of) is one of the prepositions that requires the genitive case [§39]. *15. der Staat* (the state) and *der Bär* (the bear) belong to the mixed declension of nouns; the singular is strong: *der Staat, des Staats, dem Staat, den Staat; Der Bär, des Bärs, dem Bär, den Bär.* The plural is weak, i.e., all four cases take the ending *–en* [§15]. *16. gewöhnlicher* (usual). An adjective which follows any of the three uninflected forms of the *ein*-words (nom. masc. and neuter sing. and acc. neuter sing.) takes strong endings. An adjective which follows any inflected *ein*-word takes weak endings. The declension of adjectives, when they follow *ein*-words, is therefore referred to as "mixed" [§45, a-b]. *17. die* (they),

19 Sie haben recht. Die wilden Tiere wie Löwen, Elefanten, Bären[15] usw. scheinen in einem Park zu leben.

20 Sehen Sie doch nur die Tiger! Sie laufen frei herum. Da kann man wirklich Angst bekommen.

21 Die[17] sind ungefährlich. Ein Graben, oft mit Wasser gefüllt, trennt die Tiere im "Park" vom Publikum.

22 Nun bin ich aber vom Herumlaufen[18] sehr müde.

23 Ich möchte gern noch die Affen und Seehunde sehen. Sie sind die Komiker unter den Tieren.

24 Jetzt haben wir alles Sehenswerte gesehen. Um[11] Hunde, Katzen, Ratten und Mäuse zu sehen, braucht man nicht in den Zoo zu gehen!

25 Das war ein schöner[16] aber anstrengender[19] Tag. Es ist zu schade, dass Ihre Kusine nicht mitkommen konnte,[20] weil sie Ihrer Tante helfen musste.[21]

26 Ach, Kristine ist doch noch ein Backfisch!

27 Sie ist sehr jung,[22] aber sehr charmant.[22]

28 Verlieren[23] Sie nur nicht Ihr Herz[24] in Hamburg; in ein paar[25] Tagen fahren wir nach Berlin!

---

a demonstrative pronoun.   *18. das Herumlaufen* (the running around) is an infinitive used as a noun [§69, a].   *19. anstrengender* (strenuous) is the present participle used as an adjective and inflected accordingly.   *20. dass Ihre Kusine nicht kommen konnte* (that your cousin could not come) is a dependent clause introduced by *dass*, which is a subordinating conjunction. The *inflected* part of the verb is last, preceded by the infinitive.   *21. weil sie Ihrer Tante helfen musste*

19 zee hah'-bĕn re*ch*t. dee vil'-dĕn tee'-rĕ vee löh'-vĕn, ay-le-fan'-tĕn, bay'-rĕn unt zoh vī'-tĕr shī'-nĕn in ī'-nĕm park tsoo lay'-bĕn.

You are right. The wild animals such as lions, elephants, bears, etc. seem to live in the park.

20 zay'-ĕn zee dokh noor dee tee'-gĕr! zee low'-fĕn frī hĕ-rum! dah kan man virk'-li*ch* angkst bĕ-ko'-mĕn.

Just see the tigers! They run around free. One can really get frightened.

21 zee zint un'-gĕ-fayr-li*ch*. īn grah'-bĕn oft mit va'-sĕr gĕ-fült' trent dee tee'-rĕ im park fom poo'-blee-kum.

They are harmless. A moat, often filled with water, separates the animals in the park from the people (*lit.*, public).

22 noon bin i*ch* ah'-bĕr fom he-rum'-low-fĕn zayr müh'-dĕ.

Now, however, I am very tired from running around.

23 i*ch* möch'-tĕ gern nokh dee a'-fĕn unt zay'-hun-dĕ zay'-ĕn. zee zint dee koh'-mi-kĕr un'-tĕr dayn tee'-rĕn.

I would still like to see the monkeys and the seals. They are the comedians among the animals.

24 yetst hah'-bĕn veer a'-lĕs zay'-ĕns-vayr-tĕ gĕ-zay'-ĕn. um hun'-dĕ, ka'-tsĕn, ra'-tĕn unt moi'-zĕ tsoo zay'-ĕn browkht man ni*ch*t in dayn tsoh tsoo gay'-ĕn.

Now we have seen everything worthwhile. You don't have to go to the zoo to see dogs, cats, rats, and mice.

25 das vahr īn shöh'-nĕr ah'-bĕr an'-shtreng-ĕn-dĕr tahk. es ist tsoo shah'-dĕ das ee'-rĕ kuh-zee'-nĕ ni*ch*t mit'-ko-mĕn kon'-tĕ, vīl zee ee'-rĕr tan'-tĕ hel'-fĕn mus'-tĕ.

That was a beautiful but strenuous day. It's too bad that your cousin couldn't come with us because she had to help your aunt.

26 akh, kri-stee'-nĕ ist dokh nokh īn bak'-fish.

Oh, Christine is still only a teenage girl (*lit.*, "fried fish").

27 zee ist zayr yung, ah'-bĕr zayr shar-mant'.

She's very young but very charming.

28 fĕr-lee'-rĕn zee noor ni*ch*t eer herts in ham'-burk; in īn pahr tah'-gĕn fah'-rĕn veer nakh bĕr-leen'.

Don't lose (*lit.*, only not) your heart in Hamburg; in a couple of days we are going to Berlin.

(because she had to help your aunt) is a dependent clause introduced by a subordinating conjunction [§55, §79]. 22. Notice again that any adjective used after *sein* (to be) is uninflected. 23. *verlieren* (to lose) is a verb with an inseparable prefix. 24. *das Herz* (the heart) has a very irregular declension. [See §16, a-b]. 25. *ein paar* (a few). *paar* written with a small *p* means "a few"; *ein Paar*, written with a capital *P*, means "a pair, a couple, two."

Zehnte Lektion

Neue Wörter für diese Lektion

die Uhr,-en (oor) — clock, watch
damit (dah-mit') — so that
der Platz,-"e (plats) — seat
endlich (ent'-li*ch*) — finally
rufen (roo'-fĕn) — to call, shout

das Abteil,-e (ap-tīl') — compartment
tüchtig (tü*ch*'-tich) — efficient
servieren (zer-vee'-rĕn) — to serve (food)
dienen (dee'-nĕn) — to serve
die Mitte,-n (mi'-tĕ) — middle

inzwischen (in-tsvi'-shĕn) — in the meantime
nicht mehr (ni*ch*t mayr) — no more
studieren (shtoo-dee'-rĕn) — to study
der Fahrplan,-"e (fahr'-plan) — timetable

der Wartesaal (var'-tĕ-zahl), die Wartesäle (var'-tĕ-zay-lĕ) — waiting room
der D-Zug,-"e (day'-tzook), Durchgangszug (dur*ch*'-gangs-tsook) — express train
der Personenzug,-"e (per-zoh'-nĕn-tsook) — local train
das Raucherabteil,-e (Raucher) (row'-khĕr-ap-tīl) — smoking compartment
Rauchen verboten (row'-khĕn fĕr-boh'-tĕn) — no smoking
der Zugführer,- (tsook'-füh-rĕr) — conductor
der Schlafwagen,- (shlahf'-vah-gĕn) — sleeping car

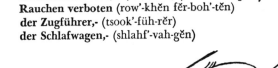

zu Abend essen (tsoo ah'-bĕnt e-sĕn) — to eat supper
treffen, sich treffen (zich tre'-fĕn), trifft (trift) — to meet
anrufen (an'-roo-fĕn), ruft an (rooft an) — to call up, telephone
wiederkommen (vee'-dĕr-ko-mĕn), kommt wieder (komt vee'-dĕr) — to return, come back
empfehlen (ĕm-pfay'-lĕn), empfiehlt (ĕm-pfeelt') — to recommend
ausserdem (ow'-sĕr-daym) — besides

IM RESTAURANT

In the Restaurant

(rĕ-stoh-rang')

das Restaurant,-s (rĕ-stoh-rang')	restaurant
der Speisewagen,- (shpī'-zĕ-vah-gĕn)	dining car
der Kellner,- (kel'-nĕr), der Ober,- (oh'-bĕr)	waiter
die Rechnung,-en (rech'-nung)	bill
das Trinkgeld,-er (tringk'-gelt)	tip
das Prozent,-e (das proh-tsent')	per cent
aufschlagen (owf'-shlah-gĕn)	to add, raise
schlägt auf (shlaykt owf')	(price)

die Bedienung,-en (bĕ-dee'-nung)	service
der Betrag,-"e (bĕ-trahk')	amount
der Rechnungsbetrag,-"e (rech'-nungs-bĕ-trahk')	amount of bill

Prosit! (proh'-zit)	Your health!	das Bier,-e (beer)	beer
		die Sauce,-n (zoh'-se)	gravy, sauce
der Wein,-e (vīn)	wine	der Kohl,- (kohl)	cabbage
der Rotwein (roht'-vīn)	red wine	der Salat,-e (zah-laht')	salad
der Weisswein (vīs'-vīn)	white wine		

der Teller,- (tel'-lĕr)	plate
das Besteck,-e (bĕ-shtek')	forks and knives
das Messer,- (me'-sĕr)	knife
die Gabel,-n (gah'-bĕl)	fork
der Suppenlöffel,- (zu'-pĕn-lö-fĕl)	tablespoon

Guten Appetit! (goo'-tĕn a-pĕ-teet')	hearty appetite
die Suppe,-n (zu'-pĕ)	soup
die Fleischbrühe,-n (flīsh'-brüh-ĕ)	broth
die Forelle,-n (foh-re'-lĕ)	trout
der Braten,- (brah'-tĕn)	roast
der Sauerbraten,- (zow'-ĕr- . . .)	sauerbraten (sweet and sour beef)

der Schweinebraten,- (shvī'-nĕ- . . .)	roast pork
die Hammelkeule,-n (ha'-mel-koi-lĕ)	leg of lamb
das Gemüse,- (gĕ-müh'-zĕ)	vegetable
die Erbsen (pl.) (erp'-sĕn)	green peas
die Kartoffel,-n (kar-to'-fĕl)	potato
der Kartoffelbrei (. . . brī)	mashed potatoes
die Bratkartoffeln (pl.) (braht'- . . .)	fried potatoes
der Nachtisch,-e (nahkh'-tish)	dessert
das Gefrorene (gĕ-froh'-rĕ-nĕ)	ice cream

CONVERSATION

1 Fahren Sie bitte direkt zum Bahnhof, Herr Smith, und lösen Sie die Billets[1] nach Berlin! Ich treffe Sie später an der Station.

2 Bitte, zwei Fahrkarten zweiter[2] Klasse nach Berlin für den D-Zug.[3] Ich möchte auch zwei Platzkarten haben, möglichst Fensterplätze. Wann kommt dieser Zug in Berlin an?

3 Um 18:15 (achtzehn fünfzehn), also ein Viertel nach sechs nach Ihrer Uhr.

4 Endlich kommen Sie. Alles ist besorgt. Wir fahren mit dem 15 Uhr 58 Zug. Ich habe noch nichts ausser einem belegten[4] Brötchen gegessen.[5]

5 Wir können im Zug zu Abend essen. Das Essen im Speisewagen ist ganz besonders gut.[6]

6 Gehen wir gleich[7] auf den Bahnsteig! Der Zug fährt bald ab.

7 "Alles einsteigen!" ruft der Zugführer. Also, schnell einsteigen!

8 Folgen Sie mir![8] Hier ist unser Abteil neben dem Speisewagen.

9 Die kleinen[9] Koffer und die beiden[9] Aktentaschen lege ich ins Gepäcknetz.

FOOTNOTES: *1. Fahrkarten (Billets) lösen*, ID., to buy tickets. 2. Ordinal numbers are inflected like adjectives: *erster Klasse, zweiter Klasse* are used here in the genitive case of the strong declension, literally meaning "of the first class," "of the second class." 3. *D-Zug* (express train) stands for *Durchgangszug*, lit., through passage train, i.e., the cars are connected for the passenger to go through and

PRONUNCIATION

1 fah'-rĕn zee bi'-tĕ dee-rekt' tsum bahn'-hohf, her *Smith*, unt löh'-zĕn zee dee bi-liets' nahkh ber-leen'. i*ch* tre'-fĕ zee shpay'-tĕr an dayr shta-tsion'.

2 bi'-tĕ, tsvī fahr'-kar-tĕn, tsvī'-tĕr kla'-sĕ nahkh ber-leen' führ dayn day'-tsook. i*ch* mö*ch*'-tĕ owkh tsvī plats'-kar-tĕn hah'-bĕn, mök'-li*ch*st fen'-stĕr-ple-tsĕ. van komt dee'-zĕr tsook in . . . an?

3 um akht'-tsayn oor fünf'-tsayn, al'-zoh īn veer'-tĕl nahkh zeks nahkh ee'-rĕr oor.

4 ent'-li*ch* ko'-mĕn zee. a'-les ist bĕ-zorkt? veer fah'-rĕn mit daym fünf'-tsayn oor akht'-unt-fünf-tsi*ch* tsook. i*ch* hah'-bĕ nokh ni*ch*ts ow'-sĕr ī'-nĕm bĕ-layk'-tĕn bröht'-*ch*ĕn gĕ-ge'-sĕn.

5 veer kö'-nĕn im tsook tsoo ah'-bĕnt e'-sĕn. das e'-sĕn im shpī'-zĕ-vah'-gĕn ist gants bĕzon'-dĕrs goot.

6 gay'-ĕn veer gli*ch* owf dayn bahn'-shtīk. dayr tsook fayrt balt ap.

7 a'-lĕs īn'-shtī-gĕn, rooft dayr tsook'-füh-rĕr. al'-zo, shnel īn'-shtī-gĕn.

8 fol'-gĕn zee meer. heer ist un'-zĕr ap'-tīl nay'-bĕn daym shpī'-zĕ-vah-gĕn.

9 dee klī'-nĕn ko'-fĕr unt dee bī'-dĕn ak'-tĕn-ta-shĕn lay'-gĕ i*ch* ins gĕ-pek'-nets.

TRANSLATION

Please, Mr. Smith, go directly to the station and buy the tickets to Berlin. I'll meet you at the station later.

Two tickets, please, second class, to Berlin for the express train. I would also like to have two seat reservations; if possible, window seats. When will this train arrive in Berlin?

At 18:15. That is quarter past six according to your watch.

At last, you're here (*lit.,* you come). Everything is taken care of. We are going on the 15:58 train. I have not eaten anything except a sandwich.

We can eat supper on the train. Meals are especially good in the dining car.

Let us go immediately to the platform. The train is going to leave soon.

"All aboard," calls the conductor. Now, get on quickly.

Follow me. Here is our compartment, next to the diner.

I put the small suitcases and the two briecases on the baggage rack.

---

these trains are used only as express trains. *Der Personenzug* is a slow train, and each half of the cars, sometimes the compartment, is a closed off unit.   *4. belegt lit.,* overlaid, covered with. Past participle of *belegen* (to overlay, cover with), used as an adjective here.   *5. gegessen* (eaten), past participle of *essen* (to eat). The *g* after the past participle prefix *ge*– and before *essen* has crept into the

10 Das Essen wird um 5 (fünf) Uhr serviert. Lassen[10] Sie uns gleich in den Speisewagen gehen, damit wir gute[9] Plätze bekommen.

11 Nehmen Sie bitte hier Platz,[11] meine Herren. Womit kann ich dienen?

12 Bringen Sie uns zuerst eine Flasche guten[9] Rotwein! Und dann die Speisekarte.

13 Ehe der Kellner wiederkommt, müssen Sie schnell ein kleines[9] Examen bestehen, Herr Smith. Nennen Sie alles, was auf dem Tisch steht

14 Ein weisses[9] Tischtuch, riesige[9] Servietten, kleine und grosse[9] Teller, Weiss- und Rotweingläser.

15 Ist das alles?

16 Nein, beinah hätte[13] ich die Bestecke vergessen: Messer, Gabeln, Suppenlöffel und Teelöffel. Und in der Mitte steht noch ein gelber[9] Korb mit Schwarzbrot, Weissbrot und Brötchen.

17 Herr Ober![14] Ich sehe, Sie haben heute Sauerbraten, Schweinebraten und Hammelkoteletts. Was können Sie uns empfehlen?

18 Ich glaube, der Schweinebraten mit Rotkohl und Kartoffelbrei ist heute am besten.

19 Ich nehme das. Ausserdem Suppe: Fleischbrühe für mich und Tomatensuppe für den Herrn.

---

language to facilitate pronunciation. *6.* Adverbs, adjectives, and nouns closely connected with the verb follow the word order rule of the verbs with separable prefixes. Therefore, *gut* stands at the end of the main clause [§79]. *7.* The adverb of time or adverbial phrase of time precedes all other adverbs or adverbial

10 das e'sĕn virt um fünf oor zer-
veert'. la'-sĕn zee uns glĭch in
dayn shpī'-zĕ-vah-gĕn gay'-ĕn,
dah-mit' veer goo'-tĕ ple'-tsĕ bĕ-
ko'-mĕn.

The meal will be served at 5 p. m.
Let us go to the dining car immediately so that we can get
good seats.

11 nay'mĕn zee bi'-tĕ heer plats,
mī'-nĕ he'-rĕn. voh-mit' kan *ich*
dee'-nĕn?

Please be seated here, gentlemen.
(With what) may I serve you?

12 bring'en zee uns tsoo-ayrst' ī'-nĕ
fla'-shĕ goo'-tĕn roht'-vīn. unt
dan dee shpī'-zĕ-kar-tĕ.

First, please bring us a bottle of
good red wine. And then the
menu.

13 ay'-e dayr kel'-nĕr vee'-dĕr-komt,
mü'-sĕn zee shnel īn klī-nĕs ek-
sah'-mĕn bĕ-shtay'-ĕn, her *Smith.*
ne'-nĕn zee a'-lĕs, vas owf daym
tish shtayt.

Before the waiter returns you will
have to pass a short examination quickly, Mr. Smith. Name
everything that is on the table!

14 īn vī'-sĕs tish'-tookh, ree'-zi-gĕ
zer-vee-e'tĕn, klī-nĕ unt groh'-sĕ
te'·lĕr, vīs unt roht'-vīn-glay'-zĕr.

A white tablecloth, enormous
napkins, small and large plates,
white wine glasses, and red
wine glasses.

15 ist das a'-lĕs?

Is that all?

16 nin, bī-nah he'-tĕ *ich* dee bĕ-
shte'-kĕ fĕr-ge'-sĕn: me'-sĕr, gah'-
bĕln, zu'-pĕn-lö-fĕl unt tay'-lö-
fĕl. unt in dayr mi'-tĕ shtayht
nokh īn gel'-bĕr korp mit shvarts'-
broht, vīs'-broht unt bröht'-*ch*ĕn.

No. I almost forgot the silverware: knives, forks, soup-
spoons, and teaspoons. And in
the middle there is also a yel-
low basket with pumpernickel,
white bread, and rolls.

17 her oh'-bĕr. *ich* zay'-ĕ zee hah'-
bĕn hoi'-tĕ zow'-ĕr-brah-tĕn, shvī'-
nĕ-brah-tĕn unt ha'-mĕl-kot-ĕ-
lets' vas kö'-nĕn zee uns ĕm-
pfay'-lĕn?

Waiter! I see you have sauerbraten, roast pork, and lamb
chops today. What would you
recommend?

18 *ich* glow'-bĕ, dayr shvī'-nĕ-brah-
tĕn mit roht'-kohl unt kar-to'-
fĕl-brī ist hoi'-tĕ am be'-stĕn.

I think the roast pork with red
cabbage and mashed potatoes
is the best today.

19 *ich* nay'-mĕ das. ow'-sĕr-daym
zu'-pĕ: flīsh'-brüh-ĕ führ m*ich*
unt toh-mah'-tĕn-zu-pĕ führ dayn
hern.

I'll have (*lit.,* take) that. And also
soup — consomme for me and
tomato soup for the gentleman.

phrases [§79, h]. *8. folgen* (to follow) is an intransitive verb which requires the
dative [§62, b]. *9.* A variety of weak and strong adjective endings [See §43, §44,
§45]. *10. lassen* (to leave, let) is one of the verbs that take an infinitive without
zu (to): Lassen Sie uns gehen (Let us go) [§74, b]. *11. Platz nehmen* (to take a

20 Von den Fischgerichten bringen Sie mir einmal Forelle[15] mit Bratkartoffeln und eine Portion grüne Erbsen und Karotten!

21 Und zum Nachtisch Gefrorenes und Pflaumenkompott!

22 Ich bin schrecklich hungrig und werde mich durch alle Gänge hindurchessen.

23 Herr Ober, bringen Sie bitte die Rechnung! Das Essen war ausgezeichnet.

24 Wieviel Trinkgeld soll ich lassen? Zehn Prozent sind schon auf die Rechnung aufgeschlagen.

25 Die Bedienung war sehr gut. Vielleicht geben wir noch fünf Prozent des Rechnungsbetrags extra!

---

seat). Ib. The English "a" is not translated.   *12*. . . . , *was auf dem Tisch ist* (what is on the table). *was* is a relative pronoun here and introduces a dependent clause. Thus, the verb must be at the end of the sentence [§79,c].   *13. hätte* (had) is the subjunctive form of *hatte*.   *14. Ober*, abbreviation of *Oberkellner* (cap-

20 fon dayn fish'-gĕ-ri*ch*-tĕn bring'-ĕn zee meer in'-mahl fo-re'-lĕ mit braht'-kar-to-fĕln unt ī'-nĕ por-tsiohn' grüh'-nĕ erp'-zĕn unt ka-ro'-tĕn.

From the fish dishes, bring me one order of trout with fried potatoes and a portion of green peas and carrots.

21 unt tsum nahkh'-tish gĕ-froh'-rĕ-nĕs unt pflow'-mĕn-kom-pot.

And for dessert, ice cream and stewed prunes.

22 i*ch* bin shrek'-li*ch* hung'-ri*ch* unt vayr'-dĕ mi*ch* dur*ch* a'-lĕ geng'-ĕ hin-dur*ch*'-e-sĕn.

I am terribly hungry and I shall eat my way through all the courses.

23 her oh'-bĕr, bring'-ĕn zee bi'-tĕ dee re*ch*'-nung. das e'-sĕn vahr ows'-gĕ-tsī*ch*-nĕt.

Waiter, please bring me the bill. The meal was excellent.

24 vee-feel' tringk'-gelt zol i*ch* la'-sĕn? tsayn proh-tsĕnt' zint shohn owf dee re*ch*'-nung owf'-gĕ-shlah-gĕn.

How much of a tip shall I leave? Ten per cent is already added to the bill.

25 dee bĕ-dee'-nung vahr zayr goot. fee-li*ch*t gay'-bĕn veer nokh fünf proh-tsĕnt' des re*ch*'-nungs-bĕ-trahks' eks'-trah.

The service was very good. Perhaps we will give an extra five per cent of the amount of the bill.

---

tain). This is the customary address for a waiter, whether he is a captain or ordinary waiter. Usually, it is prefaced by *Herr* (i.e., *Herr Ober*), but often *Ober* alone is used.   15. *Bringen Sie mir ein Mal Forelle* (Bring me one order of trout) The indirect object is a pronoun, i.e., *Bringen Sie sie mir* (Bring me it) [§79, d].

Elfte Lektion

Neue Wörter für diese Lektion

der Schritt,-e (shrit) — step, pace
dankbar (dangk'-bahr) — grateful
klopfen (klo'-pfĕn) — to knock
herein (he-rīn') — come in

erwarten (ĕr-var'-tĕn) — to expect
still (shtil) — quiet, still
bitten um (bi'-tĕn um) — to ask for
der Rest,-e (rest) — remainder

sich erinnern (zich er-i'-nĕrn) — to remind of
bekanntmachen (bĕ-kant'-ma-khĕn), — to introduce
   macht bekannt (makht bĕ-kant')
das Zentrum, Zentren[1] (tsen'-trum, tsen'-trĕn) — center, the heart (of a city)

glücklicherweise (glük'-li-chĕr-vī'-zĕ) — fortunately
die Überraschung,-en (üh-bĕr-ra'-shung) — surprise
Platz nehmen (plats nay'-mĕn) — to take a seat
sich beziehen auf (zich bĕ-tsee'-ĕn owf) — to refer to

die Empfehlung,-en (ĕm-pfay'-lung) — recommendation
der Empfehlungsbrief,-e (ĕm-pfay'-lungs-breef) — letter of recommendation
aufnehmen (owf'-nay-mĕn), — to take in, to pick up
   nimmt auf (nimt owf')

Südamerika (züht'-a-may-ree-ka) — South America
suchen nach (zoo'-khĕn nahkh) — to look for, search for
der Mittelpunkt,-e (mi'-tĕl-pungkt) — center
der Überbringer (üh-bĕr-bring'-ĕr) — bearer
sich interessieren für — to be interested in
   (zich in-tĕ-re-see'-rĕn führ)

106

HANDEL UND WANDEL

BUSINESS LIFE (LIT. COMMERCE AND CHANGE)   (han'-děl unt van'-děl)

das Büro,-s (büh-roh')   office
der Büroraum,-··e (büh-roh'-rowm)   office (room)
das Geschäft,-e (gě-sheft')   business
das Geschäftshaus,-··er (gě-shefts'-hows)   office building,
                                                       commercial firm
exportieren (eks-por-tee'-rěn)   to export
importieren (im-port-tee'-rěn)   to import
einführen (īn'-füh-rěn)   to import, introduce

der Kredit,-e (kray-deet')   credit
bar kaufen (bahr kow'-fěn)   to buy
                                (for cash)
der Profit,-e (proh-feet')   profit
das Produkt,-e (proh-dukt')   product

die Ausfuhr,-en (ows'-foor)   export
die Einfuhr,-en (īn'-foor)   import
die Ware,-n (vah'-rě)   goods, commodity
unterschreiben (un-těr-shrī'-běn)   to sign

das Kontor,-e (kon-tohr')   office
das Privatkontor,-e (pree-vaht'-kon-tohr)   private office
der Geschäftsfreund,-e (gě-shefts'-froint)   business friend
der Geschäftszweig,-e (gě-shefts'-tsvīk)   specialty
die Branche,-n (bran'-zhě)   branch
der Artikel,- (ar-tee'-kěl)   article, commodity
der Inhaber,- (in'-hah-běr)   owner
der Teilhaber,- (tīl'-hah-běr)   partner
die Firma, Firmen (fir'-mah), (fir'-měn)   firm

die Korrespondenz,-en (ko-res-pon-dents')   correspondence
die Schreibmaschine,-n (shrīp'-ma-shee-ně)   typewriter
tippen (ti'-pěn)   to typewrite
das Stenogramm,-e (stay-noh-gram')   shorthand note
die Stenographie,-n (stay-noh-grah-fee')   shorthand
stenographieren (stay-noh-grah-fee'-rěn)   to write shorthand
die Stenotypistin,-nen (stay-noh-ti-pee'-stin) shorthand typist
diktieren (dik-tee'-rěn)   to dictate
hochachtungsvoll (hohkh'-akh-tungs-fol)   respectfully,
                                                   truly yours
übertragen (üh-běr-trah'-gěn)   to transcribe

CONVERSATION

1 Berlin! Alles aussteigen!

2 Das ist schnell[2] gegangen. Gepäckträger! Nehmen Sie diese beiden Handkoffer! Warten Sie auf uns bei der Gepäckannahme.

3 Wir geben das Gepäck vorläufig[3] zur Aufbewahrung und fahren dann morgen früh vom Hotel[4] zu meinem Vater ins Büro, wo[5] ich Sie vorstellen möchte.

4 Hier, meine Herren, sind die Gepäckzettel. Fünfzig Pfennig,[6] bitte! . . .

5 Wir nehmen die Untergrundbahn vom Hotel bis[7] zum Potsdamer[8] Platz. Dann brauchen[9] wir nur ein paar Schritte bis zum Büro zu gehen.

6 Also, das ist Berlin! Das Leben und Treiben erinnert mich beinah an New York.

7 Sie sind hier im Herzen der Stadt. In diesem Geschäftshaus hat mein Vater seine Büros. Wie Sie wissen, exportiert er Porzellan und Glaswaren aus Deutschland nach den Vereinigten[10] Staaten.

8 Ich bin Ihnen[11] sehr dankbar, dass Sie mich mit Ihrem Herrn Vater bekanntmachen wollen.[12]

9 Glücklicherweise[13] ist er gerade in Deutschland. Er kommt nur ein- bis zweimal im Jahr hierher, um[14] nach dem Rechten zu[14] sehen.

FOOTNOTES: *1.* Nouns derived from Latin and ending in *–um* belong to the mixed declension, i.e., the singular takes an *–s* in the genitive case while the plural in all cases takes *–en.*   *2. schnell* (fast), used here as an adverb and, therefore, uninflected.   *3. vorläufig* (for the time being), as an adverb of time precedes all other adverbs or adverbial phrases.   *4. Hotel,* originally a French word; therefore, the stress is retained on the last syllable, as it is in French.   *5. wo* is a

PRONUNCIATION

1 ber-leen'! a'-lĕs ows'shtī-gĕn!
2 das ist shnel gĕ-gang'-ĕn. gĕ-pek'-tray-gĕr. nay'-mĕn zee dee'-zĕ bī'-dĕn hant'-ko-fĕr. var'-tĕn zee owf uns bī dayr gĕ-pek'-an-nah-mĕ.
3 veer gay'-bĕn das gĕ-pek' fohr'-loi-fich tsoor owf'-bĕ-vah-rung unt fah'-rĕn dan mor'-gĕn früh fom hoh-tĕl' tsoo mī'-nĕm fah'-tĕr ins büh-roh', voh ich zee fohr'-shte-lĕn mö'-chtĕ.
4 heer, mī-nĕ he'-rĕn, zint dee gĕ-pek'-tse-tĕl. fünf'-tsich pfe'-nich, bi'-tĕ.
5 veer nay'-mĕn dee un-tĕr-grunt'-bahn fom hoh-tel' bis tzum pots'-da-mĕr plats. dan brow'-khĕn veer noor īn pahr shri'-tĕ bis tsum büh-roh' tsoo gay'-ĕn.

6 al'-zoh, das ist ber'-leen'. das lay'-bĕn unt trī'-bĕn er-i'-nĕrt mich bī-nah' an New York.
7 zee zint heer im her'-tsĕn dayr shtat. in dee'-zĕm gĕ-shefts'-hows hat mīn fah'-tĕr zī'-nĕ büh-rohs'. vee zee vi'-sĕn, eks-por-teert' ayr por-tsĕ-lahn' unt glas'-vah-rĕn ows doitsh'-lant nahkh dayn fĕr-ī'-nik-tĕn shtah'-tĕn.
8 ich bin ee'-nĕn zayr dangk'-bahr, das zee mich mit ee'-rĕm hern fah'-tĕr bĕ-kant'-ma-khĕn vo'-lĕn.
9 glük'-li-chĕr-vī'-zĕ ist ayr gĕ-rah'-dĕ in doitsh'-lant. ayr komt noor īn bis tsvī mahl im yahr heer-hayr', um nahkh daym rech'-tĕn tsoo zay'-ĕn.

TRANSLATION

Berlin! All out!
That went fast. Porter! Take both of these suitcases! Wait for us at the baggage window.

We'll check the baggage for the time being and tomorrow morning we'll go from the hotel to my father's office, where I would like to introduce you.
Gentlemen, here are the tickets (lit., slips) for your luggage. Fifty pennies please.
We will take the subway from the hotel to Potsdam Square. Then we only need to walk a few steps to the office.

So, this is Berlin! The hustle and bustle almost reminds me of New York.
You are in the heart of the city here. My father's offices are in this office building. As you know, he exports china and glassware from Germany to the United States.

I am very grateful that you want me to become acquainted with your father.
Fortunately he is in Germany just now. He comes here only once or twice a year to look after things (lit., in order after the right things to look).

subordinating conjunction; therefore, the inflected part of the verb stands at the end of the clause [§56].   6. Monetary units usually do not change their form in the plural. *Mark* never changes in the plural: *eine Mark*, one mark, *fünf Mark*, five marks. *Pfennig* is sometimes used in the plural: *fünf Pfennige* five pennies, in which case one rather thinks of the five individual coins [§52, c].   7. *bis* (as far as, till, to) is a preposition requiring the accusative case but is used mostly with

10 Diesen Korridor entlang sind die Büroräume meines Vaters. Dies ist sein Privatkontor. Ich klopfe.

11 Herein! Du, Hans? Was für eine[15] Überraschung! Ich habe dich erst nächste Woche erwartet. Wie geht es Mutter?

12 Hallo, Vater! Mutter geht es sehr gut. Sie lässt dich herzlich grüssen! Was macht das Geschäft?

13 So, so! In den Sommermonaten ist es etwas still. Wer[16] ist dieser Herr, Hans?

14 Dies ist Herr Smith, mein Freund und Reisegefährte.

15 Freut mich sehr. Nehmen Sie bitte Platz. Wie gefällt Ihnen[17] Deutschland?

16 Danke, so weit sehr gut.

17 Herr Smith möchte dich um einen Empfehlungsbrief an einen deiner Geschäftsfreunde in Frankfurt bitten.

18 Das mache ich gern. In welcher Branche sind Sie? Worauf[18] soll sich die Empfehlung beziehen?[19]

19 Mein Vater möchte mich bald als Teilhaber in sein Geschäft aufnehmen. Wir importieren Kaffee, Tee und Kakao aus Südamerika.

20 Und nun suchen Sie nach[19] Waren, die Sie aus Deutschland nach Amerika einführen können.

---

another preposition.   *8.* Adjectives can be derived from proper names of cities by the addition of the suffix *—er: Potsdam—Potsdamer; Berlin—Berliner.* Such adjectives do not take any inflectional ending and are written with a capital letter.

10 dee'-zĕn ko'-ree-dohr ent-lang' zint dee büh-roh'-roi-mĕ mī'-nĕs fah'-tĕrs. dees ist zīn pree-vaht'-kon-tohr. *ich* klo'-pfĕ an.

My father's offices are along this corridor. This is his private office. I'll knock.

11 he-rīn'. doo hans? vas führ ī'-nĕ üh-bĕr-ra'-shung. *ich* hah'-bĕ dich ayrst nay*ch*'-stĕ vo'-khĕ ĕr-var'-tĕt. vee gayt es mu'-tĕr?

Come in! You, Hans? What a surprise! I didn't expect you until next week. How is mother?

12 ha-loh', fah'-tĕr. mu'-tĕr gayt es zayr goot. zee lest di*ch* herts'-li*ch* grü'-sĕn. vas macht das gĕ-sheft'?

Hello, Father! Mother is very well. She sends you her best regards (*lit.,* she lets you heartily greet). How is business (*lit.,* what does the business do)?

13 zoh, zoh! in dayn zo'-mĕr-moh-nah'-tĕn ist es et'-vas shtil. vayr ist dee-zer her, *hans?*

So, so! In the summer months it is somewhat quiet. Who is this gentleman, Hans?

14 dees ist her *Smith,* mīn froint unt rī'-zĕ-gĕ-fayr'-tĕ.

This is Mr. Smith, my friend and traveling companion.

15 froit mi*ch* zayr. nay'-mĕn zee bit'-tĕ plats. vee gĕ-felt' ee'-nĕn doitsh'-lant?

Pleased to meet you. Please, be seated (*lit.,* take you please seat). How do you like Germany?

16 dang-ke, zoh vīt zayr goot.

Thank you, very well so far.

17 her *Smith* möch'-tĕ di*ch* um ī'-nĕn em-pfay'-lungs-breef an ī'-nĕn dī'-nĕr gĕ-shefts'-froin'-dĕ in frangk'-furt bi'-tĕn.

Mr. Smith would like to ask you for a letter of recommendation to one of your business associates in Frankfort.

18 das ma'-khĕ i*ch* gern. in vel'-*ch*ĕr bran'-chĕ zint zee? voh-rowf' zol zi*ch* dee em-pfay'-lung bĕ-tsee'-ĕn?

I'll gladly do that. In which branch of business are you? To what shall the recommendation refer?

19 mīn fah'-tĕr möch'-tĕ mi*ch* balt als tīl'-hah-bĕr in zīn gĕ-sheft' owf'-nay-mĕn. veer im-por-tee'-rĕn ka'-fay, tay unt ka-kah'-oh ows züt'-a-may-ree-kah.

My father would like to take me into the business as a partner soon. We import coffee, tea, and cocoa from South America.

20 unt noon zoo'-khĕn zee nahkh vah'-rĕn, dee zee ows doitsh'-lant nahkh a-may'-ree-kah īn'-füh-rĕn kö'-nĕn.

And now you are looking for articles which you can import into America from Germany.

---

9. *brauchen* (to need) takes an infinitive without *zu.*   10. *Vereinigten,* past participle of *vereinigen* (to unite), used as an adjective and inflected accordingly. 11. *dankbar sein* (to be grateful) requires the dative case.   12. *dass* (that) sub-

21 Ganz recht! Wir dachten an[20] Lederwaren, und Frankfurt und Offenbach am Main sind die Mittelpunkte für solche Artikel.

22 Entschuldigen Sie mich bitte einen Augenblick! Fräulein Kruse, wollen Sie bitte ein Stenogramm aufnehmen:

Das Kuvert:

Herrn Walter Fischer[21]
Frankfurt a. Main
Bahnhofstrasse 10

Berlin, den 20. Juli 19 . . .

Der Brief:

Sehr geehrter Herr Fischer![22]

Der Überbringer dieses,[23] Herr Robert Smith aus New York, interessiert sich[24] für den Export und Import von Waren zwischen Deutschland und den Vereinigten Staaten von Amerika. Sein Vater ist Inhaber eines gut eingeführten[25] Importhauses und würde[26] gern neue Artikel zur Einfuhr aufnehmen.

Vielleicht können Sie Herrn[27] Smith behilflich sein. Er ist ein Freund meines Sohnes, und ich kann ihn bestens empfehlen.

Hochachtungsvoll

23 Fräulein Kruse, übertragen[28] Sie diesen Brief sofort auf der· Schreibmaschine. Den Rest der heutigen Korrespondenz diktiere ich später.

---

ordinating conjunction, therefore, the changeable part of the verb stands at the end of the clause with the infinitive preceding it. *bekannt* (known) follows the word order of the separable prefix [§79].   *13. Glücklicherweise* (fortunately). *Weise* (manner) is used to form adverbs from adjectives [§53, d].   *14. um . . . zu* (in order to), is always used with the infinitive of a verb. This combination must be used whenever a definite purpose is expressed.   *15. Was für (eine)* (What a, what

21 gans re*ch*t. veer dakh'-tĕn an lay'-dĕr-vah-rĕn unt frangk'-furt unt o'-fĕn-bakh am mīn zint dee mi'-tĕl-pungk-tĕ führ zol'-*ch*ĕ ar-tee'-kĕl.

Exactly (*lit.,* completely right)! We were thinking of leather goods, and Frankfort and Offenbach-on-the-Main are the centers for such articles.

22 ĕnt-shul'-di-gĕn zee mi*ch* bi'-tĕ ī'-nĕn ow'-gĕn-blik. — froi'-līn *Kruse*, vo'-lĕn zee bi'-tĕ īn stay-noh-gram' owf-nay'-mĕn:
das kuh-vayrt': hern val'-tĕr fi'-shĕr. frank'-furt am mīn. bahn'-hohf-shtrah-sĕ tsayn. ber-leen' dayn tsvan'-tsik-sten yoo'-lee, noin'-tsayn-hun-dĕrt. dayr breef: zayr gĕ-ayr'-tĕr her *Fischer*. dayr üh-bĕr-bring'-ĕr dee'-zĕs, her roh'-bert *Smith* ows *New York*, in-tĕ-re-seert' *zich* führ dayn eks-port' unt im-port' fon vah'-rĕn tsvi'-shĕn doitsh'-lant unt dayn fer'-ī'-nik-tĕn shtah'-tĕn fon a-may'-ree-kah. zīn fah'-tĕr ist in'-hah-bĕr ī-nes goot īn'-gĕ-führ-tĕn im-port'-how-zĕs unt vür'-dĕ gern noi'-ĕ ar-tee'-kĕl tsoor īn'-foor owf'-nay-mĕn.
fee'-līcht kö'-nĕn zee hern *Smith* bĕ-hilf'-*lich* zīn. ayr ist īn froint mī'-nĕs zoh'-nĕs, unt i*ch* kan een be'-stĕns ĕm-pfay'-lĕn. hohkh'-akh-tungs-fol.

Excuse me a moment, please. Miss Kruse, will you please take dictation:

The envelope:
    Mr. Walter Fischer
    10 Bahnhof Street
    Frankfort-on-the-Main

The letter:
    Berlin, July 20, 19....
My dear Mr. Fischer:
The bearer of this letter, Mr. Robert Smith of New York, is interested in the export and import of goods between Germany and the United States of America. His father is the owner of a well-established import firm and would like to add new articles for import.
Perhaps you could be of some help to Mr. Smith. He is a friend of my son and I can recommend him highly.
    Very truly yours,

23 froi'-līn *Kruse*, üh-bĕr-trah'-gĕn zee dee'-zĕn breef zoh-fort' owf dayr shrīp'-ma-shee-nĕ. dayn rest dayr hoi'-ti-gĕn ko-rĕs-pon-dents' dik-tee'-rĕ i*ch* shpay'-tĕr.

Miss Kruse, transcribe this letter on the typewriter immediately. I will dictate the rest of today's correspondence later.

kind of) [§33, a, b]. *16. Wer* (who) is an interrogative pronoun in the nominative singular. The interrogative pronoun is inflected much the same as the article *der*. There is only one interrogative referring to masculine and feminine, singular and plural. The neuter interrogative is *was* (what). *17.* The dative is used in German. *18. Worauf* (to what), interrogative compound of *wo* (where) and *auf,* the preposition necessary in the idiomatic expression *sich beziehen auf*

24 Ich danke Ihnen[29] vielmals, Herr Miller.

25 Nun überlassen[28] wir Vater seiner Arbeit. Kommen Sie, Herr Smith!

26 Leider, bin ich jetzt sehr beschäftigt.[30] Sie können sich inzwischen Berlin ansehen.

27 Wir treffen uns dann heute abend in unserem Stamm-lokal am Kurfürstendamm. Ich rufe dich noch an.

28 Noch einen Augenblick,[31] Hans! Wen[16] könnten[32] wir für heute abend noch einladen?

29 Wie wäre[33] es mit Vetter Jürgen? Er ist immer ein guter Gesellschafter.

30 Jürgen ist leider nicht in Berlin. Er ist auf einer Geschäftsreise in Österreich.

31 Mit wem[16] könnten wir sonst gehen?

32 Bleiben wir lieber unter uns. Das ist gemütlicher. Also, auf Wiedersehen.

(to refer to). An *r* is inserted between *wo* and any prefix beginning with a vowel: *worin* (in what), *woraus* (from what), but *womit* (with what).   *19. suchen nach* (to look for). Id.   *20. denken an* (to think of). Id.   *21.* Form of address written on envelope.   *22.* Formal salutation to a person who does not belong to a circle of friends. The space between the date and salutation should be very generous, almost half a page. The punctuation after the formal address is an exclamation mark. A comma may be used instead of the exclamation mark but, in that case, the first word of the letter would begin with a small letter. In a formal business letter no salutation is used.   *23. dieses* (of this), used instead *dieses Schreiben.* *24. sich interessieren für* (to be interested in). Id., *lit.,* interest oneself for. *25. eingeführten* (established), past participle of *einführen* (to establish), used as an adjective.   *26. würde,* subjunctive of *wurde* (became), is used to form the conditional mood: *würde aufnehmen* (would add, take up), *würde arbeiten*

24 *ich* dang'-kĕ ee'-nĕn feel'-mahls, her *Miller.*

Thank you very much, Mr. Miller.

25 noon üh-bĕr-la'-sĕn veer fah'-tĕr zī'-nĕr ar'-bīt. ko'-mĕn zee, her *Smith.*

Now we will leave Father to his work. Come, Mr. Smith!

26 lī'-dĕr, bin *ich* yetst zayr bĕ-sheft'-tikt. zee kö'-nĕn *zich* in-tsvi'-shĕn ber-leen' an'-zay-ĕn.

Unfortunately, I am very busy right now. In the meantime, you can look around Berlin.

27 veer tre'-fĕn uns dan hoi'-tĕ ah'-bĕnt in un'-zĕ-rĕm shtam'-lohkahl am kur-für-stĕn-dam'. *ich* roo'-fĕ *dich* nokh an.

Then we shall meet tonight in our favorite haunt on Kurfürstendamm. I'll call you.

28 nokh ī'-nĕn ow'-gĕn-blik, hans! vayn kön'-tĕn veer führ hoi'-tĕ ah'-bĕnt nokh īn'-lah-dĕn?

Just a moment, Hans. Whom else could we invite for tonight?

29 vee vay'-rĕ es mit fe'-tĕr yür'-gĕn? ayr ist i'-mĕr īn goo'-tĕr gĕ-zel'-shaf-tĕr.

How about Cousin George? He is always good company (*lit.,* a good companion).

30 yür'-gĕn ist lī'-dĕr ni*ch*t in berleen'. ayr ist owf ī'-nĕr gĕ-shefts'-rī-zĕ in öh'-stĕ-rīch.

Unfortunately, George is not in Berlin. He is on a business trip in Austria.

31 mit vaym kön'-tĕn veer zonst gay'-ĕn?

Whom can we go with then (otherwise)?

32 blī'-bĕn veer lee'-bĕr un'-tĕr uns. das ist gĕ-müht'-li-*ch*ĕr. al'-zoh, owf vee'-dĕr-zayn.

Let us rather keep by ourselves. That is more agreeable. Well, good-bye.

(would work) [§77 a].   27. *Herrn Smith. Herr* belongs to the weak noun declension and is always inflected, except in the nominative case.   28. *übertragen* (transcribe). *Über* (over) is one of the doubtful prefixes like *um* (around), *unter* (under), *wieder* (again). Here, the prefix is inseparable because it is used figuratively [§68, c].   29. *danken* (to thank) is intransitive and requires the dative case as object [§62].   30. *beschäftigt* (busy, occupied), past participle of *beschäftigen* (to occupy), used as predicate adjective. Note word order: adjectives used with *sein* (to be) stand at the end of the sentence, i.e., they follow the rule for word order for separable prefixes [68, b].   31. *einen Augenblick* (a moment) is in the accusative case because it is an expression of extent of time [24 d, 2].   32. *könnten* (could), subjunctive form of *konnte.*   33. *wie wäre es* (how would it be), subjunctive of *war* (was) [§76].

Zwölfte Lektion

Neue Wörter für diese Lektion

stehen bleiben (shtay'-ĕn blī'-bĕn) — to stop
stellen (shte'-lĕn) — to set, put
sicher (zi'-chĕr) — sure,-ly
meistens (mī'-stĕns) — mostly, usually

das Hotel,-s (hoh-tĕl') — hotel
meinen (mī'-nĕn) — to mean
gründlich (grünt'-lich) — thorough,-ly
reinigen (rī'-ni-gĕn) — to clean
zwischen (tsvi'-shĕn) — between
zu Fuss (tsoo foos) — on foot, walk

der Wald,-¨er (valt) — forest, woods
der Weg,-e (vayk) — way, road, path
reparieren (re-pah-ree'-rĕn) — to repair
die Reparatur,-en (re-pah-rah-toor') — repairs
verlässlich (fĕr-les'-lich) — dependable

zahlen (tsah'-lĕn) — to pay
die Weile,-n (vī'-lĕ) — the while
halten (hal'-tĕn) — to hold, keep
auf und ab (owf unt ap) — back and forth

einmal (īn'-mahl) — once
ziemlich (tseem'-lich) — rather
froh (froh) — happy, glad
lebhaft (layp'-haft) — lively
stören (shtöh'-rĕn) — to disturb
strecken (shtre'-kĕn) — to stretch

sich umsehen (zich um'-zay-ĕn) — to look around
abholen (ap'-hoh-lĕn), holt ab (hohlt ap') — to call for
herausgeben (he-rows'-gay-bĕn), gibt heraus (gipt he-rows') — to give change, give up

erledigen (ĕr-lay'-di-gĕn) — to take care of
nachdem (nahkh-daym') — after (conj.)
herumfahren (he-rum'-fah-rĕn) fährt herum (fayrt he-rum') — to ride around
fröhlich (fröh'-lich) — cheerful, merry, happy

116

DIE TAGESZEITEN • BEIM UHRMACHER

THE TIME, AT THE
    WATCHMAKER

(tah'-gĕs-tsī-tĕn,
bĭm oor'-ma-khĕr)

die Uhr,-en (oor)	watch, clock
die Taschenuhr,-en (ta'-shĕn-oor)	pocket watch
die Armbanduhr,-en (arm'-bant-oor)	wrist watch
die Turmuhr,-en (turm'-oor)·	tower clock
die Standuhr,-en (shtant'-oor)	grandfather clock
der Wecker,- (ve'-kĕr)	alarm clock

der Uhrmacher,- (oor'-ma-khĕr)	watchmaker
die Uhrmacherwerkstatt,-"en (. . .-verk-shtat)	watchmaker's shop
die Werkstatt,-"en (verk'-shtat)	workshop

das Werk,-e (verk)	works
die Feder,-n (fay'-dĕr)	feather, spring
die Uhrfeder (oor'-fay-dĕr)	watch spring
die Feder springt (fay'-dĕr shpringkt)	the spring breaks

WIEVIEL UHR IST ES?

WHAT TIME IS IT?

(vee-feel' oor'ist es)

die Stunde,-n (shtun'-dĕ)	hour
die Minute,-n (mee-noo'-tĕ)	minute
die Sekunde,-n (zay-kun'-dĕ)	second

ein Uhr (īn oor)	one o'clock
zwei Uhr (tsvī . . .)	two o'clock
halb zwei (halp tsvī)	half past one
Viertel nach drei (feer'-tĕl nahkh drī)	quarter past three
zehn Minuten vor vier (tsayn mee-noo'-tĕn for feer)	ten minutes to four
ein Viertel vor sechs (īn feer'-tĕl fohr zeks)	a quarter to six

nachgehen (nahkh'-gay-ĕn), geht nach (gayt nahkh')	to be slow (watch)
vorgehen (fohr'-gay-ĕn), geht vor (gayt fohr')	to be fast (watch)
richtiggehen (rich'-tich-gay-ĕn), geht richtig (gayt rich'-tich)	to be right
falschgehen (falsh'-gay-ĕn), geht falsch (gayt falsh)	to be wrong
aufziehen (owf'-tsee-ĕn), zieht auf (tseet owf')	to wind
schlagen (shlah'-gĕn)	to strike, beat

CONVERSATION

1 Nun haben wir Zeit, uns ein bisschen in Berlin umzusehen.[1] Wieviel Uhr ist es?[2]

2 Ich habe halb zehn. Aber ich bin nicht ganz sicher. Meine Uhr geht meistens nach.[3]

3 Meine Uhr steht.[3] Als[4] ich sie heute morgen aufziehen wollte, knackte etwas.

4 Die Turmuhr schlägt gerade dreiviertel (ein Viertel vor) zehn. Einen Augenblick! Ich werde meine Uhr stellen. Jetzt geht sie richtig.[3] Diese Turmuhren gehen auf die Minute, ja, beinah auf die Sekunde richtig.

5 Wir gehen zuerst zu Fuss nach *Unter den Linden*.[5] Dort sehen wir das Brandenburger Tor und den Tiergarten.[6]

6 Ich würde auf dem Weg gern meine Uhr zum Reparieren[7] bringen.

7 Gut, hier in der Potsdamer Strasse[8] kenne ich einen Uhrmacher, der[9] sehr verlässlich ist.

8 Ist dies die Uhrmacherwerkstatt, die[9] Sie meinen?

9 Ja, treten wir ein!

10 Guten Tag! Wollen Sie sich bitte meine Armbanduhr ansehen. Sie ist heute morgen stehengeblieben.

FOOTNOTES: *1. umsehen* (to look around) is a verb with a separable prefix. If *zu* is used with verbs which have separable prefixes, the *zu* stands between the separable prefix and the verb proper.   *2. Wieviel Uhr ist es?* (what time is it). ID., *lit.,* How much clock is it?   *3.* In German the clock or watch, *die Uhr,* is almost personified: *sie geht* (she goes, walks); *sie steht* (she stands); *sie ist stehengeblieben* (she has stopped); *sie geht vor* (she walks [goes] ahead); *sie geht nach* (she walks [goes] after); *sie geht nicht* (she does not go); *gehen auf die Minute* ("walk" on the minute); *geht richtig* ("walks" correctly); *geht falsch*

PRONUNCIATION	TRANSLATION

PRONUNCIATION

1 Noon hah'-bĕn veer tsīt, uns în bis'-*ch*ĕn in ber-leen' um'-tsoo-zay-ĕn. vee'-feel' oor ist es?

2 i*ch* hah'-bĕ halp tsayn. ah'-bĕr i*ch* bin ni*ch*t gants zi'-*ch*ĕr. mī'-nĕ oor gayt mī'-stĕns nahkh.

3 mī'-nĕ oor shtayt. als i*ch* zee hoi'-tĕ mor'-gĕn owf'-tsee-ĕn vol'-tĕ knak'-tĕ et'-vas.

4 dee turm'-oor shlaykt gĕ-rah'-dĕ drī'-feer-tĕl (īn' feer-tĕl fohr) tsayn. ī'-nĕn ow'-gĕn-blik. i*ch* vayr'-dĕ mī'-nĕ oor shte'-lĕn. yetst gayt zee ri*ch*'-ti*ch*. dee'-zĕ turm'-oo-rĕn gay'-ĕn owf dee mee-noo'-tĕ yah bī-nah' owf dee zay-kun'-dĕ ri*ch*'-ti*ch*.

5 veer gay'-ĕn tsoo-ayrst' tsoo foos nahkh "un'-tĕr dayn lin'-dĕn". dort zay'-ĕn veer das "bran'-dĕn-bur-gĕr tohr" unt dayn "teer'-gar-tĕn".

6 i*ch* vür'-dĕ owf daym vayk gern mī'-nĕ oor tsum re-pah-ree'-rĕn bring'-ĕn.

7 goot heer in dayr pots'-da-mĕr shtrah'-sĕ ke'-nĕ i*ch* ī'-nĕn oor'-ma-khĕr dayr zayr fĕr-les'-li*ch* ist.

8 ist dees dee oor'-ma-khĕr-verk-shtat dee zee mī'-nĕn?

9 yah, tray'-tĕn veer īn.

10 goo'-tĕn tahk. vo'-lĕn zee zi*ch* bi'-tĕ mī'-nĕ arm'-bant-oor an'-zay-ĕn? zee ist hoi'-tĕ mor'-gĕn shtay'-ĕn-gĕ-blee-bĕn.

TRANSLATION

Now we have time to look around Berlin a little. What time is it? I have half past nine. But I'm not quite sure. My watch is usually slow.

My watch has stopped. When I wanted to wind it this morning, something snapped. The tower clock is just striking a quarter to ten. Just a moment! I'll set my watch. Now it's right. These tower clocks are correct to the minute, yes, even to the second.

First we'll walk (*lit.*, go on foot) to *Unter den Linden*. There we'll see the Brandenburger Gate and the *Tiergarten*.

On the way, I'd like to take my watch for repairs.

Good. I know a watchmaker here on Potsdamer Street who is very dependable.
Is this the watchmaker's shop that you mean?
Yes, let's step in.
How do you do. Would you please look at my wrist watch? It stopped this morning.

("walks" incorrectly). *4. als* (when) introduces a dependent clause. Therefore, the inflected part of the verb is placed at the end of the clause and the infinitive precedes it. The main clause has inverted word order because it follows the dependent clause [79, b]. *5. Unter den Linden* (under the linden trees), the most famous avenue of Berlin, a very wide boulevard with linden trees planted on both sides. Many palaces, embassies, the state opera, art galleries, cafes, and elegant stores used to be located on this avenue; the university is still to be found there today. *6. Brandenburger Tor,* a triumphal arch that is a landmark of

11 Die Feder ist gesprungen. Die Uhr ist schmutzig und muss gründlich gereinigt werden.

12 Wieviel wird die Reparatur kosten, und wann kann ich die Uhr wiederhaben?[10]

13 Die Reparatur wird zwischen acht und zehn Mark[11] kosten. Sie können die Uhr in drei Tagen abholen.

14 Ich zahle Ihnen gleich fünf Mark an. Können Sie mir aus 100 (hundert) Mark herausgeben[12]?

15 Ja, hier sind 95 (fünfundneunzig) Mark heraus.[13] Dies ist die Quittung.

16 Wir essen nun schnell zu Abend.[14] Ich habe meinen Vater angerufen, der[9] uns um 9 Uhr im Café am Kurfürstendamm erwartet.[9]

17 Der Kurfürstendamm ist eine sehr bekannte und interessante Strasse, nicht wahr?

18 Das stimmt! Er scheint die Eleganz der Geschäfte der 5.[15] (Fünften) Allee, die Breite der Parkallee mit dem Nachtleben der 42. (Zweiundvierzigsten)[15] Strasse zu verbinden.

19 Viele grosse Kinos, elegante Speisehäuser, Bier-Restaurants, Kleinkunstbühnen[16] (Kabaretts) und auch Theater sind zu beiden Seiten der Strasse.

Berlin. It is an entrance gate to the *Tiergarten.* The *Tiergarten* is a former forest in which German princes hunted, but now is a beautiful public park.   7. *zum Reparieren* (for repairs), *lit.,* for repairing. The infinitive *reparieren* (to repair) is used as a neuter noun.   8. *Potsdamer Strasse,* Potsdam Street. *Die Strasse* (the street) and *der Platz* (the square) usually form a compound noun with the proper name of a street. For example, *Friedrichstrasse* (Frederick Street); *Schillerplatz* (Schiller Place). However, if the name of the street is derived from the name of a city or country, it is not compounded but is written separately and followed

11 dee fay'-dĕr ist gĕ-shprung'-ĕn. dee oor ist shmu'-tsi*ch* unt mu̧s grünt'-li*ch* gĕ-rī'-nikt vayr'-dĕn.

12 vee'-feel' virt dee re-pah-rah-toor' ko'-stĕn unt van kan i*ch* dee oor vee'-dĕr-hah'-bĕn?

13 dee repah-rah-toor' virt tsvi'-shĕn akht unt tsayn mark ko'-stĕn. zee kö-nĕn dee oor in drī tah'-gĕn ap'-hoh-lĕn.

14 i*ch* tsah'-lĕ ee'-nĕn glī*ch* fünf mark an. kö'-nĕn zee meer ows hun'-dĕrt mark he-rows'-gay-bĕn?

15 yah heer zint fünf'-unt-noin'-tsi*ch* mark he-rows'. dees ist dee kvi'-tung.

16 veer e'-sĕn noon shnel tsoo ah'-bĕnt. i*ch* hah'-bĕ mī'-nĕn fah'-tĕr an'-gĕ-roo-fĕn, dayr uns um noin oor im ka-fay' am koor-für-stĕn-dam' ĕr-var'-tĕt'.

17 dayr koo-für-stĕn-dam' ist ī'-nĕ zayr bĕ-kan'-tĕ unt in-tĕ-re-san'-tĕ shtrah'-sĕ ni*ch*t vahr?

18 das shtimt. ayr shīnt dee ay-le-gans' dayr gĕ-shef'-tĕ dayr fünf'-tĕn a-lay' dee brī'-tĕ dayr park'-a-lay mit daym nakht'-lay-bĕn dayr tsvī-unt-feer'-tsik-stĕn shtrah'-sĕ tsoo fĕr-bin'-dĕn.

19 fee'-lĕ groh'-sĕ kee'-nohs, ay-le-gan-'tĕ shpī'-zĕ-hoi-zĕr beer'-re-stoh-rangs, klīn-kunst'-büh-nĕn (ka-bah-rays') unt owkh tay-ah'-tĕr zint tsoo bī'-dĕn zī'-tĕn dayr shtrah'-sĕ.

The spring is broken. The watch is dirty and must be thoroughly cleaned.

How much will the repairs cost and when may I have the watch back?

The repairs will cost between eight and ten marks. You may call for the watch in three days.

I'll pay five marks down right now. Can you give me change from one hundred marks?

Yes, here are ninety-five marks. Here is the receipt.

We'll eat supper quickly. I called my father, who expects us at 9:00 o'clock in the cafe on the Kurfürstendamm.

The Kurfürstendamm is a very well known and interesting street, isn't it?

That's right. It seems to combine the elegance of the shops of Fifth Avenue, the width of Park Avenue, and the night life of Forty-Second Street.

There are many large movie-houses, high class restaurants, beer gardens, cabarets, and also theaters on both sides of the street.

---

by *Strasse* as illustrated by *Potsdamer Strasse*. 9. *der* (who) is a relative pronoun. which therefore must agree in number and gender with its antecedent; however, it takes the case required by its function in the subordinate clause. In *der sehr ver-lässlich ist, der* refers to *Uhrmacher* and is the subject of the clause. In *die Sie meinen, die* refers to *Werkstatt* and, as object, is in the accusative case. A relative pronoun introduces a subordinate clause; therefore dependent word order is re-quired [§79, c]. 10. Any compound with a verb (such as *kennenlernen*) or any adverb, adjective, noun, etc. closely connected with a verb in idea, is treated like

20 Dort sitzt mein Vater schon in dem Vorgarten-Café. Diese Vorgarten-Cafés sind ebenso[17] charakteristisch für Berlin wie für Paris.

21 Guten Abend, Herr Miller! Wir haben Sie doch nicht warten lassen?

22 Nein, ich bin gerade gekommen.—Herr Ober, bringen Sie mir ein grosses Glas helles Bier, Münchner,[18] bitte!

23 Ich möchte[19] einen Kognak und ein Glas Wasser.

24 Und ich nehme eine Zitronenlimonade sowie einmal Apfelkuchen mit Schlagsahne.

25 Die Musik ist sehr gut. Die Kapellen in diesen Cafés[20] sind auf ziemlich künstlerischer Höhe.

26 Im allgemeinen werden Auszüge aus bekannten Opern und Operetten, sowie auch moderne Musik gespielt.

---

a separable prefix as far as word order is concerned. *11. zehn Mark* (ten marks). Monetary units do not take a plural. *12. herausgeben* (to give change), *lit.*, give out from. *13. heraus* (out from); *geben* (give) is understood. *14. zu Abend essen* (to eat supper). ID., *lit.*, to eat to evening. Also *zu Mittag essen* (to eat dinner), *lit.*, to eat to noon. *15. zweiundvierzigsten.* Ordinals are adjectives and, therefore, take adjective endings. Usually ordinals are indicated by a period after the number and are not written out. See §51, b. *16. Kleinkunstbühnen,*

20 dort zitst mīn fah'-tĕr shohn in daym fohr'-gar-tĕn-ka-fay. dee'-zĕ fohr'-gar-tĕn-ka-fays zint ay'-bĕn-zoh kah-rak-tĕ-ris'-tish führ berleen' vee führ pah-rees'.

There is my father sitting at the sidewalk cafe. These sidewalk cafes are just as characteristic of (lit., for) Berlin as of (lit., for) Paris.

21 goo'-tĕn ah'-bĕnt, her Miller. veer hah'-bĕn zee dokh nicht var'-tĕn la'-sĕn?

Good evening, Mr. Miller. I hope we haven't kept you waiting.

22 nīn, ich bin gĕ-rah'-dĕ gĕ-ko'-mĕn. her oh'-bĕr, bring'-ĕn zee meer īn groh'-sĕs glahs he'-lĕs beer, münch'-nĕr bi'-tĕ.

No, I have just arrived. Waiter, bring me a large glass of light beer, Münchner, please!

23 ich möch'-tĕ ī-nĕn kon'-iak unt īn glahs va'-sĕr.

I'd like cognac and a glass of water.

24 unt ich nay'-mĕ ī'-nĕ tsee-troh'-nĕn-li-moh-nah-dĕ zoh-vee' īn'-mahl a'-pfĕl-koo-khĕn mit shlak'-zah-nĕ.

And I'll have a lemonade and also apple cake with whipped cream.

25 dee moo-zeek' ist zayr goot. dee ka-pe'-lĕn in dee'-zĕn ka-fays' zint owf tseem'-lich künst'-lĕ-ri-shĕr höh'-ĕ.

The music is very good. The orchestras in these cafes have rather high artistic standards.

26 im al-gĕ-mī'-nĕn vayr'-dĕn ows'-tsüh-gĕ ows bĕ-kan'-tĕn oh'-pĕrn unt oh-pĕ-re'-tĕn zoh-vee' owkh moh-der'-nĕ moo-zeek' gĕ-shpeelt'.

In general, selections from well-known operas and operettas, as well as modern music, are played.

---

lit., little art stages.   17. ebenso...wie (just as...as), almost the same as so... wie (as...as) [§48]. These expressions are used in comparing things of equal value.   18. Münchner (Munich). Bier (beer) is understood.   19. A modal auxiliary is sometimes used without an infinitive if the inference is clear [§72, a].   20. Note the difference in spelling and pronunciation between Kaffee (coffee) and Café (restaurant). The Café is usually used by families, friends, business associates. as a gathering place.

Dreizehnte Lektion

Neue Wörter für diese Lektion

Es tut mir leid (es toot meer līt)	I am sorry
Was fehlt Ihnen? (vas faylt ee'-něn)	What is the matter with you?
der Fall,-"e (fal)	case
auf alle Fälle (owf a'-lě fe'-lě)	in any case, in any event

das Telefon,-e (tay'-lě-fohn),	telephone
der Fernsprecher,- (fern'-shpre-*ch*ěr)	
die Telefonnummer,-n (tay'-lě-fohn-nu-mer)	telephone number
das Telefonbuch,-"er (. . . bookh)	telephone book

die Leitung,-en (lī'-tung)	line, connection
aufsuchen (owf'-zoo-khěn),	to look up, to seek (for)
sucht auf (zookht owf)	
worüber (voh-rüh'-běr)	what of, what
der Schmerz,-es,-en (shmerts)	pain

erhöhen (ěr-höh'-ěn)	to increase, elevate
messen (me'-sěn), **misst** (mist)	to measure
aufmachen (owf'-ma-khěn),	to open
macht auf (makht owf')	
wenigstens (vay'-nik-stěns)	at least

fast (fast)	almost	**besetzt** (bě-zetst')	occupied, busy
nötig (nöh'-ti*ch*)	necessary		
erreichen (ěr-rī'-*ch*ěn)	to reach	**klagen** (klah'-gěn)	to complain
vergehen (fěr-gay'-ěn)	to perish	**stecken** (shte'-kěn)	to put, stick
schwitzen (shvi'-tsěn)	to sweat		
weh tun (vay' toon)	to hurt, pain	**danach** (da-nahkh')	after that
		eher (ay'-ěr)	rather

124

BEIM ARZT • BEIM ZAHNARZT

AT THE DOCTOR'S, DENTIST'S   (bīm ahrtst, tsahn'-ahrtst)

der Arzt,-"e (ahrtst)	doctor	das Rezept,-e (ray-tsept')	prescription
der Besuch,-e (bĕ-zookh')	visit	das Fieber (fee'-bĕr)	fever

die Sprechstunde,-n (shpre*ch*'- shtun-dĕ)   office hour
das Wartezimmer,- (vahr'-tĕ-tsi-mĕr)   waiting room
der Kopfschmerz,-en (kopf'-shmerts)   headache
sich erkälten (*zich* ĕr-kel'-tĕn)   to catch cold
die Entzündung,-en (ĕn-tsün'-dung)   inflammation
das Honorar,-e (hoh-noh-rahr')   fee
die Medizin,-en (may-dee-tseen')   medicine
die Apotheke,-n (a-poh-tay'-kĕ)   drugstore
gute Besserung (goo'-tĕ be'-sĕ-rung)   speedy recovery

untersuchen (un-tĕr-zoo'-khĕn)   to examine, investigate
die Untersuchung,-en (un-tĕr-zoo'-khung)   examination
der Blutdruck (bloot'-druk)   blood pressure
der Krankenwagen,- (krang'-kĕn-vah-gĕn)   ambulance
das Krankenhaus,-"er (krang'-kĕn-hows)   hospital
verschreiben (fĕr-shrī'-bĕn)   to prescribe
der Zahnarzt,"e (tsahn'-ahrtst)   dentist
die Zahnschmerzen (*pl.*) (tsahn'-shmer-tsĕn)   toothache
die Röntgenaufnahme,-n (rönt'-gĕn-owf-nah-mĕ)   x-ray
die Plombe,-n (plom'-bĕ)   filling (tooth)
herausfallen (he-rows'-fa-lĕn), fällt heraus (felt . . .)to fall out
das Loch,-"er (lokh)   hole, cavity

DER MENSCHLICHE KÖRPER

THE HUMAN BODY   (mensh'-li-*ch*ĕ kör'-pĕr)

das Bein,-e (bīn)	leg	das Auge,-n (ow'-gĕ)	eye
der Arm,-e (arm)	arm	das Gesicht,-e (gĕ-*zich*t')	face
der Finger,- (fing'-ĕr)	finger	die Backe,-n (ba'-kĕ)	cheek
der Fuss,-"e (foos)	foot	der Zahn,-"e (tsahn)	tooth
der Zeh,-en (tsay)	toe	die Zunge,-n (tsung'-ĕ)	tongue
der Hals,-"e (hals)	throat, neck	der Nerv,-en (nerf)	nerve
		der Rücken,- (rü'-kĕn)	back
der Mund,-"er (munt)	mouth	der Magen,- (mah'-gĕn)	stomach
die Nase,-n (nah'-zĕ)	nose	das Herz,-en (hayrts)	heart
das Ohr,-en (ohr)	ear	die Leber (lay'-bĕr)	liver

CONVERSATION

1 Heute müssen Sie mich entschuldigen, Herr Miller. Ich fühle mich[1] gar nicht wohl.

2 Das tut mir leid.[2] Was fehlt Ihnen[3] denn?

3 Ich weiss auch nicht recht. Alle Glieder tun mir weh.[4]

4 Soll ich nicht einen Arzt kommen lassen?[5]

5 Oh, nein! Das ist nicht nötig. Ich habe kein Fieber. Gehen Sie ruhig Ihren Geschäften nach!

6 Nehmen Sie einige Aspirintabletten und versuchen Sie zu schwitzen!

7 Auf alle Fälle[6] lassen Sie mir die Adresse und Telefonnummer eines Arzts.

8 Doktor Friedrich Burkhard in der Potsdamer Strasse ist sehr gut. Sie finden ihn im Telefonbuch.

9 Vielen Dank! Ich gehe zuerst noch einmal[7] ins Bett.

10 Sie können mich den ganzen Tag[8] in meines Vaters Büro erreichen.

11 Keine Angst, Herr Miller, "Unkraut vergeht nicht." Auf Wiedersehen! . . .

12 . . . Verbinden Sie mich bitte mit Nummer 32 45 68 (zweiunddreissig fünfundvierzig achtundsechzig).[9]

13 Die Leitung ist besetzt. Wollen Sie einen Augenblick[8] warten.

FOOTNOTES: *1. sich fühlen* (to feel), used reflexively when referring to one's health or well-being.   *2. Das tut mir leid* (I am sorry). ID., *lit.*, That makes me suffer.   *3. Was fehlt Ihnen* (What is the matter with you)? ID., *lit.*, What is missing to you?   *4. Alle Glieder tun mir weh* (All my limbs ache). ID., *lit.*, All

PRONUNCIATION	TRANSLATION

1 hoi'-tĕ mü'-sĕn zee mi*ch* ĕnt-shul'-di-gĕn, her *Miller*. i*ch* füh'-lĕ mi*ch* gar ni*ch*t vohl.

Today you must excuse me, Mr. Miller. I don't feel at all well.

2 das toot meer līt. vas faylt ee'-nĕn den?

I'm sorry. What is the matter with you (*lit.*, what is missing to you)?

3 i*ch* vīs owkh ni*ch*t re*ch*t. a'-lĕ glee'-dĕr toon meer vay.

I don't know myself. All my limbs ache.

4 zol i*ch* ni*ch*t ī'-nĕn ahrtst ko'-mĕn la'-sĕn?

Shouldn't I call a doctor (*lit.*, shouldn't I let come a doctor)?

5 oh nīn. das ist ni*ch*t nöh'-ti*ch*. i*ch* hah'-bĕ kīn fee'-bĕr. gay'-ĕn zee roo'-i*ch* ee'-rĕn gĕ-shef'-tĕn nahkh.

Oh, no! That is not necessary. I have no fever. Go on about your business without concern (*lit.*, calmly).

6 nay'mĕn zee ī'-ni-gĕ as-pi-reen'-ta-ble-tĕn unt vĕr-zoo'-khĕn zee tsoo shvi'-tsĕn.

Take a few aspirin tablets and try to perspire.

7 owf a'-lĕ fe'-lĕ la'-sĕn zee meer dee a-dre'-sĕ unt tay'-lĕ-fohn-nu-mĕr ī'-nĕs ahrtsts.

In any event, leave me the address and telephone number of a physician.

8 dok'-tohr free-'dri*ch* *Burkhard* in dayr pots'-da-mĕr shtrah'-sĕ ist zayr goot. zee fin'-dĕn een im tay'-lĕ-fohn-bookh.

Dr. Frederic Burkhard in Potsdamer Street is very good. You will find him in the telephone book.

9 fee'-lĕn dangk. i*ch* gay-ĕ tsoo-ayrst nokh īn'-mahl ins bet.

Many thanks. First, I'll go back to bed again.

10 zee kö'-nĕn mi*ch* dayn gan-tsĕn tahk in mī'-nĕs fah'-tĕrs büh-roh' e-rī'-*ch*ĕn.

You can reach me at my father's office all day long.

11 kī'-nĕ angkst, her *Miller*, un'-krowt fĕr-gayt' ni*ch*t. owf vee'-dĕr-zayn.

Don't worry, Mr. Miller, "weeds don't perish." Good-bye.

12 fĕr-bin'-dĕn zee mi*ch* bi'-tĕ mit nu'-mĕr tsvī'-unt-drī'-si*ch* fünf'-unt-feer'-tsi*ch* akht-unt-ze*ch*'-tsi*ch*.

Please connect me with number 32 45 68.

13 dee lī'-tung ist bĕ-zetst'. vo'-lĕn zee ī'-nĕn ow'-gĕn-blik var'-tĕn?

The line is busy. Will you wait a moment?

---

limbs do hurt to me. The dative is often used in German to indicate the possessor when the possessive adjective is used in English.   *5. einen Arzt kommen lassen* (to call a doctor). *Lassen* used in the meaning of "to cause something to."   *6. auf alle Fälle* (in any case). ID., *lit.*, on all cases.   *7. noch einmal* usually means

14 Hallo! Hallo! Doktor Burkhard?—Hier ist Herr Smith. Wann haben Sie heute Sprechstunde?[10] Von 4-6 (vier bis sechs)? Gut, ich werde Sie heute nachmittag aufsuchen.

15 Herr Smith? — Nehmen Sie bitte einen Moment[8] im Wartezimmer Platz!

16 Treten Sie ein, Herr Smith! Worüber[11] klagen Sie?

17 Ich habe Schmerzen im ganzen Körper, in den Armen und Beinen; ja, der Schmerz geht sogar bis in die Finger und Zehen. Der Rücken tut mir[4] auch weh.

18 Lassen Sie mich den Puls fühlen! Und stecken Sie bitte das Thermometer unter die Zunge!

19 Habe ich Fieber?

20 Sie haben erhöhte Temperatur.

21 Sie haben sich nur stark erkältet.[12] Machen Sie bitte den Mund auf! Sagen Sie: Ah!

22 Der Hals ist entzündet, und die Mandeln sind auch geschwollen.

23 Im Backzahn haben Sie aber ein grosses Loch. Ich würde Ihnen empfehlen, gleich zu einem Zahnarzt zu gehen.

24 Was bin ich Ihnen schuldig, Herr Doktor?

25 Mein Honorar für eine gründliche Untersuchung ist 20 (zwanzig) Mark.

"once again." *Sagen Sie das noch einmal.* "Say that (once) again. Repeat that." *8. den ganzen Tag* (all day) *lit.,* the whole day. Extent of time is expressed by the accusative case in German [§24, d]. **9.** The use of letters or words in telephone numbers has been discontinued in Germany; instead, sets of numbers in pairs are

14 ha-loh' ha-loh' dok'-tohr Burk-hard? — heer ist her *Smith*. van hah'-bĕn zee hoi'-tĕ shpre*ch*'-shtun-dĕ? fon feer bis zeks? — goot *ich* vayr'-dĕ zee hoi'-tĕ nahkh'-mi-tahk owf'-zoo-khĕn.

15 her *Smith*? — nay'-mĕn zee bi'-tĕ ī'-nĕn moh-ment' im var'-tĕ-tsi-mĕr plats.

16 tray'-tĕn zee īn, her *Smith*. voh-rüh'-bĕr klah'-gĕn zee.

17 *ich* hah'-bĕ shmer'-tsĕn im gan'-tsĕn kör'-pĕr in dayn ar'-mĕn unt bī'-nĕn; yah, dayr shmerts gayt zoh-gahr' bis in dee fing-ĕr unt tsay'-ĕn. dayr rü'-kĕn toot meer owkh vay.

18 la'-sĕn zee m*ich* dayn puls füh'-lĕn. unt shte'-kĕn zee bi'-tĕ das ter-moh-may'-tĕr un'-tĕr dee tsung'-ĕ.

19 hah'-bĕ *ich* fee'-bĕr?

20 zee hah'-bĕn er-höh'-tĕ tem-pĕ-ra-toor'.

21 zee hah'-bĕn z*ich* noor shtark er-kel'-tĕt. ma'-khĕn zee bi'-tĕ dayn munt owf. zah'-gĕn zee ah.

22 dayr hals ist ĕn-tsün'-dĕt unt dee man'-dĕln zint owkh gĕ-shvo'-lĕn.

23 im bak'-tsahn hah'-bĕn zee ah'-bĕr īn groh'-sĕs lokh. *ich* vür'-dĕ ee'-nĕn ĕm-pfay'-lĕn gl*ich* tsu ī'-nĕm tsahn'-ahrtst tsoo gay'-ĕn.

24 vas bin *ich* ee'-nĕn shul'-di*ch*, her dok-tor'-

25 mīn hoh-noh-rahr' führ ī'-nĕ grünt'-li-*ch*ĕ un-tĕr-zoo'-khung ist tsvan'-tsi*ch* mark.

Hello! Hello! Doctor Burkhard? This is Mr. Smith. When are your office hours today? From four to six? Good, I'll see you this afternoon (*lit.*, look you up).

Mr. Smith? Please be seated in the waiting room for a minute.

Step in, Mr. Smith. What is your complaint (*lit.*, about what complain you)?

I have pains in my whole body, in my arms and legs; the pain even goes to my fingers (*lit.*, as far as into the fingers) and toes. My back also hurts.

Let me feel your pulse. And please put the thermometer under your tongue.

Do I have a fever?
You have a slight temperature.

You only have a bad (*lit.*, strong) cold. Please open your mouth. Say, "Ah!"
Your throat is inflamed and also your tonsils are swollen.
You have a large cavity in your back tooth. I would advise you to go to a dentist immediately.

What do I owe you, doctor?

My fee for a thorough examination is twenty marks.

---

used. *10. die Sprechstunde* (the office hour). *Lit.*, speaking hour. *11. worüber* (about what), a compound interrogative: *wo–r–über* not referring to a person. *klagen über* (to complain of, about). *12. sich erkälten* (to catch a cold, to have a cold). ID., *lit.*, to cold oneself. *13. dreimal* (three times), *viermal* (four times),

26 Lassen[5] Sie dieses Rezept in der Apotheke anfertigen.
Nehmen Sie die Medizin dreimal[13] am Tag und bleiben
Sie zwei Tage im Bett! ...

27 Herr Doktor Burkhard hat Sie
mir empfohlen. Wollen Sie
bitte meine Zähne unter-
suchen.

28 Nehmen Sie bitte auf diesem
Stuhl Platz! Machen Sie den
Mund weit auf! Die Vorder-
zähne sind in Ordnung;[14] die
Backzähne auch, ausser einem.

29 Ich hatte mir[4] vor meiner Reise die Zähne plombieren
und reinigen lassen.[5]

30 Aus dem einen Backzahn ist die Plombe herausgefallen.
Tut das weh?

31 Ein bisschen. Der Nerv scheint entzündet zu sein.

32 Ich mache Ihnen eine provisorische Einlage.

33 Kommen Sie wieder, wenn Sie ganz gesund sind! Dann
werde ich eine Röntgenaufnahme machen.

34 Dann können Sie den Zahn gleich plombieren, nicht
wahr?

35 Hoffentlich! Auf Wiedersehen und gute Besserung![15]

---

etc. written as one word.   *14. in Ordnung sein* (to be all right). ID., *lit.,* to be in
order.   *15. gute Besserung* (speedy recovery) ID., *lit.,* good betterment, improve-
ment.

26 la'-sĕn zee dee'-zĕs ray-tsept' in dayr a-poh-tay'-kĕ an'-fer-ti-gĕn. nay'-mĕn zee dee may-dee-tseen' drī'-mahl am tahk unt blī'-bĕn zee tsvī tah'-gĕ im bet.

27 her dok'-tohr *Burkhard* hat zee meer ĕm-pfoh'-lĕn. vo'-lĕn zee bi'-tĕ mī'-nĕ tsay'-nĕ un-tĕr-zoo'-khĕn.

28 nay'-mĕn zee bi'-tĕ owf dee'-zĕm shtool plats. ma'-khĕn zee dayn munt vīt owf. dee for'-dĕr-tsay-nĕ zint in ord'-nung; dee bak'-tsay-nĕ owkh, ow'-sĕr ī'-nĕm.

29 ich ha'-tĕ meer for mī'-nĕr rī'-zĕ dee tsay'-nĕ plom-bee'-rĕn unt rī'-ni-gĕn la'-sĕn.

30 ows daym ī'-nĕn bak'-tsahn ist dee plom'-bĕ he-rows'-gĕ-fa-lĕn. toot das vay?

31 īn bis'-*ch*ĕn. dayr nerf shīnt ent-tsün'-dĕt tsoo zīn.

32 ich ma'-khĕ ee'-nen ī'-nĕ proh-vee-zoh'-ri-shĕ īn'-lah-gĕ.

33 ko'-mĕn zee vee'-dĕr ven zee gans gĕ-zunt' zint. dan vayr'-dĕ *ich* ī'-nĕ rönt'-gĕn-owf-nah-mĕ ma'-khĕn.

34 dan kö'-nĕn zee dayn tsahn glī*ch* plom-bee'-rĕn ni*ch*t vahr?

35 ho'-fĕnt-li*ch*. owf vee'-dĕr-zayn unt goo'-tĕ be'-sĕ-rung.

Have this prescription made up in the drugstore. Take the medicine three times a day and stay in bed for two days.

Dr. Burkhard recommended you to me. Will you please examine my teeth?

Please be seated on this chair. Open your mouth wide. Your front teeth are all right; the back teeth also, except for one.

Before my trip, I had my teeth filled and cleaned.

The filling has fallen out of one of your back teeth. Does it hurt?

A little. The nerve seems to be inflamed.
I'll make a temporary filling for you.
Come again when you are completely recovered (*lit.*, healthy). Then I shall take an x-ray.

Then you will be able to fill the tooth immediately, won't you?
I hope so. Good-bye and a speedy recovery.

Vierzehnte Lektion

Neue Wörter für diese Lektion

senden (zen'-děn)	to send	**nebenan** (nay-běn-an')	next door
ledig (lay'-di*ch*)	unmarried	**der Kamm,-ᵉe** (kam)	comb
die Stirn,-en (shtirn)	forehead	**kämmen** (ke'-měn)	to comb
der Nacken,- (na'-kěn)	neck	**voll** (fol)	full
schneiden (shnī'-děn)	to cut	**das Schild,-er** (shilt)	sign

entweder . . . oder (ěnt-vay'-děr, oh'-děr)   either . . . or
da (dah) (*conj.*)   since (reason), inasmuch as

an Ort und Stelle (an ort unt shte'-lě)   at one's destination, on the very spot

kreuzen (kroi'-tsěn)   to cross (a street)

freundlich (froint'-li*ch*)   friendly, kind
die Leute (*pl.*) (loi'-tě)   people
innerhalb[1] (i'-něr-halp)   within
ausserhalb (ow'-sěr-halp)   outside of
hinaus (hi-nows')   out, outside (to go)

weitergehen (vī'-těr-gay-ěn), **geht weiter** (gayt vī'-těr)   to go on
einbiegen (īn'-bee-gěn), **biegt ein** (beekt īn')   to turn into
aufschreiben (owf'-shrī-běn), **schreibt auf** (shrīpt owf')   to write down

in der Nähe (in dayr nay'-ě)   near, in the neighborhood
nach ausserhalb (nahkh ow'-ser-halp)   leading out
verbunden sein (fěr-bun'-děn zīn)   to be obliged

hinten (hin'-těn)   in the rear, behind
hierher (heer-hayr')   here (direction to place)
die Verabredung,-en (fěr-ap'-ray-dung)   appointment
die Gemahlin,-nen (gě-mah'-lin)   wife
vorgehen (fohr'-gay-ěn), **geht vor** (gayt fohr')   to go on

EIN ZIMMER MIETEN • BARBIER UND FRISEUSE

RENTING A ROOM, BARBER
AND HAIRDRESSER

(īn tsi'-mĕr mee'-tĕn,
bar-beer' unt free-zöh'-zĕ)

das Zimmer,- (tsi'-mĕr)	room
das Einzelzimmer (īn'-tsĕl-tsi-mĕr)	single room
das Vorderzimmer (for'-dĕr-tsi-mĕr)	front room
das Hinterzimmer (hin'-tĕr-tsi-mĕr)	back room
das Handgeld (hant'-gelt)	deposit
möblieren (möh-blee'-rĕn)	to furnish

die Miete,-n (mee'-tĕ)	rent
eintragen (īn'-trah-gĕn)	to register
trägt ein (traykt īn)	
möbliert (möh-bleert')	furnished

der Barbier,-e (bar-beer')	barber
der Friseur,-e (free-zöhr')	hairdresser, m.
die Friseuse,-n (free-zöh'-zĕ)	hairdresser, f.
das Barbiergeschäft,-e (bar-beer'-gĕ-sheft)	barber shop
der Barbierladen,-·· (bar-beer'-lah-dĕn)	
das Frisiergeschäft,-e (free-zeer'-gĕ-sheft)	beauty shop
der Frisiersalon,-s (free-zeer'-za-long)	

frisieren (free-zee'-rĕn)	to dress hair
der Haarschnitt,-e (hahr'-shnit)	haircut
die Maniküre,-n (ma-nee-kühr'-ĕ)	manicure
maniküren (ma-nee-küh'-rĕn)	to manicure
der Nagel,-·· (nah'-gĕl)	nail
die Nagelpolitur,-en (nah'-gĕl-po-lee-toor)	nail polish

die Gesichtsmassage,-n (gĕ-zichts'-ma-sah-zhĕ)	face massage
die Schläfe,-n (shlay'-fĕ)	temple
der Scheitel,- (shī'-tĕl)	parting (of hair), crown
der Hinterkopf,-··e (hin'-tĕr-kopf)	back of head
das Haarwasser,- (hahr'-va-sĕr)	hair wash, hair tonic
das Haaröl,-e (hahr'-öhl)	hair oil
rasieren (rah-zee'-rĕn)	to shave
das Rasiermesser,- (rah-zeer'-me-sĕr)	razor

das Haar,-e (hahr)	hair	Kopf waschen (kopf . . .)	to shampoo
bleichen (blī'-chĕn)	to bleach	bürsten (bür'-stĕn)	to brush
färben (fer'-bĕn)	to dye	die Bürste,-n (bür'-stĕ)	brush
waschen (va'-shĕn)	to wash		

CONVERSATION

1 Hier ist das Reisebüro. Können Sie mir bitte ein gutes Hotel, eine Pension oder vielleicht ein nettes möbliertes Zimmer empfehlen?

2 Gern. Ich schreibe Ihnen einige Adressen auf. Sie sind alle in der Nähe, innerhalb[1] der Stadt.

3 Ich bin Ihnen sehr verbunden.[2] Zuerst werde ich ein Hotel versuchen.

4 Guten Tag! Haben Sie ein Einzelzimmer frei?

5 Wir haben noch zwei Zimmer, eins ist ein Vorderzimmer mit Bad.

6 Wieviel kostet dieses Zimmer?

7 Der Preis ist 12 (zwölf) Mark den Tag.[3] Das andere Zimmer ist ein Hinterzimmer. Es hat kein Bad und kommt auf sechs Mark den Tag.

8 Ich möchte mir doch noch etwas anderes ansehen.

> Möbliertes Zimmer
> zu vermieten

9 Ich sah Ihr Schild am Fenster und würde mir gern das Zimmer ansehen. Ist es ein Vorderzimmer?

10 Ja, es ist ein grosses, helles Zimmer mit zwei Fenstern nach der Strasse im ersten Stock.

11 Das Zimmer gefällt mir sehr. Es hat nur kein Bad. Wieviel kostet es die Woche[3]?

FOOTNOTES: *1. innerhalb* (within) and *ausserhalb* (outside of) are two prepositions that require the genitive case. *2. Ich bin Ihnen sehr verbunden.* (I am very much obliged to you). ID., *lit.,* I am to you very linked. *3.* In expressions such as *den Tag* (a day), *den Monat* (a month), *die Woche* (a week), *das Jahr* (a

Pronunciation

1 heer ist das rī'-zĕ-büh-roh. kö'-nen zee meer bi'-tĕ in goo'-tĕs hoh-tĕl', ī'-nĕ pang-ziohn' oh'-der fee-li*ch*t' in ne'-tĕs möh-bleer'-tĕs tsi'-mĕr ĕm-pfay'-lĕn?

2 gern. i*ch* shrī'-bĕ ee'-nĕn ī'-ni-gĕ ah-dre'-sĕn owf. zee zint a'-lĕ in dayr nay'ĕ i'-nĕr-halp dayr shtat.

3 i*ch* bin ee'-nĕn zayr fĕr-bun'-dĕn. tsoo-ayrst' vayr'-dĕ i*ch* in hoh-tel' fĕr-zoo'-khĕn.

4 goo'-tĕn tahk. hah'-bĕn zee in in'-tsĕl-tsi-mĕr frī?

5 veer hah'-bĕn nokh tsvī tsi'-mĕr, ins ist in for'-dĕr-tsi-mĕr mit baht.

6 vee-feel' ko'-stĕt dee'-zĕs tsi'-mĕr?

7 dayr prīs ist tsvölf mark dayn tahk. das an'-dĕ-rĕ tsi'-mĕr ist in hin'-tĕr-tsi-mĕr. es hat kīn baht unt komt owf zeks mark . . .

8 i*ch* mö*ch*'-tĕ meer dokh nokh et.-vas an'-dĕ-rĕs an'-zay-ĕn.

möh-bleer'-tĕs tsi'-mĕr tsoo fĕr-mee'-tĕn.

9 i*ch* zah eer shilt am fen'-stĕr unt vür'-dĕ meer gern das tsi'-mĕr an'-zay-ĕn. ist es in for'-dĕr-tsi-mĕr?

10 yah es ist in groh'-sĕs, he'-lĕs tsi'-mĕr mit tsvī fen'-stĕrn nahkh dayr shtrah'-sĕ im ayr'-stĕn shtok.

11 das tsi'-mĕr gĕ-felt' meer zayr. es hat noor kīn baht. vee-feel' ko'-stĕt es dee vo'-khĕ?

Translation

Here is the travel bureau. Can you please recommend a good hotel, a boarding house, or perhaps a nice furnished room?

Gladly. I will write down a few addresses. They are all in the neighborhood, within the city.

I'm very much obliged to you. First I'll try a hotel.

Good day. Do you have a single room?

We still have two rooms, one a front room with bath.

How much is (*lit.,* costs) this room?

The price is twelve marks a day. The other room is a back room. It doesn't have a bath and it rents (*lit.,* costs) for six marks a day.

I would still like to look at something else.

Furnished Room
to Let

I saw your sign in the window and I would like to look at the room. Is it a front room?

Yes, it is a large, light room on the first floor with two windows facing (*lit.,* to the) the street.

I like the room very much. The only thing is that it has no bath (*lit.,* it has only no bath). How much does it cost a week?

year), *Es kostet eine Mark das Pfund* (it costs one mark a pound), the definite article is used in German [§9, c]. *4.* Private rooms are very frequently rented with breakfast included in Germany. This breakfast, however, consists only of coffee, rolls, and butter. *5.* Notice the meaning of *noch ein* (one other, another).

12 20 Mark (zwanzig) die Woche[3] mit Frühstück. Mit allen Mahlzeiten kostet es 55 (fünfundfünfzig) Mark.

13 Ich miete das Zimmer mit Frühstück[4] auf eine Woche. Wo ist das Badezimmer?

14 Hier auf diesem Korridor; es wird ausser Ihnen nur noch von einem[5] Herrn benutzt.[6] Wollen Sie mir bitte ein Handgeld von fünf Mark geben?

15 Natürlich! Ich lasse[7] das Gepäck hierher[8] senden. Wo ist bitte der nächste Barbier?

16 Gehen Sie diese Strasse rechts hinunter[8] und dann um die Ecke. Sie können den Laden nicht verfehlen.

17 Womit kann ich Ihnen dienen, mein Herr?

18 Ich möchte mir[9] das Haar schneiden lassen.[7]

19 Wie, bitte? Sie wollen eine Verabredung für Ihre Frau Gemahlin treffen?

20 Meine Frau? Ich bin noch ledig. Ah! Nun verstehe ich. Ich bin in einem Damen-Frisiersalon. Was für Instrumente sind das?

21 Mit diesen Apparaten machen wir den Damen Dauerwellen; an jenen Tischen werden sie manikürt und dort sind die Waschbecken.

22 Der richtige Laden ist wohl nebenan.

23 Wollen Sie mir[9] bitte das Haar schneiden und mich rasieren. Ich möchte mir[9] auch den Kopf waschen lassen.

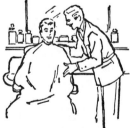

Geben Sie mir noch eine Tasse Kaffee (Give me another cup of coffee). But: *Geben Sie mir eine andere Tasse Kaffee* (Give me a different cup of coffee).   6. *Es*

12 tsvan'-tsi*ch* mark dee vo'-kh*ě* mit früh'-shtük. mit a'-l*ě*n mahl'-tsī-t*ě*n ... fünf'-unt-fünf-tsi*ch* mark.

13 i*ch* mee'-t*ě* das tsi'-m*ě*r mit früh'-shtük owf ī'-n*ě* vo'-kh*ě*. voh ist das bah'-d*ě*-tsi-m*ě*r?

14 heer owf dee'-z*ě*m ko'-ree-dohr; es virt ow'-s*ě*r ee'-n*ě*n noor nokh fon ī'-n*ě*m hern b*ě*-nutst'. vo'-l*ě*n zee meer bi'-t*ě* īn hant'-gelt fon fünf mark gay'-b*ě*n.

15 na-tühr'-li*ch*. i*ch* la'-s*ě* das g*ě*-pek' heer-hayr' zen'-d*ě*n. voh ist bi'-t*ě* dayr nay*ch*'-st*ě* bar-beer'?

16 gay̆'-*ě*n zee dee'-z*ě* shtrah'-s*ě* rechts hi-nun'-t*ě*r unt dan um dee e'-k*ě*. zee kö'-n*ě*n dayn lah'-d*ě*n ni*ch*t f*ě*r-fay'-l*ě*n.

17 voh-mit' kan ... dee'-n*ě*n ...

18 i*ch* mö*ch*'-t*ě* meer das hahr shnī'-d*ě*n la'-s*ě*n.

19 vee, bi'-t*ě*? zee vo'-l*ě*n ī'-n*ě* f*ě*r-ap'-ray-dung führ ee'-r*ě* frow g*ě*-mah'-lin tre'-f*ě*n?

20 mī'-n*ě* frow? i*ch* bin nokh lay'-di*ch*. ah noon f*ě*r-shtay'-*ě* i*ch*. i*ch* bin in ī'-n*ě*m dah'-m*ě*n-free-zeer-zah-long. vas führ in-stroo-men'-t*ě* zint das?

21 mit dee'-z*ě*n a-pah-rah'-t*ě*n ma'-kh*ě*n veer dayn dah'-m*ě*n dow'-*ě*r-ve-l*ě*n; an yay'-n*ě*n ti'-sh*ě*n vayr'-d*ě*n zee ma-nee-kührt' unt dort zint dee vash'-be-k*ě*n.

22 dayr ri*ch*'-ti-g*ě* lah'-d*ě*n ist vohl nay-b*ě*n-an'.

23 vo'-l*ě*n zee meer bi'-t*ě* das hahr shnī'-d*ě*n unt mi*ch* ra-zee'-r*ě*n. i*ch* mö*ch*'-t*ě* meer owkh dayn kopf va'-sh*ě*n la'-s*ě*n.

Twenty marks a week with breakfast. With all meals, it comes to fifty-five marks.

I'll rent this room with breakfast for a week. Where is the bathroom?

Here on this floor. It is used by only one other gentleman. Please give me a deposit of five marks?

Of course. I'll have my luggage sent here. Where is the nearest barber shop, please?

Go down this street to the right and then around the corner. You can't miss the shop.

How can I serve, you, sir?

I would like to have my hair cut.

I beg your pardon (*lit.*, how, please)? You wish to make an appointment for your wife?

My wife? I'm still unmarried. Ah, now I understand. I'm at a ladies hairdressing establishment. What kind of instruments are those?

With these machines we give the ladies permanent waves — at those tables they are manicured, and there are the washbasins.

The right shop is probably next door.

Will you please cut my hair and shave me. I would also like a shampoo (*lit.*, have my head washed).

---

wird benutzt von einem Herrn. (It is used by a gentleman.) This is the passive mood of the verb. In German the present passive is formed by the present tense

24 Wie wünschen Sie den Haarschnitt, sehr kurz oder etwas voll?

25 Um die Schläfen und im Nacken kurz, aber am Hinter-kopf und auf dem Kopf lassen Sie es ziemlich voll.

26 Auf welcher Seite tragen Sie den Scheitel?

27 Rechts. Kämmen und bürsten Sie das Haar recht glatt, aber brauchen Sie bitte kein Haaröl.

28 Sehen Sie bitte in diesen Spiegel! Ist es so recht?

29 Gerade richtig. Danke!

---

of *werden* (to become) and the past participle of the verb. In English, "to be," *sein,* is used as auxiliary. The preposition *von,* which requires the dative case, is used in German and it is translated in English by "by" [§75, a].   7. Notice again the meaning of *lassen* (to have done, to cause to be done).   *8. hierher, lit.,* here to; *hinunter, lit.,* down there. In German, direction is indicated by *her* (here or hither), *hin* (there or thither): *Kommen Sie her!* "Come here." *Gehen Sie dahin!*

24 vee vün'-shĕn zee dayn hahr'-shnit, zayr kurts oh'-dĕr et'-vas fol?

How do you want your hair cut, very short or somewhat full?

25 um dee shlay'-fĕn unt im na'-kĕn kurts ah'-bĕr am hin'-tĕr-kopf unt owf daym kopf la'-sĕn zee es tseem'-lich fol.

Around the temples and at the neckline short, but at the back and on top of the head (*lit.,* on the head) leave it rather full.

26 owf vel'-chĕr zī'-tĕ trah'-gĕn zee dayn shī'-tĕl?

On which side do you part your hair (*lit.,* on which side do you wear your parting)?

27 rechts. ke'-mĕn unt bür'-stĕn zee das hahr recht glat ah'-bĕr brow'-khĕn zee bi'-tĕ kīn hahr'-öhl.

On the right. Comb and brush my hair very smooth, but don't use any hair oil, please.

28 zay'-ĕn zee bi'-tĕ in dee'-zĕn shpee'-gĕl. ist es zoh recht?

Please look into this mirror. Is it all right this way?

29 gĕ-rah'-dĕ rich'-tich. dang'-kĕ.

Just right, thank you.

"Go there." *Woher kommt er?* "Where does he come from?" *Wohin geht sie?* "Where does she go to?" *Er geht die Treppe hinauf.* "He goes upstairs (that is, away from the speaker)." *Er kommt die Treppe herunter.* "He comes downstairs (that is, toward the speaker)." 9. The dative case used here for the possessive adjective in English.

Fünfzehnte Lektion

Neue Wörter für diese Lektion

alt (alt)	old	der Wert,-e (vayrt)	value, worth
bisher (bis-hayr')	up to now	der Dichter,- (dich'-tĕr)	poet
wählen (vay'-lĕn)	to choose	benutzen (bĕ-nu'-tsĕn)	to use
einfach (īn'-fakh)	simple	riskieren (ris-kee'-rĕn)	to risk
dasselbe (das-zel'-bĕ)	the same	reizend (rī'-tsĕnt)	charming
tagelang (tah'-gĕ-lang)	for days	sofort (zoh-fort')	immediately
das Wort,-"er (vort)	word	die Träne,-n (tray'-nĕ)	tear

ungern (un'-gĕrn) — not like, reluctantly
geradeüber (gĕ-rah-dĕ-üh'-bĕr) — opposite, just across
überraschen (üh-bĕr-ra'-shĕn) — to surprise
die Form,-en (form) — form (denomination), shape

der Ausländer,- (ows'-len-dĕr) — foreigner
die Geburt,-en (gĕ-burt') — birth
die Geburtsstätte,-n (gĕ-burts'-shte-tĕ) — place of birth
die Kindheit,-en (kint'-hīt) — childhood
vergiessen (fĕr-gee'-sĕn) — to spill

der Besuch,-e (bĕ-zookh') — visit
einen Besuch machen (ī'-nĕn . . . ma'-khĕn) — to pay a visit

die Geschichte,-n (gĕ-shich'-tĕ) — history, story
geschichtlich (gĕ-shicht'-lich) — historical
beeindrucken (bĕ-īn'-dru-kĕn) — to impress
aufbauen (owf'-bow-ĕn), baut auf (bowt owf') — to rebuild, to build up, to erect
der Bau,-s (bow), die Bauten (bow'-tĕn) — building, structure, style
zurückkehren (tsoo-rük'-kay-rĕn), kehrt zurück (kayrt tsoo-rük') — to return
benachrichtigen (bĕ-nahkh'-rich-ti-gĕn) — to notify, to inform
die Polizei (poh-lee-tsī') — police

AUF DER BANK • AUF DER POST

AT THE BANK, AT THE POST OFFICE   (bangk, post)

die Bank,-en (bangk)   bank
die Mark (mark)   mark
der Schein,-e (shīn)   bill
der Scheck,-s (shek)   check

die Summe,-n (zu'-mě)   sum,
                              amount
der Brief,-e (breef)   letter
die Karte,-n (kar'-tě)   card, ticket

die Gesellschaft,-en (gĕ-zel'-shaft)   company, party
das Geld,-er (gelt)   money *pl.;* funds
wechseln (vek'-zĕln)   to change, exchange
umwechseln (um'-vek-zĕln),   to change for
  wechselt um (vek'-zĕlt um')
einwechseln (īn'-vek-zĕln),   to give in exchange
  wechselt ein (vek'-zĕlt īn)
das Kleingeld (klīn'-gelt)   small change
der Pfennig,-e (pfe'-ni*ch*)   penny
der Betrag,-"e (bĕ-trahk')   amount
der Abzug,-"e (ap'-tsook)   deduction, discount
die Gebühr,-en (gĕ-bühr')   fee
der Kurs,-e (kurs)   rate of exchange

telegrafieren (tay-le-grah-fee'-rĕn)   to telegraph
das Telegramm,-e (tay-le-gram')   telegram
das Formular,-e (for-moo-lahr')   form, blank

schreiben (shrī'-bĕn)   to write
das Papier,-e (pa-peer')   paper
die Feder,-n (fay'-der)   pen
die Tinte,-n (tin'-tě)   ink
ausfüllen (ows'-fü-lĕn)   to fill out
  füllt aus (fült ows')
das Schreibpult,-e (shrīp'-pult)   writing desk
der Bleistift,-e (blī'-shtift)   pencil
die Füllfeder,-n (fül'-fay-dĕr)   fountain pen

die Briefmarke,-n (breef'-mar-kĕ)   stamp
der Briefumschlag,-"e (breef'-um-shlak)   envelope
die Postkarte,-n (post'-kar-tě)   postal card
der Luftpostbrief,-e (luft'-post-breef)   air-mail letter
der Luftpostleichtbrief,-e (luft-post-lī*ch*t'-breef)   air letter
einschreiben (īn'-shrī-bĕn), schreibt ein (shrīpt īn')   to register
der eingeschriebene Brief (īn'-gĕ-shree-bĕ-nĕ breef)   registered letter
  der Einschreibebrief,-e (īn'-shrī-bĕ-breef)

CONVERSATION

1 Guten Morgen, Herr Smith! Wie haben Sie geschlafen? Was für ein Programm haben Sie heute?

2 Ich habe wie immer gut geschlafen. Heute werde ich mir das Goethehaus ansehen. Aber zuerst muss ich auf die Bank gehen.

3 Gleich hier um die Ecke ist eine grosse Bank.

4 Vielen Dank! Bis auf heute abend! . . .

5 Ich möchte 100 (hundert) Dollar[1] in deutsche Mark umwechseln. Wie steht die Mark heute?

6 Der heutige Kurs ist DM 4,20[2] (vier Mark zwanzig) für einen Dollar. In welcher Form wünschen Sie das Geld?

7 Geben Sie mir drei Hundertmarkscheine, einen Fünfzigmarkschein, fünf Zehnmarkscheine und den Rest in Kleingeld!

8 Von den 420 (vierhundertzwanzig) Mark kommt noch eine kleine Wechselgebühr[3] in Abzug.

9 Sie lösen auch Reiseschecks ein, nicht wahr?

10 Aber, natürlich! Über[4] welchen Betrag ist Ihr Scheck?

11 Danke! Ich möchte ihn nicht heute einlösen. Können Sie mir bitte sagen, wo das nächste Postamt ist?

12 Geradeüber im Hauptbahnhof ist ein Postamt.

13 Wo kann ich bitte ein Telegramm aufgeben? Wieviel kostet das[5] Wort nach Berlin und nach New York?

FOOTNOTES: *1.* Since monetary units do not take a plural ending in German, *100 Dollar* is also in the singular.   *2. DM 4,20.* Note that in German a comma is used to set off the *Mark* from the *Pfennig* as against the American period between dollars and cents. Moreover, the capitals *DM* are placed *before* the total instead of the

PRONUNCIATION

1 goo'-tĕn mor'-gĕn, her *Smith!* vee hah'-bĕn zee gĕ-shlah'-fĕn? vas führ in proh-gram'. . . .

2 ich hah'-bĕ vee i'-mĕr goot gĕ-shlah'-fĕn . . . hoi'-tĕ vayr'-dĕ ich meer das göh'-tĕ-hows an'-zay-ĕn. ah'-bĕr tsoo-ayrst' mus ich owf dee bangk gay'-ĕn.

3 glich heer um dee e'-kĕ ist i'-nĕ groh'-sĕ bangk.

4 fee'-lĕn dangk! bis owf hoi'-tĕ. . . .

5 ich möch'-tĕ hun'-dĕrt do'-lahr in doit'-shĕ mark um'-vek-zĕln. vee shtayt dee mark hoi'-tĕ?

6 dayr hoi'-ti-gĕ kurs ist feer mark tsvan'-tsich führ i'-nĕn do'-lahr. in vel'-chĕr form vün'-shĕn zee das gelt?

7 gay'-bĕn zee meer dri hun'-dĕrt-mark-shi-nĕ, i'-nĕn fünf'-tsich-mark-shin, fünf tsayn'-mark-shi-nĕ unt dayn rest in klin'-gelt.

8 fon dayn feer'-hun-dert-tsvan'-tsich mark komt nokh i'-nĕ kli'-nĕ vek'-zĕl-gĕ-bühr in ap'-tsook.

9 zee löh'-zĕn owkh ri-zĕ-sheks in nicht vahr?

10 ah'-bĕr na-tühr'-lich. üh'-bĕr vel'-chĕn bĕ-trahk' ist eer shek?

11 dang'-kĕ ich möch'-tĕ een nicht hoi'-tĕ in'-löh-zĕn. kö-nen zee meer bi'-tĕ . . . naych'-stĕ post'-amt ist?

12 gĕ-rah'-dĕ-üh'-bĕr im howpt'-bahn-hohf ist in post'-amt.

13 voh kan ich bi'-tĕ in tay-le-gram' owf'-gay-bĕn? vee-feel' ko'-stĕt das vort nahkh. . . .

TRANSLATION

Good morning, Mr. Smith. How did you sleep? What kind of a program do you have today?

I slept well, as always. Today I will look at the Goethe house. But first I must go to the bank.

Right here around the corner is a large bank.

Many thanks. Until tonight.

I would like to change a hundred dollars into German marks. What is the rate of exchange for the mark today?

Today's rate of exchange is four marks twenty (M 4.20) for a dollar. In which form do you want the money?

Give me three hundred-mark bills, one fifty-mark bill, and five ten-mark bills, and the remainder in small change.

There is still a small exchange fee to be deducted from the 420 marks.

You also cash travelers' checks, don't you?

Of course. For what amount is your check?

Thank you. I don't want to cash it today. Please, where is the nearest post office?

There's a post office right across the street in the main terminal.

Please, where can I send a telegram? How much do you charge per word to Berlin and to New York?

---

dollar sign ($) used in the United States *before* the amount. *3. Wechselgebühr.* *Lit.,* exchange fee. *4. über welchen Betrag* (for which amount). *Lit.,* over which amount. *5. kostet das Wort* (costs . . . a word). The definite article instead of the indefinite article is used in German in this and similar phrases [§9, c]. *6.*

14 Nach Berlin oder irgendeinem[6] Ort in Deutschland kostet es 15 (fünfzehn) Pfennig, nach New York 30 (dreissig) Pfennig das[5] Wort; zehn Wörter sind das Minimum. Dies ist der Schalter für Telegramme.

15 Füllen Sie dieses Telegrammformular aus. Auf dem Schreibpult drüben finden Sie Papier, Feder, Tinte und Löschblatt. Sie können auch mit Bleistift schreiben. Vergessen Sie nicht den Absender!

16 Danke, ich habe meine Füllfeder bei[7] mir. Ich würde auch gern einige Briefmarken kaufen.

17 Es tut mir leid, aber Briefmarken erhalten Sie am nächsten Schalter.

18 Wieviel kostet ein einfacher Brief und ein Luftpostbrief nach den Vereinigten Staaten?

19 Ein einfacher Brief kostet DM—,40[2] (vierzig Pfennig) und ein Luftpostbrief DM—,60 (sechzig Pfennig) bis fünf Gramm. Es gibt[8] auch Luftpostleichtbriefe für DM—,50 (fünfzig Pfennig), wenn Sie nicht soviel schreiben wollen.

20 Geben Sie mir bitte fünf Luftpostmarken, zehn Luftpostleichtbriefe und drei Dreissigpfennig-Briefmarken.

21 Hallo, Fräulein Kruger! Was machen Sie denn hier?

22 Dasselbe[9] wie Sie; ich sehe mir das Goethehaus an, schon zum dritten Mal.

---

irgendeinem (any one) is a pronominal adjective. *Irgend* (any) is undeclinable; *einem* is in the dative case. *ein* in this compound is inflected like the article.   7. *bei mir* (with me). *Lit.*, at me.   8. *es gibt* (there are) is used in German to refer to something in a general, indefinite way. *Es sind* is used for "there are" if it refers

14 nahkh ber-leen' oh'-dĕr eer'-gent-ī-nĕm ort in doitsh'-lant ko'-stĕt es fünf'-tsayn pfe'-ni*ch*, nahkh *New York* drī'-si*ch* pfe'-ni*ch* das vort; tsayn vör'-tĕr zint das mi'-nee-mum. dees ist dayr shal'-tĕr führ tay-le-gra'-mĕ.

15 fü'-lĕn zee dee'-zĕs tay-le-gram'-for-moo-lahr' ows. owf daym shrīp'-pult drüh'-bĕn fin'-dĕn zee pa-peer', fay'-dĕr, tin'-tĕ und lösh'-blat. zee kö'-nĕn owkh mit blī'-shtift shrī'-bĕn. fĕr-ge'-sĕn zee ni*ch*t dayn ap'-zen-dĕr.

16 dang'-kĕ *ich* hah'-bĕ mī'-nĕ fül'-fay-dĕr bī meer. *ich* vür'-dĕ owkh gern ī'-ni-gĕ breef'-mar-kĕn . . .

17 es toot meer līt ah'-bĕr breef'-mar-kĕn er-hal'-tĕn . . . shal'-tĕr.

18 vee-feel' ko'-stĕt īn īn'-fa-khĕr breef unt īn luft'-post-breef nahkh dayn vĕr-ī'-nik-tĕn shtah'-tĕn?

19 īn īn'-fa-khĕr breef ko'-stĕt drī-si*ch* pfe'-ni*ch* unt īn luft'-post-breef ze*ch*'-tsi*ch* pfe'-ni*ch* bis fünf gram. es gipt owkh luft'-post-lī*cht*'-bree-fĕ führ fünf'-tsi*ch* pfe'-ni*ch* ven zee ni*ch*t zoh-feel' shrī'-bĕn vo'-lĕn.

20 gay'-bĕn zee meer bi'-tĕ fünf luft'-post-mar-kĕn, tsayn luft-post-li*cht*'-bree-fĕ unt drī drī'-si*ch* pfe'-ni*ch* breef'-mar-kĕn.

21 ha-loh' froi'-līn *Kruger*. vas ma'-khĕn zee den heer?

22 das-zel'-bĕ vee zee; *ich* zay'-ĕ meer das göh'-tĕ-hows an, shohn tsum drī'-tĕn mahl.

To Berlin or to any other place in Germany, it is fifteen pennies a word; to New York thirty pennies a word. Ten words are the minimum. This is the window for telegrams.

Fill out this telegram form. On the writing desk over there you'll find paper, pen, ink, and a blotter. You may also use a pencil. Don't forget your return address.

Thank you. I have my fountain pen with me. I would also like to buy a few stamps.

I am sorry, but you get stamps at the next window.

How much do an ordinary letter to the United States and an air mail letter cost?

An ordinary letter costs thirty pennies and an air mail letter up to five grams, sixty. We also have air letter sheets for fifty pennies if you don't want to write so much.

Please give me five air-mail stamps, ten air letters (or aero-grams; *lit.,* air-mail light letters) and three thirty-penny stamps.

Hello, Miss Kruger! What are you doing here?

The same as you; I am looking at the *Goethehaus* (already) for the third time.

to a definite number or something definite [§78, d]: *Es sind fünf Stühle in diesem Zimmer* (There are five chairs in this room). *9. dasselbe* (the same) is a demonstrative compound pronoun, which can be used in all genders, cases, and numbers [§31, d]. *10.* Goethe was born 1749 in Frankfort-on-the-Main and died

23 Dies ist also das Haus, in dem der grösste deutsche Dichter Johann Wolfgang von Goethe[10] am 28. August 1749
geboren wurde.[11]

24 Es ist ein grosses, aber nicht sehr schönes Gebäude, doch
für die Deutschen hat es grossen gefühlsmässigen Wert.

25 In diesem Dachzimmer hat Goethe geschlafen, gelernt,
geträumt, und manche Träne ist hier von ihm während
seiner Kindheit und Jugend vergossen worden.[12]

26 Ist das Originalhaus nicht 1944 (neunzehnhundertvier-
undvierzig) durch Bomben zerstört worden[13]?

27 Ja, leider! Aber es ist wieder nach dem Originalplan aufgebaut worden. Soweit als möglich wurden auch die
alten Steine benutzt.

28 Ich erinnere mich[14] jetzt, dass amerikanische Universi-
täten und auch einzelne Amerikaner eine gewisse Summe
zum Neubau beigetragen haben.

29 Das stimmt, Fräulein Kruger.

30 Es ist spät geworden. Ich muss ins Hotel zurückkehren.

31 Vielen Dank für Ihre reizende Gesellschaft. Wir werden
Sie morgen aufsuchen.

1832 in Weimar. He is one of the greatest lyric poets of the world. He wrote
dramas, novels, and scientific treatises. His greatest work, which has been uni-
versally translated, is his philosophical drama, *Faust*, the tragedy of modern
man.   *11. geboren wurde* (was born), past tense of the passive voice referring to
a person who is not living any longer. *Er ist geboren*—"He was born" (*lit.*, he is
born); present tense is used if the person referred to is alive [§67 b, 1, 2].   *12.
ist . . . von ihm . . . vergossen worden*—"was shed (*lit.*, has been shed) by him.
Present perfect tense of the passive. To form the passive voice, the different tenses

23 dees ist al'-zoh das hows in dạym dayr gröh'-stĕ doit'-shĕ dich'-tĕr yoh'-han volf'-gang fon göh'-tĕ am akht'-unt-tsvan-tsik-stĕn owgust' zeep'-tsayn-hun-dĕrt-noinunt-feer-tsich gĕ-boh'-rĕn vur'-dĕ.

So, this is the house in which the greatest German poet, Johann Wolfgang von Goethe, was born on August 28th, 1749!

24 es ist īn groh'-sĕs dokh nicht zayr shöh'-nĕs gĕ-boi'-dĕ ah'-bĕr führ dee doit'-shĕn hat es groh'-sĕn gĕ-fühls'-may-si-gĕn vayrt.

It is a big but not very beautiful building, yet it has great sentimental value for the Germans.

25 in dee'-zĕm dakh'-tsi-mĕr hat göh'-tĕ gĕ-shlah'-fĕn, gĕ-lernt', gĕtroimt' unt man'-chĕ tray'-nĕ ist heer fon eem vay'-rĕnt zī'-nĕr kint'-hīt unt yoo'-gĕnt fĕr-go'-sĕn vor'-dĕn.

In this attic room, Goethe slept, studied, dreamed, and many a tear was shed by him here during his childhood and youth.

26 ist das o-ree-gee-nahl'-hows nicht noin'-tsayn-hun-dĕrt-feer-untfeer'-tsich durch bom'-bĕn tsĕrshtöhrt' vor'-dĕn?

Wasn't the original house destroyed by bombs in 1944?

27 yah lī'-dĕr. ah'-bĕr es ist vee'-dĕr nahkh daym o-ree-gee-nahl'-plahn owf'-gĕ-bowt vor'-dĕn. zoh-vīt' als möhk-lich vur'-dĕn owkh dee al'-tĕn shtī'-nĕ bĕ-nutst'.

Yes, alas! But it has been rebuilt according to the original plan. And also, the original stones were used as far ạs possible.

28 ich ĕr-i'-nĕ-rĕ mich yetst das a-may-ree-kah'-ni-shĕ oo-nee-vĕr-zee-tay'-tĕn unt owkh īn-tsĕl-nĕ a-may-ree-kah'-nĕr ī'-ne gĕ-vi'-sĕ zu'-mĕ tsum noi'-bow bī'-gĕ-trah-gĕn hah'-bĕn.

I remember now that American universities and also individual Americans contributed a certain sum for its rebuilding.

29 das shtimt . . .

That is correct, Miss Kruger.

30 es ist shpayt gĕ-vor'-dĕn. ich mus ins hoh-tel' tsoo-rük'-kay-rĕn.

It has grown late. I must return to the hotel.

31 fee'-lĕn dangk führ ee'-rĕ rī'-tsĕn-dĕ gĕ-zel'-shaft. veer vayr'-dĕn zee mor'-gĕn owf'-zoo-khĕn.

Thanks for your charming company. We will see (lit., seek out) you tomorrow.

---

of *werden* are used with the past participle of the verb. The ge– of the past participle of *werden*, however, is dropped. The agent of the passive is expressed by *von* with the dative case. **13.** *durch Bomben zerstört worden.*—the house was (has been) destroyed by bombs. If the agent of a sentence in the passive is not a living being, the preposition *durch* (through), which requires the accusative case, is used [§75, c]. **14.** *sich erinnern, sich erinnern an* reflexive verb, "to remember, to recall."

Sechzehnte Lektion

Neue Wörter für diese Lektion

obgleich (op-gli*ch*')	although	**bereit** (bĕ-rīt')	ready
der Wind,-e (vint)	wind		
der Dienst,-e (deenst)	service	**derb** (derp)	heavy, coarse
niedlich (neet'-li*ch*)	dainty, pretty		
weit (vīt)	far	**ebenfalls** (ay'-bĕn-fals)	likewise, too
		raten (rah'-tĕn)	to advise, guess

die Autotour,-en (ow'-toh-toor)   auto trip
die Vorbereitung,-en (fohr'-bĕ-rī-tung)   preparation
Vorbereitungen treffen (. . . tre'-fĕn)   to make arrangements

der Ausverkauf,-"e (ows'-fĕr-kowf)   sale
verlängern (fĕr-leng'-ĕrn)   to lengthen
aufreissen (owf'-rī-sĕn), **reisst auf** (rīst owf')   to tear open, rip
abnützen (ap'-nü-tsĕn), **nützt ab** (nütst ap')   to wear out
einziehen (īn'-tsee-ĕn), **zieht ein** (tseetīn')   to lace, pull in
beilegen (bī'-lay-gĕn), **legt bei** (laykt bī)   to add, enclose
ausprobieren (ows'-proh-bee-rĕn),   to try out
   probiert aus (proh-beert' ows)

das heisst (abbr. **d.h.**) (das hīst)   that is
gratis (grah'-tees)   free of charge
losfahren (lohs'-fah'-rĕn),   to start
   fährt los (fayrt lohs')
vorschlagen (fohr'-shlah-gĕn),   to suggest
   schlägt vor (shlaykt fohr')
erschrecken (ĕr-shre'-kĕn), **erschrickt** (ĕr-shrikt')   to be frightened
numerieren (nu-mĕ-ree'-rĕn)   to number
sich umdrehen (*z*ich um'-dray-ĕn),   to turn around
   dreht sich um (drayt *z*ich um')

148

DAMENKLEIDUNG • BEIM SCHUHMACHER

LADIES' WEAR, AT THE
SHOEMAKER'S

(dah'-mĕn-klī-dung, bīm
shoo'-ma-khĕr)

das Kleid,-er (klīt)	dress	die Taille,-n (ta'-liĕ)	waist
die Bluse,-n (bloo'-zĕ)	blouse	der Saum,-"e (zowm)	hem, seam
der Rock,-"e (rok)	skirt	die Länge,-n (leng'-ĕ)	length
der Sweater,- (tsve'-tĕr)	sweater		

die Damenkonfektion (dah'-mĕn-kon-fek-tsiohn)	ladies' wear store
der Damenmantel,-" (dah'-mĕn-man-tĕl)	lady's coat
der Regenmantel,-" (ray'-gĕn-man-tĕl)	raincoat
der Regenschirm,-e (ray'-gĕn-shirm)	umbrella
der Strumpf,-"e (shtrumpf)	stocking
gut stehen (goot shtay'-ĕn)	to suit well, to be becoming
gut sitzen (goot zi'-tsĕn)	to fit well
schlecht sitzen (shlecht zi'-tsĕn)	to fit badly
die Veränderung,-en (fĕr-en'-dĕ-rung)	alteration, change

rosa (roh'-zah)	pink	blau (blow)	blue
grau (grow)	gray	weiss (vīs)	white

der Schuhmacher,- (shoo'-ma-khĕr)	shoemaker
das Schuhleder,- (shoo'-lay-dĕr)	shoe leather
der Absatz,-"e (ap'-zats), }	heel
der Hacken,- (ha'-kĕn) }	
schiefgetreten (sheef'-gĕ-tray-tĕn)	worn down
der Schnürsenkel,- (shnühr'-zen-kĕl)	shoelace
die Schuhe putzen (shoo'-ĕ pu'-tsĕn)	to shine shoes

die Sohle,-n (zoh'-lĕ)	sole	nähen (nay'-ĕn)	to sew, to stitch
besohlen (bĕ-zoh'-lĕn)	to sole		
die Naht,-"e (naht)	seam	besorgen (bĕ-zor'-gĕn)	to attend to
nageln (nah'-gĕln)	to nail		

führen (füh'-rĕn)	to carry (in stock)
die Sendung,-en (zen'-dung)	shipment
hereinbekommen (he-rīn'-bĕ-ko-mĕn),	to get in
bekommt herein (bĕ-komt' he-rīn')	

CONVERSATION

1 Wie weit sind wir mit den Vorbereitungen für unsere Autotour? Von Frankfurt haben wir genug gesehen, nicht wahr, meine Damen?

2 Sie haben recht. Wir müssen aber noch allerlei besorgen, wenn wir übermorgen losfahren wollen.

3 Gut! Wir sehen uns um sechs Uhr im Hotel wieder. . . .

4 Wohin[1] wollen Sie zuerst gehen, Fräulein Barnett. Ich brauche nicht viel.

5 Vielleicht könnten[2] wir in ein Damenkonfektionsgeschäft gehen.

6 An der Zeil[3] kenne ich ein sehr feines Geschäft. Es führt Damenkleider, Damenmäntel und auch Hüte.

7 Womit kann ich den Damen dienen?

8 Ich möchte mir gern Sportkleider ansehen. Ich suche nach einem einfachen, aber schicken Kleid.

9 Wir haben gerade eine neue Sendung hereinbekommen. Ich glaube, es ist gerade das, was Sie suchen.

10 Ich würde dieses Kleid nehmen, wenn es nicht so teuer wäre.[4] Haben Sie nichts Billigeres[5]?

11 Wie gefällt Ihnen dieses Kleid? Wir haben es in allen Farben: weiss, rosa, grau, grün, dunkelblau und so weiter.

FOOTNOTES: *1. Wohin* (where "to"). Direction must always be indicated by the particle *–hin* (toward a place) or *–her* (from a place). *Wohin gehen wir?* (Where do we go?), *Woher kommen Sie?* (Where do you come from?). *Wo* alone means

PRONUNCIATION

1 vee vīt zint veer mit dayn fohr'-bĕ-rī-tung-ĕn führ un'-zĕ-rĕ ow'-toh-toor? fon frangk'-furt hah'-bĕn veer gĕ-nook' gĕ-zay'-ĕn, nicht vahr, mī'-nĕ dah'-mĕn?

2 zee hah'-bĕn recht. veer mü'-sĕn ah'-bĕr nokh a'-lĕr-lī' bĕ-zor'-gĕn ven veer üh'-bĕr-mor-gĕn lohs'-fah-rĕn vo'-lĕn.

3 goot. veer zay'-ĕn uns um zeks oor im hoh-tĕl' vee'-dĕr.

4 voh-hin' vo'-lĕn zee tsoo-ayrst' gay'-ĕn, froi'-līn *Barnett.* ich brow'-khĕ nicht feel.

5 fee-licht' kön'-tĕn veer in īn dah'-mĕn-kon-fek-tsiohns-gĕ-sheft gay'-ĕn.

6 an dayr tsīl ke'-nĕ ich īn zayr fī'-nĕs gĕ-sheft'. es führt dah'-mĕn-klī-dĕr, dah'-mĕn-men-tĕl unt owkh hüh'-tĕ.

7 voh-mit' kan ich dayn dah'-mĕn dee'-nĕn?

8 ich möch'-tĕ meer gern shport'-klī-dĕr an'-zay-ĕn. ich zoo'-khĕ nahkh ī'-nĕm īn'-fa-khĕn ah'-bĕr shi'-kĕn klīt.

9 veer hah'-bĕn gĕ-rah'-dĕ ī'-nĕ noi'-ĕ zen'-dung he-rīn'-bĕ-ko-mĕn. ich glow'-bĕ es ist gĕ-rah'-dĕ das, vas zee zoo'-khĕn.

10 ich vür'-dĕ dee'-zĕs klīt nay'-mĕn ven es nicht zoh toi'-ĕr vay'-rĕ. hah'-bĕn zee nichts bi'-li-gĕ-rĕs?

11 vee gĕ-felt' ee'-nĕn dee'-zĕs klīt? veer hah'-bĕn es in a'-lĕn far'-bĕn: vīs, roh'-za, grow, grühn, dun'-kĕl-blow unt zoh vī'-tĕr.

TRANSLATION

How far are we with preparations for our auto trip? We have seen enough of Frankfort, ladies, haven't we?

You are right. However, we have to attend to all kinds of things if we want to start day after tomorrow.

All right! We'll see each other again at the hotel at six o'clock.

Where do you want to go first, Miss Barnett? I do not need much.

Perhaps we could go to a store specializing in ladies' wear.

I know a very fine store on the *Zeil.* It carries ladies' dresses, ladies' coats, and hats, too.

What can I do for you, ladies?

I would like to look at sport dresses. I am looking for a simple, but chic dress.

We just received a new shipment. I think this is just what you are looking for.

I would take this dress if it were not so expensive. Don't you have anything cheaper?

How do you like this dress? We have it in all colors, white, pink, gray, green, dark blue, and so forth.

"where (place)." *Wo sind Sie?* (Where are you?).   *2. könnten* (could) subjunctive form derived from the past indicative *konnte* [§76].   *3. die Zeil,* the main street in Frankfort, where many elegant stores are situated. Crowds can be seen surging

12 Das hellblaue Kleid gefällt mir am besten. Welche Grösse brauche ich?

13 Vielleicht probieren Sie Grösse 38 (achtunddreissig) oder 40 (vierzig)[6] an. Erschrecken Sie nicht; die Grössen werden hier anders als in Amerika numeriert.

14 Diese Farbe steht Ihnen[7] ausgezeichnet. Drehen Sie sich bitte einmal herum. Das Kleid sitzt sehr gut.[8]

15 Ich nehme dieses Kleid. Nun brauche ich noch einen Rock, eine Bluse und vieleicht einen Sweater.

16 Diese Röcke sind sehr preiswert, ebenso jene Blusen. Wir haben auch einen aussergewöhnlichen Ausverkauf in Mänteln.

17 Nein, ich möchte[9] heute keinen Mantel. Der Rock ist sehr hübsch, wenn er nur besser passte.[10] Könnten[11] Sie die Taille etwas enger machen?

18 Ich lasse die Schneiderin sofort kommen. Ist die Länge des Rocks so recht, oder sollen wir ihn etwas verlängern? Veränderungen sind gratis.

19 Machen Sie einen breiteren Saum! Ich trage meine Röcke gern kurz. Jene Bluse packen Sie bitte auch ein, obgleich ich lieber etwas mit langen Ärmeln gehabt hätte.[12]

---

up and down the street especially in the afternoon.   *4. Ich würde dieses Kleid nehmen, wenn es nicht so teuer wäre* (I would take this dress if it were not so expensive). This is a contrary-to-fact statement and is formed similarly in German and in English. For the first part of the statement (which is actually the conclusion of the sentence here, although it precedes the clause of condition), the present conditional mood is used. The condition (introduced by "if") is expressed by the

12 das hel'-blow-ĕ klīt gĕ-felt' meer am be'-stĕn. vel'-*ch*ĕ gröh'-sĕ brow'-khĕ *ich?*

I like the light blue dress best. Which size do I need?

13 fee-lī*ch*t' proh-bee'-rĕn zee gröh'-sĕ akht'-unt-drī-si*ch* oh'-dĕr feer'-tsi*ch* an. ĕr-shre'-kĕn zee ni*ch*t; dee gröh'-sĕn vayr'-dĕn heer an'-dĕrs als in a-may'-ree-ka nu-mĕ-reert'.

Try size thirty-eight or forty. Don't be frightened; the sizes run differently here from the ones in America.

14 dee'-zĕ far'-bĕ shtayt ee'-nĕn ows'-gĕ-tsī*ch*-nĕt. dray'-ĕn zee *zich* bi'-tĕ īn'-mahl he-rum'! das klīt zitst zayr goot.

This color suits you perfectly. Please turn around. The dress fits you very well.

15 ich nay'-mĕ dee'-zĕs klīt. noon brow'-khĕ *ich* nokh ī'-nĕn rok, ī'-nĕ bloo'-zĕ unt fee-lī*ch*t' ī'-nĕn sve'-tĕr.

I'll take this dress. Now, I still need a skirt, a blouse, and perhaps a sweater.

16 dee'-zĕ rö'-kĕ zint zayr prīs'-vayrt ay'-bĕn-zoh yay'-nĕ bloo'-zĕn. veer hah'-bĕn owkh ī'-nĕn ow-sĕr-gĕ-vöhn'-li*ch*-ĕn ows'-fĕr-kowf in men'-tĕln.

These skirts, as well as those blouses, are very reasonable. We also have a special sale on coats.

17 nīn *ich* mö*ch*'-tĕ hoi'-tĕ kī'-nĕn man'-tĕl. dayr rok ist zayr hüpsh ven ayr noor be'-sĕr pa'-stĕ. kön'-tĕn zee dee tal'-iĕ et'-vas eng'-ĕr ma'-khĕn?

No, I don't want a coat today. The skirt is very pretty, if only it fitted better. Could you make the waistband a little tighter (*lit.*, more narrow)?

18 *ich* la'-sĕ dee shnī'-dĕ-rin zoh-fort' ko'-mĕn. ist dee leng'-ĕ des roks zoh re*ch*t oh'-dĕr zo'-lĕn veer een et'-vas fĕr-leng'-ĕrn? fĕr-en'-dĕ-rung-ĕn zint grah'-tees.

I'll have the dressmaker come immediately. Is the length of the skirt right, or shall we make it a little longer? Alterations are free of charge.

19 ma'-khĕn zee ī'-nĕn brī'-tĕ-rĕn zowm. *ich* trah'-gĕ mī'-nĕ rö'-kĕ gern kurts. yay'-nĕ bloo'-zĕ pa'-kĕn zee bi'-tĕ owkh īn op'-glī*ch* *ich* lee'-bĕr et'-vas mit lang'-ĕn er'-mĕln gĕ-hahpt' he'-tĕ.

Make a wider hem. I like to wear my skirts short. Please wrap up that blouse also, although I would have preferred something with long sleeves.

subjunctive of the verb derived from the past tense indicative: *war* (was) becomes *wäre* (were). The word order follows the general rule: *wenn* (if) introduces a dependent clause; therefore, the inflected part of the verb is at the end [§77]. **5.** *nichts Billigeres* (nothing cheaper). The comparative of the adjective *billig* (cheap) is used as a neuter noun. **6.** Sizes for dresses in Germany run differently from American sizes. German size 38 is about American size 14; 40, about 16; 42, about

20 Wie finden Sie diese Sporthüte, Fräulein Barnett? Sie sind schick und praktisch. In Wind und Wetter wird uns solch ein Hut gute Dienste tun.

21 Senden Sie bitte alles an: Fräulein Lois Barnett, Hotel Frankfurter Hof. . . .

22 Ich muss diese derben Schuhe zum Schuhmacher bringen.

23 Hier ist eine Schuhmacherwerkstatt. Ich möchte[9] diese Schuhe besohlen lassen.

24 Die Absätze sind auch schiefgetreten.[13] Soll ich neue Absätze machen? Einige Nähte sind ebenfalls aufgerissen.

25 Machen Sie alle nötigen Reparaturen! Benutzen Sie recht starkes Sohlenleder.

26 Die Schnürsenkel sind schon sehr abgenützt. Soll ich neue Schnürsenkel einziehen?

27 Ja, bitte. Legen Sie noch ein Paar Schnürsenkel extra bei und putzen Sie auch die Schuhe! . . .

28 So, da sind wir wieder zusammen! Einen Wagen haben wir gemietet. Wir mussten 500 (fünfhundert) Mark als Sicherheit hinterlegen und sind nun beinah pleite.

18, etc. *7. Diese Farbe steht Ihnen ausgezeichnet.* (This color suits you excellently). ID., *lit.,* This color stands to you . . ." *8. gut sitzen* (to fit well). ID., *lit.,* sits well. *9. möchte* (would like). Subjunctive used in polite expressions, derived from *mochte,* past tense indicative of *mögen* (to like, to want). This subjunctive has been used in the conversations again and again [§76]. *10. passte* is here the subjunctive of the weak verb *passen,* expressing present tense: *wenn er nur besser passte* (if only it fitted better) [§77]. *11. könnten* (could). Subjunctive used in

20 vee fin'-děn zee dee'-zě shport-hüh'-tě, froi'-līn Barnett? zee zint shik unt prak'-tish. in vint unt ve'-těr virt uns zolch in hoot goo'-tě deen'-stě toon.

How do you like (lit., find) these sport hats, Miss Barnett? They are chic and practical. A hat like this will come in very handy (will do us good service) in wind and bad weather.

21 zen'-děn zee bi'-tě a'-lěs an: froi'-līn loh'-is Barnett, hoh-těl' frangk'-fur-těr hohf.

Please send everything to Miss Lois Barnett, Hotel Frankfurter Hof.

22 ich mus dee'-zě der'-běn shoo'-ě tsum shoo'-ma-khěr bring'-ěn.

I must take these heavy shoes to the shoemaker's.

23 heer ist ī'-ně shoo'-ma-khěr-verk-shtat.—ich möch'-tě dee'-zě shoo'-ě bě-zoh'-lěn la'-sěn.

Here is a shoemaker's repair shop. I should like to have these shoes resoled.

24 dee ap'-ze-tsě zint owkh sheef'-gě-tray-těn. zol ich noi'-ě ap'-ze-tsě ma'-khěn? ī'-ni-gě nay'-tě zint ay'-běn-fals owf'-gě-ri-sěn.

The heels are also worn down. Shall I put on new heels? A few seams are also ripped.

25 ma'-khěn zee a'lě nöh'-ti-gěn rě-pa-rah-too'-rěn. bě-nu'-tsěn zee recht shtar'-kěs zoh'-lěn-lay-děr.

Make all the necessary repairs. Use very strong leather for the soles.

26 dee shnühr'-zeng-kěl zint shohn zayr ap'-gě-nütst. zol ich noi'-ě shnühr'-zeng-kěl īn'-tsee-ěn?

The shoelaces are quite frayed. Shall I put in new laces?

27 yah bi'-tě. lay'-gěn zee nokh īn pahr shnühr'-zeng-kěl eks'-trah bī unt pu'-tsěn zee owkh dee shoo'-ě.

Yes, please. Add an extra pair of shoelaces and also shine my shoes.

28 zoh dah zint veer vee'-děr tsoo-za'-měn. ī'-něn vah'-gěn hah'-běn veer gě-mee'-tět. veer mu'-stěn fünf'-hun-děrt mark als zi'-chěr-hīt hin-těr-lay'-gěn unt zint noon bī'-nah plī'-tě.

So, here we are together again. We rented a car. We had to deposit five hundred marks as security and we're almost bankrupt.

the same way as explained in Note 9. *12. lieber gehabt hätte* (would have preferred). The past perfect subjunctive of *haben* and the comparative of adverb *gern* (like), *lieber* (rather), are used. *13. sind schiefgetreten* (are worn down). In this phrase the so-called "false" passive is used. The past participle of the verb is used like an adjective, describing the condition of the shoes [§75, f]. *14. Wir hätten einen amerikanischen Wagen genommen, wenn einer dagewesen wäre.* (We should have taken an American car if one had been there). Here, we have

29 Raten Sie, was für ein Auto wir gemietet haben? Einen Volkswagen. Wir hätten einen amerikanischen Wagen genommen, wenn einer dagewesen wäre.[14]

30 Wir haben über diesen Volkswagen in den Staaten gelesen. Nun können wir ihn selbst ausprobieren.

---

a contrary-to-fact statement expressing past tense. In the German sentence, the condition as well as the conclusion is expressed by the past perfect in the subjunc-

29 rah'-tĕn zee vas führ ĭn ow'-toh   Guess what kind of car we rented.
   veer gĕ-mee'-tĕt hah'-bĕn? ĭ'-nĕn   A *Volkswagen*. We would have
   folks'-vah-gĕn. veer he'-tĕn ĭ'-nĕn   taken an American car if one
   a-may-ree-kah'-ni-shĕn   vah'-gĕn   had been there.
   gĕ-no'-mĕn ven ĭ'-nĕr dah'-gĕ-vay-
   zĕn vay'-rĕ.

30 veer hah'-bĕn üh'-bĕr dee'-zĕn   We read about this *Volkswagen*
   folks-vah-gĕn in dayn shtah'-tĕn   in the States. Now, we can try
   gĕ-lay'-zĕn. noon kö'-nĕn veer een   it out ourselves.
   zelpst ows'-proh-bee-rĕn.

tive, while in English the conditional of the verb must be used for the condition.
In German, either form is permissible [§77].

17 Siebzehnte Lektion

HINAUS IN DIE FERNE![1]

FRÄULEIN KRUGER: Endlich sind wir soweit und können die Stadt mit dem Verkehr, dem Lärm, den vielen Menschen und den Einkäufen hinter uns lassen. Ich bin wirklich ganz erschöpft.

HERR SMITH: Die Damen brauchten nur für ihre Schönheit sorgen, die wir aber auch jetzt voll und ganz geniessen können. Wir Männer haben wirklich schwer arbeiten müssen, um die technische Seite der Reise in Schwung zu bringen. Der Benzintank ist voll, die Reifen sind aufgepumpt, das Gepäck ist im Kofferraum verstaut, und unsere beiden Damen sitzen auch bequem im Auto, nicht wahr? Also können wir starten.

FRÄULEIN BARNETT: Ach, alles ist herrlich! Die Deutschen haben so viele reizende Wanderlieder. Wie wäre es, wenn wir unsere "Autowandertour"[2] mit einem Volkslied oder einem Wanderlied beginnen? Eines meiner Lieblingslieder ist: "Der frohe Wandersmann" von Eichendorff. Es ist so voller Freude und Liebe zur Natur.

FOOTNOTES: *1.* Lit., "out into the distance." *2.* "auto-hiking-trip." *3.* Josef von Eichendorff (1788-1857), German poet of that period of German literature known as *Romanticism,* which was the predominant literary trend throughout the early part of the 19th century. *4.* The first stanza of the poem "The Happy

HERR MILLER: Sie haben schon viel in der kurzen Zeit gelernt und Ihr Geschmack ist ausgezeichnet. Josef von Eichendorff[3] ist einer der bekanntesten Lyriker der Romantik,[3] dieser Literaturperiode, die so reich an lyrischen Dichtern war. Aber "Grau, teurer Freund, ist alle Theorie, und grün des Lebens goldner Baum" hat schon Goethe im *Faust* gesagt. Darum theorisieren wir nicht weiter, sondern singen lieber. Eins, zwei, drei:

> "Wem Gott will rechte Gunst erweisen,
> Den schickt er in die weite Welt;
> Dem will er seine Wunder weisen
> In Berg und Wald und Strom und Feld."[4]

FRÄULEIN KRUGER: Das war wirklich schön. Inzwischen sind wir aus der Stadt heraus und in der freien Natur. Wohin geht die Reise zuerst? Wir mussten soviel besorgen und haben den Herren alle Reisepläne überlassen. Wie es sich auch gehört, nicht wahr, Herr Miller?

HERR MILLER: Ich entnehme aus[5] dieser Frage, dass Sie endlich die Superiorität des männlichen Geschlechts anerkennen. Danke sehr! Wir haben uns mit Landkarten, Autobahnkarten, Hotel-Führern usw. bewaffnet. Es war schwer, sich für eine bestimmte Tour zu entscheiden, da Süddeutschland und Österreich überall so schön sind. Wir mussten uns leider nach der begrenzten Zeit richten; acht bis zehn Tage sind sehr wenig. Ich kenne Bayern und Österreich sehr gut, und so habe ich Herrn Smith nur etwas beraten.

HERR SMITH: Herr Miller war sehr freundlich und hat mir sehr viel überlassen. Eine Reise planen, ist schon halb eine Reise machen. Wir werden versuchen, die Natur mit der Kultur zu vereinigen; an beiden ist gerade dieser Teil des Landes so reich. So fahren wir erst direkt nach Bayreuth,[6] wo wir ein bis zwei Tage bleiben werden. Dann machen wir kurz in Nürnberg[7] halt, und wir fahren dann von dort nach München weiter. Dann . . .

Wanderer": "The one to whom God wants to grant a special favor/He sends into the wide world./He will then show him His wonders/In mountain, forest, stream, and field."   *5. entnehmen aus* (to understand). Id., *lit.,* "to take out from."   6. A small city in Northern Bavaria, idyllically situated; seat of the famous Wagnerian

FRÄULEIN BARNETT: Bitte, nicht weiter, Herr Smith. Ich lasse mich gern überraschen und plane nicht gern voraus. Sich einfach treiben lassen, ist der grösste Reiz der Wanderlust. Bayreuth, die Stadt der Festspiele, die Stadt Richard Wagners![8] Vielleicht *Parsifal* an Ort und Stelle, wo die Uraufführung stattfand, hören können! Zweimal habe ich diese Oper in New York gehört.[9]

FRÄULEIN KRUGER: Freuen Sie sich nicht zu früh, Fräulein Barnett. Soviel ich weiss, sind diese Opern immer ausverkauft, und die Plätze müssen lange vorher reserviert werden. Von überallher[10] kommen Ausländer und natürlich auch Deutsche jedes Jahr nach Bayreuth, um diesen Festspielen beizuwohnen.

HERR MILLER: Ich habe eine Überraschung für Sie. Schon von Berlin aus habe ich Plätze für uns bestellt, denn ich wollte

dieses Jahr unbedingt wieder nach Bayreuth fahren. Besonders da sich Wieland Wagner, der Enkel Richard Wagners, zu einem der grössten Theatergenies der Gegenwart entwickelt hat. Von Anfang an bis zum heutigen Tage war die Leitung des Festspielhauses in den Händen der Familie Wagner.

HERR SMITH: Sie haben das sogar mir verschwiegen. Woher wussten Sie, dass wir zu vieren dorthin fahren würden?

HERR MILLER: Ich hatte eine Ahnung, dass die Schiffsbekanntschaft nicht eine vorübergehende[11] Freundschaft sein würde. Ausserdem kann man zwei Karten für *Parsifal* jederzeit loswerden. Ja, meine Damen, heute abend werden wir *Parsifal* in Bayreuth hören!

FRÄULEIN BARNETT: Herr Miller, Sie sind grossartig. Ich bin

---

festivals.   7. A picturesque old city in Bavaria, also known for its industries, especially metal work and toys.   8. Richard Wagner (1813-1883), great German composer of operas, creator of the "music drama."   9. In German an opera is "heard," a drama is "seen."   10. *von überallher* (from all over).   11. *vorübergehend* (transitory), present participle of *vorübergehen* (to pass by) used as adjective. 12. *Der reine Tor wird "durch Mitleid wissend."* The pure fool becomes wise

Ihnen sehr dankbar. Für mich ist Wagners letzte Oper auch seine grösste. Aber das ist natürlich Geschmackssache. Nicht nur die Musik, sondern auch die Idee bezaubert mich. Der reine Tor wird "durch Mitleid wissend."[12]

> "Gesegnet sei dein Leiden,
> das Mitleids höchste Kraft
> und reinstens Wissens Macht
> dem zagen Toren gab."[13]

FRÄULEIN KRUGER: Richard Wagner war im 19. Jahrhundert, und ist heute noch, eine viel umstrittene Gestalt, als Mensch und auch als Künstler. Er wollte die Ideen der deutschen Romantik[3] verwirklichen und das Gesamtkunstwerk[14] schaffen. Herr Smith, Sie sagten mir in Frankfurt, dass Sie sich für Wagner interessieren und viel über ihn gelesen haben. Vielleicht können Sie uns helfen. Ganz klar sind mir seine Ideen nicht.

HERR SMITH: Wenn Sie sich wirklich dafür interessieren, bin ich gern dazu bereit. Wagner strebte dem Ideal der Romantik nach, alle Künste im Gesamtkunstwerk zu vereinen. Das Wortdrama, die Musik, die Tanzkunst, die Malerei im Bühnenbild,  höchste Schauspielkunst, Religion und Philosophie, ja, sogar politische Tendenzen sollten zu einer Einheit im Musikdrama verschmelzen. Wagner komponierte nicht nur die Opern, sondern schrieb seine eigenen Librettos; er war ein grosses Theatergenie, und seine Opern zeigen auch den Einfluss der philosophischen und politischen Strömungen seiner Zeit.

FRÄULEIN BARNETT: In *Tristan und Isolde* erkenne ich Schopenhauers[15] Idee, dass alles Leben Leiden ist. Erlösung vom

through compassion.   *13.* "Blessed be thy suffering/That gave pity's highest might/And the power of purest knowledge/To a timid fool."   *14. das Gesamtkunstwerk,* a harmony of all the arts, ideas and emotions.   *15.* Artur Schopenhauer (1788-1860), famous German philosopher, who exerted a great influence on the ideology of the latter part of 19th century. His main work, *The World as Will*

Leiden ist nur möglich, wenn man den Willen zum Leben verneint, d.h. also, stirbt. Der Ausdruck dieser Idee ist Isoldes Liebestod—der Tod ist "höchste Lust."[16] *Der Ring des Nibelungen*[17] scheint mir jedoch nur eine Verherrlichung des heroisch-germanischen Menschen, des "Übermenschen" zu sein.

HERR SMITH: Oh, nein, das ist eine ganz falsche Interpretation. Hier findet man starke Spuren der Revolution von 1848,[18] an der Wagner aktiv teilgenommen hat. Er musste nach der Schweiz fliehen, um nicht verhaftet zu werden. Wagner versucht, den Fluch der Macht und des Goldes zu zeigen. Die Macht und das Gold wird durch den Ring symbolisiert, um dessen Besitz die Götter, Riesen und Zwerge mit allen Mitteln kämpfen. Die Gier nach Macht korrumpiert sogar die Welt der Götter, und diese müssen schliesslich untergehen. Auch die Idealgestalten der Liebe; Brünnhilde und Siegfried, werden das Opfer dieser Welt des Lugs und Trugs,[19] des Kampfs um die Macht. Nur in der Liebe liegt vielleicht die Rettung:

"Nicht Gut und Gold
noch göttliche Pracht;
nicht Haus, nicht Hof
noch herrlicher Prunk;
nicht trüber Verträge
trügender Bund,
nicht heuchelnder Sitte
hartes Gesetz:
selig in Lust und Leid
lässt—die Liebe nur sein.[20]

HERR MILLER: Genug der Kultur—"zurück zur Natur!" Sonst werden wir noch ganz sentimental. Sehen Sie nur, wie schön die Landschaft hier geworden ist. Wir nähern uns allmählich Bayreuth.

---

and *Idea,* reveals his pessimistic philosophy.   *16. höchste Lust* (highest bliss). Isolde's last words before she wills herself to die.   *17.* A music drama by Wagner in four parts.   *18.* A revolution which began in France and inflamed the greater part of Western Europe.   *19. Lug und Trug.* ID., lying and cheating.   *20.* Wagner had written several versions for the end of the fourth opera of the Ring, *Götterdämmerung* ("The Twilight of the Gods"). In the first, the existing world of the Gods (as symbol) is irrevocably destroyed. The version quoted above sounds

FRÄULEIN KRUGER: Wie entzückend dieses Städtchen liegt. Kein Wunder, dass Wagner gerade diesen Ort für sein Theater gewählt hat. Es ist entfernt von den Hauptverkehrsstrassen. Hoffentlich bekommen wir noch Hotelzimmer.

HERR MILLER: Verlassen Sie sich nur auf Ihren wandelnden Reiseführer.[21] Ich habe telegrafisch Zimmer von Frankfurt aus bestellt, da ich fürchtete, dass wir während der Festspiele zu lange nach Unterkunft hätten suchen müssen. In diesem Hotel steigen wir ab. Ich schlage vor, dass wir uns alle gut ausruhen. Wir haben viele Meilen[22] hinter uns.

FRÄULEIN BARNETT: Besonders Sie als Fahrer müssen sicherlich sehr müde sein. Bis nachher, bei der *Parsifal*-Vorstellung!

---

a more hopeful note, expressed by Brünnhilde: "Neither possessions and gold,/Nor godlike splendor,/Nor house, nor estate,/Nor brilliant pomp,/Nor deceitful alliances/ Based on tarnished treaties,/Nor rigid laws/Of a hypocritical moral;/Only Love blesses us/In joy and sorrow."   *21. der wandelnde Reiseführer* (the walking travelers' guide book).   *22.* A German mile is about seven and a half kilometers, an English mile only one and a half.

 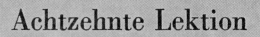

INS MITTELALTER HINEIN!

FRÄULEIN KRUGER: Guten Morgen, allerseits! Wir beherzigen[1] wirklich das Sprichwort: "Morgenstunde hat Gold im Munde!"[2] Vorgestern fuhren wir um sechs Uhr morgens von Frankfurt los, heute starten wir um sieben.

HERR MILLER: Glaubten Sie, Fräulein Kruger, eine "Auto-wandertour" wäre nur ein Vergnügen? Heute müssen wir noch München erreichen und vorher einen Abstecher[3] nach Nürnberg machen. Herr Smith, Sie übernehmen vielleicht zuerst das Steuer.

FRÄULEIN KRUGER: Fräulein, Herr; Herr, Fräulein! Warum nennen wir uns nicht gut amerikanisch beim Vornamen? Wir kommen sonst ganz germanisiert nach Amerika zurück. Ich heisse Marion; Fräulein Barnett, Lois.

HERR MILLER: Sehr angenehm. Ich heisse Hans. Darf ich Ihnen meinen Freund Robert vorstellen? Marion, das ist die beste Idee, die Sie bisher gehabt haben!

ROBERT: Wollen wir nicht gleich Brüderschaft trinken?[4] Die deutsche Zeremonie dafür ist sehr verlockend.[5]

LOIS: Nein, nicht jetzt, vielleicht in Amerika. Erstens haben

---

FOOTNOTES: *1. beherzigen,* a verb derived from *das Herz* (the heart); therefore it means "to take to heart."   *2.* A German proverb: "The early bird catches the worm." *Lit.* The morning hour has gold in its mouth.   *3. Abstecher* (short excursion, side-trip).   *4.* A customary procedure when two people agree to change from the polite form of address to the familiar *du*-form. See Lesson 20.   *5. verlockend*

164

wir keinen Wein und zweitens; nah, Sie wissen schon.[4] Sprechen wir von etwas anderem. Was erwartet uns in Nürnberg?

HANS: Dort kommen wir direkt ins deutsche Mittelalter hinein. Viel von dem alten Teil der Stadt ist zwar im letzten Krieg zerstört, aber vieles ist schon wieder aufgebaut worden. Wie man bei Bayreuth sofort an Richard Wagner denkt, so denkt man bei Nürnberg an Albrecht Dürer,[6] den grössten deutschen Maler des 15.-16. Jahrhunderts.

MARION: Bitte, Hans, nicht schon so früh am Morgen einen Vortrag! Ich möchte erst versuchen, ein bisschen Schlaf nachzuholen.

LOIS: Ach, ja! Ich würde auch gern noch von *Parsifal*, dieser einzigartigen Vorstellung und den Eindrücken in Bayreuth träumen.

ROBERT: Uns Männern ist das schon recht. Wir können uns besser auf die Autobahn konzentrieren.[7]

(*In Nürnberg*)

HANS: So, nun verlassen wir die Neustadt und kommen aus dem modernen, industriellen Nürnberg zur Altstadt. Die Burg Nürnberg, an der wir gerade vorbeikommen, existierte schon im 11. Jahrhundert. Wie alle Städte des Mittelalters war auch Nürnberg eine Festung und wurde von einer Ringmauer umgeben, die von Brücken, Türmen und Toren unterbrochen wird. Ein Graben läuft aussen um diese Mauer. Diese Befestigungen haben sich bis in die Neuzeit erhalten. Natürlich wurden sie oft teilweise zer-

(tempting). 6. Albrecht Dürer (1471-1528).   7. *sich konzentrieren auf* (to concentrate on). ID.   8. *Fachbauwerk,* timber framework filled with masonry. 9. The German artisan of the 15th and 16th centuries, rigidly organized in the guild system, followed his trade during the week, but met his fellow-artisans on Sundays to cultivate the arts of poetry and music. In many cities, especially in

stört, aber die Stadt sorgte dafür, dass sie immer wieder repariert wurden. Innerhalb dieser Mauer befindet sich die Altstadt mit den schönsten alten Bauwerken.

LOIS: Plötzlich sieht man sich aus der kahlen Wirklichkeit in die Romantik des Mittelalters versetzt; man glaubt in einer Märchenwelt zu sein. Sehen Sie nur die entzückenden Häuser im Fachwerkbau[8] und mit Giebeln. Jeden Augenblick erwartet man, dass Hans Sachs,[9] der Schuhmacher und Meistersinger, aus einem Haus und Evchen Pogner aus dem gegenüberliegenden Haus tritt. Natürlich denke ich hier wieder an "meinen" Wagner und seine Oper *Die Meistersinger von Nürnberg*.[10]

ROBERT: Wollen Sie sich bitte jetzt meiner Führung durch Nürnberg anvertrauen! Ich habe doch den Baedeker[11] nicht umsonst studiert. Dies, meine Damen, ist das Dürer-Haus, in dem der grosse Maler und Graphiker gelebt hat und auch gestorben ist. Dieses Haus wurde auch während des Kriegs zerstört, aber es ist inzwischen wieder aufgebaut worden. Hier befinden sich viele Originalwerke von Albrecht Dürer. Kommen Sie herein, und sehen Sie sich die Bilder an!

MARION: Robert, Sie sind ja ein Wunder! Albrecht Dürers Gemälde, Zeichnungen und Kupferstiche — Originale und Kopien—findet man in vielen Ländern. Zum Beispiel seine Selbstbildnisse und Kupferstiche,[12] wie "Ritter, Tod und Teufel."

LOIS: Oh, natürlich! Jetzt fällt mir ein, dass die rührend schöne Zeichnung *Betende Hände* von Dürer ist und als Karte, besonders zur Weihnachtszeit, überall in Amerika verkauft wird, nicht wahr?

Southern Germany. *Singschulen* (schools for singing) were formed. At certain intervals meetings were held in churches on Sunday afternoon where singing matches took place. The classification of apprentice, journeyman, master was adopted from the guild system. Whoever wrote his own lyrics and also invented his own melody became a "master singer." Hans Sachs (1494-1576) in Nürnberg was the most gifted of these master singers.   10. Richard Wagner's only comic opera.   11. Well-known as a tourists' guide book for Germany and other countries of Europe.   12. *Kupferstiche*, engravings on copper.   13. *gen Himmel*

ROBERT: Das stimmt! Warten Sie, bitte, ich habe noch mehr gelernt. In Nürnberg sind viele Denkmäler der deutschen Gotik des Spätmittelalters. Sehen Sie hier die St. Lorenzkirche mit ihren vielen Türmen und Türmchen, die gen[13] Himmel zu streben scheinen? Nun kommen wir an dem "Schönen Brunnen" vorbei, einem Meisterwerk gotischer, filigranfeiner Arbeit. Das schönste Monument dieser Zeit ist vielleicht das Sebaldusgrab, das von Peter Vischer[14] und seinen Söhnen geschaffen wurde. Es befindet sich hier in dieser im gotischen Stil gebauten Kirche des heiligen Sebaldus. Es gibt hier noch viel Schönes zu sehen. Beinah jedes Haus scheint uns heute ein Kunstwerk.

HANS: Bravo, Robert! Sie haben Ihre Lektion gut gelernt. So werde ich vom Lehrer zum Schüler degradiert. Dies sind wirklich Meisterwerke gotischer Feinarbeit und Schönheit. Zeit spielte damals keine Rolle.

MARION: Das ist alles sehr schön und interessant, aber jetzt streike ich und gehe keinen Schritt weiter. Meine armen Füsse! Ausserdem wollen wir heute noch nach München. Ist es Ihnen recht, wenn wir uns wieder auf den Weg machen?

HANS: Wir sind wohl alle bereit, nicht wahr? Ich möchte vorschlagen, dass wir uns morgen München in zwei Gruppen ansehen. Marion und ich halten uns an die Natur. Wir besuchen das berühmte Hofbräuhaus, wo wir Münchner Bier in München

---

(toward heaven). *Gen,* an old form of *gegen* (against, toward), is used only in a few set phrases.   14. Peter Vischer, the elder (1455-1529), and Peter Vischer, the younger (1487-1528), members of a famous family of bronze founders. 15. A famous public park, laid out in 1789.   *16.* Church of Our Lady. 17. "Onion towers" because they are shaped like onions.   *18. Portier* (doorman). But his functions go far beyond those of a person in a similar position in an American hotel. The bellboys, elevator men, porters, etc. are under his jurisdiction. He also possesses and dispenses a wealth of information on the local points of

trinken und Weisswürstchen dazu essen. Wir sitzen natürlich im Garten, in der "Natur"! Nachher sehen wir uns den Englischen Garten[15] an, während Sie beide sich der Kultur hingeben können. In München gibt es viele Gemäldesammlungen; Sie können auch Bauten im gotischen und im Barockstil bewundern, an denen München so reich ist. Die Frauenkirche[16] mit den unvollendeten Zwiebeltürmen[17] ist sehenswert.

ROBERT: Damit bin ich schon von ganzem Herzen einverstanden. Und die Damen? Sie nicken! Also, ja!

HANS: Wir sind an Ort und Stelle, alles aussteigen!

LOIS: Hans, wir können doch nicht in diesem eleganten Hotel absteigen; so wie wir aussehen?

MARION: Das macht gar nichts, Lois. Wir sind amerikanische Touristen und werden in Hotels und Gasthäusern gern gesehen.

PORTIER:[18] Was wünschen die Herrschaften?

HANS: Ich hatte telefonisch zwei Doppelzimmer mit Bad, Telefon und allen Bequemlichkeiten auf den Namen Miller bestellt.

PORTIER: Ja, die Zimmer sind für Sie reserviert. Hier sind die Schlüssel. Der Liftboy wird Ihr Gepäck nehmen und Sie auf Ihre Zimmer führen.

ROBERT: Sie sind einfach grossartig, Hans. Aber warum haben Sie Zimmer mit Telefon bestellt. Wir kennen doch niemand in München?

HANS: Ich wollte nun einmal Zimmer mit allem Drum und Dran[19] haben. Morgen haben wir einen schweren Tag vor uns. Endlich muss ich mein Versprechen Robert gegenüber erfüllen. Ich lade Sie alle zum Theater ein.

---

interest and amusement. *19. mit allem Drum und Dran.* ID.: with all the trimmings. *20.* A lullaby, text by Karl Simrock (1802-1876), music by Johannes Brahms (1833-1897), great German composer. There are several versions of this song in English. Free translation: "Lullaby and good night,/With roses bedight,/With lilies bestead/Is baby's wee-bed;/Lay thee down now and rest,/May thy slumber be blessed." Literal translation: "Good evening, good night,/With roses

ROBERT: Das ist sehr nett von Ihnen. So werden wir uns alle gleich auf unsere Zimmer zurückziehen.

LOIS:

> "Guten Abend, gut' Nacht,
> Mit Rosen bedacht,
> Mit Näglein besteckt,
> Schlüpf' unter die Deck'.
> Morgen früh, wenn Gott will,
> Wirst du wieder geweckt."[20]

(Nach dem Theater)

MARION: Setzen wir uns noch ein wenig in die Hotelhalle und lassen Sie uns plaudern! Nach solch einer eindrucksvollen Aufführung wie dieser *Faust,* erster Teil, kann man doch nicht schlafen. Hier ist eine gemütliche Ecke.

ROBERT: Darf ich Ihnen eine Zigarette anbieten, Marion? Ich weiss, Lois, Sie rauchen nicht. Einen Augenblick, ich gebe Ihnen Feuer. Das Feuerzeug funktioniert nicht. Hier ist ein Streichholz.

LOIS: Die Gretchentragödie[21] in *Faust* ist an sich mächtig, aber die Schauspieler haben auch Ausserordentliches geleistet. Ich bin noch ganz aufgewühlt. Faust hat seine Seele dem Teufel verschrieben. Können Sie mir noch einmal kurz die Idee des Pakts geben, Hans?

---

bedight/With carnations bestead,/Slip under the cover./Tomorrow morning, God willing,/You'll be awakened again."   *21.* Margarete, a very young, innocent girl, falls in love with Faust, who, with the help of the devil, undermines the purity of her character and then seduces her. Faust also loves her, but must leave the city because he has killed Margarete's brother in a duel. He returns to free her from jail (again with the help of the devil), where she is awaiting execution.

HANS: Das lässt sich schwer in ein paar Worten sagen, da die Idee des Pakts durch *Faust I* und *II* geht.[22] Faust symbolisiert den modernen Menschen, der wissen möchte, "was die Welt im Innersten zusammenhält".[23] Der Teufel verspricht seine Hilfe, um dieses Streben zu befriedigen. Dafür erhält der Teufel Fausts Seele nach dem Tod, wenn er zum Augenblick sagt: "Verweile doch! du bist so schön".[24] In Faust zeigt sich die Tragik des Dualismus im Menschen; das Triebhafte und Ideale oder Göttliche sind im stetigen Kampf um seine Seele.

ROBERT: Ich glaube, gerade der moderne Mensch empfindet diesen Zwiespalt besonders stark. Zu diesem Konflikt kommt noch der unstillbare Trieb nach Erkenntnis und Wissen, der seit der Renaissance[25] solche Dimensionen angenommen hat und zum heutigen "Atomischen Zeitalter" führte.

HANS: So stürmt nun der durch den Teufel verjüngte[26] Faust durch die Welt; geniesst und leidet und sündigt; erlebt die höchste Seligkeit der Liebe und richtet Gretchen zugrunde.[27] Er sinkt in die Tiefen des Bösen und steigt zur göttlichen Idee hinauf, um wieder tiefer zu fallen. Er will mit Hilfe des Teufels alles erfahren: Liebe, Reichtum, Macht, Schönheit, Kunst, Wissen und schliesslich intensive Arbeit. Der Teufel wartet auf den Augenblick, wenn Faust zufrieden sein wird. Aber vergeblich! Noch im Alter von 100 Jahren, kurz vor dem Tode, hat Faust grandiose Zukunftspläne.[28] Deshalb verliert der Teufel seinen Pakt. Die Engel bringen seine Seele in den Himmel nach der Idee des Herrn[29]:

---

her penalty for destroying their illegitimate child in a fit of desperation. She refuses to be freed by Faust, because she wants to atone for her sins.   22. The tragedy *Faust* consists of two parts. The first part is concerned mainly with Faust's love for Margarete (or Gretchen) and her fate. The second part treats universal and philosophic problems of modern man.   23. *der wissen möchte, "was die Welt im Innersten zusammenhält"* (he wished to know what holds the world together in its innermost core).   24. *wenn er zum Augenblicke sagt: "Verweile doch du bist so schön"* (if he says to the moment, "Tarry a while thou art so beautiful").   25. *Renaissance (lit.,* born again) is a revival of the classical influence which began in the 15th century in Italy from whence it spread over Western Europe.   26. *der durch den Teufel verjüngte Faust.* Lit., the by the devil rejuvenated Faust. A participial phrase is frequently used in German and is best translated by a relative clause in English: "Faust who has been rejuvenated by

"Wer immer strebend sich bemüht
Den können wir erlösen."[30]

ROBERT: Etwas Wichtiges haben Sie jedoch nicht erwähnt, nämlich die Idee der letzten zwei Zeilen, womit der zweite Teil des *Faust* endet.

"Das Ewig-Weibliche
Zieht uns hinan."[31]

Gretchens Liebe, die auch nach ihrem Tode nicht ihre Kraft verloren hat, wirkte mit, um Faust zu erlösen.

LOIS: Ist das nicht schön, Marion? Wenn ich nach Amerika zurückkomme, werde ich tüchtig Goethe lesen.

HANS: Es ist natürlich unmöglich, überhaupt kurz eine Idee von einem Werk zu geben, mit dem sich Goethe 60 Jahre beschäftigt hat. Als ungefähr 22jähriger begann er das Drama. Die Gretchen-Tragödie stammt aus dieser Zeit. Er arbeitete hier und da daran; liess es wieder liegen, bis sein Dichterfreund Friedrich Schiller[32] ihn anregte und ermunterte, dass er es später nach Schillers Tod vollendete.

MARION: Diese Freundschaft der beiden grössten deutschen Dichter ist einzigartig in der Geschichte der Literatur. Über zehn Jahre lebten sie im engsten Ideenaustausch und unter gegenseitiger künstlerischer Anregung, meistens in Weimar: Friedrich Schiller, der grösste deutsche Dramatiker, und Goethe, der grösste Lyriker und das letzte Universalgenie.[33]

---

the devil."   *27. zugrunde richten* (to ruin). ID. *lit.*, to direct toward the ground. *28.* Faust is stricken by blindness, but his restless mind and his inner eye visualize an accelerated reclaiming of land from the ocean—work that has occupied him the whole latter part of his life—and on this regained land he would want to settle a free people on free soil. (Goethe thought of America whose development interested him in his old age.) Now at the age of one hundred, blind and alone, he utters, almost ecstatically, the following words: "With a free people stand on a free soil./To such a moment past me fleeting,/Tarry, I'd cry, thou art so fair." In German, however, the subjunctive is used, *dürft' ich sagen* (might I say). *29. der Herr,* here means "the Lord."   *30.* "Whoever tirelessly strives to higher levels we can save."   *31.* "The eternal essence of womanhood leads us on." Most of the *Faust* quotations in these footnotes are from Bayard Taylor's translation. *32.* Friedrich von Schiller (1759-1805), leading German dramatist, who wrote

ROBERT: Kein Wunder, dass das kleine Städtchen in Mitteldeutschland trotz der krummen Gässchen und holprigen Pflastersteine der geistige und kulturelle Mittelpunkt seiner Zeit wurde. Es zog viele grosse Männer aus anderen Ländern in seinen Bann. Für die späteren Generationen wurde es zum Symbol der Humanität und Kultur.

LOIS: Nun wird es mir plötzlich klar, warum die Nationalversammlung nach der Revolution von 1918 gerade in Weimar stattfand. Der Geist der Humanität jener Zeit zeigt sich teilweise in der Weimarer Verfassung von 1919, die hier gegeben wurde.

HANS: Das war damals wieder eine kritische Periode in der deutschen Geschichte. Nach der Niederlage von 1918 bestand die Gefahr, dass sich das im Jahre 1871[34] vereinigte Deutsche Reich[35] wieder auflösen würde. Man wählte diese Stadt für den ersten Reichstag nach dem Krieg, um die Gegensätze zwischen Norden und Süden etwas auszugleichen und auch als Symbol eines liberalen, demokratischen Deutschlands, das neue Hoffnungen im Volke erwecken sollte.

MARION: Wohin haben wir uns verloren? Wir sind doch noch in München, der Hauptstadt von Bayern, in der schönsten deutschen Grosstadt. Hier scheint sich alles zu vereinigen; intensives Kulturleben und Industrie mit Naturschönheit in nächster Umgebend; und dazu kommt noch die sprichwörtliche bayrische Gemütlichkeit. Nach ungefähr drei Stunden Autofahrt ist

mostly historical tragedies: *Don Carlos, Maria Stuart, The Maiden of Orleans,* etc. Idealist, exponent of the idea of freedom, he was strongly influenced by the outstanding German philosopher Immanuel Kant (1724-1804).   33. A universal genius is one who embraces a wide range of pursuits and interests. Goethe was a great lyric poet and dramatist, wrote outstanding novels, painted, was well versed in science, wrote scientific treatises of value, held positions as secretary of different

man mitten in den Bayrischen Alpen. Wissen Sie, wie spät es inzwischen geworden ist? Es ist nach eins, und es ist höchste Zeit, dass wir zu Bett gehen.

LOIS: Das war ein sehr interessanter, anregender Abend. Aber jetzt heisst's:[36] Gute Nacht, allerseits!

departments of his dukedom; for many years he also directed the theater of Weimar. 34. The year of the unification of all German states.   35. das im Jahre 1871 vereinigte Deutsche Reich. Lit., the in the year 1871 united German Empire. This participial phrase is best translated by a relative clause: "the German Empire that was united in the year 1871."   36. heisst's—heisst es, lit. "it means."

19 Neunzehnte Lektion

DIE FAHRT NACH SÜDEN

LOIS: Der Volkswagen macht seinem guten Ruf alle Ehre. Bisher haben wir keine Panne gehabt.

HANS: Sch! Lois, malen Sie den Teufel nicht an die Wand![1] Ich muss zugeben, der Wagen fährt gut. Der Benzinverbrauch ist sehr gering, was bei den Benzinpreisen auch sehr nötig ist. Ein Liter Benzin kostet DM—,— und da ungefähr vier Liter auf die Gallone gehen, kommt eine Gallone Benzin umgerechnet auf $.—.

MARION: Es ist doch herrlich, so durch die Alpen zu fahren. Hohe Bergriesen mit schneebedeckten Gipfeln und grüne Täler; um jede Biegung der Autobahn bietet sich ein neues Panorama. Keines ist dem vorhergehenden ähnlich. Bald sausen wir durch einen Tunnel, und bald sind wir hoch über Tälern und Bergseen, und die reizend gelegenen Dörfchen liegen zu unseren Füssen. Die hohen, weissen Kirchtürme sieht man schon von weitem.

ROBERT: Ich muss auch gestehen, so schön habe ich es mir nicht vorgestellt. Je weiter wir nach Süden kommen, desto schöner wird die Natur.

LOIS: Der Kontrast zwischen dem Gewaltigen und dem Lieblichen übt einen eigenartigen Reiz aus. Könnten wir heute nicht

FOOTNOTE: *1. den Teufel an die Wand malen. Lit.*, to paint the devil on the wall. By praising one might tempt fate. *2. Rast machen* (to stop). ID., *lit.*, to make a rest. *3. unberufen* (knock wood). *4.* A proverb: "Don't praise the day

174

in einem der niedlichen Gasthäuser, die an uns vorbeihuschen, Rast machen?[2]

HANS: Aber gewiss! Ich möchte auch den Wagen einmal nachsehen lassen. Plötzlich höre ich verdächtige Geräusche. Lois, wir haben nicht "unberufen"[3] gesagt, als wir den Wagen lobten.

MARION: Ja, ja, "Man soll den Tag nicht vor dem Abend loben."[4] Vielleicht können wir das Angenehme mit dem Nützlichen[5] verbinden. Lois und ich ruhen uns im Gasthaus aus, während Sie und Robert einen Mechaniker suchen.

ROBERT: Die Gleichberechtigung der Geschlechter[6] ist wirklich ein Segen für die Frauen und macht uns Männern das Leben soviel leichter, nicht wahr?

LOIS: Das stimmt! Unsere Mütter hätten das grosse Opfer, als Reisebegleiterinnen zu fungieren, gar nicht bringen *dürfen.* Da sehe ich gerade, was wir suchen. Könnten Sie hier halten?

HANS: Also meine Damen, Sie sitzen bequem im Gärtchen unter schattigen Bäumen, und wir können uns beruhigt von den "Opfern" trennen.

LOIS: Wie charmant dieses Gasthaus mit dem überhängenden Dach, dem Balkon, der um das ganze Haus zu gehen scheint, aussieht. Überall sind Blumen. Das Eigenartigste sind jedoch die buntbemalten Fensterläden.

MARION: Diese Bauart ist charakteristisch für die Bauern- und Wohnhäuser in Bayern und Österreich. Je tiefer wir in die Alpen hineinkommen, desto hübscher und bunter werden die bemalten Fensterläden; ja, sogar ganze Mauern sind oft mit bunten

---

before the evening (has come)." *5. das Angenehme mit dem Nützlichen verbinden* (to combine the agreeable with the useful). *6. die Gleichberechtigung der Geschlechter* (the equality of the sexes). *7. Heiligenbilder* (images of saints). *8. einen Spaziergang machen.* ID., to take a walk. *9. sich die Zeit vertreiben.*

Bildern, meistens Heiligenbildern,[7] bedeckt. Sehen Sie nur die dralle Kellnerin in bayrischer Tracht. Hier ist alles echt!

Lois: Ach, ich hätte nie gedacht, dass meine erste Deutschlandreise so wunderbar sein würde!

Marion: Besonders, wenn man dabei noch sein Herz verloren hat. Passen Sie auf, dass es nicht die letzte Deutschlandreise wird!

Lois: Warum? Dann machen wir eben unsere Hochzeitsreise hierher. Ich scherze natürlich, soweit ist es noch nicht. Aber tun Sie nur nicht so blasiert! Hans hat auch Eindruck auf Sie gemacht.

Marion: Wir haben Glück gehabt. Beide sind patente Kerle, intelligent und lustig. Vielleicht machen wir einen kleinen Spaziergang[8] um den See, bis unsere Herren wiederkommen. . . .

Hans: Hallo, hoffentlich haben Sie sich die Zeit während unserer Abwesenheit gut vertrieben.[9] Es waren nur Kleinigkeiten an dem Wagen zu reparieren.

Robert: Lassen Sie mich berichten, Hans. Eine neue "deutsche" Welt hat sich mir an der Tankstelle aufgetan. Also, das Wasser im Kühler musste aufgefüllt werden. Die Reifen des Autos waren schlapp, und jetzt sind sie aufgepumpt und stramm. Die Gänge mussten geölt, die Kupplung angezogen werden, und die Birne des Rückenlichts war ausgebrannt. Die Zünder, die Lichtmaschine und die Bremsen sind in Ordnung. Ausserdem ist das kein Auto, sondern ein Kraftwagen, d.h. "power car."

Lois: Was das alles auch bedeuten könnte, weiss ich nicht. Aber der arme Kraftwagen! Es überrascht mich nur, dass er unterwegs nicht auseinandergefallen ist.

Hans: Sie haben Ihre Weisheit verschwendet, Robert. Wie wenig doch Frauen von der Mechanik verstehen! Nun sind wir auf die höchsten Berge vorbereitet. Steigen Sie ein; Salzburg wartet auf uns! Wir kommen durch Berchtesgaden,[10] wo wir ganz kurz Station machen werden. Und da heisst es, Rucksack und derbe Schuhe herausnehmen! Von Berchtesgaden wandern wir zum Königsee.

Id., to pass the time.   *10.* One of the most beautiful Bavarian towns and health resorts, near the Austrian border.   *11.* First stanza of a wanderer's song by Wilhelm Müller (1794-1827), a German lyric poet: "To wander is the desire of

MARION: Endlich machen wir eine Wanderung, mit Essen und Trinken im Rucksack und Picknick im Walde.

ROBERT: Diese Wanderung durch den Wald war so erfrischend und eine Erholung vom Autofahren und durch die Strassenlaufen.

LOIS: Aber der Rückweg! Nein, ich klage nicht. Der Königsee ist überwältigend und auch, wie soll ich es ausdrücken? Der Anblick erfüllt mich mit einer heiligen Scheu. Wie kommt das? Besonders jetzt im Motorboot in der Mitte des Sees!

HANS: Dies ist, glaube ich, der einzige Bergsee dieser Art. Er ist auf allen Seiten von riesigen Bergen umgeben, die manchmal bis in den See hineinreichen. Man fühlt sich als Mensch so klein vor den mächtigen Bergen, dem Schweigen dieser Abgeschlossenheit und der sonnenlosen und doch klaren Atmosphäre. Die Schatten der Berge fallen auf den See, sodass er ganz schwarz erscheint.

MARION: So, die Rückwanderung kann beginnen. Mit Hilfe eines munteren Wanderlieds können wir diesen Eindruck wieder abschütteln und vergessen, dass wir müde sind:

"Das Wandern ist des Müllers Lust;
   Das Wandern!
Das muss ein schlechter Müller sein,
Dem niemals fiel das Wandern ein,
   Das Wandern."[11]

HANS: Die österreichische Grenze haben wir hinter uns. Wir nähern uns Salzburg, einer der charmantesten Städte Europas. Die Lage in einem lieblichen Tal zwischen hohen Bergen und die schönen Bauten, meistens im Barock und Renaissance Stil,

---

the miller, to wander./It must be a poor miller/To whom it has never occurred to wander, to wander." *12.* Wolfgang Amadeus Mozart (1756-1791), the greatest Austrian composer, famous for his operas, *The Marriage of Figaro, Don Giovanni, The Magic Flute,* etc. *13. über alle Berge sein* (to be far away). *Lit.,* "to be over

geben Salzburg ein eigenartiges Gepräge. Wolfgang **Amadeus** Mozart[12] hätte sich keinen schöneren Geburtsort aussuchen können. Leider beginnen die Salzburger Musikfestspiele erst Ende Juli, und bis dahin sind wir schon über alle Berge.[13]

LOIS: Das ist zu schade. So müssen wir uns mit dem Besuch von Mozarts Geburtshaus begnügen. Vielleicht haben wir in Wien Gelegenheit *Don Juan, Die Zauberflöte* oder eine andere Oper von Mozart zu hören.

> "Wien, Wien, nur du allein
> Sollst stets die Stadt meiner Träume sein ..."[14]

ROBERT: Wie schön Wien liegt! Wir kommen jetzt von den österreichischen Alpen in den Wiener Wald; zu unseren Füssen sehen wir Wien und darüber hinaus die viel besungene Donau.

MARION: Und sofort denkt man an Johann Strauss[15] und seine

Walzer: "Geschichten aus dem Wiener Wald" und "An der schönen blauen Donau" und seine echt Wiener Operette *Die Fledermaus.* Nichts hat Wien in der ganzen Welt so einen romantischen Schimmer gegeben wie Strauss' Musik.

LOIS: *Die Fledermaus* in englischer Sprache wird oft in amerikanischen Opernhäusern aufgeführt.

HANS: Wie oft hat meine Grossmutter mit leuchtenden Augen von der Zeit erzählt, als Johann Strauss Gastdirigent in Berlin war und seine Walzer selbst dirigierte!

MARION: Lange ehe Wien die Walzerstadt wurde, war es schon eine berühmte Musikstadt. Mozart lebte jahrelang in Wien und starb auch hier. Josef Haydn[16] verbrachte den grössten Teil seines Lebens in Wien; Franz Schubert[17] wurde in Wien ge-

---

all mountains.   *14.* From a song by R. Sieczynski, Austrian composer: "Vienna, Vienna, thou alone shall always be the city of my dreams." Copyright 1914 by Adolf Robitschek, copyright renewed and assigned to Harms, Inc. Reprinted by permission. *15.* Johann Strauss (1825-1899), the greatest Austrian composer of waltzes and operettas, often called the Waltz King.   *16.* Josef Haydn (1732-1809), Austrian

boren; Ludwig van Beethoven[18] kam zu seiner weiteren Ausbildung unter Josef Haydn nach Wien und blieb dort bis an sein Ende. Und so kann man noch viele Namen berühmter Komponisten, die durch Wien angezogen wurden, bis in die Gegenwart hinein aneinanderreihen.

ROBERT: Wien ist solch eine alte schöne Stadt. Ihre Wurzeln reichen bis ins Altertum. Schon von 77 nach Christi bis ins 6. Jahrhundert war es eine befestigte Siedlung der Römer. Wien sieht auf eine beinahe tausendjährige Geschichte als Weltstadt zurück. Es wurde zur Mittlerin der Kulturen des Südens, Ostens und Westens und später auch des Nordens. Wien war schon eine bedeutende Stadt im Mittelalter, zu einer Zeit, als Berlin nur ein Fischerdorf war.

LOIS: Ich habe mich auch über Wien informiert. Von 1556-1806 war es die deutsche Kaiserstadt, der Sitz des "Heiligen Römischen Reichs Deutscher Nation."[19] Und natürlich war es auch die Hauptstadt des Kaiserreichs Österreich-Ungarn, das nach dem ersten Weltkrieg von den Alliierten aufgelöst wurde. Heute ist es die Hauptstadt des Bundesstaats Österreich.

MARION: Da die Geschichte Österreichs bis ins Altertum reicht, findet man Bauwerke aus den verschiedenen Zeiten. Die berühmte Ringstrasse ist auf den früheren Festungswällen angelegt worden und schliesst, wie die Ringmauer in Nürnberg, die Altstadt ein. Wenn wir jetzt die Kärntnerstrasse, die elegante Hauptstrasse von Wien, hinuntergehen, kommen wir zur St. Stephanskirche, deren Bau im 13. Jahrhundert begonnen wurde. Dieser

composer, wrote operas, symphonies, oratorios, etc.   17. Franz Schubert (1797-1828), great Austrian composer of songs, symphonies, etc.   18. Ludwig van Beethoven (1770-1827), foremost German composer of symphonies, the opera *Fidelio*, chamber music, etc.   19. "The Holy Roman Empire of the German Nations," officially dissolved by Napoleon in 1806.   20. Style of architecture

Dom, mit seinem zum Himmel strebenden Turm, ist das Wahrzeichen Wiens.

ROBERT: Was für ein herrliches Beispiel der gotischen Baukunst diese Kirche ist! Das ist wirklich das schönste Bauwerk, das ich bisher gesehen habe. Die gotische Feinarbeit, die graziösen Türme und Türmchen, die Spitzbögen und das massive Fundament verbinden sich zu einem Ganzen von Grazie und Majestät.

HANS: Sie finden hier auch die schönsten Schlösser, wie zum Beispiel Schönbrunn in Wien; weltliche und kirchliche Bauten in Hülle und Fülle aus der Renaissance, dem Rokoko und solche mit byzantinischen[20] Einflüssen. Sie müssen mich aber jetzt entschuldigen. Die langen Fahrten durch die Alpen und das Übernachten in manchmal nicht zu modernen Gasthäusern haben mich stark übermüdet. Ich gehe ins Hotel zurück und lege mich eine Weile hin.

LOIS: Aber natürlich entschuldigen wir Sie. Unser Hauptchauffeur muss doch neue Kräfte sammeln. Wir wandern inzwischen in der Stadt herum und sehen uns die Staatsoper, das Burgtheater usw. wenigstens von aussen an. Denn leider ist es auch hier nichts mit einer Oper von Mozart. Für die Salzburger Musikfestspiele kamen wir zu früh, für die Wiener zu spät.

(Im Prater)

MARION: So sitzen wir also wirklich unter schönen, alten Bäumen im Prater, von dem wir soviel gehört haben, und der in Liedern besungen wird, und trinken Tiroler Landwein.

LOIS: Es herrscht eine fröhliche, beschwingte Stimmung in diesem Vergnügungspark. Da ist ein Riesenrad, dort ein Karussel, weiter fort eine Berg- und Talbahn und Musik. Die Menschen lachen, singen, plaudern und scherzen, und doch ist es nicht wirklich laut. Die Wiener scheinen so leichtlebig und sorglos zu sein. Auch das öffentliche Leben spielt sich scheinbar reibungslos und gemütlich ab.

---

developed in the Eastern Roman Empire or Byzantine Empire — Constantinople (Istanbul) in the 5th and 6th centuries. *21. Neureicher* (newly rich). **22.** Franz Grillparzer (1791-1872), great Austrian poet and dramatist, also wrote short

HANS: Ich glaube, wir täuschen uns über den wahren Charakter der Wiener. Unter der Fröhlichkeit verbirgt sich doch eine gewisse Melancholie. Vielleicht ist diese leichte Resignation das Resultat einer alten Kultur. Berlin ist gewissermassen ein "Neureicher"[21] unter den europäischen Grosstädten; es ist soviel jünger als Wien. Der Berliner ist lauter, aktiver und aggressiver und ziemlich frei von Sentimentalität.

ROBERT: Vielleicht ist gerade Franz Grillparzer,[22] Österreichs grösster Dramatiker, in seinem Wesen und seinen Werken der typische Wiener. Er neigte zur Melancholie und resignierte früh; nur fehlte ihm die fröhliche Seite des Wiener Temperaments.

LOIS: Mir wird auch ganz melancholisch zu Mut. Ist es Wien, unsere Unterhaltung oder der Landwein?

HANS: Alles drei. Dazu kommt noch, dass wir am Ende unserer schönen Tour sind. Morgen fahren wir wieder gen Norden, und bald müssen wir uns trennen. Sie müssen nach Frankfurt zurück, und Robert und ich fahren von dort weiter nach Berlin.

MARION: Trösten wir uns wieder mit ein paar Zeilen aus einem Volkslied:

"In der Heimat, in der Heimat,
Da gibt's ein Wiedersehn."[23]

---

stories.   23. Part of a German marching song that originated among the soldiers in World War I: "At home (the homeland), at home, There'll be a reunion (a seeing again)."

20

Zwanzigste Lektion

EIN GEMÜTLICHER ABEND

HANS: Hallo, Mutter. Darf ich dir Fräulein Kruger und Fräulein Barnett vorstellen?

FRAU MILLER: Guten Tag, meine Damen! Ich habe schon soviel von Ihnen gehört, und ich freue mich sehr, Ihre Bekanntschaft zu machen. Willkommen, Robert! Wollen Sie bitte alle Platz nehmen!

MARION: Wir danken Ihnen sehr für Ihre liebenswürdige Einladung.

FRAU M.: Oh, es ist nur ein Kaffeeklatsch am Abend. Es lässt sich gemütlicher am runden Tisch bei Kaffee, Kuchen und belegtem Brot plaudern, nicht wahr, Robert?

ROBERT: Ich erinnere mich noch mit Vergnügen an meinen ersten Besuch und die Schwierigkeiten, die mir das Wort "Kaffeeklatsch" sowie die deutsche Sprache bereiteten und heute . . .

FRAU M.: . . . sprechen Sie wie ein geborner Deutscher. Ich wollte nicht nur die beiden Damen kennenlernen, sondern ich möchte mit Ihnen auch gern Reiseerlebnisse austauschen. Greifen Sie bitte zu, und lassen Sie sich nicht weiter nötigen![1]

FOOTNOTES: *1. greifen Sie bitte zu, und lassen Sie sich nicht nötigen* (please, help yourself and don't wait to be asked). *2. der Neuling* (the novice, "greenhorn"). *3. drunter und drüber.* Id., topsy-turvy. *4. die Ätzungen* (the etchings). *5. so schnell wie möglich* (as quickly as possible). *6. der Eingeweihte*

182

Lois: Ihr Sohn erzählte uns, dass Sie schon viele Male den Ozean gekreuzt haben. Ich bin nur ein Neuling.[2]

Hans: Oh, meine Mutter war nicht immer so erfahren und vielgereist. Sie ist das erste Mal auf ihrer Hochzeitsreise in Deutschland gewesen.

Frau M.: Hans, fängst du schon wieder an, mich zu necken?

Hans: Mutter, hüte dich vor diesem Wort! Erinnerst du dich nicht daran, zu was für Missverständnissen es führen kann? Mutter und Vater lernten auf einer Reise nach Deutschland eine junge Amerikanerin auf dem Schiff kennen, mit der Vater gern scherzte. Sie sprach nur gebrochenes Deutsch, und eines Tages sagte Mutter: "Lassen Sie sich nicht immer von meinem Mann necken, necken Sie ihn auch!"

Frau M.: Woraufhin das junge Mädchen mich entsetzt ansah, sich umdrehte und uns während der ganzen Reise nicht mehr kannte. Wir konnten uns dies gar nicht erklären, bis Hans uns später die Erklärung gab.

Marion: Das ist sehr komisch. Meine Mutter hat auch etwas Ähnliches erlebt. Sie machte mit meiner Schwester zwei oder drei Jahre nach dem Zusammenbruch von 1946 eine Reise nach Deutschland. Alles ging noch ziemlich drunter und drüber.[3] Die Not war gross, Kunstwerke wurden gestohlen oder gefunden und verkauft usw. Meine Mutter und Schwester sahen sich ein Gebäude in Innsbruck an und sprachen Englisch miteinander. Plötzlich trat ein Mann mit einer Mappe unterm Arm an meine Mutter heran und flüsterte ihr in gebrochenem Englisch ins Ohr: "Gnädige Frau, wollen Sie sich nicht meine Ätzungen[4] ansehen?" Die beiden brachen in schallendes Gelächter aus, und der arme Mann entfernte sich so schnell wie möglich,[5] indem er sich ein paarmal kopfschüttelnd umsah.

Robert: Ja, unser Slang ist für nicht Eingeweihte[6] eine Fremdsprache. Man braucht eigentlich ein besonderes Wörterbuch dafür. So schön die Reise auch war, ist man doch froh,

(the adept, "the one in the know"). *7. verschont bleiben.* Id., to be spared. *8. ein Dankopfer* (a "thank-offering," thanksgiving). *9. sich vererben auf.* Id., to be passed on. *10. teilnehmen an.* Id., to participate in. *11. sich vorbereiten auf.* Id.. to prepare for. *12.* about 1768-1775. *13.* Ludwig Uhland (1787-1862).

wieder einen Abend in einem amerikanischen Heim verleben
zu können und Erlebnisse auszutauschen. Was hat den grössten
Eindruck in Deutschland auf Sie gemacht, Frau Miller?

FRAU M.: Das ist schwer zu sagen. Vielleicht die Passionsspiele
in Oberammergau, Bayern.

MARION: Erzählen Sie uns bitte davon. Da diese Passionsspiele
nur alle zehn Jahre stattfinden, hatten wir keine Möglichkeit, sie
auf unserer Reise zu sehen. Ich weiss nur, dass diese Aufführun-
gen auf ein Gelübde aus dem Jahr 1634 zurückgehen.

FRAU M.: Es herrschte damals in ganz Europa eine grosse Pest,
und die Einwohner dieses kleinen Dorfes gelobten, dass sie alle
zehn Jahre die Passion Christi aufführen würden, wenn das Dorf
von der Pest verschont bliebe.[7] Da dies geschehen war, hielten
die Bewohner ihr Gelübde bis auf den heutigen Tag. Es ist also
ein Dankopfer.[8] Alle Rollen werden nur von Dorfbewohnern
gespielt. Die Rollen vererben sich oft vom Vater auf[9] den Sohn.
Fast das ganze Dorf nimmt an diesem religiösen Spiel teil[10] und

bereitet sich ein bis zwei
Jahre darauf vor.[11] Die
Knaben lassen sich das Haar
wachsen, die Männer, das
Haar und die Bärte. Alle
Versuche, die Oberammer-
gauer Passionsspiele nach
Amerika zu bringen, sind
bisher vergeblich gewesen.
Mir ist diese Aufführung,
die tagelang dauerte, unvergesslich geblieben. Und was
hat Ihnen am besten ge-
fallen, Fräulein Barnett?

LOIS: Bayreuth und die *Parsifal*-Aufführung, da ich nun einmal eine Wagnerianerin bin; aber dann kommt gleich an
zweiter Stelle Wien. Es scheint die Urheimat der Musik zu sein.

German writer known for his lyric poetry.   14. Robert Schumann (1810-1856),
one of the great German composers of the 19th century, wrote songs, symphonies,
etc.   15. Felix Mendelssohn-Bartholdy (1809-1847), German composer, wrote
songs, sonatas, concertos, symphonies, music to *A Midsummer Night's Dream*, etc.

Es singt und klingt dort überall, selbst die Sprache ist weich und melodiös. Schubert, der Vater des modernen Lieds, ist so ganz und gar der wahre Sohn Wiens.

HANS: Vieles kam zusammen, um das deutsche Lied zu schaffen. Die Wiederentdeckung des Volkslieds war für die Literatur zur Zeit des jungen Goethe[12] von grosser Bedeutung. Die Dichter der Romantik brachten die lyrische Dichtung zu höchster Blüte. Josef von Eichendorff, Ludwig Uhland,[13] Wilhelm Müller, um nur einige zu nennen, kommen in ihren Gedichten der Einfachheit des Volkslieds nahe.

ROBERT: Und die grossen Komponisten dieser Zeit wie Franz Schubert, Robert Schumann,[14] und später Felix Mendelssohn[15] und Johannes Brahms sowie viele andere, vertonten viele dieser Gedichte. Diese bisher einmalige Vereinigung grosser Musik mit ebenbürtiger[16] Lyrik schuf die deutschen Lieder, die sich die Welt erobert haben.

FRAU M.: Unter den grossen Lyrikern dürfen wir Heinrich Heine[17] nicht vergessen. Wenige Lieder sind so tief in das Volk eingedrungen, wie zum Beispiel "Die Lorelei," bei der Heines Lyrik und die Musik von Silcher zu einer schönen Einheit verschmolzen sind.

MARION: Das ist ein Lied, das wir auch alle kennen und singen, nicht wahr? Ludwig van Beethoven, der Komponist der grossen Symphonien, hat in seiner letzten Symphonie, der neunten, Friedrich von Schillers "Lied an die Freude" für seinen Jubel-Chor: Die Hymne an die Freundschaft und Brüderlichkeit, verwandt.

LOIS: Es ist nur ein Jammer, dass gerade viele von den ganz grossen Komponisten jung gestorben sind oder unter einem schweren Schicksal leiden mussten. Mozart starb im Alter von 35. Jahren, Schubert lebte nur bis zum 31. Jahr. Schumann wurde mit 44 Jahren geisteskrank und Beethoven mit 42 Jahren vollkommen taub. Trotz der Taubheit arbeitete er weiter an seinen

---

16. *ebenbürtig* (equal in value).   17. Heinrich Heine (1797-1856), German lyric poet.   18. See Lesson 18.   19. Proverb: Practice makes perfect. *Lit.*, Practice makes the master.   20. *es rührend finden* (to find it touching).   21. A folksong, writer and composer unknown: "Thou, thou art in my heart;/Thou, Thou art

Kompositionen, die er selbst nicht mehr hören konnte. Die 9. Symphonie entstand während dieser Zeit.

HANS: Robert, ich weiss, Sie spielen gut Klavier. Vielleicht können wir ein paar Lieder singen, wenn Sie uns auf dem Klavier begleiten. Hier liegt ein Volkslieder-Album auf dem Klavier.

FRAU M.: Das ist eine reizende Idee. Zuerst wollen wir unsere Gläser füllen und auf die Zukunft und unsere nächste Europareise trinken. Prosit! Entschuldigen Sie mich bitte, ich muss ein wenig in der Küche nach dem Rechten sehen.

ROBERT: Das ist der Augenblick, auf den ich seit unserer Rückkehr nach Amerika gewartet habe. Lois, lösen Sie Ihr Versprechen ein! Hans, füllen Sie die Gläser von neuem!

LOIS: Mein Versprechen?[18] Ich weiss von nichts.

ROBERT: Tun Sie nur nicht so unschuldig. Wir sind jetzt in Amerika; wir haben Wein; es fehlt nur noch das "Brüderschaft trinken."

HANS: Wollen wir uns den beiden nicht anschliessen, Marion?

MARION: Gern. Wir sind ja schon solch *alte* Freunde.

ROBERT: Aufpassen, nun kommt die Zeremonie! Jeder nimmt das Glas in die rechte Hand und hebt den Arm! Lois, kommen Sie ein bisschen näher! Nun haken wir die Arme ein, dann trinken wir gleichzeitig. Soweit hat es gut geklappt! Jetzt kommt der Brüderschaftskuss.

HANS: Nun müssen wir die Zeremonie wiederholen. Denn Lois und ich wollen uns doch auch duzen, nicht wahr? Ausserdem: "Übung macht den Meister."[19]

---

in my mind;/Thou, thou causeth me much sorrow;/ Thou dost not know;/ How much I love thee./Yes, yes, yes, yes, thou dost not know/How much I love thee." 22. First stanza of the poem *Heidenröslein* (Wild Rose) by Goethe: Literal trans-

ROBERT: Zu schade, dass man nicht mehrere Male Brüder-schaft trinken kann!

MARION: Was wird nur deine Mutter sagen, wenn wir uns plötzlich alle duzen?

HANS: Sie wird es nicht merken; wir singen!

FRAU M.: Ich finde es ja rührend,[20] dass Sie mit dem Singen auf mich gewartet haben.

HANS: Aber, Mutter, dass war doch ganz selbstverständlich! Womit beginnen wir? Vielleicht mit einem Volkslied, von dem man weder den Dichter noch den Komponisten kennt? Es ist Ihnen recht? Ja! Eins, zwei, drei:

> "Du, du liegst mir im Herzen;
> Du, du liegst mir im Sinn.
> Du, du machst mir viel Schmerzen,
> Weisst nicht, wie gut ich dir bin . . .
> Ja, ja, ja, ja, weisst nicht,
> Wie gut ich dir bin."[21]

ROBERT: Das ist ein reizendes Lied. Ich finde es so nett, dass man sich darin duzt. Auf der nächsten Seite folgt "Heidenrös-lein" von Goethe. Wollen Sie dieses Lied singen?

HANS: Wenn es Ihnen allen recht ist, singen wir zuerst die volkstümliche Melodie—der Name des Komponisten ist schon beinah ganz vergessen—und dann singen wir es in der Vertonung von Franz Schubert. Also, bitte; eins, zwei, drei:

> "Sah' ein Knab, ein Röslein steh'n;
> Röslein auf der Heiden.
> War so jung und morgenschön;
> Lief er schnell, es nah zu seh'n;
> Sah's mit vielen Freuden.
> Röslein, Röslein, Röslein, Röslein rot,
> Röslein auf der Heiden."[22]

---

lation: "A boy saw a little rose;/Little rose on the heather./ (It) was so young and beautiful like the early morning./He went quickly to see it closely./He beheld it with great joy./Little rose, little rose, little rose red;/Little rose on the heather."

Reference Grammar

ALTHOUGH ALL the necessary grammatical explanations for each of the Twenty Lessons have been provided in the footnotes of the lessons, a complete REFERENCE GRAMMAR is given here for the convenience of the student. Each part of speech (the Article, Noun, Verb, etc.) is explained thoroughly in all its uses. Therefore, should the student wish complete information about any point of grammar, he can easily find it in this handy REFERENCE GRAMMAR.

Study Plan for
Reference Grammar

SINCE THE MATERIAL of the REFERENCE GRAMMAR is not arranged in order of difficulty or frequency of occurrence, but is classified by subjects (the Article, Noun, Adjective, etc.), it is suggested that the student refer to and study the following paragraphs along with each lesson, for guidance in the grammatical points covered in each lesson. The easiest way of locating any paragraph (§) is to flip through the pages of the grammar watching for the § number which is in bold face alongside the page number.

Lesson I   The definite article §1. The present tense of verbs §61. Gender of nouns §19. The plural of nouns §10. The verb *sein* §59. Possessive adjectives §30.

Lesson II   The indefinite article §6. Stem vowel change of verbs §65-b. Reflexive verbs §27. Inverted word order §53-e. Imperative mood of verbs §70. Verbs with separable prefixes §68.

Lesson III   Comparison of adjectives §47. *der*-words §5. Prepositions taking the dative case §37. Modal auxiliary verbs §71, §72.

Lesson IV   Strong and weak verbs §61. Prepositions taking either the dative case or the accusative case §38.

Lesson V   Present perfect tense of weak verbs §64-c,d. Past tense of weak verbs §64-b. Past tense of *sein* §59. Past tense of strong verbs §65-b, §67-b. Past tense of *haben* §59. Prepositions taking the accusative case §36. Numerals §51.

Lesson VI   Expressions of time §52-a. Verbs conjugated with *haben* and *sein* §63-a,b. Present tense of strong verbs §65-a.

Lesson VII   Prepositions requiring the genitive case §39. Transitive and intransitive verbs §62. Position of the infinitive §79-f. Word order of dependent clauses §79-c. Formation of the future tense §60-d. Word order with coordinating conjunctions §79-a. Conjugation of modal auxiliaries §76. Strong declension of the adjective §43. Pronominal compounds §26.

Lesson VIII   Strong, weak, and mixed declensions of nouns §10-§15. Weak adjective declensions §44. Inseparable and separable prefixes §68-a,b. Past participle used as an adjective §69-c.

Lesson IX   Indefinite pronouns §35. Mixed declension of adjectives §45. Infinitive used as a noun §69-a. Nouns irregularly declined §16.

Lesson X   Ordinal numbers §51-c. Position of adverbs of time §78-h. Intransitive verbs taking the dative case §62-c. Infinitives without *zu* §69-e. Subjunctive mood §76.

Lesson XI   Formation of adverbs §53. Inflection of interrogative pronouns §32. Formation of the conditional tenses §77-a.

Lesson XII   Relative pronouns §34. Adverbial conjunctions §58. Uses of the genitive case §22. Translations of "when" §57.

Lesson XIII   Uses of the dative case §23. Adjective endings §42.

Lesson XIV   Uses of the accusative case §24. Formation of the passive voice §75-a.

Lesson XV   Impersonal expressions §78. Demonstrative pronouns §31. Tenses of the passive voice §75-b. Expressions denoting monetary units §52-c.

Lesson XVI   Use of the subjunctive §76-d. Comparison of adjectives §47. The false passive §75-f. Declension of the comparative and superlative §50.

Lesson XVII   Prepositions with the infinitive and *zu* §40. Compound nouns §26. Coordinating conjunctions §54.

Lesson XVIII   Expressions of measure §52-d. Contractions of prepositions §41. *wissen* and *lassen* §74. Review strong verbs.

Lesson XIX   Pronouns with intransitive verbs §28. Comparison of equal and unequal degrees §48. Subordinating conjunctions §55. Review regular and irregular weak verbs.

Lesson XX   Adverbial conjunctions §58. Reciprocal pronouns §29. Uses of the modal auxiliaries §73. Idiomatic expressions.

REFERENCE GRAMMAR
Table of Contents

THE ARTICLE

THE NOUN

The Article (Der Artikel)

§ 1 The Definite Article

a. The definite article is an adjective that in German agrees in number, gender, and case with the noun it modifies. There are three definite articles in German, which indicate the three different genders—masculine, feminine, and neuter.

MASCULINE	FEMININE	NEUTER
der **Vater**	*die* **Mutter**	*das* **Kind**
the father	*the* mother	*the* child

In German even inanimate objects take a masculine, feminine, or neuter article.

der **Stuhl**	*die* **Schule**	*das* **Schiff**
the chair	*the* school	*the* ship

Therefore, every noun must be learned with its proper article.

b. The endings *-chen* and *-lein* change any noun into a neuter noun, regardless of its original gender. These endings are used to form diminutives and terms of endearment.

die **Magd**	*das* **Mädchen**
the maid	*the* girl (little maid)
die **Frau**	*das* **Fräulein**
the woman	*the* miss (little woman)
der **Mann**	*das* **Männlein**
the man	*the* little man
	das **Männchen**
	the little man

When *-chen* or *-lein* are added, the stem vowel of the original noun, if *a, o, u,* or *au,* takes an umlaut: *ä, ö, ü, äu.*

c. The noun in German always takes a capital letter.

§ 2 The Article and the Noun

In German the noun and the pronoun have three genders. Each of the three genders has four cases expressing the different relationships of the noun or pronoun to the rest of the words in the sentence. As far as the noun is concerned, these case changes are indicated primarily by case changes in the article.

§ 3 Declension of the Definite Article with Nouns

a. The declension of the definite article with nouns in the singular is as follows:

	MASCULINE	FEMININE	NEUTER
NOM.:	*der* **Vater**	*die* **Mutter**	*das* **Mädchen**
	the father	*the* mother	*the* girl
GEN.:	*des* **Vaters**	*der* **Mutter**	*des* **Mädchens**
	of the father	*of the* mother	*of the* girl
DAT.:	*dem* **Vater**	*der* **Mutter**	*dem* **Mädchen**
	to, for the father	*to, for* the mother	*to, for* the girl
ACC.:	*den* **Vater**	*die* **Mutter**	*das* **Mädchen**
	the father	*the* mother	*the* girl

General rules for the declension of nouns in the singular:

1. All neuter nouns and most masculine nouns take an *s* in the genitive singular.

2. In monosyllabic nouns, an *e* is often inserted before the *s* in the genitive:

des Mannes
of the man

des Kindes
of the child

But this *e* is *never* inserted in polysyllabic words.

3. In nouns ending in *s* or *tz*, an *e* must be inserted before the s of the genitive:

des Fusses
of the foot

des Schatzes
of the treasure

4. Only the accusative masculine article differs in form from the nominative. The feminine and neuter accusatives are the same as the nominative.

5. The genitive and the dative forms of feminine articles are alike.

6. Feminine nouns never take an ending in the singular.

b. All three genders have the same article declension in the plural. The declension of the definite article with nouns in the plural is as follows:

	MASCULINE	FEMININE	NEUTER
NOM.:	*die* **Väter**	*die* **Mütter**	*die* **Mädchen**
	the fathers	*the* mothers	*the* girls
GEN.:	*der* **Väter**	*der* **Mütter**	*der* **Mädchen**
	of the fathers	*of the* mothers	*of the* girls
DAT.:	*den* **Vätern**	*den* **Müttern**	*den* **Mädchen**
	to, for the fathers	*to, for the* mothers	*to, for the* girls
ACC.:	*die* **Väter**	*die* **Mütter**	*die* **Mädchen**
	the fathers	*the* mothers	*the* girls

General rules for the declension of nouns in the plural:

1. The nominative and accusative cases of the article are alike.

2. All nouns take an *n*-ending in the dative plural. However, if the noun happens to end in an *n,* another *n* is not added in the dative plural.

§ 4   Basic Uses of Cases

a. The nominative case indicates the subject of the sentence.

> **Der Vater wohnt in Deutschland.**
> *The father* lives in Germany.

The predicate noun or pronoun after the verb *sein* (to be) is also in the nominative case.

> **Herr Miller ist *der Lehrer.***
> Mr. Miller is *the teacher.*

b. The genitive case indicates possession and is usually translated by "of the."

> **Die Mutter *des Kind(e)s* wohnt hier.**
> The mother *of the child* lives here.

> **Der Bruder *des Vaters* ist gekommen.**
> The brother *of the father* (or *the father's* brother) has come.

c. The dative case is used for the indirect object of the verb and is usually translated by "to the" or "for the."

> **Die Frau gibt *dem Sohn* ein Stück Kuchen.**
> The woman gives a piece of cake *to the son.*

> **Er kauft *dem Vater* einen Hut.**
> He buys *the father (for the father)* a hat.

d. The accusative is used for the direct object of the verb.

> **Ich kaufte *den Hut.***
> I bought *the hat.*

§ 5   The *der*-words

The declension of articles must be thoroughly mastered, since the inflection of adjectives, the different types of pronouns, etc. will refer back to article declension.

a. There are two unique groups of modifiers which serve to indicate a noun as distinct from other parts of speech. These are classified separately from the regular adjectives because they take their declensions from the definite and indefinite articles respectively.

b. The first group to be considered is the *der*-words, so called because they follow almost exactly the declension of the definite articles *der, die, das*. There are six *der*-words:

dieser	**jeder**	**solcher**
this	each	such (a)
jener	**welcher**	**mancher**
that	which	many a

The ending -*er* already indicates the nominative masculine singular case. Therefore the stems to which the inflectional endings are added are: *dies-, jen-, jed-, welch-, solch-, manch-*.

The *der*-words are declined in the singular as follows:

Nom.:	*dieser* **Mann**	*diese* Frau	*dieses* Kind
	this man	*this* woman	*this* child
Gen.:	*dieses* **Manns***	*dieser* Frau	*dieses* Kinds*
Dat.:	*diesem* **Mann***	*dieser* Frau	*diesem* Kind*
Acc.:	*diesen* **Mann**	*diese* Frau	*dieses* Kind

The *der*-words are declined in the plural as follows and the endings are the same for all genders:

Nom.: *diese* **Männer, Frauen, Kinder**
these men, women, children

Gen.: *dieser* **Männer, Frauen, Kinder**
of *these* men, women, children

Dat.: *diesen* **Männern, Frauen, Kindern**
to (for) *these* men, women, children

Acc.: *diese* **Männer, Frauen, Kinder**
these men, women, children

All six of the *der*-words are declined according to the above model. By comparing the article endings [see §3, a, b] with the paradigm of *dieser*, the following slight deviations from the *der* declension will be noticed:

1. In the nominative and accusative feminine, singular, and plural, the *i* of the article is dropped.

2. In the nominative and accusative neuter singular, the *a* of the article changes to *e*.

---

* Formerly, monosyllabic nouns, masculine and neuter, of the strong declension required an *e* before the genitive *s* of the singular (*des Mannes* "of the man", *des Kindes* "of the child"), and an *e* ending in dative singular (*dem Manne* "to the man", *dem Kinde* "to the child"). Today, these forms are usually used only in elevated language and style.

§ 6   The Indefinite Article

The indefinite article is similar to the definite article since it must also agree in number, gender, and case with the noun it modifies. The complete declension of *ein* (a) in the singular and *kein* (no) in the plural follows:

DECLENSION OF THE SINGULAR

	MASCULINE	FEMININE	NEUTER
NOM.:	*ein* **Mann** *a* man	*eine* **Frau** *a* woman	*ein* **Kind** *a* child
GEN.:	*eines* **Mann(e)s** *of a* man	*einer* **Frau** *of a* woman	*eines* **Kind(e)s** *of a* child
DAT.:	*einem* **Mann(e)** *to, for a* man	*einer* **Frau** *to, for a* woman	*einem* **Kind(e)** *to, for a* child
ACC.:	*einen* **Mann** *a* man	*eine* **Frau** *a* woman	*ein* **Kind** *a* child

DECLENSION OF THE PLURAL

	MASCULINE	FEMININE	NEUTER
NOM.:	*keine* **Männer** *no* men	*keine* **Frauen** *no* women	*keine* **Kinder** *no* children
GEN.:	*keiner* **Männer** *of no* men	*keiner* **Frauen** *of no* women	*keiner* **Kinder** *of no* children
DAT.:	*keinen* **Männern** *to, for no* men	*keinen* **Frauen** *to, for no* women	*keinen* **Kindern** *to, for* no children
ACC.:	*keine* **Männer** *no* men	*keine* **Frauen** *no* women	*keine* **Kinder** *no* children

The declension of the indefinite article is similar to that of the *der*-words (like *dieser*). The indefinite article differs from the declension of *dieser* in three instances: the masculine and neuter nominative singular and the neuter accusative singular do not take a case ending. All other cases, singular and plural, follow the declension of *dieser*.

§ 7   The *ein*-words

The possessive adjectives [see §8, a b] and the indefinite article *ein* (a) with its negative *kein* (no) are grouped together as *ein*-words, since they follow the declension of *ein* and *kein*. The complete list of the *ein*-words follows:

ein a	**kein** no
mein my	**unser** our
dein your (familiar)	**euer** your (familiar plural)
sein his	**ihr** their
ihr her	**Ihr** your (polite sing. & plur.)
sein its	

The *ein*-words are declined in the singular as follows:

MASCULINE

NOM.: *ein (kein, mein, dein, sein, ihr, unser, euer, ihr, Ihr)* Mann

GEN.: *eines (keines, meines, deines, seines, ihres, unseres*, eueres*, ihres, Ihres)* Mann(e)s

DAT.: *einem (keinem, meinem, deinem, seinem, ihrem, unserem, euerem*, ihrem, Ihrem)* Mann

ACC.: *einen (keinen, meinen, deinen, seinen, ihren, unseren, eueren, ihren, Ihren)* Mann

FEMININE

NOM.: *eine (keine, meine, deine, seine, ihre, unsere, euere, ihre, Ihre)* Frau

GEN.: *einer (keiner, meiner, deiner, seiner, ihrer, unserer, euerer, ihrer, Ihrer)* Frau

DAT.: *einer (keiner, meiner, deiner, seiner, ihrer, unserer, eurer, ihrer, Ihrer)* Frau

ACC.: *eine (keine, meine, deine, seine, ihre, unsere, eurere, ihre, Ihre)* Frau

NEUTER

NOM.: *ein (kein, mein, dein, sein, ihr, unser, euer, ihr, Ihr)* Kind

GEN.: *eines (keines, meines, deines, seines, ihres, unseres, eueres, ihres, Ihres)* Kind(e)s

DAT.: *einem (keinem, meinem, deinem, seinem, ihrem, unserem euerem, ihrem, Ihrem)* Kind

ACC.: *ein (kein, mein, dein, sein, ihr, unser, euer, ihr, Ihr)* Kind

The *ein*-words are declined in the plural as follows:

NOM.: *keine* Männer, Frauen, Kinder

GEN.: *keiner* Männern, Frauen, Kinder

DAT.: *keinen* Männern, Frauen, Kindern

ACC.: *keine* Männer, Frauen, Kinder

§ 8 Possessive Adjectives

a. A possessive adjective modifies a noun like any ordinary adjective and, therefore, it has all the characteristics of the adjective in German, namely:

1. It must agree in gender, number, and case with the noun it modifies.

2. Like an adjective, it can be used as a noun.

3. Possessive adjectives, however, do not follow the adjective declension. They are declined like the indefinite article *ein* and its negative *kein*. Therefore, the possessive adjectives and the indefinite article are grouped together under the category of *ein*-words.

---

* In *unser* (our) and *euer* (your) the *e* is often dropped before the *r* of the stem when a case ending is added.

b. The basic or stem form of the possessive adjective indicates the possessor to which it refers:

POSSESSIVE ADJECTIVE	PERSONAL PRONOUN
mein my, refers to	**ich** I, as possessor
dein your, refers to	**du** you, as possessor
sein his, refers to	**er** he, as possessor
ihr her, refers to	**sie** she, as possessor
sein its, refers to	**es** it, as possessor
unser our, refers to	**wir** we, as possessor
euer your, refers to	**ihr** you, as possessor
ihr their, refers to	**sie** they, as possessor
Ihr your, refers to	**Sie** you, as possessor

c. In German, however, the stem of the possessive adjective requires case endings according to the gender, number, and case of the noun that follows it.

Ich habe *mein* Buch.
I have *my* book.

Sie hat *ihren* Bleistift.
She has *her* pencil.

Wir lieben *unsere Mütter*.
We love *our* mothers.

***Unser* Vater ist nicht hier.**
Our father is not here.

Ich kenne *Ihren* Mann nicht.
I do not know *your* husband.

§ 9   Idiomatic Use of Articles

a. The definite article is used in German:

1. With the seasons, the months, and the days of the week.

Im *(in + dem)* Januar ist es meistens sehr kalt.
In January it is usually cold.

Wir fahren im *(in + dem)* Sommer auf das Land.
We shall go to the country *in* Summer.

Die Schule ist am *(an + dem)* Sonnabend geschlossen.
School is closed *on* Saturday.

2. In expressing the date:

Heute ist *der* 20. Oktober.
Today is October 20th.

Berlin, *den* 20. Oktober 19...
Berlin, October 20th, 19........

3. With abstract nouns:

> **Das Leben ist doch schön.**
> Life is beautiful.
>
> **Sie kämpfen für die Freiheit.**
> They are fighting for liberty.

4. With parts of the body or personal possessions when there is no doubt as to the possessor:

> **Er setzt den Hut auf.**
> He puts on *his* hat.
>
> **Sie wusch sich die Hände.**
> She washed *her* hands.

5. With proper names when they are preceded by an adjective:

> **der kleine Fritz**   **die arme Marie**
> *little* Fred   *poor* Mary

Otherwise, the article is omitted.

> **Fritz ist klein.**   **Marie ist arm.**
> Fred is small.   Mary is poor.

6. After the prepositions *in* (in, into), *nach* (after), *vor* (before), *zu* (to), in such expressions as:

> **Sie gehen in die Schule.**   **Sie sind in der Schule.**
> They go *to* school.   They are *in* school.
>
> **nach dem Abendessen**   **vor dem Frühstück**
> *after* supper   *before* breakfast
>
> **zum (zu + dem) Frühstück**
> *for* breakfast

7. With feminine countries (countries are usually neuter in German):

> **die Schweiz**   **die Türkei**
> Switzerland   Turkey
>
> **die Tschechoslowakei**
> Czechoslovakia

8. If the name of the country is always used in the plural, a plural form of the definite article *must* precede it:

> **die Vereinigten Staaten**   **die Niederlande**
> the United States   the Netherlands

9. With names of streets and squares:

> **Er wohnt in der Parkstrasse [am (an + dem) Potsdamer Platz].**
> He lives in Park Street (on Potsdamer Square).

10. The article, definite or indefinite, and possessive adjectives must be repeated if the nouns connected are of different genders:

> **mein Vater und meine Mutter**
> *my* father and mother
>
> **der Mann und die Frau**
> *the* man and woman

11. Before *meist* (most):

die meister Leute
most people

b. The indefinite article is omitted in German:

1. In referring to vocation, nationality, occupation, etc.:

Er ist Arzt.
He is *a* physician.

BUT:

Er ist *ein* guter Arzt.
He is *a* good physician.

Meine Mutter ist Amerikanerin.
My mother is *an* American.

Der junge Mann ist Student.
The young man is *a* student.

Meine Freundin ist Witwe.
My friend is *a* widow.

2. In certain phrases:

Ich habe Kopfschmerzen (Zahnschmerzen).
I have *a* headache (*a* toothache).

c. The definite article instead of the indefinite article is used:

Zweimal *die* Woche geht er ins Kino.
Twice *a* week he goes to the movies.

Das Zimmer kostet sechs Mark *den* Tag.
The room costs six marks *a* day.

Die Äpfel kosten 20 Pfennig *das* Pfund.
The apples cost twenty pennies *a* pound.

The Noun (Das Hauptwort)

§ 10   The Declension of Nouns

The declension of nouns is perhaps the most difficult aspect of German grammar. Nouns are classified according to the endings and forms which they take in the plural. There are three declensions:

1. Strong declension

2. Weak declension

3. Mixed declension

a. The strong declension is so called because the nouns belonging to this declension add different endings in the plural and the stem vowel is often modified in the plural by an umlaut.

1. All masculine and neuter nouns of the strong declension are distinguished by an *s* ending in the singular genitive.

2. Feminine nouns, whether strong or weak, take no ending in the singular.

3. The dative plural of all strong nouns is formed by adding -*n* or -*en* to the nominative plural of the noun. If the noun happens to end in -*n*, the -*(e)n* of the dative plural is not added:

das Mädchen	die Mädchen	den Mädchen
the girl	the girls	to the girls (dative plural)

b. The strong declension is subdivided into three classes:

1. The first class does not add an ending in the plural.

2. The second class adds -*e* to the nominative singular to form the plural.

3. The third class adds -*er* to the nominative singular of the noun to form the plural.

§ 11 Class I of the Strong Declension

a. No ending is added (except -*n* in the dative plural) and the stem vowel of the masculine noun frequently takes an umlaut, *a* changing to *ä*, *o* to *ö*, *u* to *ü*, and *au* to *äu*.

SINGULAR

NOM.:	der Vater	der Bruder	der Vogel
	the father	the brother	the bird
GEN.:	des Vater	des Bruders	des Vogels
DAT.:	dem *Vater*	dem Bruder	dem Vogel
ACC.:	den Vater	den Bruder	den Vogel
NOM.:	der Wagen	das Mädchen	die Mutter
	the car	the girl	the mother
GEN.:	des Wagens	des Mädchens	der Mutter
DAT.:	dem Wagen	dem Mädchen	der Mutter
ACC.:	den Wagen	das Mädchen	die Mutter

PLURAL

NOM.:	die Väter	die Brüder	die Vögel
GEN.:	der Väter	der Brüder	der Vögel
DAT.:	den Vätern	den Brüdern	den Vögeln
ACC.:	die Väter	die Brüder	die Vögel
NOM.:	die Wagen	die Mädchen	die Mütter
GEN.:	der Wagen	der Mädchen	der Mütter
DAT.:	den Wagen	den Mädchen	den Müttern
ACC.:	die Wagen	die Mädchen	die Mütter

b. To Class I belong:

1. Only masculine and neuter nouns; there are, however two exceptions: *die Mutter* and *die Tochter*.

2. All masculine and neuter nouns ending in -*el*, -*en*, -*er*.

3. All diminutives ending in *-chen* and *-lein,* which are always neuter.

4. Neuter nouns with the prefix *ge-* and suffix *-e: das Gemüse* (the vegetable), *die Gemüse* (the vegetables).

There are no monosyllabic nouns in this class.

§ 12 Class II of the Strong Declension

a. This plural is formed by adding *-e* to the nominative singular of the noun. Most nouns of this class require an umlaut, except the neuter nouns.

SINGULAR

NOM.:	der Sohn	die Hand	das Jahr
	the son	the hand	the year
GEN.:	des Sohns	der Hand	des Jahrs
DAT.:	dem Sohn	der Hand	dem Jahr
ACC.:	den Sohn	die Hand	das Jahr

NOM.:	die Nacht	der Tag	der Monat
	the night	the day	the month
GEN.:	der Nacht	des Tags	des Monats
DAT.:	der Nacht	dem Tag	dem Monat
ACC.:	die Nacht	den Tag	den Monat

PLURAL

NOM.:	die Söhne	die Hände	die Jahre
GEN.:	der Söhne	der Hände	der Jahre
DAT.:	den Söhnen	den Händen	den Jahren
ACC.:	die Söhne	die Hände	die Jahre

NOM.:	die Nächte	die Tage	die Monate
GEN.:	der Nächte	der Tage	der Monate
DAT.:	den Nächten	den Tagen	den Monaten
ACC.:	die Nächte	die Tage	die Monate

NOTE: *Tag, Jahr,* and *Monat* are three of the most commonly used nouns which do not take an umlaut in the plural.

b. To Class II belong:

1. Many nouns of one syllable, predominantly masculine nouns, some neuter, and also a few feminine nouns.

2. Nouns of more than one syllable, masculine, neuter, and feminine, ending in *-ig, -ing, -ling, -nis* (here the *s* is doubled before the plural ending: *-isse*) , *-sal, -kunft.*

3. Compound nouns in which the last component consists of a monosyllabic noun belonging to Class II:

der Zu*fall*	der Blei*stift*
the coincidence	the pencil

§ 13   Class III of the Strong Declension

a. The nominative plural of this class is formed by adding *-er* to the nominative singular. The stem vowel always takes an umlaut.

SINGULAR

NOM.:	der Mann	das Kind	das Haus
	the man	the child	the house
GEN.:	des Manns	des Kinds	des Hauses
DAT.:	dem Mann	dem Kind	dem Haus
ACC.:	den Mann	das Kind	das Haus

NOM.:	das Land	der Irrtum
	the land	the error
GEN.:	des Lands	des Irrtums
DAT.:	dem Land	dem Irrtum
ACC.:	das Land	den Irrtum

PLURAL

NOM.:	die Männer	die Kinder	die Häuser
GEN.:	der Männer	der Kinder	der Häuser
DAT.:	den Männern	den Kindern	den Häusern
ACC.:	die Männer	die Kinder	die Häuser

NOM.:	die Länder	die Irrtümer
GEN.:	der Länder	der Irrtümer
DAT.:	den Ländern	den Irrtümern
ACC.:	die Länder	die Irrtümer

b. To Class III belong:

1. Primarily monosyllablic neuter nouns, but also a few masculine nouns.

2. There are no feminine nouns in this class.

3. All nouns with the suffix *-tum*.

c. The most important monosyllabic nouns of this class include:

NEUTER

das Bild	das Feld	das Land	das Tal
the picture	the field	the country	the valley
das Buch	das Gras	das Licht	das Volk
the book	the grass	the light, candle	the people
das Dach	das Haus	das Lied	das Wort
the roof	the house	the song	the word
das Dorf	das Kind	das Nest	
the village	the child	the nest	
das Ei	das Kleid	das Schloss	
the egg	the dress	the castle	

MASCULINE

| der Gott | der Mann | der Wald | der Ort |
| the God | the man | the forest | the place |

§ 14 The Weak Declension of Nouns

This declension is called weak because there is no modification of the stem vowel and the plural is formed uniformly by adding -(e)n to the nominative singular in all four cases of the plural.

a. The feminine forms, which predominate in the weak declension, are as follows:

SINGULAR

Nom.:	die Frau the woman	die Tür the door	die Schule the school
Gen.:	der Frau	der Tür	der Schule
Dat.:	der Frau	der Tür	der Schule
Acc.:	die Frau	die Tür	die Schule

Nom.:	die Schwester the sister	die Schneiderin the dressmaker
Gen.:	der Schwester	der Schneiderin
Dat.:	der Schwester	der Schneiderin
Acc.:	die Schwester	die Schneiderin

NOTE: As mentioned earlier, feminine nouns never take endings in the singular.

PLURAL

Nom.:	die Frauen	die Türen	die Schulen
Gen.:	der Frauen	der Türen	der Schulen
Dat.:	den Frauen	den Türen	den Schulen
Acc.:	die Frauen	die Türen	die Schulen

Nom.:	die Schwestern	die Schneiderinnen
Gen.:	der Schwestern	der Schneiderinnen
Dat.:	den Schwestern	den Schneiderinnen
Acc.:	die Schwestern	die Schneiderinnen

NOTE: As can be seen from the example of *Schneiderinnen*, feminine nouns ending in -*in* double the *n* of this feminine suffix before the plural ending -*en* is added in order to retain the original pronunciation of short *i* of the ending -*in*.

b. Although the weak declension is fundamentally a declension of feminine nouns, it does contain a certain number of masculine nouns which take an -(e)n ending in the singular as well as in the plural, with the exception of the nominative singular.

SINGULAR

Nom.:	der Knabe the boy	der Herr the gentleman	der Mensch the human being
Gen.:	des Knaben	des Herrn	des Menschen
Dat.:	dem Knaben	dem Herrn	dem Menschen
Acc.:	den Knaben	den Herrn	den Menschen

Nom.:	der Student	der Philosoph	
	the student	the philosopher	
Gen.:	des Studenten	des Philosophen	
Dat.:	dem Studenten	dem Philosophen	
Acc.:	den Studenten	den Philosophen	

PLURAL

Nom.:	die Knaben	die Herren	die Menschen
Gen.:	der Knaben	der Herren	der Menschen
Dat.:	den Knaben	den Herren	den Menschen
Acc.:	die Knaben	die Herren	die Menschen

Nom.:	die Studenten	die Philosophen
Gen.:	der Studenten	der Philosophen
Dat.:	den Studenten	den Philosophen
Acc.:	die Studenten	die Philosophen

NOTE: When *Herr* is used before a name, to mean "Mister," it is always inflected, except in the nominative:

Herr Miller ist mein Freund.
Mr. Miller is my friend.

Ich fahre mit *Herrn* Miller nach Deutschland.
I am going to Germany with Mr. Miller.

c. To the weak declension belong:

1. Many monosyllabic feminine nouns and most feminine nouns of more than one syllable.

2. All masculine nouns ending in -e denoting masculine beings:

der Junge	**der Löwe**	**der Rabe**
the boy	the lion	the raven, crow
der Knabe		
the boy		

3. A few monosyllabic masculine nouns:

der Graf	**der Narr**	**der Mensch**
the count	the fool	the human being

4. Some foreign masculine nouns:

der Präsident	**der Philosoph**	**der Student**
the president	the philosopher	the student

§ 15   The Mixed Declension of Nouns

The name "mixed declension" indicates that this declension is a combination of the other two declensions, namely, the strong and weak declensions.

a. The singular of nouns belonging to the mixed declension is strong; i.e. the nouns take an -s, in the genitive case singular, while the plural is weak, taking -(e)n in all four cases. Since the plural of these nouns is weak, they do not take an umlaut.

SINGULAR

Nom.:	der Schmerz	der Vetter	der Doktor
	the pain	the cousin	the doctor
Gen.:	des Schmerzes	des Vetters	des Doktors
Dat.:	dem Schmerz	dem Vetter	dem Doktor
Acc.:	den Schmerz	den Vetter	den Doktor

Nom.:	das Auge	das Studium
	the eye	the study
Gen.:	des Auges	des Studiums
Dat.:	dem Auge	dem Studium
Acc.:	das Auge	das Studium

PLURAL

Nom.:	die Schmerzen	die Vettern	die Doktoren
Gen.:	der Schmerzen	der Vettern	der Doktoren
Dat.:	den Schmerzen	den Vettern	den Doktoren
Acc.:	die Schmerzen	die Vettern	die Doktoren

Nom.:	die Augen	die Studien
Gen.:	der Augen	der Studien
Dat.:	den Augen	den Studien
Acc.:	die Augen	die Studien

b. To the mixed declension belong:

1. A few *masculine* and *neuter* nouns:

der Nachbar the neighbor	**das Bett** the bed
der Bauer the farmer	**das Ende** the end
der See the lake	**das Hemd** the shirt
der Staat the state	**das Ohr** the ear

2. Some nouns derived from the Latin or Greek.

das Datum (die Daten)   **das Gymnasium (die Gymnasien)**
the date   the classical state school

das Drama (die Dramen)
the drama

3. There are no feminine nouns in the mixed declensions.

§ 16   Irregularly Declined Nouns

There are a few nouns which cannot be classified under the three main declensions.

a. The following nouns, although declined like the weak declension in the singular, also take an *-s* in the genitive singular, like strong nouns. They are weak in the plural, ending in *-(e)n,* and never take an umlaut.

SINGULAR

NOM.:	der Glaube the belief	der Name the name	das Herz the heart
GEN.:	des Glaubens	des Namens	des Herzens
NOM.:	dem Glauben	dem Namen	dem Herzen
GEN.:	den Glauben	den Namen	das Herz

NOM.:	der Wille the will	der Gedanke the thought	
GEN.:	des Willens	des Gedankens	
DAT.:	dem Willen	dem Gedanken	
ACC.:	den Willen	den Gedanken	

PLURAL

NOM.:	die Glauben	die Namen	die Herzen
GEN.:	der Glauben	der Namen	der Herzen
DAT.:	den Glauben	den Namen	den Herzen
ACC.:	die Glauben	die Namen	die Herzen

NOM.:	die Willen	die Gedanken	
GEN.:	der Willen	der Gedanken	
DAT.:	den Willen	den Gedanken	
ACC.:	die Willen	die Gedanken	

b. To this group belong a few masculine nouns ending in -e (see above examples) and the neuter noun *das Herz* (the heart).

c. A limited number of nouns, derived from foreign languages, form their plural by adding -s to the nominative singular. These nouns are strong in the singular. No feminine nouns are ever thus declined. The principal parts of some of these nouns are:

	SINGULAR	PLURAL
NOM.:	das Auto the auto	die Autos
GEN.:	des Autos	
NOM.:	das Kino the theater (film)	die Kinos
GEN.:	des Kinos	
NOM.:	das Hotel the hotel	die Hotels
GEN.:	des Hotels	
NOM.:	das Piano the piano	die Pianos
GEN.:	des Pianos	

NOTE 1: Some nouns have two different plural forms, and their meanings are different. A few examples follow:

SINGULAR	PLURAL	
das Wort the word	die Wörter the words	die Worte meaningful, connected words
das Licht the light, candle	die Lichte the candles	die Lichter the lights
die Bank the bench, bank	die Bänke the benches	die Banken the banks
das Band the ribbon (tie)	die Bänder the ribbons	die Bande the ties (of friendship)

NOTE 2: Some words also may have two different articles in which case they also have different meanings:

das Band the ribbon, tie	(see above)
der Band the volume	die Bände the volumes
der Tor the fool	die Toren the fools
das Tor the gate	die Tore the gates

d. All plurals of foreign words formed by adding -s to the nominative take -s in all cases of the plural and do not show the -n otherwise required in the dative plural.

§ 17 Principal Parts of the Noun

The declension of the German noun in the plural is rather complicated, since there are really five possibilities for the formation of the plural. It is therefore best to learn the principal parts of the most commonly used nouns.

a. The three principal parts of the noun are:

1. The nominative singular:

der Mann	die Frau	das Kind

2. The genitive singular:

des Manns	der Frau	des Kinds

3. The nominative plural:

die Männer	die Frauen	die Kinder

b. If these three cases of a noun are known, all other cases can be formed according to definite rules outlined in the sections on the declension of nouns.

§ 18 Declension of Proper Nouns

a. A proper noun is a name designating a particular person, country, city, river, etc.

1. Proper names are usually not declined in German, with the exception that they do usually take an ending in the genitive case.

> **Georgs Mutter kommt heute nicht.**
> George's mother is not coming today.
>
> **Karls Buch liegt auf dem Tisch.**
> Charles' book is lying on the table.

2. Even feminine proper names take an -s in the genitive case.

> **Maries Freundin ist in Europa.**
> Mary's girl friend is in Europe.

3. The genitive s in the declension of proper nouns is not separated from the noun by an apostrophe as in English. An apostrophe is used only as indicated below.

4. When the proper noun ends in a sibilant (-s, -sch, -ss, -z, -tz, -x), the -s is omitted and an apostrophe follows the noun.

> **Hans' und Max' Vater wohnt in Deutschland.**
> Hans's and Max's father is living in Germany.
>
> **Fritz' Schwester macht eine Reise durch Europa.**
> Fred's sister is taking a trip through Europe.

b. Sometimes the genitive s is used in expressions of place. However, the preposition *von* is generally used with a proper noun and the noun shows no change in form.

> **die Länder Europas**   **Deutschlands Dichter**
> the countries of Europe   the poets of Germany
> BUT:
>
> **die Häuser *von* Berlin**
> the houses of Berlin
>
> **die grossen Städte *von* Deutschland**
> the large cities of Germany

c. Whenever a proper noun is preceded by an adjective, the noun does not take an s in the genitive, but the article is used in the genitive.

> **Goethes Werke**
> the works of Goethe
> BUT:
>
> **die Werke *des* jungen Goethe**
> the works of young Goethe
>
> **Frau Millers Sohn**
> Mrs. Miller's son
> BUT:
>
> **der Sohn *der* alten Frau Miller**
> the son of old Mrs. Miller

d. When a title is used with a proper noun, the proper noun is in the genitive and the title is not. The proper noun, however, is uninflected when preceded by an article. But, when the title is used without the proper noun, it must be in the genitive case.

Doktor Millers Sohn
Doctor Miller's son

der Sohn des Doktor Miller
the son of Dr. Miller

BUT:

der Sohn des Doktors
the son of the doctor

König Friedrichs Feldzug
King Frederick's campaign

der Feldzug des König Friedrich
the campaign of King Frederick

BUT:

der Feldzug des Königs
the campaign of the king

e. When adjectives have become part of a proper name and follow the name, the adjectives are declined in all cases:

Karl der Grosse lebte im 8. Jahrhundert.
Charles the Great lived in eighth century.

Der Sohn Karl des Grossen war Ludwig der Fromme.
The son of Charles the Great was Ludwig the Pious.

Sie kämpften mit Karl dem Grossen.
They fought against (with) Charles the Great.

Sie lesen über Karl den Grossen.
They read about Charles the Great.

§ 19   Determining the Gender of a Noun

There are certain characteristics by which the gender of many German nouns can be determined.

a. Masculine gender can be recognized by the following:

1. Almost all nouns ending -en, except nouns derived from the infinitive, are masculine:

der Garten the garden	**der Laden** the store	**der Boden** the floor
der Faden the thread	**der Norden** the north	

2. Nouns ending in -er denoting a person, a tool, or an instrument, are masculine:

der Lehrer the teacher	**der Gärtner** the gardener	**der Künstler** the artist
der Hammer the hammer		

3. Nouns ending in -ig, ich, -ling, -mus are always masculine.

der **König**	der **Käfig**	der **Teppich**
the king	the cage	the rug
der **Frühling**	der **Neuling**	der **Nationalismus**
the spring	the novice	the nationalism
der **Idealismus**		
the idealism		

4. The seasons, days of the week, months, times of the day (except *die Nacht*) are masculine.

der **Morgen**	der **Sommer**	der **Montag**
the morning	the summer	(the) Monday
der **Abend**	der **Mai**	der **Nachmittag**
the evening	(the) May	the afternoon

b. Feminine gender can be recognized by the following:

1. Most nouns ending in -e (except nouns denoting masculine beings and a few neuters) are feminine.

die **Schule**	die **Rose**
the school	the rose

2. Nouns with the suffixes -ei, -heit, -keit, -in, -ion, -tion, -schaft, -tät, -ung are always feminine and belong to the weak declension.

die **Bäckerei**	die **Religion**	die **Freundin**
the bakery	the religion	the girl friend
die **Tapferkeit**	die **Universität**	die **Zeitung**
the bravery	the university	the newspaper
die **Verwandschaft**	die **Schönheit**	die **Nation**
the relationship	the beauty	the nation

c. Neuter gender can be recognized by the following:

1. Diminutives formed with the suffixes -chen and -lein are always neuter.

das **Mädchen**	das **Fräulein**	das **Hündchen**
the girl	(the) Miss	the little dog

2. All nouns derived from infinitives are neuter.

das **Singen**	das **Schreiben**	das **Tanzen**
the singing	the writing	the dancing

3. Nouns ending in -um and -ium are neuter.

das **Datum**	das **Studium**
the date	the study

4. All metals are neuter.

das **Silber**	das **Gold**	das **Kupfer**
(the) silver	(the) gold	(the) copper

The above rules for determining the gender of many nouns are helpful, but the best method is still to learn all nouns with the proper article, since it is impossible to determine the gender of every noun by rules.

§ 20   Compound Nouns

The German language abounds in compound nouns; for example:

das Schlafzimmer (**der Schlaf** the sleep + **das Zimmer** the room) the bedroom

die Hafergrütze (**der Hafer** oats + **die Grütze** grits) the oatmeal

der Hausherr (**das Haus** the house + **der Herr** the master) the master of the house

The last component of a compound noun is the most important word; it gives the basic meaning of the noun as a whole, while all words preceding this key word are modifiers of it. Therefore gender and declension are almost always determined by the last component of a compound noun.

der Badezimmerschlüssel (**das Bad** the bath + **das Zimmer** the room + **der Schlüssel** the key) the key to the bathroom door.

The principal parts of the declension of this compound are:

NOM. SING.:   **der Badezimmerschlüssel**
GEN. SING.:   **des Badezimmerschlüssels**
NOM. PLUR.:   **die Badezimmerschlüssel**

§ 21   Uses of the Nominative Case

The nominative case is used as:

a. The subject of a sentence.

Der Mann hat kein Geld.
The man has no money.

b. The predicate nominative, after the verb *sein,* to be.

Das Baby ist *ein Knabe.*
The baby is a *boy.*

Er ist *der Freund* meines Bruders.
He is my brother's *friend (the friend* of my brother).

§ 22   Uses of the Genitive Case

The genitive case has these uses:

a. It expresses possession and usually stands for "of the," "of my," etc. in English.

Der Vater *der Kinder* ist in Deutschland.
The father *of the children (the children's* father) is in Germany.

Der Freund *meines Bruders*
The friend *of my brother (my brother's* friend).

But, in connection with countries and cities *von* of is generally used:

Berlin ist die Hauptstadt *von Preussen.*
Berlin is the capital *of Prussia.*

Der Hafen *von Hamburg* ist sehr bekannt.
The harbor *of Hamburg* is well known.

b. It is used after certain prepositions. [See §39].

Trotz seiner Erkältung geht er ins Theater.
In spite of his cold, he is going to the theater.

c. It expresses indefinite time.

Eines Tages besuchte er uns.
One day he visited us.

Eines Morgens trat er in mein Zimmer.
One morning he stepped into my room.

§ 23   Uses of the Dative Case

The dative case has these uses:

a. As indirect object often translated with "to" or "for" in English.

Sie gibt dem Bruder ein Buch.
She gives a book to her (the) brother.

b. After certain prepositions which always require the dative case. [See §37].

Nach dem Abendessen schläft er.
After supper he sleeps.

c. After "doubtful" prepositions if they indicate a place where something is or takes place. [See §38].

Sie wohnen in diesem Haus.
They are living in this house.

Er ging in dem Zimmer auf und ab.
He went back and forth in the room.

d. After "doubtful" prepositions in expressions of time.

am Morgen
in the morning

in der Nacht
at night

im 12. Jahrhundert
in the 12th century

vor einem Jahr
a year ago

im Frühling
in spring

im Februar
in February

e. As the sole object after certain verbs.

antworten answer	**folgen** follow	**gleichen** resemble
begegnen meet	**gefallen** please	**helfen** help
danken thank	**gehören** belong to	**passen** fit, suit
dienen serve	**gehorchen** obey	**schaden** harm
(er)scheinen appear	**genügen** suffice	**(ver)trauen** trust
fehlen be missing	**glauben** believe	

Er antwortet der Mutter.
He answers his (the) mother.

Ich danke dem Mann für die Blumen.
I thank the man for the flowers.

Die Schuhe passen *meinem Sohn* nicht.
The shoes do not fit *my son.*

f. In the so-called "dative of interest," used very commonly in German with expressions concerning feeling, reactions, etc.

Wie geht es *Ihnen?*
How are you?

Es tut *mir* leid.
I am sorry.

Es ist *mir* recht.
It suits me (It is all right with me.)

§ 24   Uses of the Accusative Case

The accusative case is used:

a. As the direct object of a verb.

Sie liest *das Buch.*
She reads *the book.*

Er hat *einen Brief* geschrieben.
He wrote (has written) *a letter.*

b. After certain prepositions which always require the accusative. [See §36].

Dieser Hut ist *für deinen Vater.*
This hat is *for your father.*

Wir gingen *ohne den Bruder* ins Theater.
We went to the theater *without our (the) brother.*

c. After "doubtful" prepositions if they indicate a motion toward a place. [See §38].

Sie kommen *in das Haus.*
They are coming *into the house.*

Das Mädchen geht *an das Fenster* und sieht *in den Garten.*
The girl goes *to the window* and looks at *(into)* the garden.

d. In expressions of time.

1. Definite time without preposition:

Diesen Sommer fahre ich nach Deutschland.
This summer, I am going to Germany.

2. Extent of time or duration:

Wir haben *den ganzen Tag* gearbeitet.
We worked (have worked) *all day.*

Sie sind schon *einen Monat* in Berlin.
They have been (already) in Berlin a month.

e. To express wishes and salutations.

Guten Morgen!
Good morning!

Gute Nacht!
Good night!

Herzlichen Gruss!
Best regards! (*lit.,* Hearty greeting!)

The Pronoun (Das Pronom)

§ 25   Personal Pronouns

a. There are three genders of personal pronouns in German.

MASCULINE	FEMININE	NEUTER
er	sie	es
he	she	it

b. The declension of personal pronouns is as follows:

SINGULAR

	1ST PERSON	2ND PERSON	3RD PERSON		
NOM.:	ich	du	er	sie	es
	I	you	he	she	it
GEN.:	(meiner)	(deiner)	(seiner)	(ihrer)	(seiner)
	of me	of you	of him	of her	of it
DAT.:	mir	dir	ihm	ihr	ihm
	to me	to you	to him	to her	to it
ACC.:	mich	dich	ihn	sie	es
	me	you	him	her	it

PLURAL

				POLITE FORM
NOM.:	wir	ihr	sie	Sie
	we	you	they	you
GEN.:	(unser)	(euer)	(ihrer)	(Ihrer)
	of us	of you	of them	of you
DAT.:	uns	euch	ihnen	Ihnen
	to us	to you	to them	to you
ACC.:	uns	euch	sie	Sie
	us	you	they	you

1. The forms of the genitive case have been put in parenthesis because they are rarely used in modern German.

2. The endings of the third person, singular and plural, are similar to the equivalent case endings of the definite article: *der—er, die—sie, das—es.* Accusative:*den—ihn, die—sie, das—es.* Dative: *dem—ihm, der—ihr, dem—ihm, den—ihnen,* etc.

3. Notice that the pronoun "you" can be translated three ways in German:

(a) The *du* form, the so-called familiar form singular, is used in addressing the Deity, a member of the family, a close friend, a child, a pet. It corresponds to the old English form "thou."

(b) The plural of *du* is *ihr* and is used in speaking to more than one person mentioned under *a* above.

(c) *Sie* is the so-called polite form, used in addressing mere acquaintances or strangers, whether singular or plural. It has the same form as the third person plural, and to distinguish it from this form it is written with a capital letter. It should be noted that in German one must be on very intimate terms with a person before changing from *Sie* to *du*. If in any doubt as to which form is suitable, use *Sie*.

c. Personal pronouns are affected by the same rule as are the nouns for which they stand; i.e., a pronoun changes its form according to the gender, case, and number of the noun it replaces:

Der Sohn geht mit *dem Vater*.
The son goes with *his* father.

Er geht mit *ihm*.
He goes with *him*.

Die Mutter grüsst *die Frau*.
The mother greets *the woman*.

Sie grüsst *sie*.
She greets *her*.

d. The grammatical gender (masculine, feminine, or neuter) rather than the natural gender of things determines the gender of the corresponding pronoun:

Der Tisch ist braun.	**Er ist braun.**
The table is brown.	*It is brown.*
Die Mutter sieht die Kabine.	**Sie sieht sie.**
The mother sees the cabin.	*She sees it.*
Die Frau gibt dem Kind einen Apfel.	**Sie gibt ihn ihm.**
The woman gives an apple to the child.	*She gives it to him.*

e. However, when pronouns are substituted for *das Mädchen* and *das Fräulein*, the feminine form of the personal pronoun is used, although grammatically speaking, these words are of neuter gender.

Sie sprechen mit *dem Mädchen*.	**Sie sprechen mit *ihr*.**
They are speaking with *the girl*.	They are speaking with *her*.
Kennen Sie *das Fräulein?*	**Kennen Sie *sie?***
Do you know *the lady?*	Do you know *her?*

§ 26 Pronominal Compounds

a. Pronominal compounds constitute the only exception to the general rule that the pronoun (whether it refers to a person or an object) agrees with the grammatical gender, number, and case of the noun it replaces.

1. Whenever a personal pronoun referring to an object or idea is used in English after a preposition, e.g. "of it", "with it", etc., in German *da* is used instead of the proper pronoun and the

preposition is compounded with this particle: *davon, damit,* etc.
These compounds can never refer to people.

> **Er schreibt mit der Feder.**
> He writes with the pen.
>
> **Er schreibt *damit.***
> He writes *with it.*

BUT:

> **Er hat die Feder.**
> He has the pen.
>
> **Er hat *sie.***
> He has it.
>
> **Die Kinder spielen mit den Puppen.**
> The children are playing with the dolls.
>
> **Sie spielen *damit.***
> They are playing *with them.*
>
> **Sie sprachen von der Reise.**
> They spoke about the trip.
>
> **Sie sprachen *davon.***
> They spoke *about it.*
>
> **Sie sitzt auf dem Stuhl.**
> She is sitting on the chair.
>
> **Sie sitzt *darauf.***
> She is sitting *on it.*

2. If the preposition begins with a vowel, an *r* is inserted between
da and the preposition:

> **da + r + an = daran**
> **da + r + auf = darauf**

b. These compound pronouns are not declined and can refer either
to the dative or to the accusative case, singular or plural.

c. Once again, note the difference between the two pairs of sentences that follow.

> **Sie denken an den Freund.**
> They are thinking of their (the) friend.
>
> **Sie denken an ihn.**
> They are thinking *of him.*

BUT:

> **Sie denken an die schöne Reise.**
> They are thinking of the beautiful trip.
>
> **Sie denken *daran.***
> They are thinking *of it.*

§ 27   The Reflexive Pronoun with Verb

a. The reflexive pronoun is a direct object referring back to the
subject and most such pronouns are in the accusative case. How-

ever, the third person singular and plural and also the polite forms have a special reflexive pronoun, *sich*.

b. The reflexive verb is either weak or strong and is conjugated accordingly.

sich freuen to be glad	*sich* waschen to wash oneself
ich freue *mich* I am glad	ich wasche *mich* I wash myself
du freust *dich* you are glad	du wäschst *dich* you wash yourself
er freut *sich* he is glad	er wäscht *sich* he washes himself
wir freuen *uns* we are glad	wir waschen *uns* we wash ourselves
ihr freut *euch* you are glad	ihr wascht *euch* you wash yourselves
sie freuen *sich* they are glad	sie waschen *sich* they wash themselves
Sie freuen *sich* you are glad	Sie waschen *sich* you wash yourself

c. Verbs are used reflexively in German more often than in English, and many verbs which are reflexive in German are not reflexive in English. They are often used when the passive would be used in English.

sich setzen to sit down	*sich* freuen to be glad	*sich* interessieren to be interested

§ 28 Pronouns with Intransitive Verbs

a. Intransitive verbs followed by the dative case require pronouns in the dative too, except in the forms of third person, singular and plural, when *sich* is used.

sich helfen	to help oneself
ich helfe *mir* I help myself	wir helfen *uns* we help ourselves
du hilfst *dir* you help yourself	ihr helft *euch* you help yourselves
er hilft *sich* he helps himself	sie helfen *sich* they help themselves
	Sie helfen *sich* you help yourselves

b. Only *mir* and *dir* differ from the reflexive pronouns in the accusative case.

c. Since the dative case *mir, dir,* etc. is often translated in English by "for me," "to me," etc., the reflexive pronoun frequently expresses possession, translated in English with the possessive adjective:

Ich wasche *mir* die Hände.
I wash *my* hand (*lit.,* I wash *for me* the hands).

Du wäschst *dir* die Hände.
You wash *your* hands.

Er wäscht *sich* die Hände.
He washes *his* hands.

Wir waschen *uns* die Hände.
We wash *our* hands.

Ihr wascht *euch* die Hände.
You wash *your* hands.

Sie waschen *sich* die Hände.
They wash *their* hands.

Sie waschen *sich* die Hände.
You wash *your* hands.

Note the difference between these two sentences:

Sie kauft *sich* ein Kleid.
She buys a dress *for herself.*

Sie kauft *ihr* ein Kleid.
She buys a dress *for her.*

§ 29   Reciprocal Pronouns

The two reciprocal pronouns are *selbst* and *einander.*

a. *selbst* (herself, himself, themselves, etc.), used to stress or emphasize a fact or statement.

Er hat es *selbst* gesagt.
He has said it *himself.*

Sie machen sich die Kleider *selbst*.
They make their dresses *themselves.*

BUT:

Sie machen sich die Kleider.
They make their own dresses. (*lit.* They make themselves the dresses.)

b. *einander* (each other).

Sie sehen *einander* oft.

OR:

Sie sehen *sich* oft.
They often see each other.

c. *selbst* and *einander* are not reflexive pronouns and never change their form, that is, they are not declined.

§ 30   Possessive Adjectives Used as Pronouns

a. The possessive adjectives can be used as possessive pronouns.

Sie braucht ihre Feder und ich *meine*.
She needs her pen and I (need) *mine.*

Er schreibt mit seinem Bleistift und sie schreibt mit *ihrem*.
He writes with his pencil and she writes with *hers.*

b. They are inflected like *ein*-words, but the three cases of the singular masculine nominative, singular neuter nominative, and singular neuter accusative take an ending when the possessive adjective is used as a pronoun.

Ist das Ihr Hut, Herr Miller? Nein, das ist nicht meiner; es ist Ihrer.
Is that your hat, Mr. Miller? No, that is not *mine;* it is *yours.*

Wessen Kind ruft er; seins oder Ihrs?
Whose child does he call, *his* or *yours?*

Nehmen Sie mein Buch! Danke, ich habe mein(e)s.
Take my book. Thank you, I have *mine.*

Ihr Haus ist grösser also unsers.
Your house is larger than *ours.*

§ 31   Demonstrative Pronouns

The demonstrative pronouns are used instead of nouns and point out more emphatically the person or thing referred to.

a. The most common demonstrative pronouns in German are:

1. *dieser* (this one), referring to a person, thing, idea, near the speaker.

2. *jener* (that one), referring to a person, thing, etc., farther away from the speaker.

Dieser Berg ist hoch, *jener* ist nicht so hoch.
This mountain is high; *that* one is not so high.

Dieser hat es nicht getan sondern *jener*.
This one did not do it but *that one* (did).

War es dieses Kind? Nein, es war *jenes*.
Was it this child? No, it was *that one.*

The demonstrative pronouns *dieser* and *jener* are declined like the demonstrative adjective *dieser* (this).

b. Definite articles are also used as demonstrative pronouns and are then inflected like relative pronouns.

Dem kann ich das nicht geben.
To *him*, I am not able to give it.

Denen ist nicht zu helfen.
Those cannot be helped.

Der hat es nicht getan.
He did not do it.

c. *Dies* and *das* are often used uninflectedly at the beginning of a sentence when used as demonstratives:

Dies ist mein Freund.   **Das sind meine Schwestern.**
This is my friend.   *Those* are my sisters.

d. There are two demonstrative compound pronouns:

1. *Derselbe* (the same), compound of the definite article *der* and *selbe* (same). Therefore, the first part of the compound is de-

clined like the definite article; *selbe* takes the weak adjective declension:

	MASCULINE	SINGULAR FEMININE	NEUTER	PLURAL
NOM.:	*derselbe* the same	*dieselbe*	*dasselbe*	*dieselben*
GEN.:	*desselben*	*derselben*	*desselben*	*derselben*
DAT.:	*demselben*	*derselben*	*demselben*	*denselben*
ACC.:	*denselben*	*dieselbe*	*dasselbe*	*dieselben*

2. *Derjenige* (he who), rarely used in modern German, is declined in the same manner as *derselbe*.

§ 32   Interrogative Pronouns

a. Interrogative pronouns are used in asking questions. Their case endings correspond closely to the case endings of the definite article *der*.

	MASCULINE AND FEMININE	NEUTER
NOM.:	wer who	was what
GEN.:	wessen whose	(no genitive or dative form)
DAT.:	wem whom, to whom, for whom	
ACC.:	wen whom	was what

1. The nominative, dative, and accusative cases are like the forms of the definite article; the genitive case is different because -*sen* is added to the usual ending, *wes*+*sen*=*wessen*.

2. There is only one form in each of the four cases as in English, whether masculine or feminine, singular or plural.

Wer ist das?
Who is that (man *or* woman)?

Wessen Hut ist das?
Whose hat is this?

Wem haben Sie das Buch gegeben?
To whom have you given the book?

Mit wem sprechen Sie?
With *whom* are you speaking?

Wen sehen Sie?
Whom do you see?

Was hat er Ihnen gestern gesagt?
What did he tell you yesterday?

b. Questions expressed in English by "what" and a preposition, i.e., questions referring to an object, an idea, or an event, such as "of what", "with what", "on what", etc., are translated in German by *wovon, womit, worauf,* etc. In each case the interrogative *wo* is used with the required preposition. If the preposition happens to start with a vowel, an *r* is inserted between *wo* and the preposition to facilitate pronunciation: *worauf, woran, worin,* etc.

c. In the following sets of questions and answers, notice the difference in choice of interrogative when a person is referred to and when a thing or idea is referred to.

PERSON: **An *wen* denken Sie? Ich denke an meine Mutter in Amerika.**
Of *whom* are you thinking? I am thinking of my mother in America.

THING OR IDEA: ***Woran* denken Sie? Ich denke an den schönen gestrigen Tag.**
Of *what* are you thinking? I am thinking of the beautiful day yesterday.

PERSON: **Mit *wem* sprechen Sie? Ich spreche mit meinem Lehrer.**
With *whom* are you speaking? I am speaking with my teacher.

THING: ***Wovon* sprachen Sie? Wir sprachen von dem neuen Drama.**
Of *what* were you talking? We were talking about (of) the new drama.

§ 33 Interrogative Pronoun *was*, with *für*

a. In the expression *was für* (what kind of), *für* has no prepositional force and does not affect *ein* or the following noun. The word following takes whichever case the syntax of the sentence requires.

b. Where more than one object or person is referred to, *ein* is dropped.

***Was für* ein Mädchen ist sie?**
What kind of girl is she?

Mit *was für* einem Wagen fahren Sie?
In (with) *what kind of* car do you travel?

***Was für* Bücher haben Sie da?**
What kind of books do you have there?

§ 34 Relative Pronouns

A relative pronoun refers to its antecedent, thus establishing a relationship between this antecedent and the following clause, the so-called relative clause.

a. The declension of the relative pronoun in German is very similar to the declension of the definite article.

	SINGULAR			PLURAL
	MASCULINE	FEMININE	NEUTER	
NOM.:	der	die	das	die
	who	who	that, which	who, which
GEN.:	dessen	deren	dessen	deren
	whose	whose	of which	whose, of which
DAT.:	dem	der	dem	denen
	to whom	to whom	to which	to whom, to which
ACC.:	den	die	das	die
	whom	whom	that, which	whom, which

Der Mann, *der* dort steht, heisst Müller.
The man *who* is standing there is called Müller.

Die Frau, *deren* Tochter ich kenne, wohnt hier.
The woman *whose* daughter I know lives here.

Das ist das Kind, *dem* sie den Apfel gegeben hat.
That is the child to *whom* she gave the apple.

Der Hut, *den* er heute trägt, ist alt.
The hat *that* he is wearing today is an old one (*lit.*, is old).

Der Schreibtisch, an *dem* er sitzt, gehört mir.
The desk he is sitting at belongs to me.

Die Frauen, mit *denen* ich gestern gesprochen habe, sind meine Kusinen.
The women with *whom* I spoke yesterday are my cousins.

Das Mädchen, *das* die Arbeit heute nicht beenden kann, muss morgen wiederkommen.
The girl *who* cannot finish the work today must return tomorrow.

b. The uses of the relative pronoun are determined by the following rules:

1. The relative pronoun agrees in gender and number with its antecedent, i.e., the preceding noun to which it refers but its case is determined by its grammatical significance in the relative clause.

2. The relative clause is a dependent clause; therefore, the word order is transposed or "dependent", i.e., the verb is at the end of the clause. It is always the inflected (the changeable) part of the verb which comes last:

Der Mann, der dort *steht*, heisst Müller.
Das ist das Kind, dem sie den Apfel gegeben *hat*.
Das Mädchen, das die Arbeit heute nicht beenden *kann*, muss morgen wiederkommen.

3. The main clause into which the relative clause is inserted follows the general rule for word order.

4. The relative clause is always set off from the main clause by commas.

5. The relative pronoun can never be omitted in German as is often done in English.

NOTE: There is another form of the relative pronoun, *welch-* (which), not as commonly used as the form based on the article. The paradigm follows:

	SINGULAR			PLURAL
	MASCULINE	FEMININE	NEUTER	
NOM.:	welcher	welche	welches	welche
GEN.:	dessen	deren	dessen	deren
DAT.:	welchem	welcher	welchem	welchen
ACC.:	welchen	welche	welches	welche

The forms of the four genitives, singular and plural, are missing and therefore the forms of the relative pronoun derived from the article must be substituted.

c. When relative pronouns refer to an unknown or indefinite antecedent, they have the same form as interrogative pronouns, namely:

Nom.:	**wer** he who, whoever	**was** what, whatever, that
Gen.:	**wessen** whose	
Dat.:	**wem** whomever, to whom	
Acc.:	**wen** whomever, whom	**was** what, whatever, that

Unknown Antecedents:

Wer einmal lügt, dem glaubt man nicht.
He who lies once is never believed.

Wem ich glauben soll, weiss ich nicht.
I don't know whom to believe (*lit.,* Whomever I shall believe I do not know.)

Was ich habe, gehört dir.
Whatever I possess belongs to you.

Indefinite Antecedents:

Alles, was sie darüber gehört hat, stimmt.
All (*that*) she heard about it is correct.

Das ist das Schönste, was ich je gehabt habe.
That is the most beautiful thing (*that*) I have ever had.

§ 35   Indefinite Pronouns

There are three classes of indefinite pronouns; some are undeclined, some are partly declined and some have a complete declension.

a. The following indefinite pronouns are never inflected:

1. *man* (one, they, or people) is only used in the singular as subject of a verb.

Man trinkt viel Wasser in Amerika.
People drink much water in America.

Man sagt so etwas nicht.
One does not say such a thing.

2. *etwas* (something) and *nichts* (nothing) are used as subject and object, etc.

Haben Sie etwas Kaffee?
Have you *a little* coffee?

But:

Ja, etwas kann ich Ihnen geben.
Yes, I can give you *some*.

Etwas wird daraus werden.
Something will come of it.

Aus nichts kann nichts entstehen.
From nothing, nothing can arise.

3. *etwas* and *nichts* are used as indefinite antecedent of a relative pronoun.

Sie gibt ihm etwas, was sie leicht entbehren kann.
She gives him something which she easily can spare.

Sage mir etwas, was ich noch nicht gehört habe.
Tell me something (that) I have not heard.

Nichts, was er sagt, glaube ich.
I believe nothing he says.

4. *etwas* and *nichts* are also used with a neuter noun derived from an adjective.

Dies ist etwas sehr Schönes.
This is something very beautiful.

Ich muss etwas Gutes haben.
I must have something good.

b. Some indefinite pronouns are inflected in the genitive case only and because of their very meaning can be used only in the singular.

1. *jemand* (someone, somebody) and *niemand* (no one, nobody).

Jemand spricht draussen.
Someone is talking outside.

Ich höre jemands Stimme.
I am hearing someone's voice.

Das Buch gehört niemand.
The book belongs to no one.

Das ist niemands Angelegenheit.
That is nobody's business.

2. *jedermann* (everybody, everyone).

Jedermann kann nicht nach London fahren.
Everyone cannot go to London.

Warum sprechen Sie mit jedermann?
Why do you speak to everyone?

Das ist nicht jedermanns Sache.
That is not everyone's taste.

c. Some indefinite pronouns are declined like definite articles, i.e. the pronouns derived from *ein-* words are inflected in all cases. Some of these indefinite pronouns are:

1. *einer* (one), *keiner* (none, nobody), *jeder* (each one), which are inflected only in the singular.

Einer von ihnen muss recht haben.
One of them must be right.

Eines der Kinder hat einen Ball.
One of the children has a ball.

Haben Sie mit einem gesprochen?
Did you speak to one of them?

Ich kann jetzt mit *keinem* verhandeln.
I am not able to deal with *anyone* now.

Sie sagten, *keiner* hätte es getan.
They said *nobody* had done it.

***Jedes* hat sein Gutes.**
Everything has its good points.

***Jeder* hat seinen eigenen Geschmack.**
Each one has his own taste.

2. *beide* (both), an indefinite pronoun that is used only in the plural and follows the declension of the strong or weak adjective.

Fahren *beide* nach Deutschland?
Are *both* going to Germany?

Keiner von *beiden* geht ins Museum.
Neither one *of the two* is going to the museum.

Die Eltern *beider* sind gestorben.
The parents *of both (of them)* have died.

3. *wenig* (little) and *viel* (much) can be fully inflected. However, in the singular they are often uninflected.

Sie hat *wenig* erlebt.
She has experienced *little*.

Er kann aus *wenig viel* machen.
He can make *much* out of *little*.

Sie haben *viel* vollbracht.
You accomplished *a lot*.

Ein *weniges* wird genügen.
A *little* will suffice.

4. *wenige* (few, a few) and *viele* (many), the plurals of *wenig* (little) and *viel* (much), respectively, are declined like the plural of the definite article.

Eine wahre Freundschaft ist nur mit *wenigen* möglich.
A true friendship is possible with *a few only*.

Die Meinung *vieler* ist nicht immer richtig.
The opinion *of many* is not always correct.

5. *all (all)* and *alle* (all of them). *all* is often used as a pronoun in the neuter singular, meaning "everything."

***Alles* gebe ich dir.**	**Sie ist mein ein und *alles*.**
I shall give you *everything*.	She is my one and *all*.

all is also used as an indefinite antecedent of a relative pronoun:

Das ist *alles*, was ich habe.
That is *all* (that) I have.

Es ist nicht *alles* Gold, was glänzt.
All is not gold that glitters.

alle (all of them) is declined like an article in the plural:

Grüsse *alle* von mir.
Regards from me to *all* (of them).

Nein, mit *allen* können wir nicht gehen.
No, we cannot go with *all* (of them).

The Preposition (Die Präposition)

In German, prepositions are followed by definite cases and are grouped according to the cases they require. There are four groups:

1. Prepositions followed by the accusative case.
2. Prepositions followed by the dative case.
3. Prepositions followed by either the dative or the accusative case.
4. Prepositions followed by the genitive case.

§ 36 Prepositions Requiring the Accusative Case

The seven prepositions requiring the accusative are:

a. *bis* (to, till). Often takes another preposition.

> **Wir fahren *bis* Berlin.**
> We travel *to* (*as far as*) Berlin.
>
> **Warten Sie *bis* nächsten Freitag!**
> Wait *till* next Friday.
>
> ***Bis zum* ersten habe ich kein Geld.**
> *Till* the first, I have no money.

b. *durch* (through).

> **Er geht *durch* den Garten.**
> He is going *through* the garden.

c. *für* (for).

> **Dies Buch ist *für* dich.**
> This book is *for* you.

d. *gegen* (against).

> **Was haben Sie *gegen* den Mann?**
> What have you *against* the man?

e. *ohne* (without).

> **Sie gingen *ohne* den Bruder ins Theater**
> They went to the theater *without* their (the) brother.

f. *um* (around, at).

> **Sie fuhren mit dem Auto *um* den See.**
> They drove *around* the lake with the car.
>
> ***Um* vier Uhr.**
> *At* four o'clock.

g. *wider* (against), rarely used in modern German.

> **Wer nicht für mich ist, ist *wider* (gegen) mich.**
> Whoever is not for me is *against* me.

§ 37 Prepositions Requiring the Dative Case

The eight important prepositions requiring the dative are:

a. *aus* (out of, from).

> **Er kommt *aus* dem Zimmer.**
> He comes *out of* the room.

Wir trinken *aus* einem Glas.
We are drinking *from* a glass.

b. *ausser* (except, beside).

Alle waren da *ausser* meiner Schwester.
All were there *except* my sister.

Ich war *ausser* mir vor Schmerz.
I was *beside* myself with pain.

c. *bei* (at, near, at the house of).

Sie ist *bei* der Arbeit.
She is *at* work.

Potsdam ist *bei* Berlin.
Potsdam is *near* Berlin.

Sie wohnt *bei* ihrer Tante.
She is living *at* her aunt's *house.*

Er ist *beim* Arzt.
He is *at the* doctor's (*house*).

d. *mit* (with).

Kommen Sie *mit* mir nach Hause!
Come home *with* me.

e. *nach* (after, to a country or city).

***Nach* dem Essen gehe ich aus.**
After dinner I'll go out.

Wann fahren Sie *nach* Deutschland?
When are you going *to* Germany?

f. *seit* (since, in expressions of time).

***Seit* dem 1. April habe ich sie nicht gesehen.**
I have not seen her *since* April 1.

g. *von* (from, of, by).

Dies Buch ist *von* mir.
This book is *from* me.

Die Hauptstadt *von* Deutschland
The capital of Germany

Ein Gedicht *von* Goethe
A poem by Goethe

h. *zu* (to, to the house of).

Ich gehe *zu* meinem Onkel.
I am going *to* my uncle's (house).

Heute muss ich *zum* Zahnarzt gehen.
Today I must go *to the* dentist's.

§ 38   Prepositions Taking Either Dative or Accusative Case

a. There are nine prepositions which take either the dative or accusative; they are therefore called the "doubtful prepositions." Before using these prepositions, these questions must always be asked:

1. "Does the preposition indicate location (or place) where an

object is," or "where action takes place?" If the answer is "yes," the *dative* case follows.

> **Wo liegt das Papier? Es liegt *auf dem* Tisch.**
> Where does the paper lie? It is lying *on* the table.

> **Wo spielen die Kinder? Sie spielen *in dem* Garten.**
> Where are the children playing? They are playing *in* the garden.

> **Wo gehen Sie spazieren? Ich gehe *im* Park spazieren.**
> Where do you talk a walk? I take a walk *in* the park.

2. "Does the preposition imply motion to a place?" If the answer is "yes," then the *accusative* is used.

> **Wohin legt er das Papier? Er legt es *auf den* Tisch.**
> Where (to) does he lay the paper? He is laying it *on* the table.

> **Wohin gehen die Kinder? Die Kinder gehen *in den* Park.**
> Where (to; "whither") do the children go? The children are going into the park.

> **Der Mann trägt das Sofa *in das* Wohnzimmer.**
> The man is carrying the sofa into the living room.

b. The nine "doubtful" prepositions are:

1. *an* (at, to, up to an object).

> **Er steht *am* Fenster. Sie geht *an das* Fenster.**
> He is standing *at* the window. She is going *to* the window.

2. *auf* (on, upon, on top of).

> **Die Lampe steht *auf dem* Tisch.**
> The lamp is standing *on* the table.

> **Er stellt die Lampe *auf den* Tisch.**
> He places the lamp *on the* table.

3. *hinter* (behind, in back of).

> **Sie steht *hinter mir*.**
> She is standing *behind me.*

> **Sie stellt sich *hinter mich.***
> She places herself *behind me.*

4. *in* (in, into).

> **Sie sind *in dem* Zimmer.**
> They are *in the* room.

> **Sie kommen *in das* Zimmer.**
> They are coming *into the* room.

5. *neben* (beside, next to).

> **Er sitzt *neben seinem* Onkel.**
> He is sitting *next to his* uncle.

> **Er setzt sich *neben seinen* Onkel.**
> He sits down *next to his* uncle.

6. *über* (over, above).

> **Ein Bild hängt *über dem* Bett.**
> A picture hangs *over the* bed.

> **Ich hänge das Bild *über das* Bett.**
> I am hanging the picture *over the* bed.

> **Ein Musiker wohnt *über ihm*.**
> A musician is living *above him.*

7. *unter* (under, among).

Unter dem Schreibtisch steht der Papierkorb.
Under the desk stands the waste basket.

Sie legt das Papier *unter den* Bleistift.
She puts the paper *under the* pencil.

Unter den Gästen sind viele Amerikaner.
Among the guests are many Americans.

8. *vor* (before, in front of, ago).

Sie steht *vor dem* Spiegel.
She is standing *before the* mirror.

Sie geht *vor den* Spiegel.
She is going *in front of the* mirror.

Vor einem Jahr ist er nach Amerika gekommen.
A year ago he came to America.

9. *zwischen* (between).

Er sitzt *zwischen meiner* Mutter und mir.
He is sitting *between my* mother and me.

Er setzt sich *zwischen meine* Mutter und mich.
He sits down *between my* mother and me.

§ 39   Prepositions Taking the Genitive Case

a. Four important prepositions which take the genitive case are:

1. *anstatt, statt* (instead of).

Anstatt meines Vaters ging mein Bruder ins Konzert.
Instead of my father, my brother went to the concert.

2. *trotz* (in spite of).

Trotz des schlechten Wetters blieb er nicht zu Hause.
In spite of the bad weather, he did not stay home.

3. *während* (during).

Während des Tages arbeitet er in einem Büro.
During the day he works in an office.

4. *wegen* (because of).

Ich konnte *wegen meiner Erkältung* nicht ausgehen.
I could not go out *because of my cold.*

b. Other, less common prepositions requiring the genitive case are given below:

ausserhalb outside of	**um . . . willen** for the sake of
diesseits on this side of	**oberhalb** above
innerhalb inside of, within	**unterhalb** below
jenseits on the other side of	

§ 40   Prepositions with the Infinitive and *zu*

a. Three prepositions are used with the infinitive of verb plus *zu*; they are: *anstatt* (instead of), *ohne* (without), *um* (in order to).

Anstatt ins Theater *zu gehen*, besuchte er seine Tante.
Instead of going to the theater, he visited his aunt.

Er verliess das Haus, *ohne sich umzusehen*.
He left the house *without looking back*.

Wir besuchten unsere Kusine, *um* ihren Verlobten kennenzulernen.
We visited our cousin *in order to meet* her fiancé.

NOTE: Notice the difference in usage between German and English after *anstatt* and *ohne*. In German these two prepositions require the infinitive with *zu* in these phrases. In English they are followed by the gerund: "going", "looking".

b. *um ... zu* (in order to), with the infinitive must always be used in German when a definite purpose is to be expressed. In English, "in order to" with the infinitive or simply the infinitive alone may be used.

§ 41   Contractions of Prepositions

Some prepositions contract with the definite article in the dative or accusative case:

an dem	am	von dem	vom
an das	ans	zu dem	zum
in dem	im	zu der	zur
in das	ins	auf das	aufs

The Adjective (Das Adjektiv)

§ 42   Undeclined and Declined Adjectives

a. UNDECLINED ADJECTIVES.

Adjectives are *not* declined in the following instances:

1. After the verb *sein* (to be) as a predicate adjective:

Das Mädchen ist *gut*.
The girl is *good*.

Der Knabe ist *gut*.
The boy is *good*.

2. After *werden* (to become, get) and a few verbs not frequently used:

Sie wird *alt*.
She is getting *old*.

Er wird *alt*.
He is getting *old*.

3. When an adjective is derived from names of cities the adjective is formed by adding -er to the noun.

ein *Berliner* Theater
a Berlin theater

das *Münchner* Bier
the Munich beer

4. When an adjective is used as an adverb:

Das Mädchen schreibt *gut.*   **Der Knabe liest *gut.***
The girl writes *well.*   The boy reads *well.*

b. DECLINED ADJECTIVES.

Adjectives are declined according to the gender, number, and case of the nouns or their equivalents which they modify. Adjectives are declined when they precede the nouns which they modify.

Das *gute* Mädchen schreibt einen Brief.
The *good* girl is writing a letter.

Ein *guter* Knabe liest ein Buch.
A *good* boy is reading a book.

Adjectives are classified according to the endings they take. There are three declensions of adjectives in German: *strong, weak,* and *mixed.*

§ 43   The Strong Adjective Declension

SINGULAR

	MASCULINE	FEMININE	NEUTER
NOM.	*guter* **Vater**	*gute* **Mutter**	*gutes* **Kind**
	good father	*good* mother	*good* child
GEN.	*guten* **Vaters**	*guter* **Mutter**	*guten* **Kinds**
DAT.	*gutem* **Vater**	*guter* **Mutter**	*gutem* **Kind**
ACC.	*guten* **Vater**	*gute* **Mutter**	*gutes* **Kind**

PLURAL

NOM.	*gute* **Väter**	*gute* **Mütter**	*gute* **Kinder**
GEN.	*guter* **Väter**	*guter* **Mütter**	*guter* **Kinder**
DAT.	*guten* **Vätern**	*guten* **Müttern**	*guten* **Kindern**
ACC.	*gute* **Väter**	*gute* **Mütter**	*gute* **Kinder**

a. In analyzing the strong declension of the adjective, note that all cases in the singular and plural, except those of the genitives of the masculine and neuter singular, are declined like *dieser* [§5].

b. The masculine and neuter genitives take the ending *-en* in the singular.

c. Any adjective can be used with any masculine, feminine, or neuter noun, but the adjective must agree with its noun.

d. Strong adjective endings are used whenever the adjective is not preceded by a definite article or by one of the inflected *ein*-words; i.e. only the three uninflected cases of the *ein-words,* masculine nominative singular, neuter nominative singular, neuter accusative singular, are followed by an adjective of the strong declension:

ein *guter* Vater, ein *gutes* Kind, ein *gutes* Kind

e. In other words, the noun must have a modifier which establishes the relationship of the noun or its equivalent to the rest of the words in a sentence, by clearly showing its gender, number, and case.

Therefore, the adjective must take over wherever the preceding word is uninflected.

§ 44   The Weak Adjective Declension

SINGULAR

	MASCULINE	FEMININE	NEUTER
NOM.	der *gute* Vater the *good* father	die *gute* Mutter the *good* mother	das *gute* Kind the *good* child
GEN.	des *guten* Vaters	der *guten* Mutter	des *guten* Kinds
DAT.	dem *guten* Vater	der *guten* Mutter	dem *guten* Kind
ACC.	den *guten* Vater	die *gute* Mutter	das *gute* Kind

PLURAL

	MASCULINE	FEMININE	NEUTER
NOM.	die *guten* Väter	die guten Mütter	die *guten* Kinder
GEN.	der *guten* Väter	der *guten* Mütter	der *guten* Kinder
DAT.	den *guten* Vätern	den *guten* Müttern	den *guten* Kindern
ACC.	die *guten* Väter	die *guten* Väter	die *guten* Kinder

a. The principal ending of the weak declension of the adjective is *-en*. There are five cases, however, which take the ending *-e*; namely, the three nominative singulars, and the accusative singulars of the feminine and neuter cases. In all other cases, the inflective ending is *-en*.

b. The weak adjective declension is used whenever the adjective is preceded by one of the *der*-words or one of the *ein*-words that has a distinct case ending.

§ 45   The Mixed Adjective Declension

a. After *ein*-words [see § 7, b] the declension of the adjective is mixed, i.e., it is declined primarily like the weak declension but there are three cases where it takes strong endings.

b. Since the nominative singular masculine and the nominative and accusative neuter cases of the *ein*-words are not inflected, these three cases are followed by an adjective of the strong declension:

SINGULAR

	MASCULINE	FEMININE	NEUTER
NOM.	ein *guter* Vater a *good* father	eine *gute* Mutter a *good* mother	ein *gutes* Kind a *good* child
GEN.	eines *guten* Vaters	einer *guten* Mutter	eines *guten* Kinds
DAT.	einem *guten* Vater	einer *guten* Mutter	einem *guten* Kind
ACC.	einen *guten* Vater	eine *gute* Mutter	ein *gutes* Kind

PLURAL

	MASCULINE	FEMININE	NEUTER
NOM.	keine *guten* Väter	keine *guten* Mütter	keine *guten* Kinder
GEN.	keiner *guten* Väter	keiner *guten* Mütter	keiner *guten* Kinder
DAT.	keinen *guten* Vätern	keinen *guten* Müttern	keinen *guten* Kindern
ACC.	keine *guten* Väter	keine *guten* Mütter	keine *guten* Kinder

§ 46   Adjectives Used as Nouns

a. Adjectives are often used as nouns in German. If an adjective is used as a noun, it is written with a capital letter. It does not follow the declension of the noun but is declined like an adjective which precedes a noun.

ADJECTIVES:

	fremd	alt	klein
	strange	old	small

NOUNS:

SINGULAR

	MASCULINE	FEMININE	NEUTER
NOM.	der *Fremde*	die *Alte*	das *Kleine*
	the stranger	the old woman	the little one
GEN.	des *Fremden*	der *Alten*	des *Kleinen*
DAT.	dem *Fremden*	der *Alten*	dem *Kleinen*
ACC.	den *Fremden*	die *Alte*	das *Kleine*

PLURAL

NOM.	die *Fremden*	die *Alten*	die *Kleinen*
GEN.	der *Fremden*	der *Alten*	der *Kleinen*
DAT.	den *Fremden*	den *Alten*	den *Kleinen*
ACC.	die *Fremden*	die *Alten*	die *Kleinen*

b. The three uninflected cases of the *ein*-words are followed by strong adjective endings.

NOM. MASCULINE	NOM. NEUTER	ACC. NEUTER
ein *Fremder*	ein *Kleines*	ein *Kleines*

All other cases of the *ein*-words are inflected, and any adjective used as a noun after an inflected *ein*-word takes a weak ending like any simple adjective [§45].

c. The English pronoun "one," indicating a thing or person, is not expressed in German when an adjective is used as a noun:

der *Gute*	die *Grosse*
the good one	the tall one

§ 47   Comparison of Adjectives and Adverbs

There are three degrees of comparison of the adjective and the adverb in English and in German: positive, comparative, superlative.

a. The adjective is compared in German by adding the endings *-er* *-(e)st* to the positive of the adjective as in English:

klein	kleiner	kleinst
small	smaller	smallest

Positive	Comparative	Superlative	
arm poor	ärmer	ärmst	am ärmsten
jung young	jünger	jüngst	am jüngsten
lang long	länger	längst	am längsten
reich rich	reicher	reichst	am reichsten
schön beautiful	schöner	schönst	am schönsten
langsam slow	langsamer	langsamst	am langsamsten

In the comparative and superlative, monosyllabic adjectives usually take an *umlaut (a,o,u* change to *ä,ö,ü).* There are two forms of the superlative in German. How they are used will be explained below.

b. When adjectives end in a sibilant (*-s, -ss,* or *z*) or in *d* or *t,* an *e* must be inserted before the ending *-st* to facilitate pronunciation.

Positive	Comparative	Superlative	
heiss hot	heisser	heissest	am heissesten
kurz short	kürzer	kürzest	am kürzesten
mild mild	milder	mildest	am mildesten
alt old	älter	ältest	am ältesten
weise wise	weiser	weisest	am weisesten
intelligent intelligent	intelligenter	intelligentest	am intelligentesten

c. When adjectives end in *-el* or *-er,* the *e* is dropped in the comparative.

Positive	Comparative	Superlative	
dunkel dark	dunkler	dunkelst	am dunkelsten
sauer sour	saurer	sauerst	am sauersten
selten rare	seltner	seltenst	am seltensten

§ 48 Comparison of Equal and Unequal Degrees

a. Comparison of equal degrees is expressed by *so ... wie,* as (so) ... as:

Mein Bruder ist *so* (or *ebenso*) gross *wie* mein Vater.
My brother is *as* tall *as* my father.

Er ist nicht *so* gross *wie* er.
He is not *so* tall *as* he.

b. Comparison of adjectives of different degrees is expressed by the adjective in the comparative with *als* (than).

Hans ist grösser *als* mein Bruder.
Hans is taller *than* my brother.

§ 49 Irregular Comparisons of Adjectives and Adverbs

a. Some of the most common adjectives are irregularly compared.

POSITIVE	COMPARATIVE	SUPERLATIVE	
gross great	**grösser**	**grösst**	**am grössten**
gut good	**besser**	**best**	**am besten**
hoch high	**höher**	**höchst**	**am höchsten**
nah near	**näher**	**nächst**	**am nächsten**
viel many, much	**mehr**	**meist**	**am meisten**

1. *grösst* is irregularly compared, since all other adjectives ending in *s* take an *e* before the superlative ending -*st*.

2. The *c* of the adjective *hoch* is always dropped before an inflection beginning with -*e*:

Das Haus ist *hoch*.
The house is *tall*.

BUT:

das *hohe* Haus.
the *tall* house.

Therefore, *hoch, höher,* but *höchst*.

3. *viel* when inflected means "many" and is then used as an adjective:

***viele* Kinder**
many children

viel when uninflected means "much" and is then an adverb:

Er hat *viel* gegessen.
He ate *a lot (much)*.

b. *wenig* (little) is compared regularly in German but has an irregular comparison in English. In some cases this adjective does not follow the general rule for the adjective declension:

wenig little, a few	**weniger** less	**am wenigsten** least

1. *wenig* uninflected or in the singular usually means "little" (in the plural "a few").

Er hat *wenig* Geld.   **Sie hat *wenig* Zeit.**
He has *little* money.   She has *little* time.

2. After a *der*-word or after a possessive adjective, *wenig* is always inflected. If it modifies a noun in the plural, it is also inflected:

Was mache ich mit diesem *wenigen* Geld?
What am I going to do with this *little* money?

***Wenige* Kinder spielen heute auf der Strasse.**
A few children are playing in the street today.

c. Some common adverbs are also irregularly compared.

bald soon	eher or früher	ehest or frühst	am ehesten or am frühsten
gern like	lieber	liebst	am liebsten

1. There are two comparatives and superlatives of *bald*. *eher* and *ehest* are less common and can be used only as adverbs. *früher* and *frühst* can be used as adjectives as well as adverbs.

Mein *früherer* Freund   **Ich fahre *früher*.**
My *former* friend   I am leaving *earlier*.

2. *gern* can be used only as an adverb:

Sie singt *gern*.
She *likes* to sing.

This adverb used with a verb replaces *mögen* (to like). The comparative and superlative of *gern*, however, can also be used as adjectives:

Mein *liebster* Bruder
my *favorite* brother (my *most liked* brother)

3. Adjectives are used in German as adverbs without any change from their regular adjectival form, whether positive, comparative or superlative. Where in English the suffix *-ly* is added, in German, no ending is used to distinguish adverbs from adjectives. However, adverbs are never declined.

§ 50 Declension of the Comparative and Superlative

a. Adjectives in the comparative and superlative follow the same rules that apply to the adjective in the positive as far as declension is concerned. This means that comparative and superlative adjectives after *sein* and *werden* are uninflected:

Der Mann ist *jünger*, aber die Frau ist *hübscher*.
The man is *younger*, but the woman is *prettier*.

Sie wird jeden Tag *hübscher*.
She gets (becomes) *prettier* every day.

After *sein* and *werden*, the form of the superlative with *am* is used.

Im Dezember sind die Tage *am kürzesten*.
In December the days are *the shortest*.

Im Dezember werden die Tage *am kürzesten*.
In December the days are (become) *shortest*.

b. Comparative and superlative adjectives must be declined whenever they precede a noun or its equivalent. The comparative and superlative forms represent a new stem of the adjectives to which the necessary inflectional endings are added:

der ältere Bruder
the *older* brother

des ältesten Bruders
of the oldest brother

die ältesten Brüder
the *oldest* brothers

ein älterer Bruder
an *older* brother

das kleinste Kind
the *smallest* child

des kleinsten Kinds
of the *smallest* child

die kleinsten Kinder
his *smallest* child

sein kleinstes Kind
the *smallest* children

die jüngere Schwester
the *younger* sister

der jüngeren Schwester
of the *younger* sister

meine jüngeren Schwestern
my *younger* sisters

c. The first form of the superlative given in §47 is used as an adjective when it precedes a noun:

mein *bester* Freund
my *best friend*

das *schönste* Mädchen
the *most beautiful girl*

1. However, when the adjective in the superlative is used after *sein* (to be), unless it is preceded by an article, the second form with *am . . . -en,* which indicates the dative singular neuter, must be used:

Dies Buch ist *am besten.*
This book is *best.*

Das Mädchen ist *am schönsten.*
The girl is *most beautiful.*

BUT:

Dies Buch ist *das beste.*
This book is *the best one.*

2. The adverb in the superlative must always be formed with *am . . .-en*:

Marie schreibt *gut.*
Marie writes *well.*

Hans schreibt *besser.*
Hans writes *better.*

Aber Else schreibt *am besten.*
But Elsie writes *best.*

§ 51 Numerals

Basically the formation of numbers is the same in German and in English. (For a list of numbers, see the Vocabulary of Lesson 5.)

a. CARDINAL NUMBERS.

1. The numbers from *dreizehn* (13) to *neunzehn* (19) correspond

to the English "teen" numbers. *zehn* (ten or "teen") is added to *vier, fünf, sechs, sieben, acht, neun.*

2. In *sechzehn* (16) the *s* of the basic number is dropped; in *siebzehn* (17) the *-en* is omitted before *zehn* (10) and the same changes occur in *sechzig* (60) and *siebzig* (70).

3. Every tenth number from *zwanzig* (20) on adds *-zig,* which corresponds to the English ending *-ty.*

4. In *dreissig* (30), the *z* of the suffix *-zig* changes to *ss.*

5. Numbers are not capitalized, except *die Null* (the zero), *die Million* (the million), *die Milliarde* (the billion).

6. No matter how long the numbers are, they are always written in *one word.*

 1776—siebzehnhundertsechsundsiebzig.

7. Except for *ein* (one), numbers are not declined. The cardinal number *eins* drops the *s* in *ein Uhr* (one o'clock). (But, *Es ist eins* —It is one o'clock.) Otherwise *ein* is inflected like an indefinite article, *ein Volk* could mean "*one* nation" or "*a* people," *eine Frau,* "*one* woman" or "*a* woman."

b. NUMERALS DERIVED FROM CARDINAL NUMBERS.

1. These numbers are compounded of the cardinal number and *-mal,* from *das Mal,* the time.

einmal once	**viermal** four times	**hundertmal** hundred times
zweimal twice	**zehnmal** ten times	**tausendmal** thousand times
dreimal three times	**zwanzigmal** twenty times	

2. These numbers are compounded of the cardinal number and *Fach,* meaning "fold."

einfach simple, single	**dreifach** threefold	**hundertfach** hundredfold
zweifach double	**zwanzigfach** twentyfold	

c. ORDINAL NUMBERS.

1. Ordinals are formed in German by adding *-t* to the cardinal numbers from 1-19 and *-st* to numbers from 20 on (English *-th*). *zwei* plus *t=zweit-*; the *e* in *zweite,* etc. is an adjective ending.

2. A few irregularities in the structure of the ordinals follow:

(a) *erste* (first) and *dritte* (third) are also irregular in English.

(b) In *achte* (eighth), the *t* of the stem of cardinal number is dropped before *-te* is added (as in English before *-th* eight+th=eighth).

3. A few points in the use of ordinals must be noted:

(a) Ordinal numbers are declined like adjectives.

(b) If ordinals are used in expressing dates, or in designating chapters, centuries, etc., they are not written out. The cardinal number is followed by a period, which substitutes for the ending otherwise added to change it to an ordinal.

Der wievielte ist heute?
What is today's date?

Heute ist der 1. (erste) Mai.
Today is the *first* of May.

New York, den 17. April 19....
New York, April *17th*, 19....

Gestern war der 16. April.
Yesterday was the *16th* of April.

Sie ist am 17. Oktober geboren.
She was born on the *17th* of October.

Goethe wurde am 28. August 1749 geboren.
Goethe was born on August *28*, 1749.

das 12. Kapitel
the *twelfth* chapter

4. Numerals used adverbially are formed by adding *-ens* to the stem of the ordinal number.

erstens	**zweitens**	**drittens**
firstly	secondly	thirdly

d. FRACTIONS.

1. Most fractional numbers are compound nouns, composed of a cardinal number with *-tel,* an abbreviation of *Teil* (part). These fractional numbers are not declined (see Lesson 5 for examples).

2. *Halb* is an exception. It is an adjective, declined as such, and written with a small letter.

Sie gab ihm einen *halben* Kuchen.
She gave him *half* a cake.

3. *Drittel* is irregular.

4. The *t* of *acht* is dropped before the ending *-tel.*

ein Achtel
one eighth

5. For numbers from *zwanzig* (20) and above, the ending *-stel* is added.

ein Zwanzigstel
one twentieth

e. COMBINATIONS WITH FRACTIONAL NUMBERS.

anderthalb	**dreieinhalb**	**zweiachtel**
one and a half	three and a half	two-eighths
zweieinhalb	**dreiviertel**	
two and a half	three-fourths	

f. ARITHMETIC IN GERMAN.

1. *Addition:*

Zwanzig und vierzehn ist vierunddreissig
$20+14=34$

2. *Subtraction:*

Zweiundfünfzig weniger sieben ist fünfundvierzig
$52-7=45$

3. *Multiplication:*

Acht mal neun ist zweiundsiebzig
$8 \times 9=72$

4. *Division:*

Sechsundsechzig geteilt durch sechs ist elf
$66 \div 6=11$

Acht mal (eight times), *zwei mal* (two times), etc. in connection with arithmetic are written in two words. But:

Ich bin schon *achtmal* bei ihm gewesen.
I have been to his house *eight* times already.

Zweimal die Woche geht er ins Kino.
Twice a week he goes to the movies.

§ 52   Some Practical Applications of Numbers

a. EXPRESSIONS OF TIME OF DAY.

1. The hours are expressed as follows:

um ein Uhr   **um sechs Uhr**
at one o'clock   at six o'clock

BUT:

Es ist eins (or ein Uhr).
It is one (or one o'clock).

Es ist zwölf (or zwölf Uhr).
It is twelve (or twelve o'clock).

2. In German, the progression of time in one hour by quarter hour intervals may be expressed in two ways:

(a) The typical idiomatic German, in advancing from one hour to the next, anticipates the succeeding hour as soon as the time has progressed to the first quarter, whereas in English the next hour is not anticipated until it is a quarter before the hour.

ENGLISH		GERMAN
a quarter past four:	one-quarter of the fifth hour has passed	**(ein) Viertel fünf**
half past four:	one-half of the fifth hour has passed	**halb fünf**
a quarter to five:	three-quarters of the fifth hour have passed	**drei Viertel fünf**

(b) Expressions of time resembling the English construction are also acceptable.

(ein) Viertel nach fünf
a quarter past five

(ein) Viertel vor fünf
a quarter to five

zehn Minuten nach zehn
ten after ten

fünf Minuten vor elf
five minutes to eleven

NOTE: *(ein) Viertel fünf* is a quarter past four but *(ein) Viertel nach fünf* is a quarter past *five*.

3. In timetables for railroads, air lines, steamships, etc. time is expressed on the basis of a twenty-four hour day. 18.20 *(achtzehn zwanzig)* is 6.20 p.m. 24 *(vierundzwanzig)* is 12 o'clock midnight.

b. EXPRESSIONS OF MEASURE.

In expressions of measure, masculine and neuter nouns are used in the singular after numerals, and the preposition "of" in English is not translated.

ein *Liter* Milch
a *quart* of milk

zwei *Liter* Milch
two *quarts* of milk

ein *Meter*
one *meter*

four *meters*
vier *Meter*

ein *Glas* Bier, zwei *Glas* Bier
one *glass* of beer, two *glasses* of beer

However, a feminine noun of measure is used in the singular after a singular number and in the plural after a plural number.

eine *Tasse* Kaffee
one *cup* of coffee

zwei *Tassen* Kaffee
two *cups* of coffee

eine *Kanne* Milch
one pitcher of milk

zwei *Kannen* Milk
two pitchers of milk

eine *Meile*
one mile

fünf *Meilen*
five miles

c. EXPRESSIONS DENOTING MONETARY UNITS.

All nouns denoting monetary units, whether masculine, feminine, or neuter, are used in the singular whether the number is singular or plural.

eine *Mark*
one *mark*

zwanzig *Mark*
twenty *marks*

ein *Pfund*
one *pound*

drei *Pfund*
three *pounds*

ein *Pfennig*
one *penny*

zehn *Pfennig*
ten *pennies*

The Adverb (Das Adverb)

§ 53   Formation of the Adverb

a. Whereas in English the adverb is distinguished from the adjective by the suffix *-ly* (slow, slowly), in German adverbs have no such special endings. In fact, in German almost any adjective can be used as an adverb without any change in its form.

> die *langsame* Frau
> the *slow* woman
>
> Die Frau arbeitet *langsam.*
> The woman works *slowly.*

b. There are also "pure" adverbs in German which can never be used as adjectives. These include *sehr* (very); *gern* (like); *bald* (soon).

> Er geht *sehr* schnell.
> He runs *very* quickly.
>
> Er wird *bald* hier sein.
> He will *soon* be here.

c. The adverb *gern* is used very idiomatically in German and requires some explanation. *Gern* is a modifier of a verb, but can never be used as a verb (itself). See the following examples for its use:

> Sie hat ihn sehr *gern.*
> She *likes* him very much.
>
> Sie gehen *gern* spazieren.
> They *like to* go walking.
>
> Ich singe *gern.*
> I *like to* sing.

Gern haben (to like) usually refers to a person. *Gern* with a verb other than *haben*, which shows the tense, person, and number, is translated as "to like to . . ."

d. In German, sometimes independent adverbs are formed from adjectives by adding *weise* (from *die Weise,* the manner, way) to the adjective. These adverbs were originally adverbial phrases: *glücklicher Weise* "fortunately," literally, "in the happy manner or way."

unglücklicherweise unfortunately	**wunderbarerweise** strangely, singularly
gewohnterweise customarily, in the accustomed way	**klugerweise** wisely

e. When a sentence begins with an adverb or an adverbial phrase, the word order is inverted; that is, the verb comes before the noun.

> In der Nacht *schlafe* ich.
> At night I sleep.
>
> Glücklicherweise *kam* sie nicht so früh.
> Fortunately, she did not come so early.

The Conjunction (Die Konjunktion)

Conjunctions are words used to connect sentences, clauses, phrases, and words. There are two types of conjunctions. Coordinating conjunctions connect clauses, phrases, or words of equal rank and include such words as "and," "but," and "or." Subordinating conjunctions connect dependent clauses with main clauses, and include such words as "when," "until," "although," etc.

§ 54 Coordinating Conjunctions

a. The most important coordinating conjunctions in German are:

aber	**oder**	**und**
but	or	and
denn	**sondern**	**entweder . . . oder**
for	but (on the contrary)	either . . . or

b. After coordinating conjunctions, which connect two principal or main clauses, the word order does not change. The subject comes first, the verb follows. This is called *normal word order.*

aber

Er hat eine Karte für das Theater, *aber* er kann nicht gehen.
He has a ticket for the theater, *but* he cannot go.

denn

Sie kaufte das Auto nicht, *denn* sie hatte nicht genug Geld.
She did not buy the automobile *for* she did not have enough money.

oder

Sie müssen sich beeilen, *oder* wir versäumen den Zug.
You must hurry *or* we will miss the train.

sondern is a stronger form of "but" meaning "on the contrary." The first part of the sentence must be in the negative and the subject of the clause beginning with *sondern* must refer back to the same subject as the negative clause.

Er fährt nicht nach Frankreich *sondern* er macht eine Tour durch Südamerika.
He isn't going to France, *but* he is taking a tour through South America.

Er ist nicht dumm, *sondern* faul.
He is not dumb, *but* lazy.

und

Wir fahren nach Frankfurt, *und* Sie können dann Ihren Onkel aufsuchen.
We are traveling to Frankfort *and* you can then look up your uncle.

entweder . . . oder

Entweder wir gehen sofort, *oder* wir kommen zu spät.
Either we go immediately *or* we will be too late.

§ 55 Subordinating Conjunctions

Subordinating conjunctions introduce subordinate clauses and require "dependent word order." The most common subordinating conjunctions follow:

als when, than, as	**dass** that	**ob** whether	**wenn auch** though
als ob as if	**ehe** before	**obgleich, obschon** although	**während** while
bevor before	**falls** in case	**seitdem** since (time)	**wie** how, as
bis until	**indem** while	**wann** when	**wo** where
da since (reason), as	**je . . . desto** the . . . the	**weil** because	
damit in order that	**nachdem** after	**wenn** when, if	

§ 56 Word Order with Subordinating Conjunctions

A clause connected with the main clause by a subordinating conjunction is called a dependent clause. The dependent clause requires a special word order in German, which is quite different from English, or the normal word order in a coordinate clause in German. This word order will be called "word order of the dependent clause" or "dependent word order."

a. In simple tenses, the verb proper is at the end of the subordinate clause.

> **Ich weiss, dass sie heute nicht zu Hause *ist.***
> I know that she *is* not home today.

b. In compound tenses, the inflected part comes last and the past participle or infinitive precedes it.

> **Sie erkannte ihn, obgleich sie ihn zwanzig Jahre nicht *gesehen hatte.***
> She recognized him, although she *had* not *seen* him for twenty years.
>
> **Warten Sie nicht länger, da er heute nicht mehr *kommen wird.***
> Don't wait any longer since he *will* not *come* anymore today.
>
> **Er tut es jetzt, weil er es doch *tun muss.***
> He does it now because he *has to do* it anyhow.

§ 57 Translation of "When"

The English "when" is translated in three different ways in German, when used in expressing time.

a. *Als* is used when the conjunction refers to an event or period of life in the past that occurred only once.

> **Als ich sie gestern traf, trug sie einen grünen Hut.**
> *When* I met her yesterday, she was wearing a green hat.
>
> **Als sie in München war, ging sie oft ins Museum.**
> *When* she was in Munich, she often went to the museum.

Er lebte in Deutschland, *als* er jung war.
He lived in Germany *when* he was young.

b. *Wann* is used in a question, direct or indirect.

Wann kommen Sie heute ins Geschäft?
When are you coming to the office today?

Sagen Sie mir, *wann* Sie heute ins Geschäft kommen werden.
Tell me *when* you will come to the office today.

Ich weiss nicht, *wann* ich heute ins Geschäft kommen werde.
I don't know *when* I will come to the office today.

c. *Wenn* is used in all remaining cases.

Wenn ich sie sehe, werde ich es ihr sagen.
When I see her, I shall tell it to her.

Wenn er nach Hause kam, trank er immer eine Tasse Kaffee.
Whenever he came home, he always drank a cup of coffee.

Immer *wenn* sie in München war, besuchte sie das Kunstmuseum.
Whenever she was in Munich, she visited the Museum of Art.

Wenn ich in Berlin sein werde, werde ich Ihren Vater besuchen.
When I am (lit., shall be) in Berlin, I shall visit your father.

NOTE: The German *wenn* is also used in contrary-to-fact statements for the English "if."

§ 58   Adverbial Conjunctions

There is a steadily increasing number of adverbial conjunctions in German. It often is difficult to draw a line between these conjunctions and adverbs. These adverbial conjunctions are of grammatical significance since they require inverted word rather than dependent word order as the ordinary subordinating conjunctions do. Only a few of these adverbial conjunctions are given here as examples.

damals at that time

Er kommt heute selten, *damals* kam er oft.
He seldom comes now; *at that time* he often came.

darauf thereupon

Sie lächelte, und *darauf* verliess sie das Zimmer.
She smiled, and *thereupon* she left the room.

darum
deshalb } therefore
deswegen

Ihre Mutter ist krank, *deshalb* kann sie nicht kommen.
Her mother is ill; *therefore* she cannot come.

vielleicht perhaps

Vielleicht kommt sie doch.
Perhaps she will come anyhow.

teils . . . teils partly . . . partly

Teils kann er nicht kommen, teils will er nicht.
Partly he cannot come, *partly* he does not want to come.

The Verb (Das Verb)

§ 59 The Verbs *sein, haben, werden*

There are two main classifications of verbs in German—*weak* verbs and *strong* verbs. These verbs will be discussed at length later in this section, for before we can discuss them it will be necessary to learn the various forms of the three irregular verbs which are used in the compound tenses of the other verbs. These are *sein* (to be), *haben* (to have), and *werden* (to become).

PRESENT INDICATIVE

sein   to be

ich **bin**
I *am*

du **bist**
you *are*

er ⎱ he ⎱
sie ⎰ **ist** she ⎰ *is*
es   it

wir **sind**
we *are*

ihr **seid**
you *are*

sie **sind**
they *are*

Sie **sind**
you *are*

haben   to have

ich **habe**
I *have*

du **hast**
you *have*

er ⎱ he ⎱
sie ⎰ **hat** she ⎰ *has*
es   it

wir **haben**
we *have*

ihr **habt**
you *have*

sie **haben**
they *have*

Sie **haben**
you *have*

werden   to become, get

ich **werde**
I *become*

du **wirst**
you *become*

er ⎱ he ⎱
sie ⎰ **wird** she ⎰ *becomes*
es   it

wir **werden**
we *become*

ihr **werdet**
you *become*

sie **werden**
they *become*

Sie **werden**
you *become*

PAST TENSE

ich **war**
I *was*

du **warst**
you *were*

er **war**
he *was*

wir **waren**
we *were*

ihr **wart**
you *were*

sie **waren**
they *were*

Sie **waren**
you *were*

ich *hatte* I had	wir *hatten* we had
du *hattest* you had	ihr *hattet* you had
er *hatte* he had	sie *hatten* they had
	Sie *hatten* you had

ich *wurde* I became	wir *wurden* we became
du *wurdest* you became	ihr *wurdet* you became
er *wurde* he became	sie *wurden* they became
	Sie *wurden* you became

PRESENT PERFECT TENSE

ich *bin gewesen* I have been	*habe gehabt* have had	*bin geworden* have become
du *bist gewesen*	*hast gehabt*	*bist geworden*
er *ist gewesen*	*hat gehabt*	*ist geworden*
wir *sind gewesen*	*haben gehabt*	*sind geworden*
ihr *seid gewesen*	*habt gehabt*	*seid geworden*
sie *sind gewesen*	*haben gehabt*	*sind geworden*
Sie *sind gewesen*	*haben gehabt*	*sind geworden*

PAST PERFECT TENSE

ich *war gewesen* I had been	*hatte gehabt* had had	*war geworden* had become
du *warst gewesen*	*hattest gehabt*	*warst geworden*
er *war gewesen*	*hatte gehabt*	*war geworden*
wir *waren gewesen*	*hatten gehabt*	*waren geworden*
ihr *wart gewesen*	*hattet gehabt*	*wart geworden*
sie *waren gewesen*	*hatten gehabt*	*waren geworden*
Sie *waren gewesen*	*hatten gehabt*	*waren geworden*

FUTURE TENSE

ich *werde sein* I shall be	*werde haben* shall (will) have	*werde werden* shall (will) become
du *wirst sein*	*wirst haben*	*wirst werden*
er *wird sein*	*wird haben*	*wird werden*
wir *werden sein*	*werden haben*	*werden werden*
ihr *werdet sein*	*werdet haben*	*werdet werden*
sie *werden sein*	*werden haben*	*werden werden*
Sie *werden sein*	*werden haben*	*werden werden*

FUTURE PERFECT TENSE

ich *werde gewesen sein* I *shall have been*	*werde gehabt haben* *shall have had*	*werde geworden sein* *shall have become*
du *wirst gewesen sein*	*wirst gehabt haben*	*wirst geworden sein*
er *wird gewesen sein*	*wird gehabt haben*	*wird geworden sein*
wir *werden gewesen sein*	*werden gehabt haben*	*werden geworden sein*
ihr *werdet gewesen sein*	*werdet gehabt haben*	*werdet geworden sein*
sie *werden gewesen sein*	*werden gehabt haben*	*werden geworden sein*
Sie *werden gewesen sein*	*werden gehabt haben*	*werden geworden sein*

§ 60   The Formation of the Tenses

By analyzing the six forms of the tenses in the indicative of the three irregular verbs given above, definite general rules for the formation of the tenses can be derived:

a. In English, there are three possibilities for expressing an action: "I write, I am writing, I do write." In German, however, there is only one way to express each tense. Therefore, *ich habe* means "I have, I am having, I do have;" *ich hatte:* "I had, I was having, I did have."

b. To form the present perfect tense of any verb use the present tense of *haben* or *sein* together with the part participle of the verb:

ich *habe gehabt*   ich *bin gewesen*
I *have had*   I *have been*

c. To form the past perfect tense use the past tense of *haben* or *sein* with the past participle of the verb:

ich *hatte gehabt*   ich *war gewesen*
I *had had*   I *had been*

d. To form the future tense use the present tense of *werden* (to become) with the infinitive of the verb:

ich *werde haben*   ich *werde sein*
I *shall have*   I *shall be*

e. To form the future perfect tense use the present tense of *werden* with the past participle of the verb and the infinitive of *haben* or *sein*:

ich *werde gehabt haben*   ich *werde gewesen sein*
I *shall have had*   I *shall have been*

f. The basic structure of the verb in the different tenses is alike in English and in German; but the word order differs. In German the infinitive in the compound tenses is at the end.

g. The compound tenses of all German verbs are formed according to the basic rules mentioned above. It is necessary, therefore, only to master these rules and to learn the principal parts of a verb. All other forms can then be derived from these. These principal parts are:

INFINITIVE	PRESENT	PAST	PAST PARTICIPLE
sein to be	**ist**	**war**	**(ist) gewesen**
haben to have	**hat**	**hatte**	**gehabt**
werden to become	**wird**	**wurde**	**(ist) geworden**

The principal parts are given in the third person singular.

§ 61   Weak and Strong Conjugations

a. German verbs are divided into two major groups: weak and strong conjugations. Almost all German verbs fall into one of these two groups.

1. German *weak* verbs correspond very closely to English regular verbs:

INFINITIVE	PAST	PAST PARTICIPLE
folgen to follow	**folgte** followed	**gefolgt** followed

2. German *strong* verbs correspond to the English irregular verbs:

INFINITIVE	PAST	PAST PARTICIPLE
springen to spring	**sprang** sprang	**gesprungen** sprung

The most outstanding characteristic of the German strong and the English irregular verb is the change of the stem vowel in the different tenses.

b. The weak verbs and strong verbs have these features in common:

1. All infinitives in German end in -en: *machen* (to do, make); *gehen* (to go); or -n as in *tun* (to do); *wandern* (to wander), while in English the infinitive form is indicated by the preposition "to." By dropping -en or -n respectively, the infinitive stem of a verb is obtained.

2. This infinitive stem is the basis for all tenses of the weak verb. However, only the present tense of strong verbs is based on the infinitive stem.

3. The endings of the present tense (first, second, third person, singular and plural) are the same whether the verb is weak or strong:

Singular		Plural	
1st person	ich—-*e*	1st person	wir—-*en*
2nd person	du—-*st*	2nd person	ihr—-*t*
3rd person	er—-*t*	3rd person	sie—-*en*

Weak Verb	Strong Verb
wohnen	**gehen**
to live	to go
ich **wohne**	ich **gehe**
I *live, am living, do live*	I *go, am going, do go*
du **wohnst**	du **gehst**
you *live, are living, do live*	you *go, are going, do go*
er, sie, es **wohnt**	er, sie, es **geht**
he, she, it *lives, is living, does live*	he, she, it *goes, is going, does go*
wir **wohnen**	wir **gehen**
we live	we go
ihr **wohnt**	ihr **geht**
you live	you go
sie **wohnen**	sie **gehen**
they live	they go
Sie **wohnen**	Sie **gehen**
you live	you go

4. In all of the *weak* and most of the *strong verbs* (in the *present tense*) when their infinitive stems end in *-t* or *-d*, an *e* must be inserted before a consonant ending is added: *er wartet* (he waits), *du wartest* (you wait), *er wartete* (he waited), *er hat gewartet,* (he has waited). *er findet* (he finds), *du findest* (you find), *ihr findet* (you find).

5. If the infinitive stem of a weak or strong verb ends in *-s, -ss, -z, -tz* only a *t* instead of *st* is added in the second person singular of the present tense:

reisen	**sitzen**
to travel (weak verb)	to sit (strong verb)
ich **reise**	ich **sitze**
I *travel*	I *sit*
du **reist**	du **sitzt**
you *travel*	you *sit*
er **reist**	er **sitzt**
he *travels*	he *sits*

THE VERB   [§62]   257

6. The past participle is characterized in almost all verbs by the prefix *ge-;* the participle ending of the weak verb is *-t;* the strong verb *-en*:

gewohnt   **gegangen**
lived   gone

§ 62   Transitive and Intransitive Verbs

Weak or strong verbs in the compound past tenses are conjugated either with *haben* or *sein,* depending on a definite rule. To be able to apply this rule, the terms *transitive* and *intransitive* in regard to verbs must be clearly understood.

a. A transitive verb requires a direct object; that is, the action passes from the subject directly to an object. (The direct object requires the accusative case in German.)

Sie *liest den Brief.*
She *reads the letter.*

Er *erwartet seinen Freund.*
He *is expecting his friend.*

b. An intransitive verb cannot take a direct object; that is, the verb is complete in itself and, hence, cannot pass its action on to anything or anybody else. Intransitive verbs fall into two classifications:

1. Those that take an indirect object (as sole object):

Sie *antwortet ihm.*
She *answers him.*

2. Those that must be completed by a prepositional phrase:

Wir *gehen* in den Park.
We *are going* to the park.

c. In German there are certain intransitive verbs that require an indirect object only, which is expressed by the *dative case.* These verbs include:

antworten	**scheinen**	**gefallen**	**glauben**
to answer	to seem	to please	to believe
begegnen	**fehlen**	**gehören**	**helfen**
to meet	to be missing	to belong	to help
danken	**folgen**	**geschehen**	**passen**
to thank	to follow	to happen	to fit
dienen			
to serve			

Sie *antwortet ihm* nicht.
She *does* not *answer him.*

Er *hilft seinem Sohn.*
He *helps his son.*

Sie *begegneten dem Mann.*
They *met the man.*

§ 63　Use of *haben* or *sein* in Compound Tenses

In all compound tenses (whether formed of weak or strong verbs), the question of whether to use *haben* or *sein* can be resolved by the following rules:

a. Verbs conjugated with *haben*:

1. All transitive verbs.

> **Er *hat* eine Reise *gemacht*.**
> He *made* (*has made*) a trip.
>
> **Sie *hat* den Brief *gelesen*.**
> She *read* (*has read*) the letter.
>
> **Sie *hatte* den Brief *gelesen*.**
> She *had read* the letter.
>
> **Sie *wird* den Brief *gelesen haben*.**
> She *will have read* the letter.

2. All modal auxiliaries.

> **Er *hat* das Verb *konjugieren können*.**
> He *was able* (*has been able*) *to conjugate* the verb.

3. Reflexive verbs.

> **Er *hatte* sich *gesetzt*.**
> He *had sat down*.
>
> **Sie *hatte* sich *gewaschen*.**
> She *had washed* herself.

4. Most intransitive verbs.

> **Sie *hat* ihm *geantwortet*.**
> She *has answered* him.
>
> **Er *hat* seinem Sohn *geholfen*.**
> He *helped* (*has helped*) his son.
>
> **Sie *hatten* die ganze Nacht gut *geschlafen*.**
> They *had slept* well all night.

b. Verbs conjugated with *sein*:

1. Intransitive verbs showing (a) a change from one place or condition to another, or (b) motion towards, or (c) change of status, such as *gehen* (to go), *einschlafen* (to fall asleep), *werden* (to become), *sterben* (to die).

> **Wir *sind* uns gestern auf der Strasse *begegnet*.**
> We *met* (*have met*) in the street yesterday [walking toward each other].
>
> **Der Hund *war* seinem Herrn *gefolgt*.**
> The dog *had followed* his master.
>
> **Er *ist* in den Park *gegangen*.**
> He *went* (*has gone*) to the park.
>
> **Sie *war* nicht *gekommen*.**
> She *had* not *come*.
>
> **Wir *sind* spät *eingeschlafen*.**
> We *fell* (*have fallen*) asleep late.

NOTE: The last sentence indicates a change of condition, from being awake to falling asleep. The same principle is seen in:

Er *ist* letztes Jahr *gestorben*.
He *died* last year.

2. *sein* (to be) itself and *bleiben* (to remain) are two intransitive verbs conjugated with *sein* which do not indicate any change.

Wo *bist* du gestern abend *gewesen*?
Where *were* you (*have* you *been*) last night?

Ich *war* zu Hause *geblieben*.
I *stayed* (*had remained*) at home.

c. The future tense of weak or strong verbs is formed with the present of *werden* (to become) and the infinitive of the main verb.

Ich *werde* ihn *sehen*.	**Sie *werden* morgen *kommen*.**
I *shall see* him.	They *will come* tomorrow.

d. The future perfect tense is formed with the present tense of *werden,* the infinitive of *haben* or *sein,* and the past participle of the main verb.

Ich *werde* ihn *gesehen haben*.
I *shall have seen* him.

Sie *werden* morgen *gekommen sein*.
They *will have come* tomorrow.

§ 64 Forming the Tenses of the Weak Verb

In order to form the different tenses of the weak verb, only the infinitive stem and the corresponding endings have to be known, since all tenses are based on this stem.

a. PRESENT TENSE.

wohnen to live		**machen** to do, make	
STEM: **wohn-**		STEM: **mach-**	
ich *wohne*	wir *wohnen*	ich *mache*	wir *machen*
I *live*		I *do*	
du *wohnst*	ihr *wohnt*	du *machst*	ihr *macht*
er *wohnt*	sie *wohnen*	er *macht*	sie *machen*
	Sie *wohnen*		Sie *machen*

1. In verbs whose infinitive stem ends in -*t* or -*d,* an *e* is inserted before a consonant ending is added:

warten to wait		**reden** to talk, speak	
STEM: **wart-**		STEM: **red-**	
ich warte	wir warten	ich rede	wir reden
du wartest	ihr wartet	du redest	ihr redet
er wartet	sie warten	er redet	sie reden
	Sie warten		Sie reden

2. In verbs whose infinitive stem ends in *-m* or *-n,* preceded by a consonant other than *l, m, n, r,* or *h,* an *e* is inserted before a consonant ending is added:

öffnen	to open		atmen	to breathe
STEM: öffn-			STEM: atm-	
ich öffne	wir öffnen		ich atme	wir atmen
du öffnest	ihr öffnet		du atmest	ihr atmet
er öffnet	sie öffnen		er atmet	sie atmen
	Sie öffnen			Sie atmen

This connecting *e* is necessary to facilitate pronunciation or to prevent shortening of the preceding vowel by changing an originally single consonant into a double one, as would be the case, for example, in *beten* (to pray)—*er betet* (he prays).

3. If the stem of a verb ends in *-s, -ss, -z,* or *-tz,* the second person present is formed by simply adding a *t* instead of *st* to avoid a "social gathering" of the *s*-sounds:

du reist	du setzt	du reizt
you travel	you put, set	you entice

Therefore, the second and third persons singular of these verbs are alike in form, and only the pronouns differ *(du reist, er reist,* etc.).

b. PAST TENSE.

ich -*(e)te*	ich *wohnte*	ich *wartete*	ich *öffnete*
	I *lived*	I *waited*	I *opened*
du -*(e)test*	du *wohntest*	du *wartetest*	du *öffnetest*
er -*(e)te*	er *wohnte*	er *wartete*	er *öffnete*
wir -*(e)ten*	wir *wohnten*	wir *warteten*	wir *öffneten*
ihr -*(e)tet*	ihr *wohntet*	ihr *wartetet*	ihr *öffnetet*
sie -*(e)ten*	sie *wohnten*	sie *warteten*	sie *öffneten*

c. PAST PARTICIPLE.

The past participle of weak verbs is formed by adding *ge-* before the infinitive stem and *-(e)t* at the end:

gemacht	gewartet	geatmet	gesetzt
made	waited	breathed	set, put
gewohnt	geöffnet	gereist	
lived	opened	traveled	

All verbs ending in *-ieren*—such as *korrigieren* (to correct), *diktieren* (to dictate), *marschieren* (to march)—are weak in German and form their past participle without the prefix *ge-* but end in *-t* like all past participles of the weak verbs.

PRESENT PERFECT:	PAST PERFECT:
hat *korrigiert* has *corrected*	hatte *korrigiert* had *corrected*
hat *diktiert* has *dictated*	hatte *diktiert* had *dictated*

By applying the above rules, all remaining tenses can be formed.

d. PRESENT PERFECT TENSE.

ich *habe gemacht* I *have done*	ich *habe geöffnet* I *have opened*
ich *habe gewohnt* I *have lived*	ich *bin gereist* I *have traveled*
ich *habe gewartet* I *have waited*	

e. PAST PERFECT TENSE.

ich *hatte gemacht* I *had done*	ich *war gereist* I *had traveled*
ich *hatte gewohnt* I *had lived*	

f. FUTURE TENSE.

ich *werde machen* I *shall do*	ich *werde reisen* I *shall travel*

g. FUTURE PERFECT TENSE.

ich *werde gemacht haben* I *shall have done*	ich *werde gereist sein* I *shall have traveled*

§ 65   Forming the Tenses of the Strong Verb

The outstanding characteristic of the strong verb in German is the change of the stem vowel in the principal parts: *singen* (to sing), *sang* (sang), *gesungen* (sung).

a. PRESENT TENSE.

1. The present tense of the strong verb is also based on the infinitive stem, as in the case of the weak verbs:

gehen to go	singen to sing
ich *gehe* I *go*	ich *singe* I *sing*
du *gehst*	du *singst*
er *geht*	er *singt*
wir *gehen*	wir *singen*
ihr *geht*	ihr *singt*
sie *gehen*	sie *singen*

2. But strong verbs whose stem vowels are *e, a, au* change to *i(ie)*, *ä, äu* in the second and third persons of the singular of the present tense.

(a) Sometimes the *e* of the stem vowel changes to *i*; sometimes, to *ie*:

geben to give	**sehen** to see
ich gebe I give	**ich sehe** I see
du *gibst*	**du** *siehst*
er *gibt*	**er** *sieht*
wir geben	**wir sehen**
ihr gebt	**ihr seht**
sie geben	**sie sehen**

(b) *Gehen, stehen,* and *heben,* although strong verbs with a stem vowel *e,* contrary to the rule, have no vowel change in the present tense:

gehen—du *gehst,* er *geht*   heben—du *hebst,* er *hebt*
to go   to lift

stehen—du *stehst,* er *steht*
to stand

(c) In addition to the vowel change, two verbs also double the stem consonant in the second and third persons singular of the present tense:

treten—ich *trete,* du *trittst,* er *tritt,* wir *treten,* ihr *tretet,* sie *treten*
to step

nehmen—ich *nehme,* du *nimmst,* er *nimmt,* wir *nehmen,*
                    ihr *nehmt,* sie *nehmen*
to take

(d) Vowel changes also take place in strong verbs with the stem vowels *a* and *au* in the second and third persons singular.

tragen—ich *trage,* du *trägst,* er *trägt,* etc.
to carry

laufen—ich *laufe,* du *läufst,* er *läuft,* etc.
to run

3. If there is a vowel change in the present tense (second and third persons singular) of the strong verb whose infinitive stem ends in *t* or *d,* the connecting vowel *e* is not inserted before a consonant ending:

halten to hold		**raten** to guess, advise	
ich *halte* I hold	**wir** *halten*	**ich** *rate* I guess	**wir** *raten*
du *hältst*	**ihr** *haltet*	**du** *rätst*	**ihr** *ratet*
er *hält*	**sie** *halten*	**er** *rät*	**sie** *raten*

But:

finden to find

ich *finde*	wir *finden*
I find	
du *findest*	ihr *findet*
er *findet*	sie *finden*

The vowel of the past tense always differs from the vowel of the infinitive stem in strong verbs. The endings are as follows and are added to the stem of the past tense:

b. PAST TENSE.

	gehen to go	tragen to carry	laufen to run
ich —	ich *ging* I went	trug carried	*lief* ran
du —*st*	du *gingst*	*trugst*	*liefst*
er —	er *ging*	*trug*	*lief*
wir —*en*	wir *gingen*	*trugen*	*liefen*
ihr —*t*	ihr *gingt*	*trugt*	*lieft*
sie —*en*	sie *gingen*	*trugen*	*liefen*

Note that the first and third persons take no endings and that the other endings are the same as the endings of the present tense. The stem consonant of the infinitive usually does not change, although there are a few exceptions:

1. The consonant may be *doubled* and also *changed*:

reiten to ride (on horseback)	er *reitet* he rides	er *ritt* he rode
leiden to suffer	er *leidet* he suffers	er *litt* he suffered

2. Double consonants may change to a single consonant:

kommen to come	er *kommt* he comes	er *kam* he came
bitten to beg, ask	er *bittet* he begs	er *bat* he begged

3. In a very few verbs, the consonant changes:

ziehen to pull, draw	er *zieht* he draws	er *zog* he drew

c. THE PAST PARTICIPLE.

The past participle is formed with the prefix *ge-* and the ending *-en* affixed to the new stem, the so-called *past participle stem.*

1. Some past participles have the same vowel as the infinitive:

geben	**gegeben**	**fallen**	**gefallen**
to give	given	to fall	fallen

2. Some past participles have the same vowel as the past tense:

schreiben	**schrieb**	**geschrieben**
to write	wrote	written

3. Some past participles differ from both forms:

INFINITIVE	PAST	PAST PARTICIPLE
finden	**fand**	**gefunden**
to find	found	found
liegen	**lag**	**gelegen**
to lie	lay	lain
nehmen	**nahm**	**genommen**
to take	took	taken

The above three forms are the principal parts of the verbs, on the basis of which all tenses can be derived. At the end of the grammar section, a list of the principal parts of the *strong* and *irregular* verbs will be given. The forms of the strong verbs should be gradually learned by heart. Verbs that do not appear in this list are weak. The present perfect, past perfect, and the two tenses of the future are formed regularly [§60].

PRESENT PERFECT TENSE.

ich *habe gefunden*	ich *bin gefallen*
I *have found*	I *have fallen*

PAST PERFECT.

ich *hatte gefunden*	ich *war gefallen*
I *had found*	I *had fallen*

FUTURE.

ich *werde finden*	ich *werde fallen*
I *shall find*	I *shall fall*

FUTURE PERFECT.

ich werde *gefunden haben*	ich *werde gefallen sein*
I *shall have found*	I *shall have fallen*

§ 66   Irregular Weak Verbs

A group of eight verbs are of a mixed conjugation and are called irregular weak verbs, because they take the endings of the weak conjugation but change the stem vowel of the infinitive in the past tense and past participle, from *e* to *a*, like a strong verb.

a. The principal parts of these irregular weak verbs are:

INFINITIVE	PRESENT	PAST	PAST PARTICIPLE
brennen	**brennt**	**brannte**	**gebrannt**
(to burn)			

kennen (to know)	kennt	kannte	gekannt
nennen (to name)	nennt	nannte	genannt
rennen (to run)	rennt	rannte	(ist) gerannt
senden (to send)	sendet	sandte	gesandt
wenden (to turn)	wendet	wandte	gewandt
bringen (to bring)	bringt	brachte	gebracht
denken (to think)	denkt	dachte	gedacht

1. The compound tenses of these verbs are formed with *haben,* with the exception of *rennen,* which is an intransitive verb denoting change of place, and therefore takes *sein.*

2. The past and past participle have the same vowel, *a.*

3. Notice that *bringen* and *denken* also change their stem consonant to *ch* in the past tense and the past participle.

b. The tenses of *bringen* (to bring), will serve as model for verbs of this group:

bringen   to bring

PRESENT:

ich *bringe*
I bring
du *bringst*
er *bringt*
wir *bringen*
ihr *bringt*
sie *bringen*
Sie *bringen*

PAST:

ich *brachte*
I brought
du *brachtest*
er *brachte*
wir *brachten*
ihr *brachtet*
sie *brachten*
Sie *brachten*

PRESENT PERFECT:

ich *habe gebracht*
I have brought

PAST PERFECT:

ich *hatte gebracht*
I had brought

FUTURE:

ich *werde bringen*
I shall bring

FUTURE PERFECT:

ich *werde gebracht haben*
I shall have brought

§ 67   Use of the Tenses

a. THE PRESENT TENSE.

1. The present indicative indicates not only present tense (*Er schreibt einen Brief.* He writes a letter.), but is also used to express future tense, especially in conversational German.

Sie *gehen* morgen in die Stadt.
They *are going* downtown (into the city) tomorrow.
Wann *fahren* Sie nach Hamburg?
When *are* you *going* to Hamburg?
Ich *fahre* nächsten Sommer.
I *am going* next summer.

This use of the present tense is very prevalent in conversational German, but in formal writing, the future tense would be used.

2. The present tense is used to indicate an action or state which started in the past and is still going on in the present. In English, the present perfect is used.

Wie lange *kenne*n Sie Hans?
How long *have* you *known* Hans?
Ich *kenne* ihn drei Jahre.
I *have known* him for three years.
Er *ist* zwanzig Jahre in den Vereinigten Staaten.
He *has been* in the United States for twenty years.
Sie *wartet* schon eine halbe Stunde auf ihn.
She *has been* waiting a half hour for him.
Wie lange *wohnt* er schon hier?
How long *has* he *been living* here?

b. THE PAST TENSE.

1. The past tense is often called the narrative tense and is used in German whenever two or more related events are connected to each other in time or sequence.

Gestern *traf* ich Herrn X auf der Strasse, und wir *sprachen* eine Weile mit einander.
I *met* Mr. X in the street yesterday and we *talked* with each other for a while.
Sie *schrieb* einen Brief, als er ins Zimmer *kam.*
She *was writing* a letter when he *entered* the room.

2. The past tense is used in German as well as in English to express repeated action in the past.

Sie *besuchte* uns oft.
She often *visited* us.
Er *rauchte* täglich ein Päckchen Zigaretten.
He smoked a pack of cigarettes a day.
Früher *trank* er sehr viel Kaffee.
Formerly he *drank* a lot of coffee.

c. THE PRESENT PERFECT TENSE.

1. The present perfect is used to express one isolated, unconnected fact or action in the past, while in English the simple past is employed.

Goethe *hat* viele lyrische Gedichte *geschrieben.*
Goethe *wrote* many lyric poems.

Ich *habe* **mir letzte Woche einen Hut** *gekauft.*
I *bought* myself a hat last week.

2. In everyday language, the present perfect is sometimes used to express connected events, but it is definitely considered bad in written German.

d. THE PAST PERFECT TENSE.

1. The past perfect indicates some action or fact completed in the past before another action in the past took place. English and German correspond closely in the use of the past perfect.

Sie *hatte* **den Brief** *beendet,* **als er ins Zimmer trat.**
She *had finished* the letter when he entered the room.

Er *hatte* **schon mit seinem Onkel** *gesprochen.*
He *had* spoken to his uncle *already.*

e. THE FUTURE TENSES.

1. The use of the future and future perfect tenses is similar in English and German.

Sie *werden* **ihr Ziel erreichen.**
They *will reach* their goal.

Bis heute abend *werde* **ich die Arbeit** *beendet haben.*
By this evening, I *will have finished* the work.

2. The future tenses are used idiomatically with *wohl* (probably), indicating probability.

Sie *werden* **wohl wieder zu spät** *kommen.*
They *are* probably late again.

Es *wird* **wohl wahr** *sein.*
It *is* probably true.

Er *wird* **wohl verschlafen** *haben.*
He *has* probably overslept.

§ 68   Inseparable and Separable Prefixes of Verbs

There are two types of prefixes which form a compound with a verb in German, inseparable prefixes and separable prefixes.

a. INSEPARABLE PREFIXES.

Certain prefixes form such a close tie with the verb that they never separate from it, similar to the English words "*be*come" or "*for*give". There are seven such prefixes in German; they should be learned by heart, since all other prefixes, with a few exceptions, are separable prefixes:

be-	*be*suchen to visit	*be*kommen to receive
ent- (emp-)	*ent*stehen to originate	*emp*fangen to receive

er-	**er**kennen	**er**warten
	to recognize	to expect
ge-	**ge**fallen	**ge**brauchen
	to please	to use
miss-	**miss**handeln	**miss**trauen
	to mistreat	to distrust
ver-	**ver**geben	**ver**stehen
	to forgive	to understand
zer-	**zer**reissen	**zer**brechen
	to tear	to break (completely)

1. Any prefix added to a word changes the meaning (compare in English *give* and *forgive*), but any verb thus prefixed follows the conjugation of the original verb; for example, *geben,* to give:

| INFINITIVE: | PRESENT: | PAST: | PRESENT PERFECT |
| **vergeben** | **er vergibt** | **vergab** | **hat vergeben** |

2. The *ge-* prefix of the past participle is dropped in verbs with inseparable prefixes.

| **entstanden** | **erkannt** | **vergeben** |
| originated | recognized | forgiven |

3. The synopsis of the conjugation, therefore, would be as follows (the person is changed in each tense) :

PRESENT:	PAST PERFECT:
ich *verstehe*	wir *hatten verstanden*
I understand	we had understood
PAST:	FUTURE:
du *verstandst*	ihr *werdet verstehen*
you understood	you will understand
PRESENT PERFECT:	FUTURE PERFECT:
er *hat verstanden*	sie *werden verstanden haben*
he has understood	they will have understood

4. The stem or root of verbs with inseparable prefixes is accented in pronunciation:

| **erken'-nen** | **misshan'-deln** | **verge'-ssen** |

b. SEPARABLE PREFIXES.

Separable prefixes do not form such a tight union with the verb as the inseparable ones and do separate under certain conditions:

1. In the simple tenses, the prefix separates from its verb and goes to the end of the sentence or phrase.

aufstehen   to get up

PRESENT:

Er *steht* jeden Morgen um 6 Uhr *auf*.
He *gets up* at six o'clock every morning.

PAST:

Er *stand* jeden Morgen um 6 Uhr *auf*.
He *got up* at six o'clock every morning.

IMPERATIVE:

Stehe jeden Morgen um 6 Uhr *auf!*
Get up at six o'clock every morning.

2. In a dependent clause, however, the verb must be at the end of the clause, and therefore the prefix cannot be last.

Er wünschte, morgen nicht um 6 Uhr *aufzustehen*.
He did not wish *to get up* at six o'clock tomorrow.

Ich weiss, dass er jeden Morgen um 6 Uhr *aufstehen* muss.
I know that he has *to get up* at six o'clock every morning.

3. In compound tenses, the prefix does not separate and the *ge-* of the past participle comes between prefix and verb. Otherwise, the verb is conjugated like the simple verb.

PRESENT PERFECT:

Er ist gestern um 6 Uhr *aufgestanden*.
He got *(has gotten)* up at six o'clock yesterday.

PAST PERFECT:

Er war gestern um 6 Uhr *aufgestanden*.
He *got (had gotten)* up at six o'clock yesterday.

FUTURE:

Er wird morgen um 6 Uhr *aufstehen*.
He *will get up* at six o'clock tomorrow.

FUTURE PERFECT:

Er wird morgen um 6 Uhr *aufgestanden* sein.
He *will have* gotten up at six o'clock tomorrow.

4. In verbs with separable prefixes, the prefix is accented in pronunciation:

auf'-stehen

5. The principal parts of *aufstehen* are:

INFINITIVE:	PRESENT:	PAST:	PRESENT PERFECT:
aufstehen to stand up, get up	**er steht *auf***	**er stand *auf***	**er ist *aufgestanden***

IMPERATIVE:

stehe *auf!*

c. THE "DOUBTFUL" PREFIXES.

A few prefixes are sometimes separable and sometimes inseparable.

When the verbs to which the prefixes are attached are used in a literal sense, the prefixes are separable and accented. In this case the participle prefix *ge-* comes between the separable prefix and the verb. When the meaning of the verb is figurative, however, the prefix is inseparable; the stress is on the verb, and the *ge-* is dropped.

The five most important prefixes of this group are:

1. *durch*

Das Wasser *läuft durch.*
The water *flows through.*

Das Wasser ist *durchgelaufen.*
The water *has flowed through.*

Er *durchläuft* die Welt.
He *rushes (runs) through* the world.

Er hat die Welt *durchlaufen.*
He *has traveled through* the world.

2. *um*

Sie *fasst* ihn *um.*
She *embraces* him.

Sie *hat* ihn *umgefasst.*
She *has embraced* him.

Dies *umfasst* das ganze System.
This *includes* the whole system.

Dies *hat* das ganze System *umfasst.*
This *has* the whole system *included.*

3. *über*

Er *setzt* auf einer Fähre *über.*
He *crosses* on a ferry.

Er *ist* auf einer Fähre *übergesetzt.*
He *has crossed* on a ferry.

Er *übersetzt* aus dem Deutschen.
He *translates* from German.

Er hat aus dem Deutschen *übersetzt.*
He *has translated* from German.

4. *unter*

Sie *drückt* ihn *unter.*
She *pushes* him *under* (water).

Sie *hat* ihn *untergedrückt.*
She *has pushed* him *under.*

Sie *unterdrückt* ihn.
She *suppresses* him.

Sie hat ihn *unterdrückt.*
She has *suppressed* him.

5. *wieder*

Der Knabe *holt* den Ball *wieder.*
The boy *brings* the ball *back.*

Der Knabe *hat* den Ball *wiedergeholt.*
The boy *has brought* the ball *back.*

Er *wiederholt* das Wort.
He *repeats* the word.

Er hat das Wort *wiederholt.*
He has *repeated* the word.

§ 69   Uses of the Gerund, Infinitive, and Participle

a. The gerund is used in English as a noun and is derived from the infinitive stem of a verb by adding *-ing*, e.g. *the writing, the singing*. This gerund is translated in German by the infinitive, which is then used as a neuter noun. Since the gerund and the infinitive used as nouns are derived from verbs, they are called *verbal nouns*. Almost any infinitive can be used as a neuter noun in German:

das *Kommen* und *Gehen* ..
The *coming* and *going*

das *Sehen*	das *Tanzen*	das *Singen*
the *seeing*	the *dancing*	the *singing*

With a few exceptions, e.g., *das Leben* (the life), *die Leben* (the lives), the nouns derived from the infinitive are used only in the singular.

b. The present participle is formed by adding *-d* to the infinitive:

liebend	gehend	singend
loving	going	singing

It is used in German only as adverb or adjective, not in verb formation, and is inflected like any other adjective:

die *liebende* Mutter	das *gehende* Kind
the *loving* mother	the *walking* child
der *singende* Vogel	ein *gehendes* Kind
the *singing* bird	a *walking* child

c. In addition to being used in the conjugation of the perfect tenses and the passive mood, the past participle is also used as an adjective:

die *geliebte* Mutter
the *beloved* mother

The present participle has active meaning, but the past participle used as adjective indicates passive force. In *die liebende Mutter* the mother does the loving, but in *die geliebte Mutter*, the mother is being loved. Similarly, *der singende Vogel* means "the singing bird," but *das gesungene Lied* is "the song being sung."

d. Since the present and past participles can be used as adjectives in German, it follows that, like adjectives, they can also be used as nouns with the proper article and adjective endings·

lieben	die *Liebenden*
to love	the *lovers, loving ones*
reisen	der *Reisende*
to travel	the *traveler*
geliebt	der *Geliebte*
beloved	the *beloved one* (the *one being loved*)
geschrieben	das Geschriebene
written	the *written matter* (*something that has been written*)

e. The infinitive with *zu* (to) is used:

1. In infinitive phrases:

Es freut mich, Sie zu sehen.
I am glad *to* see you.

Sie begann die Geschichte zu erzählen.
She began *to* tell the story.

Das ist schwer zu sagen.
That is difficult *to* say.

2. After certain prepositions such as *anstatt* (instead of) and *um ohne* (in order to) (indicating a purpose), and *ohne* (without):

Er blieb bis 12 Uhr, anstatt nach Hause zu gehen.
He remained until twelve o'clock instead *of* going home.

Er geht zur Bank, um Geld zu wechseln.
He goes to the bank *to (in order to)* change money.

Er kam in den Garten, ohne mich zu sehen.
He came into the garden without seeing *(to* see) me.

3. After *sein* with passive meaning.

Hier ist viel zu sehen.
Much is *to* be seen here.

Das ist leicht zu lernen.
That is easily learned.

§ 70   The Imperative Mood

The imperative mood is used in expressing a command. There are three forms of the imperative in German: two for the familiar form, singular and plural, one for polite address.

a. Whether the verb belongs to the weak or the strong conjugation, the imperative is formed by adding the following endings to the infinitive stem (there are only a few exceptions):

-e	**gehe***!*
	go (to a person addressed by *du*)
-(e)t	**geht***!*
	go (to a person addressed by *ihr*)
-en Sie	**gehen Sie***!*
	go (to a person addressed by *Sie,* singular and plural)

1. The personal pronoun of the polite form is never dropped and always follows the verbs.

2. The punctuation after the imperative is an exclamation mark.

3. Whenever the infinitive stem of a verb ends in *t* or *d* or *n* or *m* preceded by a consonant other than *l, m, n, r, h,* an *e* is inserted before the *t* ending.

warte!	**finde!**	**öffne!**
wait	find	open
wartet!	**findet!**	**öffnet!**
warten Sie!	**finden Sie!**	**öffnen Sie!**

b. A few irregular forms of the imperative must be noted:

1. The imperative of *sein* (to be):

    sei!   **seid!**   **seien Sie!**

2. Otherwise there is only one more exception to the rule for the formation of the imperative. Strong verbs which undergo a vowel change from the infinitive stem vowel *e* to *i* or *ie* in the second and third persons singular of the present tense also show this change in the form of the imperative familiar singular. The change takes place only in the *singular* and the *e* of the regular ending is dropped.

geben to give	lesen to read	nehmen to take	sehen to see
gib! give	*lies!* read	*nimm!* take	*sieh!* see
gebt!	lest!	nehmt!	seht!
geben Sie!	lesen Sie!	nehmen Sie!	sehen Sie!

All other verbs with vowel changes from *a* to *ä* and *au* to *äu* form their imperatives regularly:

tragen to carry	laufen to run
trage! carry	laufe! run
tragt!	lauft!
tragen Sie!	laufen Sie!

c. The imperatives of the reflexive verbs are as follows:

ACCUSATIVE	DATIVE
Freue *dich!* Be glad.	**Wasche *dir* die Hände!** Wash your hands.
Freut *euch!*	**Wascht *euch* die Hände!**
Freuen *Sie sich!*	**Waschen *Sie* sich die Hände!**

1. The reflexive pronoun must always be expressed in the imperative wherever a reflexive verb is used.

2. Whether the reflexive verb is followed by the accusative or the dative is shown only in the case of the pronoun of the familiar form singular:

    Freue *dich!* Wasche *dir* die Hände!

d. The imperatives of verbs with separable prefixes are as follows:

aufstehen to get up, rise	sich anziehen to get dressed
Stehe *auf!* Get up!	Ziehe dich *an!* Get dressed!
Steht *auf!*	Zieht euch *an!*
Stehen Sie *auf!*	Ziehen Sie sich *an!*

The separable prefix breaks away from the verb and is placed at the end of a phrase.

§ 71 The Modal Auxiliary Verbs

The modal auxiliary verbs are a group of six verbs which form a conjugation of their own. These verbs express possibility, wish, obligation, permission, and require the infinitive of another verb to complete the thought. Their use is highly idiomatic.

a. The six modal auxiliaries are:

dürfen	**mögen**	**sollen**
to be permitted, may	may, to like	shall, ought to
können	**müssen**	**wollen**
to be able, can	have to, must	to want, will

In English we no longer have most of the conjugational forms of the modal auxiliaries. Infinitives of the modals do not exist any longer, and substitutes for the different tenses, such as "to be able" for "can", "had to" for "must", have to be used. In German, however, forms for all tenses exist and are used.

b. The present tense of the modals differs from that of all strong and weak verbs:

dürfen	**können**	**mögen**	**müssen**	**sollen**	**wollen**
may	can	to like	must	shall	will
ich *darf*	*kann*	*mag*	*muss*	*soll*	*will*
du *darfst*	*kannst*	*magst*	*musst*	*sollst*	*willst*
er *darf*	*kann*	*mag*	*muss*	*soll*	*will*
wir *dürfen*	*können*	*mögen*	*müssen*	*sollen*	*wollen*
ihr *dürft*	*könnt*	*mögt*	*müsst*	*sollt*	*wollt*
sie *dürfen*	*können*	*mögen*	*müssen*	*sollen*	*wollen*

1. The present tense shows a vowel change in the first, second, and third person singular of all modal auxiliaries, except *sollen*.

2. The first and third persons singular do not take an ending.

3. The forms of the plural are regular; that is, they are formed on the infinitive stems and take the endings of the present tense.

c. The conjugation in the indicative of *können* (can, to be able) serves as a model for all modal auxiliaries.

PRESENT TENSE	PAST TENSE
ich *kann*	ich *konnte*
I *can*	I *could*
du *kannst*	du *konntest*
er *kann*	er *konnte*
wir *können*	wir *konnten*
ihr *könnt*	ihr *konntet*
sie *können*	sie *konnten*

PRESENT PERFECT TENSE	PAST PERFECT TENSE
ich *habe gekonnt*	ich *hatte gekonnt*
I *have been able*	I *had been able*

FUTURE TENSE	FUTURE PERFECT TENSE
Ich *werde können*	ich *werde gekonnt haben*
I *shall be able*	I *shall have been able*

d. The principal parts of the modal auxiliary verbs are as follows:

INFINITIVE	PRESENT	PAST	PAST PARTICIPLE	
dürfen (to be permitted)	darf	durfte	gedurft	dürfen
können (to be able)	kann	konnte	gekonnt	können
müssen (to have to)	muss	musste	gemusst	müssen
mögen (to like)	mag	mochte	gemocht	mögen
sollen (shall)	soll	sollte	gesollt	sollen
wollen (to will, want)	will	wollte	gewollt	wollen

e. Note these points regarding modal verb forms:

1. All modals are conjugated with *haben*.

2. In the past tense, there is a slight modification of the stem vowel. The umlaut of the infinitive is dropped in the past and past participle. *Sollen* and *wollen* keep their stem vowel.

3. Except in the present tense and the second past participle, the modals take the endings of the weak conjugation.

4. The modals have two forms of the past participle. Their uses will be explained in §72-b.

§ 72   Constructions with the Modal Auxiliary Verbs

a. In English, the modal auxiliary verb always requires an infinitive of another verb in order to complete the thought, e.g. "He can do it"; "She will not come today". In German too, the modals usually are accompanied by an infinitive.

Sie *will* heute *kommen.*	Er *kann* Deutsch *sprechen.*
She *wants to come* today.	He *can speak* German.

If, however, the inference from the preceding statement or question is clear or the meaning can be implied, the modal auxiliary is sometimes used without a dependent infinitive:

Kann er die Arbeit *machen?*	Ja, er *kann* es.
Can he do the *work?*	Yes, he *can do it.*

Wollte sie wirklich den Brief *schreiben?*	Sie *wollte* es.
Did she really want to *write* the letter?	She *wanted* to do it.

Ich *muss* fort.	Ich *kann* nicht mehr.
I *must* go away.	I *cannot* stand it any longer.

b. There are two forms of the past participle of the modal auxiliary in German: the regular past participle is formed as in a weak verb with the prefix *ge-* and the ending *-t*; and the "second" past participle which has exactly the same form as the infinitive of the verb: *können, wollen,* etc.

1. The regular past participle of the modal in compound tenses is used whenever it is not followed by a dependent infinitive:

Er hat es gekonnt.
He *has been able to do* it.

Er hatte es gekonnt.
He *had been able to do* it.

Sie hat es gewollt.
She *wanted to do* it.

Sie hat ihn nicht gemocht.
She *did* not *like* him.

2. The second form of the past participle, the same in form as the infinitive, is used when the modal is accompanied by a dependent infinitive. This is called a "double infinitive" construction.

Sie hat heute nicht kommen wollen.
She *did not want to come* today.

Er hat Deutsch sprechen können.
He *has been able to speak* German.

In an infinitive accompanying a modal auxiliary, *zu* is always omitted.

c. Word order in sentences with modal auxiliaries requires special mention:

1. In the main clause:

(a) With simple tenses, the dependent infinitive is at the end.

Ich kann nicht gehen.
I cannot *go.*

(b) With compound tenses the modal is at the end, preceded by the dependent infinitive.

Er hat nicht gehen können.
He *has* not *been able (to go).*

(c) With compound tenses, and omission of the infinitive, the past participle of the modal is last.

Er hat es nicht gekonnt.
He has not been able *(to go).*

2. In the dependent clause:

Ich weiss, dass er heute nicht hat kommen können.
I know that he *could* not *(has not been able to) come* today.

In a dependent clause which contains a modal auxiliary in a compound tense accompanied by an infinitive, the auxiliary of the past participle comes first, the dependent second, the "double infinitive" last.

This is the only exception to the *definite* rule that the inflected part of the verb comes last in a dependent clause [§56].

d. There are a number of other verbs which have some of the characteristics of the modal auxiliary verbs.

1. In structure, they belong either to the weak or the strong conjugation; the most important ones are:

INFINITIVE	PRESENT	PAST	PAST PARTICIPLE
gehen to go, walk	geht	ging	ist gegangen
heissen to order	heisst	hiess	geheissen
helfen to help	hilft	half	geholfen
hören to hear	hört	hörte	gehört
lassen to let	lässt	liess	gelassen
lehren to teach	lehrt	lehrte	gelehrt
lernen to learn	lernt	lernte	gelernt
sehen to see	sieht	sah	gesehen

2. They take an infinitive without *zu*.

3. They also require the "double infinitive" in compound tenses.

4. They conform to the same rules for word order as the modals.

> Er *half* ihm den Koffer *tragen.*
> He *helped* him *carry* the trunk.

> Er hat ihm den Koffer tragen *helfen.*
> He has *helped* him carry the trunk.

> Sie *lässt* sich ein Kleid *machen.*
> She *has (let)* a dress made.

> Haben Sie sich das Kleid in Paris machen *lassen?*
> Have you *had (let)* this dress made in Paris?

> Ich weiss, dass er hier die Vögel hat singen *hören.*
> I know that he *has heard* the birds sing here.

> Sie geht einkaufen.
> She goes shopping.

> Sie ist einkaufen gegangen.
> She went shopping.

§ 73   Uses of Modal Auxiliary Verbs

Modal auxiliaries are used highly idiomatically in German; some of the important uses follow:

a. *dürfen*—"to be permitted," often "may":

> *Darf* ich das Fenster öffnen?
> *May* I open the window?

> *Darf* (*dürfte*) ich um das Salz bitten?
> *May* I trouble (ask) you for the salt?

NOTE: *Dürfte,* the subjunctive of *dürfen,* is used for greater politeness.

b. können—"to be able, can," i.e. ability to perform or do something, "know how":

Können Sie singen?
Can you sing ?

Er *kann* nicht zur Schule gehen.
He *cannot go* to school.

Er *konnte* nicht tanzen.
He *could* not dance.

c. *mögen*—"to like, to like to"; sometimes "may":

Sie *mag* ihn nicht.
She *does* not *like* him.

Sie *möchten* gern nach Deutschland fahren.
They *would* like to go to Germany.

Das *mag* wahr sein.
That *may* be true.

NOTE 1: *Mögen,* in the meaning of "to like," is only used in the negative in modern German. This verb, especially in the positive, is gradually dying out in German. It is replaced by the adverb *gern* (like), with a verb:

Sie hat ihn *gern.*
She *likes* him.

NOTE 2: *Möchte,* the subjunctive of *mögen,* is often followed by the adverb *gern,* and, in that case, is translated by "should like to." This verb will tend to survive in certain idiomatic forms.

Sie *möchte* gern ins Theater gehen.
She *would like to* go to the theater.

d. *müssen*—"to have to, must"; indicating a drive by a force, to be compelled to (by law, etc.):

Jedes Kind *muss* mit sechs Jahren zur Schule gehen.
Every child *must* go to school at the age of six.

Ich *musste* gestern arbeiten.
I *had to* work yesterday.

Du musst *(darfst)* das nicht sagen.
You *must* not say that.

e. *sollen*—"to be expected (shall)"; signifiying a duty or moral law. In the past subjunctive, *sollen* is translated by "ought to".

Du *sollst* Vater und Mutter ehren.
Thou *shalt* honor thy father and mother.

Wir *sollten* ihn heute im Krankenhaus besuchen.
We *ought to* visit him in the hospital today.

Er *soll* eine deutsche Arbeit schreiben.
He *is to (expected to)* write a German composition.

sollen is often used where in English "to be said" or "to be supposed to" would be used:

> **Er *soll* sehr intelligent sein.**
> He *is said* to be intelligent.
>
> **Sie *sollen* in Europa sein.**
> They *are supposed* to be in Europe.

f. *wollen*—"to want, wish", is never used as auxiliary verb to form the future tense as in English:

> **Er *will* Deutsch lernen.**
> He *wants* to learn German.
>
> **Sie *wollte* ihn nicht wiedersehen.**
> She *did* not *want* to see him again.

Sometimes *wollen* means "to intend to":

> **Ich *wollte* es tun, aber ich hatte keine Zeit.**
> I *intended* to do it, but I had no time.
>
> **Sie *wollte* gerade fortgehen, als er kam.**
> She *was about* to *(intended* to) leave, when he came.

It also may mean "to claim to":

> **Er *will* reich sein.**
> He *claims* to be rich.
>
> **Sie *wollte* es gewusst haben.**
> She *claimed* to have known it.

§ 74 *Wissen* (to Know) and *Lassen* (to Let)

a. *Wissen,* to know (a fact), is a verb not easily classified in German. It is not a modal auxiliary verb but it has a conjugation similar to the modals:

PRESENT	PAST	PRESENT PERFECT
ich *weiss*	*wusste*	habe *gewusst*
du *weisst*	*wusstest*	hast *gewusst*
er *weiss*	*wusstet*	hat *gewusst*
wir *wissen*	*wussten*	haben *gewusst*
ihr *wisst*	*wusstet*	habt *gewusst*
sie *wissen*	*wussten*	haben *gewusst*

1. While the present tense is irregular in the singular and the other tenses show a vowel change to *u,* this verb otherwise follows the conjugation of the weak verb.

NOTE: The English verb "to know" is translated in three ways in German:

1. *wissen*—to know a fact:

> **Ich *weiss,* dass sie Marie heisst.**
> I *know* that her name is Marie.
>
> **Er *weiss,* wann die Ferien beginnen**
> He *knows* when the vacation begins.

2. *können*—"to be able, can," referring to physical or mental ability or skill, "to know how":

Ich *kann* Deutsch sprechen.
I am able to speak German.

Sie *kann* nicht schwimmen.
She is not *able* to swim.

Können Sie den Tisch heben?
Are you *able* to lift the table?

3. *kennen*—"to be acquainted with, to know a person or a place":

Kennen Sie Herrn Müller?
Do you know Mr. Muller?

Ich *kenne* Paris.
I know Paris.

b. *Lassen*, besides meaning "to let," may also mean "to leave," "to have something done or to cause something to be done".

Er *lässt* mich nicht arbeiten.
He *does* not *let* me work.

Lass mich in Ruhe!
Leave me in peace!

Sie *liess* einen Arzt kommen.
She *had* a doctor come.

Lassen with a reflexive infinitive means "to have something done":

Ich *lasse mir* ein Kleid machen.
I *am going* to have a dress made.

Sie *liess sich* ein Glass Wasser bringen.
She *had* a glass of water brought to her.

Sich lassen is also used instead of the English passive:

Das *lässt sich* leicht sagen.
That *can be* easily said.

§ 75   The Passive Voice

In the passive voice, the subject is acted upon or it passively suffers the action of the verb. In an active sentence the subject carries out the action:

ACTIVE:

Der Knabe schlägt den Hund.
The boy [subject] beats the dog [direct object].

PASSIVE:

Der Hund wird von dem Knaben geschlagen.
The dog [subject] is beaten [verb in passive] by the boy [the agent].

a. THE FORMATION OF THE PASSIVE.

1. To form the passive voice in German the auxiliary verb *werden* (to become) is used (as contrasted with the verb "to be" in English), to indicate the different tenses of a passive sentence. The main verb appears in form of the past participle as in English.

2. Whereas in English the preposition "by" is used to express the agent, in German usually *von* is used, followed by the dative.

3. The past participle of *werden* comes at the end of the sentence and the *ge-* of the regular form of the past participle, *geworden,*

is dropped, the form then becoming *worden.* This form is used in the present perfect, past perfect, and future perfect tenses of the passive.

Er ist geschlagen *worden.*
He has been beaten.

b. THE TENSES OF THE PASSIVE VOICE.

PRESENT:

Der Hund *wird von* dem Knaben *geschlagen.*
The dog *is beaten by* the boy.

PAST:

Der Hund *wurde von* dem Knaben *geschlagen.*
The dog *was beaten by* the boy.

PRESENT PERFECT:

Der Hund *ist von* dem Knaben *geschlagen worden.*
The dog *has been beaten by* the boy.

PAST PERFECT:

Der Hund *war von* dem Knaben *geschlagen worden.*
The dog *had been beaten by* the boy.

FUTURE:

Der Hund *wird von* dem Knaben *geschlagen werden.*
The dog *will be beaten by* the boy.

FUTURE PERFECT:

Der Hund *wird von* dem Knaben *geschlagen worden sein.*
The dog *will have been beaten by* the boy.

c. If the agent is a force or an object, the preposition *durch* (through), which takes the accusative case, is used. Otherwise, the formation of the passive voice is the same.

Die Stadt *ist durch* das Wasser *zerstört worden.*
The city *was destroyed* by water.
Der Tiger *wurde durch* eine Kugel *getötet.*
The tiger *was killed by* a bullet.

d. Basically, only transitive verbs can be changed directly into the passive voice, since only a direct objective (accusative case), never an indirect object (dative case) can be changed to the subject of the passive voice. Therefore, the so-called impersonal passive is used in German with *es* (it), as the subject and the third person singular of *werden* in the different tenses.

ACTIVE:

Die Lehrerinnen helfen den Kindern.
The teachers help the children.

PASSIVE:

***Es wird* den Kindern von den Lehrerinnen geholfen.**

OR:

Den Kindern *wird* von den Lehrerinnen geholfen.
The children are being helped by the teachers.

In sentence 1, the impersonal subject *es* (it), is used. In the second sentence, the subject *es* is understood, and consequently the verb *werden* is still used in the third person singular. The dative cannot become the subject and therefore cannot affect the number of the verb.

> **Sie hat ihm gedankt.**
> She thanked him.
>
> **Ihm *ist* von ihr *gedankt worden.***
> He is *being thanked* by her.

e. Verbs with the indefinite pronoun *man* (one, they, people) are frequently used in the passive voice in German, in which case the impersonal pronoun *es* (expressed or understood) is the subject of the sentence in the passive.

> ACTIVE: PASSIVE:
>
> *Man* **sagte.**   *Es wurde* **gesagt.**
> It was said.
>
> *Man* **tanzt und singt.**   *Es wird* **getanzt und gesungen.**
> There is dancing and singing.

If, however, the active sentence contains an adverb or adverbial phrase, e.g., *Man tanzte und sang gestern,* then the passive sentence begins with the adverb and the subject *es* (it), is understood, not expressed.

> *Gestern wurde viel* **getanzt und gesungen.**
> *Yesterday there was* much dancing and singing.
>
> *Hier wird* **Deutsch *gesprochen.***
> German *is spoken* here.

f. The "true" passive explained in the preceding paragraphs indicates an action going on at the different times, expressed by the tenses of *werden*. To point out this fact in English "is being," "was being," etc. are often used with the past participle of the verb.

> **Das Haus *wird gebaut.***
> The house *is being built.*

There is, however, a "false" passive in German, conjugated with *sein* (to be), which describes a condition or state of the subject, not an action. The past participle is used almost as a descriptive adjective. Notice the difference in meaning in the following sentences:

> FALSE PASSIVE:
>
> **Das Haus *ist* aus Stein *gebaut.***
> The house *is built* of stone.
>
> TRUE PASSIVE:
>
> **Das Haus *wurde* im Jahre 1890 *gebaut.***
> The house *was built (was being built)* in 1890.
>
> FALSE PASSIVE:
>
> **Die Tür *ist geöffnet.***
> The door *is open (opened).*

TRUE PASSIVE:

Die Tür *wird geöffnet.*
The door *is being opened.*

g. The passive voice is used less frequently in German than in English. There are many substitutes for the passive in German:

1. *Man* (one, people, they), as indefinite subject of a sentence:

Man sagt.   **Man tut das nicht.**
It is said.   It is not done.

2. The reflexive verb, which is more commonly used in German than in English.

Es *freut mich* sehr.   **Das *versteht sich.***
I *am pleased.*   That *is understood.*

Sie *interessierte sich* für ihn.
She *was interested* in him.

3. *lassen* (to let), often translated by "can" and the passive in English.

Das *lässt* sich leicht sagen.
That can *easily* be said.

4. *sein* (to be), with an infinitive and *zu.*

Das *ist zu erwarten.*
That *is* to *be expected.*

Hier *ist* alles *zu haben.*
Everything *is* to *be had* (to be gotten) here.

§ 76   The Subjunctive Mood

The indicative mood signifies an action or a state as fact; the subjunctive mood shows that something is possible, doubtful, desirable, uncertain, or contrary to fact. In German, the subjunctive is also used in an indirect statement, i.e. when something is repeated that someone said, wrote, reported, etc.

Er sagte, er *wäre* krank.
He said he is sick.

The subjunctive mood is not so often used in English as in German except in contrary to fact statements and in certain idiomatic expressions.

a. FORMATION OF THE SUBJUNCTIVE TENSES.

The personal endings are the same for all tenses of all verbs used in the subjunctive mood:

ich—-*e*   **wir—-*en***
du—-*est*   **ihr—-*et***
er—-*e*   **sie—-*en***
                Sie—-*en*

b. EXPRESSING THE PRESENT IN THE SUBJUNCTIVE.

1. There are two forms of the verb in the subjunctive mood to express present tense:

(a) One form is based on the infinitive stem:

gehen	machen	können	wissen	sein
to go	to make	to be able	to know	to be
ich *gehe*	*mache*	*könne*	*wisse*	*sei*
du *gehest*	*machest*	*könnest*	*wissest*	*seiest*
er *gehe*	*mache*	*könne*	*wisse*	*sei*
wir *gehen*	*machen*	*können*	*wissen*	*seien*
ihr *gehet*	*machet*	*könnet*	*wisset*	*seiet*
sie *gehen*	*machen*	*können*	*wissen*	*seien*

Note that *sein* is conjugated somewhat irregularly in the singular of the present subjunctive.

(b) The other form is based on the past tense stem:

ging-	macht-	konnt-	wusst-	war-	hatt-
ich *ginge*	*machte*	*könnte*	*wüsste*	*wäre*	*hätte*
du *gingest*	*machtest*	*könntest*	*wüsstest*	*wärest*	*hättest*
er *ginge*	*machte*	*könnte*	*wüsste*	*wäre*	*hätte*
wir *gingen*	*machten*	*könnten*	*wüssten*	*wären*	*hätten*
ihr *ginget*	*machtet*	*könntet*	*wüsstet*	*wäret*	*hättet*
sie *gingen*	*machten*	*könnten*	*wüssten*	*wären*	*hätten*

In the past tense stem of the subjunctive strong verbs take an umlaut whenever possible. Modal auxiliary verbs with the exception of *sollen* (shall) and *wollen* (will) also take an umlaut in the past tense of the subjunctive mood.

Weak verbs never take an umlaut in the past subjunctive mood. In the irregular weak verb, the stem vowel of the past indicative changes from *a* to *e;* in two verbs *a* changes to *ä.*

2. The two simple tenses derived from (1) the present infinitive and (2) the past indicative always present action in the subjunctive mood.

Er sieht aus, als ob er krank *sei.* **Wenn er nur hier *wäre.***
He looks as though he *were* sick. If he *were* only here!

c. COMPOUND TENSES IN THE SUBJUNCTIVE.

1. Only the compound tenses of the subjunctive mood express past action.

2. To form the compound tenses, the auxiliary verb of the present perfect, past perfect, future, and future perfect, respectively, is changed to the subjunctive form.

PRESENT PERFECT:
ich *habe* gemacht, du *habest* gemacht, er *habe* gemacht, etc.
ich *sei* gegangen, du *seiest* gegangen, er *sei* gegangen, etc.

PAST PERFECT:

ich *hätte* gemacht, du *hättest* gemacht, er *hätte* gemacht, etc.

ich *wäre* gegangen, du *wärest* gegangen, er *wäre* gegangen, etc.

FUTURE:

ich *werde* machen, du *werdest* machen, er *werde* machen, etc.

ich *werde* gehen, du *werdest* gehen, er *werde* gehen, etc.

FUTURE PERFECT:

ich *werde* gemacht *haben,* du *werdest* gemacht *haben,* er *werde* gemacht *haben,* etc.

ich *werde* gegangen *sein,* du *werdest* gegangen *sein,* er *werde* gegangen *sein,* etc.

d. THE USES OF THE SUBJUNCTIVE.

1. In indirect discourse, when repeating or reporting what somebody else said, wrote, had told, etc.:

Er sagt, dass er heute keine Zeit *habe* (or *hätte*).
He says that he *has* no time today.

Er schrieb, dass er sie letzte Woche *gesehen hätte*.
He wrote that he *had seen* her last week.

Since the indicative mood rather than the subjunctive mood is used in indirect discourse in conversational German, except in North Germany, this phase of the subjunctive mood will not be further developed here. In highly literary style, the subjunctive mood is used in indirect discourse.

2. In a wish:

PRESENT:

***Möge* sie glücklich sein!**
May she be happy!

Er *ruhe* in Frieden!
May he rest in peace!

Lang *lebe* die Freiheit!
Long *live* freedom!

***Wäre* er doch zu Hause!**
If he *were* only home!

***Hätte* ich nur Geld!**
If I only *had* money!

Wenn er es nur nicht *sähe!*
If only he would not see it!

PAST:

Hätte* sie es mir doch *gesagt.
If only she *had told* me!

Wenn er nur nicht so krank *gewesen wäre!*
If only he *had* not *been* so ill!

3. After *als ob* (as if):

PRESENT:

Sie sieht aus, als ob sie krank *wäre*.
She looks as if she *were* ill.

PAST:

Er sah aus, als ob er die ganze Nacht nicht *geschlafen hätte*.
He looked as if he *had* not *slept* all night.

Sie tat, als ob sie ihn nie *gesehen hätte*.
She acted as if she *had* never *seen* him.

4. In expressions of possibility or doubt:

Das *wäre* ein Fehler.	**Es *liesse* sich machen.**
That *would be* a mistake.	It *could be* done.
Es *könnte* wahr sein.	**Wäre es Ihnen recht?**
It *could (might)* be true.	*Would* it *be* all right with you?
Würden Sie morgen kommen?	
Would you *come* tomorrow?	

5. In polite expressions based on modal auxiliaries:

Dürfte ich um das Salz bitten?
May I *trouble* you for the salt?

Ich *möchte* Sie gern *begleiten*.
I *would like to accompany* you.

Man *sollte* so etwas nicht *sagen*.
One *should* not *say* such a thing.

6. In a command:

Lassen Sie uns jetzt gehen!
Let us go now.

Nehmen wir eine Autodroschke!
Let us take a taxi.

§ 77   The Conditional Mood

a. FORMATION OF THE CONDITIONAL TENSES.

The conditional has only two tenses, present and past.

PRESENT CONDITIONAL

1. To form the present tense of the conditional, the past subjunctive of *werden* (to become) is used, with the infinitive of the verb:

ich *würde antworten*	er *würde gehen*	sie *würde schreiben*
I *should answer*	he *would go*	she *would write*

The conditional formation is the same for all verbs, strong or weak.

ich *würde haben*	ich *würde sein*	ich *würde antworten*
I *should have*	I *should be*	I *should answer*
du *würdest haben*	du *würdest sein*	du *würdest antworten*
er *würde haben*	er *würde sein*	er *würde antworten*
wir *würden haben*	wir *würden sein*	wir *würden antworten*
ihr *würdet haben*	ihr *würdet sein*	ihr *würdet antworten*
sie *würden haben*	sie *würden sein*	sie *würden antworten*

Note that the present conditional looks like the future, with *würden* instead of *werden*.

PAST CONDITIONAL

2. To form the past conditional, the past subjunctive of *werden* is used with the past participle of the verb and the infinitive *haben* or *sein*:

ich *würde gehabt haben* I *should have had*	ich *würde gewesen sein* I *should have been*
du *würdest gehabt haben*	du *würdest gewesen sein*
er *würde gehabt haben*	er *würde gewesen sein*
wir *würden gehabt haben*	wir *würden gewesen sein*
ihr *würdet gehabt haben*	ihr *würdet gewesen sein*
sie *würden gehabt haben*	sie *würden gewesen sein*

ich *würde geantwortet haben*
I *should have answered*

du *würdest geantwortet haben*
er *würde geantwortet haben*
wir *würden geantwortet haben*
ihr *würdet geantwortet haben*
sie *würden geantwortet haben*

Note that the past conditional resembles the future perfect tense, with *würden* instead of *werden*.

b. Uses of the Conditional.

The conditional is used in German in statements that are unreal, or are mere suppositions or contrary to fact or reality.

1. *Expressing present time:*

Wenn ich Geld hätte, *würde* ich einen Wagen *kaufen*.
If I had money, I *should buy* a car.

Ich *würde* einen Spaziergang *machen*, wenn ich Zeit hätte.
I *should take* a walk, if I had time.

Wäre ich Sie, *täte* ich das nicht.
If I were you, I *should* not *do* it.

2. *Expressing past time:*

Wenn ich Geld gehabt hätte, *würde* ich mir letztes Jahr einen Wagen *gekauft haben* (or . . . hätte ich mir letztes Jahr einen Wagen *gekauft*.)
If I had had money, I *should have bought* myself a car last year.

Ich *hätte* gestern einen Spaziergang *gemacht* (or . . . Ich *würde* gestern einen Spaziergang *gemacht haben*), wenn ich Zeit gehabt hätte.
I *should have taken* a walk yesterday, if I had had time.

Wäre ich Sie gewesen, *hätte* ich das nicht getan (or . . . *würde* ich das nicht *getan haben*).
If I had been you, I *should* not *have done* it.

c. Note from the above examples that there are in German two possibilities for expressing the conclusion in a contrary-to-fact statement: by the conditional (as in English) or by the subjunctive (possible only in German).

> **Wenn ich Geld hätte, *würde ich* einen Wagen *kaufen* (... *kaufte* ich einen Wagen).**
> If I had money, I *would buy* a car.

Usually with strong verbs, the subjunctive is preferred in the conclusion. With weak verbs, however, the conditional is more commonly used in the conclusion, especially in expressing the present tense, since the forms of the indicative and subjunctive are alike in the simple tenses. There is, however, the tendency in German to use a construction of the subjunctive or conditional that definitely differs from the indicative form. But, either the subjunctive or the conditional in the conclusion is grammatically correct.

Remember that in the *wenn* or "if" clause, the conditional should never be used. This rule is also valid in English.

§ 78   Impersonal Construction of Verbs

In German many verbs are used with *es* (it) as an indefinite subject.

a. In expressions referring to phenomena of nature, as in English.

es regnet	**es donnert**
it is raining (it rains)	it is thundering (it thunders)
es schneit	**es blitzt**
it is snowing (it snows)	it is lightning (it lightens)

b. The following verbs can be used not only in the third person singular, but also in the third person plural.

1. *es gelingt* (from *gelingen* to succeed in)

> **Es gelingt ihm nicht, weiterzukommen,**
> He *does* not *succeed* in getting ahead.
>
> **Die Experimente *gelangen* ihm gut.**
> He *succeeded* well in his experiments.

2. *es geschieht* (from *geschehen* to happen)

> **Es geschieht dir recht.**
> It serves you right (*lit.*, It happens to you right).
>
> **Diese Unfälle *geschahen* vor einer Woche.**
> These accidents *happened* a week ago.

c. But other verbs are also used impersonally in German in idiomatic expressions as in English.

1. In such expressions as "it seems," "it looks," etc.:

> **Es scheint heute warm zu sein.**   **Es sieht aus, als ob ...**
> It *seems* to be warm today.   It *looks* as if ...

2. In many expressions in German referring to physical or emotional conditions (with the "dative of interest"):

Wie *geht es* Ihnen?	**Es *geht* mir gut.**
How are you?	I am well.
Es *freut* mich.	**Es *wundert* mich.**
I am glad.	I am surprised.
Es *tut* mir leid.	**Er (*sie*) *tut* mir leid.**
I am sorry.	I am sorry for him (her).
Es *gefällt* mir.	**Sie *gefallen* mir.**
I like it.	I like them.
Es *ärgert* mich.	**Die *Kinder ärgern* mich.**
It vexes me.	The children vex me.
Es *steht* Ihnen gut.	**Er (*die Hut*) *steht* Ihnen gut.**
It looks well on you.	It (the hat) looks well on you.

In the above examples, the impersonal subject *es* refers in a vague sense to something to which the speaker reacts. Therefore, when the *es* is replaced by something concrete which is then the subject of the sentence, whoever experiences the emotion or reaction is usually indicated by the dative case ("It happens to me," etc.), sometimes by the accusative.

d. Often *es* is not expressed, as in the following idiomatic phrases:

Mich friert (Es friert mich).	**Mir ist warm (Es ist mir warm).**
I am freezing.	I am warm.
Mir ist kalt (Es ist mir kalt).	
I am cold.	

e. The pronoun *es* is frequently used in German similarly to the English "there," referring to:

1. Something definite, countable:

> **Es sind 126 Schulen in dieser Stadt.**
> *There* are one hundred twenty-six schools in this city.

2. Something indefinite:

> **Es gibt viele Schulen in dieser Stadt.**
> *There* are many schools in this city.

f. The neuter *es* may also anticipate the real subject, which could be in any gender or number.

Es irrt der Mensch, solange er lebt.	**Es sind meine Freunde.**
Man errs as long as he lives.	They are my friends.

g. The impersonal pronoun *es* is also used in the passive mood.

Es wurde nur Deutsch gesprochen.	**Es wird gemacht werden.**
Only German was spoken.	It will be done.

h. The indefinite pronoun *man* (one) may be used as subject of a verb. It is always in the singular.

1. *man* can be translated as "they, people, you, one."

> **Man weiss nicht, was passieren kann.**
> *You* never know (*one* never knows) what may happen.

> **Man würde das nicht glauben.**
> *People* would not believe that.

2: Frequently the verb with *man* as subject is translated by the passive voice in English:

Man sagt.
It is said. (*People say.*)
Man muss das nicht tun.
That must not be done.
Man isst viel Fleisch in Amerika.
Much meat is eaten in America. (*People* eat much meat in America.)
Man sah sie oft im Theater.
They were often seen in the theater.

§ 79   Summary of Rules for Word Order

The verb plays a very important part in determining the word order in a sentence. The place of the verb in a clause or a sentence determines the type of word order. Whenever the position of a verb, however, is mentioned in regard to word order, the inflected part of a verb (also called "finite verb") is meant, i.e., in a simple tense the verb proper, in a compound tense the auxiliary (or helping word)· The word order is very characteristic and differs very much from English word order.

a. NORMAL WORD ORDER.

In normal word order the subject comes before the verb, as in English. This word order is used in German:

1. When the sentence begins with the subject:

Der Vater ist nicht hier.   **Sie hat zwei Söhne.**
The father is not here.   *She* has two sons.

2. After the coordinating conjunctions, because these conjunctions combine two clauses which are of the same or equal values and importance; in other words both clauses are *main* clauses.

Hans fährt nach Deutschland, *aber* die Mutter bleibt zu Hause.
Hans goes to Germany, *but* his mother remains at home.

3. After adverbs of affirmation or negation, such as *ja* (yes), *nein* (no), and *gut* (all right), since these adverbs imply a sentence understood but not expressed:

Nein, mein Bruder spricht nicht Deutsch.
No, my brother does not speak German.
Gut, wir können jetzt gehen.
All right, we can go now.

4. In a question which starts with the interrogative subject:

Wer hat das getan?
Who did that?
Welches Kind spielt auf der Strasse?
Which child is playing in the street?

5. In an indirect statement when the subordinating conjunction *dass* (that) is omitted:

Ich glaube, er hat recht.
I believe he is right.

BUT:

Ich glaube, *dass* er recht hat.
I believe *that* he is right.

6. In German an adverb or adverbial phrase cannot come between the subject and its verb as in English:

Sie geht *beinah* nie ohne ihn.
She *hardly* ever goes without him.

b. INVERTED WORD ORDER.

In inverted word order the regular position of the subject and verb is reversed; that is, the verb comes before the subject. The inverted word order is used:

1. In a question:

Haben Sie einen Bruder?
Have you a brother?

Wird sie ihn im Sommer besuchen?
Will she visit him in Summer?

Warum haben Sie ihm das gesagt?
Why did you tell him that?

2. In the imperative of the polite form of direct address:

Warten Sie einen Augenblick!   **Steigen Sie ein!**
Wait a moment!   Get in!

3. In commands:

Nehmen wir eine Droschke!
Let us take a taxi.

Fahren wir mit der Untergrundbahn!
Let us go by subway.

4. If the main clause does not start with a subject, being preceded by an adverb, an adverbial phrase, an object, or a dependent clause:

In Deutschland sagt man
In Germany ONE SAYS . . .

Morgen besuche ich Sie.
Tomorrow I SHALL VISIT you.

Dass er heute nicht kommen kann, hat er mir schon gesagt.
That he cannot come today, HE HAS already told me.

Obgleich es den ganzen Tag geregnet hat, bin ich nicht nass geworden.
Although it rained all day, I DID not GET wet.

Den Hut trage ich nicht.
That hat I AM not WEARING.

Der Tante brauchst du das nicht zu sagen.
YOU NEED not TELL that to your aunt.

Dem Hund gebe ich das Fleisch nicht.
I DO not GIVE that meat to the dog.

If something is to be stressed, there is a tendency in German to begin the sentence with the important word or phrase.

5. Usually after adverbial conjunctions:

> **Sie sind jetzt in Bayern, *deshalb* können *Sie* nicht kommen.**
> They are in Bavaria just nòw; *therefore* THEY CANNOT come.

> ***Teils* sind *sie* dagegen teils dafür.**
> Partly THEY ARE against it, partly for it.

6. In simple condition or contrary-to-fact statements, when *wenn* (if) is omitted:

> ***Irre ich* mich nicht, so wohnt er in dieser Strasse?**
> If I am not mistaken, he lives in this street.

> ***Wäre er* gesund, würde er nicht so müde sein.**
> If he were well he would not be so tired.

Similarly, in a subjunctive of wish when *wenn* is dropped:

> ***Wäre er* nur zur Zeit gekommen!**
> If only he had come in time.

7. After *als* (as), followed by the subjunctive. In German, *ob* (if), in the phrase *als ob* (as if), may be dropped, in which case the word order changes from dependent to inverted word order:

> **Er sieht aus, als sei *er* krank.**
> RATHER THAN:
> **Er sieht aus, als ob er krank *sei*.**
> He looks *as if* HE WERE sick.

8. The past participle and the infinitive are at the end of the sentence in inverted word order, as in normal word order.

c. WORD ORDER OF THE DEPENDENT CLAUSE.

A dependent clause is introduced either by a subordinating conjunction or a relative pronoun.

1. In dependent word order, the subject follows the conjunction or relative pronoun and the inflected part of the verb goes to the end of the clause, while the past participle or the infinitive precedes the finite verb.

> **Sie gehen jeden Tag baden, *während es* so warm *ist*.**
> They go bathing every day *while* it IS so warm.

> ***Nachdem wir* gegessen *hatten*, gingen wir spazieren.**
> *After* we HAD EATEN we went for a walk.

> **Der Dampfer, *mit dem* wir morgen *fahren*, ist in Deutschland gebaut worden.**
> The steamer *with which* we ARE GOING tomorrow was built in Germany.

> **Er spart Geld, *damit* er eine Reise machen *kann*.**
> He is saving (saves) money *so that he* WILL BE ABLE to take a trip.

2. When a modal auxiliary with a double infinitive in a compound tense is used in a dependent clause, then the helping verb precedes the double infinitive. All other verbs which require a double infinitive without *zu* (to) also follow this rule.

> **Ich weiss, dass er uns nicht vom Bahnhof *hat abholen können*.**
> I know that he WAS not *able* (has been *able*) to meet us at the station.

Da Sie ihn nicht *haben singen hören,* wissen Sie nicht, was für eine schöne Stimme er hat.
Since you HAVE not *heard* him *sing,* you do not know, what a beautiful voice he has.

d. POSITION OF THE DIRECT AND INDIRECT OBJECT.

1. The indirect object precedes the direct object, unless the direct object is a pronoun.

Die Mutter kauft *dem Knaben* einen Anzug.
The mother buys *the boy* a suit.

Die Mutter kauft *ihm* einen Anzug.
The mother buys *him* a suit.

Die Mutter kauft ihn *dem Knaben.*
The mother buys it *for the boy.*

Die Mutter kauft ihn *ihm.*
The mother buys it *for him.*

2. The adverb or adverbial phrase of time usually precedes the direct object. Other adverbs to be stressed also precede the direct object but not the indirect object.

Er hat sich *gestern* einen Schlips im Warenhaus gekauft.
He brought himself a tie at the department store *yesterday.*

Sie gibt ihm *heute* ein Buch.
She is going to give him a book *today.*

Sie hat dem Kind *auf der Strasse* einen Apfel gegeben.
She gave the child an apple *on the street.*

Er zeigte ihr *heute* das Bild.
He showed the picture to her *today.*

Er zeigte es ihr *heute.*
He showed it to her *today.*

e. THE POSITION OF *sich* AND ITS INFLECTED FORMS.

1. In a main clause and after coordinating conjunctions the reflexive pronoun *sich* follows right after the verb.

Sie hat *sich* die Hände gewaschen.
She washed her hands.

Ich kann nicht lange bleiben, aber ich will *mich* doch ein bisschen ausruhen.
I cannot stay long, but I want to rest for a little while.

2. In a dependent clause, a question, or a clause with inverted word order, *sich* comes directly after the subject.

Sie sagte, dass sie *sich* die Hände gewaschen hat.
She said (that) she washed her hands.

Weil Sie *sich* nicht aufs Sofa setzen, muss ich mich darauf setzen.
Since you are not going to sit down on the sofa, I have to sit on it.

Freuen Sie *sich* auf morgen?
Are you looking forward to tomorrow?

Heute haben wir *uns* noch nicht gesehen.
We have not seeen *each other* today.

f. POSITION OF THE INFINITIVE.

1. The infinitive stands last in the sentence, clause, or phrase.

(a) In a main clause and in phrases introduced by a coordinating conjunction.

(1) With compound tenses:

Er wird das Haus nicht *kaufen*.
He will not *buy* the house.

Er wird auch nächstes Jahr das Haus nicht gekauft *haben*.
Even by next year, he will not have *bought* the house.

Sie war in der Stadt, aber ich konnte sie nicht *sprechen*.
She was in town, but I could not *speak* to her.

Sie braucht den Brief nicht *schreiben*.
She does not have to *write* the letter.

(2) After infinitive phrases introduced by *um* (in order to), *anstatt* (instead of), *ohne* (without):

Sie ging zur Bäckerei, um Kuchen zu *kaufen*.
She went to the bakery *to buy* cake.

Anstatt zu *ruhen*, gingen sie in die Stadt.
Instead of *resting* they went downtown.

Er machte eine Reise, ohne viel Gepäck *mitzunehmen*.
He took a trip without *taking* much baggage.

(3) In infinitive phrases:

Sie baten ihn, zum Kaffee zu *kommen*.
They asked him *to come* for coffee.

Wir werden versuchen, Ihnen die Grammatik zu *erklären*.
We shall try *to explain* the grammar to you.

(b) In dependent clauses with a double infinitive, the infinitive of the modal auxiliary is at the end, the accompanying infinitive preceding it:

Sie sagte, dass sie das nicht hätte tun *sollen*.
She said that she *should* not have done it.

Er wusste, dass er das Haus hat verlassen *müssen*.
He knew that he *had to* leave the house.

g. POSITION OF THE PAST PARTICIPLE.

1. The past participle stands at the end of a sentence or clause.

(a) In a main clause:

Sie hat ihn gestern *gesehen*.
She *saw* him yesterday.

Er hatte den Brief *geschrieben*, als ich in das Zimmer kam.
He had *written* the letter when I entered the room.

(b) In inverted word order:

Warum hat er das *getan*?
Why did he *do* it?

Heute sind sie ins Theater *gegangen*.
They *went* to the theater today.

2. The past participle precedes the inflected part of the verb in a dependent clause.

Er sagt, dass er dem Mann gestern *geholfen* hat.
He says he *helped* the man yesterday.

Weil er den ganzen Tag *gearbeitet* hatte, war er abends sehr müde.
Since he had *worked* all day he was very tired in the evening.

h. Position of Adverbs and Adverbial Phrases.

1. Adverbs or adverbial phrases of time precede all other adverbs or adverbial phrases.

Er kommt *heute* nicht nach Hause.
He does not come home *today*.

Sie werden *heute abend* mit dem Auto nach Köln fahren.
They will go to Cologne by car *tonight*.

2. Adverbs or adverbial phrases of manner usually precede adverbs of place.

Sie ist gestern *mit ihrer Freundin* aufs Land gefahren.
She went to the country *with her friend* yesterday.

3. The place of *nicht* in a sentence is not easily covered by an iron-clad rule, and a feeling for it must be acquired gradually.

(a) In a simple sentence with a verb in simple tense, *nicht* is at the end.

Sie weiss es *nicht*.	**Geben Sie ihr das Geld *nicht!***
She does *not* know it.	Don't give her the money.

(b) In compound tenses *nicht* usually precedes the past participle and the infinitive:

Wir haben ihn heute noch *nicht* gesehen.
We have *not* seen him today.

Er wird das Buch *nicht* lesen.
He will *not* read the book.

(c) Generally, *nicht* precedes that part of speech which it negates:

Ist dieser Satz *nicht* richtig?
Is this sentence *not* correct?

Er hat mir *nicht* einen Brief, sondern eine Karte geschrieben.
He did *not* write me a letter but a card.

Das Wetter wird *nicht* besser werden.
The weather will *not* get better.

i. Position of Separable Prefixes.

1. In a main clause, question, or any clause with inverted word order, the separable prefix stands at the end in simple tenses:

Ziehen Sie sich schnell *an!*
Get dressed quickly.

Er steht jeden Morgen um 7 Uhr *auf*.
Every morning he gets *up* at seven o'clock.

Morgen sehe ich ihn *wieder*.
I shall see him *again* tomorrow.

2. In compound tenses and dependent clauses the prefix as well as *zu* with an infinitive is connected with the verb:

Er ist heute morgen um 7 Uhr *aufgestanden*.
He *got up* at seven o'clock this morning.

Ich werde ihn morgen *wiedersehen*.
I shall *see* him *again* tomorrow.

Sie sagte, dass er sich schnell *anziehen* soll.
She said that he should *get dressed* quickly.

3. The word order of the separable prefixes is used whenever the verb and its modifier form a close relationship of idea:

(a) With the verb *sein* (to be):

Die Frau ist trotz ihres Alters sehr *schön*.
The woman is very *beautiful* in spite of her age.

Die Kinder sind sehr wild aber doch *wohlerzogen*.
The children are wild, yet *well bred*.

(b) Verb with adverb:

Er liest und schreibt *sehr gut Deutsch*.
He reads and writes *German very well*.

Trinken Sie das Eiswasser nicht *so schnell!*
Don't drink the ice water *so fast*.

(c) Verb with noun:

Sie spielt den ganzen Tag *Klavier*.
She plays the *piano* all day.

Spielen Sie im Sommer gern *Tennis?*
Do you like to play *tennis* in the summer?

(d) Verb with infinitives (usually written in one word):

kennenlernen   **spazierengehen**
to get acquainted   to take a walk

Wir *lernten* uns letzten Winter in der Schweiz *kennen*.
We *became acquainted* in Switzerland last winter.

Gehen* wir jetzt ein bisschen *spazieren!
Let us take a little *walk* now.

4. In compound tenses and dependent clauses.

(a) In compound tenses:

Die Frau war früher *sehr schön* gewesen.
The woman had formerly been *very beautiful*.

Er hat sehr gut *Deutsch* gelesen und geschrieben.
He wrote and read *German* very well.

Wir haben uns letzten Winter in der Schweiz *kennengelernt*.
We *became* acquainted in Switzerland last year.

(b) In dependent clauses:

Wir wissen, dass Sie gestern im Park *spazierengegangen* sind.
We know that you *went for a walk* in the park yesterday.

Er sagte, dass er im Sommer gern *Tennis spielt*.
He said he likes to play *tennis* in the summer.

VERB LIST

The verb list is composed of four sections:

    A. Strong verbs

    B. Irregular verbs

    C. Irregular weak verbs

    D. Modal auxiliary verbs.

Weak verbs are not included because all tenses and forms of the weak verb can be derived from the stem of the infinitive by the application of definite rules given in §63.

The *principal parts,* that is to say, the infinitive, third person singular of the present indicative and past indicative, past participle, and the irregularly formed imperative, familiar form, are given. From these given forms, all other forms and tenses can be derived by the addition of appropriate endings to the required stem in accordance with rules given in §66 and §67, a—c.

The verb forms are given in the *third person singular* because this form shows any irregularity in the present and gives the past stem.

If the past participle is preceded by *ist* (third person sing. of *sein*), the compound tenses of the verb are conjugated with the appropriate form of *sein.* If the past participle alone is given, the compound tenses are conjugated with the appropriate form of *haben.*

The imperative is given in the singular familiar form only when the vowel of the infinitive stem changes from *e* to *i* in the imperative. All other imperatives are regularly formed from the infinitive. Some verbs do not have imperatives because of the nature of their meaning, i.e., modal auxiliaries have no imperatives because, obviously, an order cannot be formulated upon them.

Many new verbs can be formed by the addition of a prefix to a basic verb. These compounds follow the conjugation of the original verb and, therefore, are not listed here.

STRONG VERBS

INFINITIVE	PRESENT INDICATIVE	PAST INDICATIVE	PAST PARTICIPLE	IMPERATIVE
backen (to bake)	bäckt	buk	gebacken	
befehlen (to command)	befiehlt	befahl	befohlen	befiehl
beginnen (to begin)	beginnt	begann	begonnen	

INFINITIVE	PRESENT INDICATIVE	PAST INDICATIVE	PAST PARTICIPLE	IMPERATIVE
beissen (to bite)	beisst	biss	gebissen	
bergen (to conceal)	birgt	barg	geborgen	birg
bersten (to burst)	birst	barst	(ist) geborsten	birst
betrügen (to deceive)	betrügt	betrog	betrogen	
bewegen (to induce)	bewegt	bewog	bewogen	
biegen (to bend)	biegt	bog	gebogen	
bieten (to offer)	bietet	bot	geboten	
binden (to bind)	bindet	band	gebunden	
bitten (to beg, to ask)	bittet	bat	gebeten	
blasen (to blow)	bläst	blies	geblasen	
bleiben (to remain)	bleibt	blieb	(ist) geblieben	
braten (to roast)	brät	briet	gebraten	
brechen (to break)	bricht	brach	gebrochen	brich
dringen (to press)	dringt	drang	(ist) gedrungen	
einladen (to invite)	lädt ein	lud ein	eingeladen	
empfehlen (to recommend)	empfiehlt	empfahl	empfohlen	empfiehl
erbleichen (to turn pale)	erbleicht	erblich	(ist) erblichen	
erlöschen (to extinguish, to go out)	erlischt	erlosch	(ist) erloschen	erlisch
erschrecken (to be frightened)	erschrickt	erschrak	(ist) erschrocken	erschrick
essen (to eat)	isst	ass	gegessen	iss
fahren (to drive, ride)	fährt	fuhr	(ist) gefahren	
fallen (to fall)	fällt	fiel	(ist) gefallen	

INFINITIVE	PRESENT INDICATIVE	PAST INDICATIVE	PAST PARTICIPLE	IMPERATIVE
fangen (to catch)	fängt	fing	gefangen	
fechten (to fence)	ficht	focht	gefochten	ficht
finden (to find)	findet	fand	gefunden	
flechten (to braid)	flicht	flocht	geflochten	flicht
fliegen (to fly)	fliegt	flog	(ist) geflogen	
fliehen (to flee)	flieht	floh	(ist) geflohen	
fliessen (to flow)	fliesst	floss	(ist) geflossen	
fressen (to eat [of animals])	frisst	frass	gefressen	friss
frieren (to freeze)	friert	fror	gefroren	
gebären (to bear, give birth)	gebiert	gebar	geboren	gebier
geben (to give)	gibt	gab	gegeben	gib
gedeihen (to thrive)	gedeiht	gedieh	(ist) gediehen	
gehen (to go)	geht	ging	(ist) gegangen	
gelingen (to succeed)	gelingt	gelang	(ist) gelungen	
gelten (to be worth)	gilt	galt	gegolten	gilt
genesen (to recover)	genest	genas	(ist) genesen	
geniessen (to enjoy)	geniesst	genoss	genossen	
geschehen (to happen)	geschieht	geschah	(ist) geschehen	
gewinnen (to gain, to get)	gewinnt	gewann	gewonnen	
giessen (to pour)	giesst	goss	gegossen	
gleichen (to resemble)	gleicht	glich	geglichen	
gleiten (to glide)	gleitet	glitt	(ist) geglitten	

INFINITIVE	PRESENT INDICATIVE	PAST INDICATIVE	PAST PARTICIPLE	IMPERATIVE
glimmen (to gleam)	glimmt	glomm	geglommen	
graben (to dig)	gräbt	grub	gegraben	
greifen (to seize)	greift	griff	gegriffen	
halten (to hold)	hält	hielt	gehalten	
hängen (to hang, to be suspended)	hängt	hing	gehangen	
hauen (to hew, to strike)	haut	hieb	gehauen	
heben (to lift)	hebt	hob	gehoben	
heissen (to bid, to be called)	heisst	hiess	geheissen	
helfen (to help)	hilft	half	geholfen	hilf
klingen (to sound)	klingt	klang	geklungen	
kommen (to come)	kommt	kam	(ist) gekommen	
kriechen (to creep)	kriecht	kroch	(ist) gekrochen	
laden (to load)	lädt or ladet	lud	geladen	
lassen (to let)	lässt	liess	gelassen	
laufen (to run)	läuft	lief	(ist) gelaufen	
leiden (to suffer)	leidet	litt	gelitten	
leihen (to lend)	leiht	lieh	geliehen	
lesen (to read)	liest	las	gelesen	lies
liegen (to lie)	liegt	lag	gelegen	
lügen (to tell a lie)	lügt	log	gelogen	
meiden (to avoid)	meidet	mied	gemieden	
messen (to measure)	misst	mass	gemessen	miss

INFINITIVE	PRESENT INDICATIVE	PAST INDICATIVE	PAST PARTICIPLE	IMPERATIVE
misslingen (to fail)	misslingt	misslang	(ist) misslungen	
nehmen (to take)	nimmt	nahm	genommen	nimm
pfeifen (to whistle)	pfeift	pfiff	gepfiffen	
preisen (to praise)	preist	pries	gepriesen	
quellen (to gush, to well)	quillt	quoll	(ist) gequollen	quill
raten (to advise)	rät	riet	geraten	
reiben (to rub)	reibt	rieb	gerieben	
reissen (to tear)	reisst	riss	gerissen	
reiten (to ride)	reitet	ritt	(ist) geritten	
riechen (to smell)	riecht	roch	gerochen	
rufen (to call)	ruft	rief	gerufen	
saufen (to drink [of animals])	säuft	soff	gesoffen	
schaffen (to create)	schafft	schuf	geschaffen	
schallen (to sound)	schallt	scholl	geschollen	
scheiden (to part)	scheidet	schied	(ist) geschieden	
scheinen (to appear, to shine)	scheint	schien	geschienen	
schelten (to scold)	schilt	schalt	gescholten	schilt
schieben (to shove, to push)	schiebt	schob	geschoben	
schiessen (to shoot)	schiesst	schoss	geschossen	
schlafen (to sleep)	schläft	schlief	geschlafen	
schlagen (to strike)	schlägt	schlug	geschlagen	
schleichen (to sneak)	schleicht	schlich	(ist) geschlichen	

INFINITIVE	PRESENT INDICATIVE	PAST INDICATIVE	PAST PARTICIPLE	IMPERATIVE
schleifen (to whet, to grind)	schleift	schliff	geschliffen	
schliessen (to shut)	schliesst	schloss	geschlossen	
schmelzen (to melt)	schmilzt	schmolz	(ist) geschmolzen	schmilz
schneiden (to cut)	schneidet	schnitt	geschnitten	
schrauben (to screw)	schraubt	schrob	geschroben	
schreiben (to write)	schreibt	schrieb	geschrieben	
schreien (to cry out, to shout)	schreit	schrie	geschrieen	
schreiten (to stride)	schreitet	schritt	(ist) geschritten	
schweigen (to be silent)	schweigt	schwieg	geschwiegen	
schwellen (to swell)	schwillt	schwoll	(ist) geschwollen	schwill
schwimmen (to swim)	schwimmt	schwamm	(ist) geschwommen	
schwinden (to vanish)	schwindet	schwand	(ist) geschwunden	
schwingen (to swing)	schwingt	schwang	geschwungen	
schwören (to swear)	schwört	schwor, schwur	geschworen	
sehen (to see)	sieht	sah	gesehen	sieh
sieden (to simmer, to seethe)	siedet	sott	gesotten	
singen (to sing)	singt	sang	gesungen	
sinken (to sink)	sinkt	sank	(ist) gesunken	
sinnen (to think, to reflect)	sinnt	sann	gesonnen	
sitzen (to sit)	sitzt	sass	gesessen	
speien (to spit)	speit	spie	gespieen	
spinnen (to spin)	spinnt	spann	gesponnen	

INFINITIVE	PRESENT INDICATIVE	PAST INDICATIVE	PAST PARTICIPLE	IMPERATIVE
sprechen (to speak)	spricht	sprach	gesprochen	sprich
spriessen (to sprout)	spriesst	spross	(ist) gesprossen	
springen (to spring)	springt	sprang	(ist) gesprungen	
stechen (to prick)	sticht	stach	gestochen	stich
stehen (to stand)	steht	stand	gestanden	
stehlen (to steal)	stiehlt	stahl	gestohlen	stiehl
steigen (to ascend)	steigt	stieg	(ist) gestiegen	
sterben (to die)	stirbt	starb	(ist) gestorben	stirb
stossen (to push, to kick)	stösst	stiess	gestossen	
streichen (to stroke)	streicht	strich	gestrichen	
streiten (to argue)	streitet	stritt	gestritten	
tragen (to carry)	trägt	trug	getragen	
treffen (to hit, to meet)	trifft	traf	getroffen	triff
treiben (to drive)	treibt	trieb	getrieben	
treten (to step)	tritt	trat	(ist) getreten	tritt
trinken (to drink)	trinkt	trank	getrunken	
tun (to do)	tut	tat	getan	
verderben (to spoil)	verdirbt	verdarb	verdorben	verdirb
vergessen (to forget)	vergisst	vergass	vergessen	vergiss
verlieren (to lose)	verliert	verlor	verloren	
verzeihen (to pardon)	verzeiht	verzieh	verziehen	
wachsen (to grow)	wächst	wuchs	(ist) gewachsen	

INFINITIVE	PRESENT INDICATIVE	PAST INDICATIVE	PAST PARTICIPLE	IMPERATIVE
waschen (to wash)	wäscht	wusch	gewaschen	
weben (to weave)	webt	wob	gewoben	
weichen (to yield)	weicht	wich	(ist) gewichen	
weisen (to show)	weist	wies	gewiesen	
werben (to woo)	wirbt	warb	geworben	wirb
werfen (to throw)	wirft	warf	geworfen	wirf
wiegen (to weigh)	wiegt	wog	gewogen	
winden (to wind)	windet	wand	gewunden	
ziehen (to draw, to pull)	zieht	zog	gezogen	
zwingen (to force)	zwingt	zwang	gezwungen	

IRREGULAR VERBS (AUXILIARY VERBS)

INFINITIVE	PRESENT INDICATIVE	PAST INDICATIVE	PAST PARTICIPLE	IMPERATIVE
haben (to have)	hat	hatte	gehabt	habe
sein (to be)	ist	war	(ist) gewesen	sei
werden (to become)	wird	wurde	(ist) geworden	werde

IRREGULAR WEAK VERBS

INFINITIVE	PRESENT INDICATIVE	PAST INDICATIVE	PAST PARTICIPLE	IMPERATIVE
brennen (to burn)	brennt	brannte	gebrannt	
bringen (to bring)	bringt	brachte	gebracht	
denken (to think)	denkt	dachte	gedacht	
kennen (to know, be acquainted with)	kennt	kannte	gekannt	
nennen (to name, to call)	nennt	nannte	genannt	
rennen (to run)	rennt	rannte	(ist) gerannt	

INFINITIVE	PRESENT INDICATIVE	PAST INDICATIVE	PAST PARTICIPLE	
senden (to send)	sendet	sandte	gesandt	
wenden (to turn)	wendet	wandte	gewandt	

MODAL AUXILIARIES AND "WISSEN"

dürfen (to be allowed)	darf	durfte	gedurft	dürfen
können (can, to be able)	kann	konnte	gekonnt	können
mögen (may, to like)	mag	mochte	gemocht	mögen
müssen (must, to be compelled, have to)	muss	musste	gemusst	müssen
sollen (shall, to be to, be said to)	soll	sollte	gesollt	sollen
wollen (will, to want)	will	wollte	gewollt	wollen
wissen (to know)	weiss	wusste	gewusst	

LIST OF IDIOMATIC EXPRESSIONS

auf und ab back and forth
auf Wiedersehen good-bye,
  au revoir
gegen bar for cash
bar zahlen to pay cash
sich beschäftigen mit to occupy
  oneself with
Besorgungen machen to take care
  of a few things, to go shopping
einen Besuch machen to pay a vist
denken an *(acc.)* to think of
Der wievielte ist heute?
Den wievielten haben wir heute?
  What is today's date?
Ehre machen to do credit to
einen Eindruck machen auf
  to make an impression on
Einkäufe machen to go shopping
sich erkälten to catch cold
es fällt mir ein it occurs to me
es gibt there are
zu Abend essen to eat supper
zu Mittag essen to eat dinner
ein Examen bestehen to pass an
  examination
auf alle Fälle in any case
eine Fahrkarte lösen to buy a ticket
Was fehlt Ihnen? What is the
  matter with you?
Feuer geben to give a light
zum Frühstück for breakfast
zu Füssen liegen to lie at one's feet
zu Fuss gehen to walk
Gegensätze ausgleichen to smooth
  down antagonism
gestern abend last night
Glück haben to be lucky
glückliche Reise bon voyage
zu Hause at (one's own) home
nach Hause to (one's own) home
ich heisse my name is

heute abend tonight
heute morgen this morning
heute über acht Tage a week from
  today
Hunger haben to be hungry
sich interessieren für to be
  interested in
vor einem Jahr a year ago
leid tun *(dat.)* to be sorry
los sein to be going on, to be the
  matter
Lust haben to feel like, would like
  to
morgen früh tomorrow morning
am Morgen in the morning
in der Nacht at night
in Ordnung sein to be all right,
  to be in order
an Ort und Stelle on the very spot
Platz nehmen to take a seat,
  to sit down
recht haben to be right
recht sein *(dat.)* to be all right with
sich richten nach to depend on
Schwierigkeiten machen to cause
  difficulty
sich freuen auf *(acc.)* to look
  forward to (with joy)
gut sitzen to fit well
schlecht sitzen to fit badly
sich sorgen um to worry about
zu spät kommen to be late
einen Spaziergang machen to take
  a walk
eine Rolle spielen to play an
  important part
Station machen to stop (for a short
  time)
gut stehen *(dat.)* to be becoming,
  to suit
streben nach to strive for
suchen nach to look for

in acht Tagen   within a week
den Tisch decken   to set the table
verbunden sein *(dat.)*   to be obliged to
versetzen in *refl. v.*   to place oneself
sich die Zeit vertreiben   to while away one's time
von etwas anderem sprechen   to change the topic
von hinten nach vorne   backward
von weitem   from the distance
vor allem   primarily, above all
sich vorbereiten auf   to prepare for
Vorbereitungen treffen   to make arrangements

einen Vorschlag machen   to suggest, make a suggestion
warten auf *(acc.)*   to wait for
Was fehlt Ihnen?   What is the matter with you?
sich auf den Weg machen   to set out
weh tun *(dat.)*   to hurt, ache, pain
Wie geht es Ihnen?   How are you?
Wie heissen Sie?   What is your name?
Wieviel Uhr ist es?   What time is it?
vor einer Woche   a week ago
in den Bann ziehen   to put under a spell
zumute sein   to feel (mood)

GERMAN PROVERBS

Aller Anfang ist schwer.
All beginning is difficult.

Übung macht den Meister.
Practice makes perfect. (Practice makes the master.)

Man soll den Tag nicht vor dem Abend loben.
One should not praise the day before the evening.

Morgenstunde hat Gold im Munde.
The early bird catches the worm. (Morning hour has gold in its mouth.)

Wer zuletzt lacht, lacht am besten.
He who laughs last, laughs best.

Wer sich in Gefahr begibt, kommt darin um.
He who betakes himself into danger, perishes in it.

Wer den Schaden hat, braucht für Spott nicht sorgen.
The loser is always laughed at. (He who has the harm, does not need to worry about mockery.)

Kinder und Narren sprechen die Wahrheit.
Children and fools speak the truth.

Was ich denk' und tu,' trau' ich andern zu.
What I think and do, I believe others capable of doing.

Eine Hand wäscht die andere.
One good turn deserves another. (One hand washes the other.)

Viele Hände machen bald ein Ende.
Many hands make light work. (Many hands soon make an end.)

Besser ein Sperling in der Hand als zehn Tauben auf dem Dache.
A bird in the hand is worth two in the bush. (Better one sparrow in the hand than ten pigeons on the roof.)

Jeder für sich, Gott für uns alle.
Every one for himself and God for us all.

Jeder kehre vor seiner Tür.
Let each attend to his own business. (Each one should sweep before his own door.)

Ohne Fleiss, kein Preis.
Without diligence, no reward. (No pains, no gains.)

Wer A sagt, muss auch B sagen.
You cannot say A without saying B.

Stille Wasser sind tief.
Still water runs deep.

Was ein Häkchen werden will, krümmt sich bei Zeiten.
As the twig is bent the tree will grow. (What will become a small hook will bend in time.)

Zeit heilt alles.
Time heals all wounds (everything).

Morgen, morgen, nur nicht heute,
sagen alle faulen Leute.
Tomorrow, not today, all the lazy people say.

Andere Zeiten, andere Sitten.
Other times, other customs.

Ein gebranntes Kind scheut das Feuer.
A burned child dreads the fire.

Kleider machen Leute.
Clothes make the man (people).

Viele Köche verderben den Brei.
Too many cooks spoil the broth (cereal).

Hunger ist der beste Koch.
Hunger is the best cook.

Glück in der Liebe, Unglück im Spiel.
Lucky in love, unlucky at cards.

Bauen und Borgen, ein Sack voll Sorgen.
Building and borrowing a sack full of worrying.

Mitgefangen, mitgehangen.
Caught together, hung together.

Der Apfel fällt nicht weit vom Stamm.
Like father, like son. (The apple does not fall far from the tree trunk.)

Eile mit Weile.
The more haste the less speed. (Hurry with leisure.)

Wer andern eine Grube gräbt, fällt selbst hinein.
He who digs a pit for others, falls in himself.

Lügen haben kurze Beine.
Lies have short wings (legs).

Es ist nicht alles Gold, was glänzt.
All is not gold that glitters.

Man muss das Eisen schmieden, solange es heiss ist.
Strike while the iron is hot.

Ende gut, alles gut.
All's well that ends well.

GERMAN BUSINESS LETTER FORM

C. T. HANSEN & SOHN
Import—Export
Hamburg
Steinstrasse 10.

Herren
Schmidt & Müller
Heidenheim, a.d. Brenz
Hauptstrasse 20.   14. September 19—

Ihre Zeichen	*Ihre Nachricht*	*Unsere Nachricht*	*Unsere Zeichen*
M/F	8.9.19—	———	H/P

Betreff
Steingut-Krüge

Auf Grund Ihres Angebots vom 4. September d.J. (dieses Jahres)
bestellen wir hiermit:

500 Steingut-Krüge, Muster A, 25; Grössen 1, 2, 3 sor-
tiert, nach Ihrem Katalog No. 33, zum Preise von   1500,-M
einschliesslich Verpackung und Fracht.

Bezahlung erfolgt durch Banküberweisung nach Empfang der Ware.
Lieferung muss umgehend erfolgen, da wir die Krüge dringend für
das Weihnachtsgeschäft benötigen.

Wir interessieren uns auch für die geschliffenen Gläser, die in Ihrem
neusten Katalog auf Seite 45 abgebildet sind. Da wir diese Gläser in
grösseren Quantitäten und laufend benötigen würden, bitten wir Sie,
uns umgehend Ihre äussersten Preise für die verschiedenen Quantitäten mitzuteilen.

Hochachtungsvoll

C. T. Hansen & Sohn

Drahtwort	*Fernsprecher*	*Geschäftszeit*	*Bank*
Hanso	No. 32 36 44	8-17 Uhr	Diskonto, Hamburg

GERMAN BUSINESS LETTER FORM
(Translation)

C. T. HANSEN & SON
Import—Export
10 Steinstrasse
Hamburg

Messrs. Schmidt & Müller
20 Hauptstrasse   September 14, 19—
Heidenheim on Brenz

Your reference	*Your letter of*	*Our letter of*	*Our reference*
M/F	Sept. 8, 19—	–––––	H/P

Re: Earthenware Pitchers

Dear Sirs:

On the basis of your offer of September 4th of this year, we herewith order:

500 Earthenware pitchers, sample A 25, sizes 1, 2, 3
    assorted, according to your catalog number 33, at
    the price of   1500,-M
    packing and freight included.

Payment will be made by bank draft upon receipt of goods.

We request immediate shipment, since we need the pitchers urgently for our Christmas business.

We are also interested in the cut-glass goblets illustrated in your newest catalog on page 45. Since we would need these glasses in larger quantities and recurrently, quote your lowest prices for various quantities immediately.

Very truly yours,

C. T. Hansen & Son

Cable Address	*Telephone*	*Business Hours*	*Bank*
Hanso	No. 32 36 44	8 a.m.-5 p.m.	Diskonto, Hamburg

GUIDE TO
German Pronunciation
Part II

ACCENT

1. In most German words, the root syllable is stressed.

   lachen   (la'-khĕn)   to laugh
   gelacht   (gĕ-lakht')   laughed

2. Separable prefixes are accented.

   aufstehen (owf'-shtay-ĕn)   to get up

3. Inseparable prefixes, such as *be, emp, ent, er, ge, ver, zer,* are never accented.

   zerstören (tsĕr-shtöh'-rĕn) to destroy

4. The prefixes *un* and *ur* are usually accented.

   Unrecht   (un'-recht)   wrong
   Ursache   (oor'-za-khĕ)   cause

5. In nouns ending in *ei* or *ie* the *ei* or *ie* is accented.

   Bäckerei   (be-kĕ-rī')   bakery

6. In compound nouns, both parts are usually stressed, with the heavier accent on the first part.

   Schulbuch (shool'-bookh)   textbook

7. Foreign words in German generally retain their native accent, which is usually on the last syllable.

   Student   (shtoo-dent')

8. In all verbs ending in *-ieren* (ee'-rĕn), the first syllable of the ending *-ieren* is stressed rather than the root of the verb.

   studieren (shtoo-dee'-rĕn) to study

313

9. In adverbial compounds, the second part is usually accented.

damit	(dah-mit')	with it
davon	(dah-fon')	of it, from it

THE GLOTTAL STOP

Very important in acquiring a proper German pronunciation is an understanding of the use of the glottal stop. The *glottal stop* is an explosive release of the breath such as occurs in English before words like "up" and "off" in a command: "Up you go!" or "Off with you!"

Before every word starting with a vowel, the German speaker seems to take a short breath that prevents the linking of the last consonant of one word with the initial vowel of the following word. In English, however, there is the tendency to take the last consonant of the preceding word over to the first vowel of the next word. Therefore, "a nice man" and "an iceman" or "an ounce" and "announce" can hardly be distinguished when spoken.

In German, every word is an independent unit and must be spoken as such: *als alter Arbeiter* (als/ al'-tĕr/ ar'-bĭ-tĕr) as an old worker.

This glottal stop is even heard, though slightly fainter, in the same word, between prefix and stem: *beantworten* (bĕ/-ant'-vor-tĕn) to answer.

Since this glottal stop gives the language the staccato rhythm for which it is noted, it should be religiously observed to acquire a proper German accent.

GENERAL RULES ABOUT LENGTH OF VOWELS

SHORT VOWELS

1. Vowels followed by more than one consonant are generally short:

Stadt	(shtat)	city
Butter	(bu'-tĕr)	butter
kommen	(ko'-mĕn)	to come

LONG VOWELS

1. Vowels before a single consonant or in words of one syllable ending in a vowel are long (exception: see rule 4 for short vowels) :

Vater	(fah'-tĕr)	father
Schaf	(shahf)	sheep
gehen	(gay'-ĕn)	to go
da	(dah)	there
du	(doo)	you
so	(zoh)	thus
zu	(tsoo)	to

SHORT VOWELS	LONG VOWELS

2. Vowels are short in some words of one syllable, especially in little particles:

an	(an)	at
in	(in)	in
das	(das)	the
des	(des)	of the

2. Vowels are long in the definite article *der* and its declension (except *des*):

der	(dayr)	the (m.)
dem	(daym)	to the
den	(dayn)	the

3. Vowels in unstressed syllables are usually short but distinct:

Anfang	(an'-fang)	begin
Teppich	(te'-pi*ch*)	rug

3. Vowels are long before silent *h:*

Sohn	(zohn)	son
Huhn	(hoon)	chicken
sehen	(zay'-ĕn)	to see

4. *e* in unstressed syllables is always short and a weak sound:

e —	Rose	(roh'-zĕ)	rose
el —	Enkel	(eng'-kĕl)	grandson
em —	Harlem	(har'-lĕm)	Harlem
en —	kommen	(ko'-mĕn)	to come
er —	Vater	(fah'-tĕr)	father
be —	bekom-men	(bĕ-ko'-mĕn)	to receive
ge —	gefallen	(gĕ-fa'-lĕn)	to please

4. Vowels are long when doubled and pronounced as *one* long sound:

Haar	(hahr)	hair
See	(zay)	sea
Boot	(boht)	boat

5. *ie* is one long vowel pronounced *ee*:

nie	(nee)	never
die	(dee)	the
lieben	(lee'-bĕn)	to love

6. Before *ch* and double *s*, the vowel may be short or long:

kochen	(ko'-khĕn)	to cook,	but	Kuchen	(koo'-khĕn)	cake
Fluss	(flus)	river,	but	Fuss	(foos)	foot

SYLLABICATION

1. A single consonant between vowels goes with the following vowel.

lesen = le-sen	(lay'-zĕn)	to read
Bruder = Bru-der	(broo'-dĕr)	brother

2. If there are two or more consonants in the middle of a word, the last consonant goes with the following vowel.

Mutter = Mut-ter   (mu'-tĕr)   mother
finden = fin-den   (fin'-dĕn)   to find
besser = bes-ser   (be'-sĕr)   better

3. *ck* is treated like *kk,* and when the word is separated into syllables the *c* changes to *k.*

Rücken = Rük-ken   (rü'-kĕn)   back

4. Compound words are divided into their component parts.

Sonntag = Sonn-tag   (zon'-tahk)   Sunday
Grossvater =   (grohs'-fah-tĕr)   grandfather
Gross-va-ter

5. The combinations *ch, ph, sch, st, th* (representing one sound) are never divided, but always go with the following vowel.

machen = ma-chen   (ma'-chĕn)   to make
waschen = wa-schen   (va'-shĕn)   to wash
Laster = La-ster   (la'-stĕr)   vice

6. In words of foreign origin, *b, d, g, k, p, t,* when followed by *l* or *r,* go with the next syllable.

Republik = Re-pu-blik   (ray-pu-bleek')   republic

CAPITALIZATION

1. All nouns and words used as nouns begin with a capital regardless of their position in the sentence.

der Vater
the father

das Neue
the new

das Gehen
the walking

Der *Vater* arbeitet.
The *father* works.

Das *Gehen* fällt der *Mutter* schwer.
Walking is difficult for Mother.

2. The polite form of the personal pronoun second person, *Sie* (zee) you, and its corresponding possessive forms, *Ihr* (eer) your, and *Ihre* (ee'-rĕ) yours, are always written with a capital.

Geben Sie mir *Ihr* Buch.
Give me *your* book.

3. In correspondence, the familiar pronouns of address and their corresponding possessives are written with capitals.

Wie geht es *Dir* und *Deiner* Mutter?
How are *you* and *your* mother?

Herzlichst *Dein* **Freund Emil**
Sincerely, *your* friend Emil

4. The pronoun of the first person singular, *ich* (*ich*) I, is written with a small letter except at the beginning of a sentence.

5. Adjectives denoting nationality are written with a small initial letter, except in fixed titles or proper names.

    die *deutsche* **Grammatik**
    the *German* grammar

BUT:

    das *Deutsche* **Reich**
    the *German* Empire

PUNCTUATION

German punctuation follows a set of rather ironclad rules. In general, the punctuation is determined along grammatical lines, in contrast to English, where marks of punctuation, especially the comma, are used according to thought groups.

The period, the question mark, the colon, and the semi-colon are used similarly in English and in German. However, a colon is also used to introduce a statement or question in direct discourse (in English, a comma is used) :

    Er sagte: "Heute kann ich Sie nicht besuchen."
    He said, "Today I cannot visit you."

An exclamation mark is used after the introductory phrase of a letter.

    Lieber Hans!
    Dear Hans,

    Sehr geehrter Herr!
    My dear Sir,

Alternatively, a comma may now be used after a salutation, in which case the first word of the letter, card, etc. begins with a small letter.

    Liebe Lois,
        schon lange wollte ich Dir schreiben.
    Dear Lois,
        For a long time I have wanted to write to you.

An exclamation point is used after a command and after expressions of joy and surprise.

    Kommen Sie bitte herein!
    Please come in.

    Lassen Sie uns jetzt gehen!
    Let us go now.

    Was für ein schöner Tag!
    What a beautiful day!

The greatest difference between English and German is in the use of the comma. Generally speaking, a phrase that contains a subject and verb (and often other parts of speech as well) is thought of as being substantially similar to a sentence and, therefore, is set apart by commas. Therefore, every clause introduced by either a co-ordinating conjunction or a subordinating conjunction which contains a subject and a verb is set off by commas from the rest of the sentence.

> **Ich gehe heute ins Konzert, oder ich bleibe zu Hause.**
> Today I am going to a concert or I will remain at home.
> **Sie weiss, dass es nicht wahr ist.**
> She knows that it is not true.

Every relative clause, whether restrictive or non-restrictive, is enclosed by commas.

> **Die Frau, die nach Europa fährt, wohnt hier.**
> The lady who went to Europe lives here.
> **Dies ist der Knabe, mit dem ihr Sohn gestern gespielt hat.**
> This is the boy with whom her son played yesterday.

Infinitive phrases accompanied by an object or modifier are set off by a comma.

> **Die Hauptsache ist jetzt, ihn wieder gesund zu machen.**
> The main thing now is to make him well again.
> **Er ist gewohnt, früh aufzustehen.**
> He is used to getting up early.

In sentences in which *um . . . zu, ohne . . . zu, anstatt . . . zu* occur, a comma precedes *um, ohne,* or *anstatt.*

> **Sie ging in den Laden, um sich ein Kleid zu kaufen.**
> She went to the store in order to buy herself a dress.

Contrary to English, adverbial phrases at the beginning of the sentence are not set off by commas.

> **Gestern abend habe ich ihn auf der Strasse getroffen.**
> Last night, I met him in the street.

Words or phrases in a series are separated by commas as in English; the last item of the series connected by *und* or *oder* is not preceded by a comma.

> **Sie kaufte einen Mantel, zwei Hüte, Strümpfe und ein Paar Schuhe.**
> She bought a coat, two hats, stockings, and a pair of shoes.

German-English Dictionary*

A

Abend,-e *m.* evening
Abendmahl,-e *n.* supper
aber but
abfahren *st.v.* to start, to depart
Abfahrt,-en *f.* departure
abholen to call for; to go to meet
abnützen to wear out
Absatz,-͏e *m.* heel
abschütteln to shake off
abspielen *refl.* to proceed; to take place
absteigen *st.v.* to check in
Abteil,-e *n.* compartment
Abteilung,-en *f.* department
Abwesenheit,-en *f.* absence
abziehen *st.v.* to subtract, take off
Abzug,-͏e *m.* deduction, discount
addieren to add
Adler,- *m.* eagle
Adresse,-n *f.* address
ähnlich similar
Ahnung,-en *f.* premonition
Aktentasche,-n *f.* brief case
all, alle all
Allee,-n *f.* avenue
allein alone
allerlei all kinds of things
allerseits to all
alles everything

allgemein general
in allgemeinen in general
allmählich gradually
Alpen *pl.* Alps
als than, when
alt old
Alter,- *n.* age
Altertum,-͏er *n.* antiquity
Amerika *n.* America
Amerikaner,- *m.* American (the)
amerikanisch *adj.* American
amüsieren *refl.* to have a good time
an at, to, on
ander other
anderes different
anderthalb (eineinhalb) one and a half
anbieten *st.v.* to offer
Anblick,-e *m.* view, sight
anerkennen to recognize
Anfang,-͏e *m.* beginning
anfangen *st.v.* to begin
angebrochen opened, started
Angelegenheit,-en *f.* affair, matter
angenehm pleasant, pleased
angezogen werden *st.v.* to be attracted
Angst,-͏e *f.* fear
Ankunft,-͏e *f.* arrival
anlangen to arrive
anlegen to construct

---

*In the German-English and English-German dictionaries that follow, these points should be noted: Strong verbs are indicated by *st. v.*; irregular verbs, by *irr. v.*; irregular weak verbs, by *irr. w.v.*; reflexive verbs, by *refl.* For nouns, plurals are shown by endings added to the stem, and vowel changes, where necessary, are indicated by an umlaut preceding the ending (e.g., *Haus,-͏er*). The genitive case is indicated only in the case of mixed declension nouns and irregularly declined nouns.

annehmen *st.v.* to accept, assume
anregen to stimulate
Anregung,-en *f.* stimulation
anrufen *st.v.* to call up, telephone
anschliessen *refl. st. v.* to join
ansehen *refl. st. v.* to look at
anstatt instead of
anstimmen to begin to sing
anstrengend strenuous
anvertrauen *refl.* to entrust oneself
to
anziehen *st.v.* to dress, to tighten
(screw)
sich . . . to get dressed
Anzug,-"e *m.* suit
Apfel,-" *m.* apple
Apfelmus *n.* applesauce
Apotheke,-n *f.* apothecary,
drugstore
Apparat,-e *m.* apparatus
April *m.* April
Arbeit,-en *f.* work
arbeiten to work
arm poor
Arme,-e *m.* arm
Armbanduhr,-en *f.* wristwatch
Ärmel,- *m.* sleeve
Art,-en *f.* type, kind
Artikel,- *m.* article, commodity
Arzt,-"e *m.* physician
atmen to breathe
auch also, too
auf on, upon, to
auf Wiedersehen good-bye, au revoir
aufbauen to build up
aufbewahren to store, check
zum Aufbewahren for checking
(baggage)
auffüllen to fill up
aufführen to perform
Aufführung,-en *f.* performance
aufgeregt excited
aufgewühlt sein to be wrought up
aufhängen *st.v.* to hang up
auflösen to dissolve
aufmachen to open
aufnehmen *st.v.* to take in, to pick
up
aufpassen to watch, pay attention,
look after
aufpumpen to pump up

aufreissen *st.v.* to tear open, rip
aufschlagen *st.v.* to add, to raise
(the price), to open (a book)
aufschliessen *st.v.* to unlock
aufschreiben *st.v.* to write down
aufsetzen to put on, to set upon
aufsparen to save for
aufstehen *st.v.* to get up, rise
aufsuchen to look up
aufwachen to wake up
aufziehen *st.v.* to wind (watch)
Auge,-s,-n *n.* eye
Augenblick,-e *m.* moment
Augenbraue,-n *f.* eyebrow
August *m.* August
aus out of, from
Ausbildung,-en training,
development
Ausdruck,-"e *m.* expression
ausdrücken to express
auseinanderfallen *st.v.* to fall apart
Ausfuhr,-en *f.* export
ausfüllen to fill out
ausgebrannt burned out
Ausgang,-"e *m.* exit
ausgezeichnet excellent
ausgleichen *st.v.* to adjust, equalize
Auskunftsstelle,-n *f.* information
desk
Ausländer,- *m.* foreigner
Ausländerin,-nen *f.* foreigner
auspacken to unpack
ausprobieren to try out
ausruhen *refl.* to rest, to take a rest
ausschalten to switch off, to turn off
aussehen *st.v.* to look, to appear
aussen outside
Aussenkabine,-n *f.* outside cabin
ausser beside(s), except
ausserdem besides
ausserhalb outside of
ausserordentlich extraordinary
ausspielen to lead (card game)
aussteigen *st.v.* to descend, get off
aussuchen to pick out, select
austauschen to exchange
ausüben to exert
Ausverkauf,-"e *m.* sale
ausverkauft sold out
Auswanderer,- *m.* emigrant
Ausweispapiere *pl.* identification
papers

auszupfen to pluck
Auto,-s *n.* automobile
Autobahn,-en *f.* highway (auto)
Autobahnkarten,-n *f.* road map
Automobil,-e *n.* automobile
Autotour,-en *f.* auto trip

B

Backe,-n *f.* cheek
Backfisch,-e *m.* girl in her teens, adolescent girl
Backpflaume,-n *f.* prunes
Backzahn,-ᵉ *m.* back tooth
Badetuch,-ᵉr *n.* bath towel
Badezimmer,- *n.* bathroom
Bahnhof,-ᵉe *m.* station (railroad)
Bahnsteig,-e *m.* platform
bald soon, presently
Balkon,-s *m.* balcony
Bank,-en *f.* bank
Bann,- *m.* spell
Barbier,-e *m.* barber
Barbiergeschäft,-e *n.* barber shop
Barbierladen,- *m.* barber shop
Base,-n *f.* cousin, feminine
Bau,-s,-ten *m.* building, structure, style
Bauart,-en *f.* architecture
bauen to build
Bauer,-s,-n *m.* farmer, peasant
Baukunst *f.* architecture
Baum,-ᵉe *m.* tree
Bauwerk,-e *n.* building
Bayern Bavaria
bayrisch Bavarian
bedecken to cover
bedeuten to mean
bedeutend significant
Bedeutung,-en *f.* importance
Bedienung,-en *f.* service
beilegen to add, enclose
beeilen *refl.* to hurry
beeindrucken to impress
befestigt fortified
Befestigung,-en *f.* fortification
befinden *refl. st.v.* to be
befriedigen to satisfy
beginnen *st.v.* to begin
begleiten to accompany
begnügen mit *refl.* to be content with

begrenzt limited
bei at the house of, by, at
beide both
Bein,-e *n.* leg
beinah(e) almost
beitragen *st.v.* to contribute
beiwohnen to attend
bekannt known, familiar
Bekannte,-n *m. & f.* acquaintance
bekanntmachen to introduce
Bekanntschaft,-en *f.* acquaintance
bekommen *st.v.* to get, receive
bemerken to notice
benachrichtigen to notify, inform
Benzin *n.* gasoline
Benzintank,-e *m.* gas tank
Benzinverbrauch *m.* gasoline consumption
beobachten to watch, observe
bequem comfortable
Bequemlichkeit,-en *f.* comfort
beraten *st.v.* to give advice
bereit ready, prepared
bereiten to cause; to prepare
bereits already
Berg-und Talbahn,-en *f.* roller coaster
Bergriese,-n *m.* very high mountain
Bergsee,-n *m.* mountain lake
berichten to report
beruhigt comforted
berühmt famous
beschäftigen to occupy
beschwingt winged
besetzt busy, crowded
besingen *st.v.* to sing of
Besitz,-e *m.* possession
besohlen to put soles on
besonders especially
besorgen to attend to, get
besser better
Besserung, gute speedy recovery
Bestecke *pl.* knives, forks, and spoons
bestehen *st.v.* to exist
bestellen to order, give a message
bestimmt definite
Besuch,-e *m.* visit
besuchen to visit
beten to pray
Betrag,-ᵉe *m.* amount, sum
Bett,-s,-en *n.* bed

bevor *conj.* before
bewaffnet provided; armed
Bewegung,-en *f.* motion
bewölkt sein to be cloudy
bewundern to admire
bezahlen to pay
bezaubern to enchant
beziehen auf *refl.st.v.* to refer to
Biegung,-en *f.* turn
Bier,-e *n.* beer
Bild,-er *n.* picture
bilden to form
billig cheap
Birne,-n *f.* pear; electric bulb
bis till, until, to
bisher up to now
bisschen, ein some, a little
bitte please; you are welcome
bitten *st.v.* to beg, ask for
bitten um to ask for
bitter bitter
blau blue
bleiben *st.v.* to remain, stay
bleichen *st.v.* to bleach
Bleistift,-e *m.* pencil
Blitz,-e *m.* lightning
blitzen to lighten, flash
Blume,-n *f.* flower
Blumenkohl,-e *m.* cauliflower
Bluse,-n *f.* blouse
Blutdruck *m.* blood pressure
Blüte,-n *f.* height; flower; blossom
Bohne,-n *f.* bean
   grüne Bohnen *pl.* green beans
Böse *n.* evil, bad
böse sein to be angry
Branche,-n *f.* branch, specialty
Bratkartoffeln *pl.* fried potatoes
brauchen to need
braun brown
Brei *m.* cereal (hot)
breit broad
Bremse,-n *f.* brake
Brett,-er *n.* board
Brief,-e *m.* letter
Briefmarken,-n *f.* stamp
Briefumschlag,-"e *m.* envelope
bringen *irr.w.v.* to bring
Brote,-e *n.* bread, loaves of bread
Brötchen,- *n.* roll
Brücke,-en *f.* bridge
Bruder,-" *m.* brother

Brüderlichkeit *f.* fraternity
Brüderschaft,-en *f.* good fellowship
Brunnen,- *m.* fountain
buntbemalt painted in many colors
Burg,-en *f.* stronghold
Büro,-s *n.* office
Büroraum,-"e office room
Bürste,-n *f.* brush
bürsten to brush
Bus,-se *m.* bus
Büstenhalter,- *m.* brassiere
Butter *f.* butter
Butterbrot,-e *n.* bread and butter

D

da *conj.* since (reason), inasmuch
da *adv.* there; then
Dach,-"er *n.* roof
damals at that time
Dame,-n *f.* lady
Damenkonfektion *f.* store specializing in ladies clothes
Damenmantel,-" *m.* lady's coat
damit so that; with that, with it
Dampfer,- *m.* steamer
danach after that
dankbar grateful
danke thanks, thank you
danken to thank
dann then
darbieten *st.v.* to offer
darüber over it, above it
darum therefore
das the *n.*; that, which
dass *conj.* that
dasselbe the same
Datum, Daten *n.* date
dauern to last
Dauerwelle,-n *f.* permanent wave
davon from it, of it
dazu to that, to it
Deck,-e *m.* deck
denken *irr.w.v.* to think
Denkmal,-"er *n.* monument
denn *conj.* because, for
der the *m.*; who
derb heavy, coarse
Deutsche *m. & f.* (the) German
Deutschland *n.* Germany
Dezember *m.* December
Dichter,- *m.* poet

die the *f.*; who
dienen to serve
Dienst,-e *m.* service
Dienstag,-e *m.* Tuesday
dies this
dieser this, this one
diktieren to dictate
doch still, yet
Donner,- *m.* thunder
Donnerstag,-e *m.* Thursday
Dorf,-¨er *n.* village
dort there
drall robust
Drittel, ein a third
Drogist,-en *m.* druggist
Droschke,-n *f.* taxi, cab
drüben over there, yonder
drücken to pinch, press
dunkel dark
dunkelblau dark blue
durch through, by
Durchgang,-¨e *m.* way through,
   passage
D-Zug,-¨e (Durchgangszug) express
   train
dürfen *mod.* to be permitted, may
duzen to call a person thou

E

ebenfalls also
ebenso just so, just, the same
echt real, genuine
Ecke,-n *f.* corner
ehe before
eher rather
Ei,-er *n.* egg
eigen own
eigenartig odd, peculiar
ein a, one
einbiegen *st.v.* to turn into
eindringen *st.v.* to penetrate
Eindruck,-¨e *m.* impression
eindrucksvoll impressive
einfach simple, plain
Einfachheit *f.* simplicity
einfallen *st.v.* to occur, to interrupt
Einfamilienhaus,-¨er *n.* one-family
   house
einflössen *st.v.* to instill, inspire
Einfluss,-¨e *m.* influence
Einfuhr,-en *f.* import

einführen to import, introduce
Eingang,-¨e *m.* entrance
einhaken to interlock
Einheit,-en *f.* unit, unity
einige few, a few
Einkauf,-¨e *m.* purchase
   Einkäufe machen to go shopping
einladen *st.v.* to invite
Einladung,-en *f.* invitation
einlösen to redeem
einmal once
einmalig happening once
einpacken to pack
Einreiseerlaubnis,- *f.* permit of
   entry
einschalten to switch on, to turn on
einschlafen *st.v.* to fall asleep
Einschreibebrief,-e *m.* registered
   letter
einschreiben *st.v.* to register
einsteigen *st.v.* to get into; to enter
einstellen auf to be geared to
eintreten *st.v.* to enter
Eintritt,-e *m.* entrance
Eintrittskarte,-n *f.* admission ticket
einverstanden sein to agree
Einwanderer,- *m.* immigrant
einwechseln to give in exchange
Einwohner,- *m.* inhabitant
Einzelzimmer,- *n.* single room
einziehen *st.v.* to lace, pull in
einzig only
einzigartig unique
Eisenbahn,-en *f.* railroad
Eiswasser *n.* ice water
Eltern *pl.* parents
empfehlen *st.v.* to recommend
Empfehlung,-en *f.* recommendation
Empfehlungsbrief,-e *m.* letter of
   recommendation
empfinden *st.v.* to feel
Ende,-s,-n *n.* end
enden to end
endlich at last, finally
eng narrow, light
Engel,- *m.* angel
England *n.* England
Engländer,- *m.* Englishman
Enkel,- *m.* grandson
entfernt remote
entlang along

entschuldigen to excuse
entsetzt horrified
entweder . . . oder either . . . or
entzünden to inflame
Entzündung,-en *f.*...inflammation
entwickeln develop
er he
Erbse,-n *f.* pea
  grüne Erbsen *pl.* green peas
Erdbeere,-n *f.* strawberry
Erdgeschoss,-e *n.* ground floor
erfahren *st.v.* to experience
erfrischend refreshing
erfüllen to fulfill
erhalten *st.v.* to preserve; to receive
erhöhen to increase
Erholung *f.* recreation
erinnern *refl.* to remind of
erkennen *irr.w.v.* to perceive, see, know, understand, recognize
Erkenntnis,-se *f.* understanding; perception
erklären to explain
Erklärung,-en *f.* explanation
erleben to experience
Erlebnis,-se *n.* adventure, experience
erledigen to take care of
erlösen to save
Erlösung *f.* deliverance
ermuntern to encourage
ernst serious, earnest
erobern to conquer
erreichen to reach
erscheinen *st.v.* to appear
erschöpft exhausted
erschrecken *st.v.* to be frightened
erst not till; at first
erstens firstly
erwachsen grown-up
erwarten to expect
erzählen to tell, relate
es it
Essen,- *n.* food, meal, eating
essen *st.v.* to eat
Essig *m.* vinegar
Esszimmer,- *n.* dining room
etwas a little, some
Europa *n.* Europe
Examen,- *n.* examination
existieren to exist
exportieren to export

F

fahren *st.v.* to ride, to travel
Fahrer,- *m.* driver
Fahrkarte,-n *f.* ticket
Fahrplan,-e *m.* timetable
Fahrrad,-er *n.* bicycle
Fahrstuhl,-e *m.* elevator
Fahrt,-en *f.* trip
Fall,-e *m.* case
falls in case
falsch false
  . . . gehen to be wrong (watch)
Farbe,-n *f.* color
färben to dye
fast almost
Februar *m.* February
Feder,-n *f.* feather, spring
fehlen to be missing, lacking
Fenster,- *n.* window
Fensterladen,- *m.* shutter
Ferne *f.* distance
Fernsprecher,- *m.* telephone
fertig ready, finished
festschnallen *refl.* to buckle on, fasten
Festspiel,-e *n.* festival
Festung,-en *f.* fortress
Festungswall,-e *m.* rampart
Feuer *n.* fire
Feuerzeug,-e *n.* lighter
Fieber *n.* fever
Figur,-en *f.* figure (shape)
Film,-e *m.* film
Filzhut,-e *m.* felt hat
finden *st.v.* to find
Finger,- *m.* finger
Firma, Firmen *f.* firm
Fisch,-e *m.* fish
Fischerdorf,-er *n.* fishing village
Fischgericht,-e *n.* fish course
Flasche,-n *f.* bottle
Fleisch *n.* meat, flesh
Fleischbrühe,-n *f.* meat broth
fliehen *st.v.* to flee
Fluch,-e *m.* curse
Flügel *m.* grand piano
Flughafen *m.* airport
Flugkarte,-n *f.* flight ticket
Flugplatz,-e *m.* airfield
Flugzeug,-e *n.* airplane
Flunder,-n *f.* flounder

Fluss,-"e *m.* river
flüstern to whisper
folgen to follow
Form,-en *f.* form, shape
förmlich formal
Formular,-e *n.* form, blank
Fracht,-en *f.* freight
Frachtdampfer *m.* freighter
Frachtschiff,-e *n.* freighter
fragen to ask
Frankreich *n.* France
Franzose,-n *m.* Frenchman
Frau,-en *f.* woman, wife, Mrs.
frei free
Freitag,-e *m.* Friday
Fremdenverkehr *m.* tourist trade
Fremdenzimmer *n.* guest room
Fremdsprache,-n *f.* foreign language
Freude,-n *f.* joy
freuen *refl.* to be glad, to rejoice
Freund,-e *m.* friend
Freundin,-nen *f.* friend
freundlich kind, friendly
Freundschaft,-en *f.* friendship
Frikassee von Huhn *n.* chicken
  fricassee
frisch fresh
Friseur,-e *m.* hairdresser
Friseuse,-n *f.* hairdresser
frisieren to dress a person's hair
Frisiersalon,-s *m.* hairdressing salon
Frisiertisch,-e *m.* dressing table
Frisur,-en *f.* dressing of the hair;
  hair-do
froh happy, glad
fröhlich cheerful, merry, happy
Fröhlichkeit *f.* cheerfulness
früh early
früher formerly, earlier
Frühling,-e *m.* spring
Frühstück,-e *n.* breakfast
fühlen to feel
  sich . . . to feel (well, etc.)
führen to lead, carry (store)
Führung,-en *f.* guidance
füllen to fill
Füllfeder,-n *f.* fountain pen
fungieren to act
für for
fürchten to fear
  sich . . . vor to be afraid of
Fuss,-"e *m.* foot

G

Gabel,-n *f.* fork
Gang,-"e *m.* course, dish; passage-
  way; gear (car)
ganz complete(ly), all
Garderobe,-n *f.* wardrobe
Gardine,-n *f.* curtain
Garten,-" *m.* garden
Gässchen,- *n.* alley
Gast,-"e *m.* guest
Gasthaus,-"er *n.* restaurant
Gatte,-n *m.* husband
Gaumen,- *m.* gum
Gebäude,-n *n.* building
geben *st.v.* to give, deal (cards)
  es gibt there are
geboren born
Gebrauch,-"e *m.* use, custom
gebrochen broken
Gebühr,-en *f.* fee
Geburt,-en *f.* birth
Geburtsstätte,-n place of birth
Gefahr,-en *f.* danger
gefallen *st.v.* to like,
  to be pleased
Gefrorenes *n.* ice cream
gegen against, toward
Gegensatz,-"e *m.* antagonism;
  contrast
gegenseitig mutual
gegenüber opposite
Gegenwart *f.* presence, present
  (tense)
Geheimnis,-se *n.* secret
gehen *st.v.* to go, walk
gehören to belong
gehören *refl.* to be proper
Geist,-er *m.* spirit; intellect
geisteskrank insane
geistig intellectual
Gelächter,- *n.* laughter
Geld *n.* money
Gelee,-s *n.* jelly
Gelegenheit,-en *f.* opportunity
geloben to vow
Gelübde,- *n.* vow
Gemahlin,-nen *f.* wife
Gemälde,- *n.* painting
Gemäldesammlung,-en *f.* collection
  of paintings
gemeinsam joint, in common

gemütlich cozy, comfortable, congenial
Gemütlichkeit f. joviality
geniessen st.v. to enjoy
genug enough
Gepäck n. baggage
  das ... aufgeben to check the luggage
Gepäckannahme,-n f. luggage office
Gepäcknetz,-e n. luggage rack
Gepäckträger,- m. porter
Gepäckzettel,- m. baggage label
Gepräge,- n. feature
gerade just now, exactly
geradeaus straight ahead
geradeüber just across, opposite
Geräusch,-e n. noise
gering little, small, slight
gern gladly, like
Geschäft,-e n. business
Geschäftsfreund,-e m. business connection
Geschäftshaus,-"er n. commercial firm, office building
Geschäftsreise,-n f. business trip
Geschäftszweig,-e m. specialty, branch
geschehen st.v. to happen
Geschichte,-n f. story, history
geschichtlich historical
Geschlecht,-er n. sex, gender
Geschmack,-"e m. taste
Geschmacksache f. matter of taste
Gesellschaft,-en f. company, party
Gesicht,-er n. face
Gestalt,-en f. figure
gestehen st.v. to confess
gestern yesterday
Getränk,-e n. beverage
gewaltig powerful, mighty
gewiss certain
gewissermassen so to say
Gewitter,- n. thunderstorm
Giebel,- m. gable
Gier f. greed
Gipfel,- m. peak, top, summit
Glas,-"er n. glass
Glaswaren pl. glassware
glauben to believe, think
gleich directly, immediately
Gleichberechtigung f. equality
gleichzeitig at the same time

Glied,-er n. limb
Glück n. happiness
glücklich happy, fortunate
glücklicherweise fortunately
gnädige Frau madame
golden of gold
göttlich divine
Graben,- m. ditch
graben st.v. to dig
gratis free of charge
gratulieren to congratulate
grau gray
Grenze,-n f. frontier, borders
gross great, large
grossartig grand
Grösse,-n f. size
Grösse,-n f. size, height; greatness
Grosstadt,-"e f. metropolis
Grossvater,-" m. grandfather
grün green
Gründer,- m. founder
gründlich thorough, thoroughly
Gruppe,-n f. group
grüssen to greet, send regards
Grütze,- f. cereal (hot)
Gummischuh,-e m. rubber, rubbers
gut good, well

H

Haar,-e n. hair
Haaröl,-e n. hair oil
Haarwasser,- n. hair tonic
haben irr.v. to have
Hacken,- m. heel
Hafen,-" m. harbor
Hafenstadt,-"e f. seaport
Haferbrei m. oatmeal
halb half
Halbes, ein a half
Hälfte, die the half
Hals,-"e m. throat, neck
halten st.v. to hold, keep, stop
haltmachen to stop
Hammelkeule,-n f. leg of lamb
Hammelkotelett,-s n. lamb chop
Handelsstadt,-"e f. commercial city
Handgeld,-er n. deposit
Handgepäck,-e n. hand luggage
Handkoffer,- m. suitcase
Händler,- m. dealer
Handschuh,-e m. glove

Handtuch,-"er *n.* towel (hand)
hart hard
hässlich ugly
Hauptbahnhof,-"e main terminal
Hauptstadt,-"e *f.* capital
Hauptstrasse,-n *f.* main street
Hauptverkehrsstrasse,-n *f.* main road
Haus,-"er *n.* house
Hausfrau,-en *f.* housewife
heben *st.v.* to lift, raise
heilig holy
Heimat,-en *f.* native country
Heimweh *n.* homesickness
heissen *st.v.* to be called, named
helfen *st.v.* to help
hell light, bright
hellblau light blue
herantreten an *st.v.* to step up to
herausfallen *st.v.* to fall out
herausgeben *st.v.* to give change, to give up
herauskommen *st.v.* to come out; to be one's turn
herausnehmen *st.v.* to take out
Herbst,-e *m.* fall
herein Come in!
hereinbekommen *st.v.* to get in
Herr,-en *m.* master, gentleman, Mister
Herrenwäsche *pl.* men's underwear and shirts
Herrenzimmer,- *n.* den (room)
herrlich splendid
herrschen to reign, prevail
herumfahren *st.v.* to ride around
herumlaufen *st.v.* to run around
Herz,-ens,-en *n.* heart
herzlich cordially, heartily
heute today
heutig today's, present
hier here
hierher here (direction to place)
Hilfe *f.* help
Himbeereis *n.* raspberry ice
Himmel,- *m.* sky, heaven
hinauf upward
hinaufsteigen *st.v.* to step up, ascend
hinaus out, outside (go), out into
hinein into
hineinreichen to reach into

hingeben *refl. st.v.* to indulge
hinten in the rear, behind
hinter behind
Hinterkopf,-"e back of the head
Hinterzimmer,- *n.* backroom
hinunter downward
hinuntergehen *st.v.* to go down
hoch high
hochachtungsvoll respectfully, truly yours
Hochbahn,-en *f.* elevated railroad
Hochzeitsreise,-n *f.* wedding trip
hoffentlich I hope, it is to be hoped
holprig uneven
Honorar,-e *n.* fee
hören to hear, listen
Hose,-n *f.* trousers, pants
Hotel,-s hotel
Hotelhalle,-n *f.* hotel lobby
hübsch pretty, nice
gebratene Huhn,-"er *n.* roast chicken
Hühnersuppe,-n *f.* chicken soup
Hund,-e *m.* dog
Hundermarkschein,-e *m.* hundred mark bill
Hunger *m.* hunger
hungrig hungry
Hut,-"e *m.* hat
Hutabteilung,-en *f.* hat department
hüten *refl. w.v.* to be careful

I

ich I
Idee,-n *f.* idea
Ideenaustausch,-"e *m.* exchange of ideas
immer always
importieren to import
in in, into
indem while
Inhaber,- *m.* owner
innerhalb within
interessant interesting
inzwischen in the meantime
irgendeinmal at one time or another
Italien *n.* Italy
Italiener,- *m.* Italian

J

ja yes
Jacke,-n f. jacket
jagen to hunt
Jahr,-e n. year
jahrelang for years
Jahrhundert,-e n. century
Jammer,- m. calamity
Januar m. January
je ... desto the ... the
jedenfalls in any case, by all means
jeder each one, each
jederzeit any time
jener that one
jetzt now
Jubel m. jubilation
Jugend f. youth (period of life)
Juli m. July
jung young
Junge,-n m. boy
Juni m. June

K

Kabarett,-s n. cabaret
Kabine,-n f. cabin, stateroom
Kabinenkoffer,- m. stateroom trunk
Kabinennummer,- f. cabin number
Kaffee m. coffee
Käfig,-e m. cage
Kajüte,-n f. cabin, stateroom
kahl bleak, bare
Kaiser,- m. emperor
Kaiserreich,-e n. empire
Kalbsbraten,- m. roast of veal
Kalbsleber f. calf's liver
Kamel,-e n. camel
Kamm,-"e m. comb
kämmen to comb
Kampf,-"e m. struggle
kämpfen to fight
Kapelle,-n f. band
  (of musicians)
Karotte,-n f. carrot
Karpfen,- m. carp
Karte,-n f. card, ticket
  Karten mischen to shuffle cards
  Karten spielen to play cards
Kartoffel,-n f. potato
Kartoffelbrei m. mashed potatoes
Kartoffelklösse, pl. potato
  dumplings

Karton,-s m. carton
Käse,- m. cheese
Katze,-n f. cat
kaufen to buy
kaum hardly
Kekse f. cookies
Kellner,- m. waiter
Kellnerin,-nen f. waitress
kennen irr.w.v. to know (a person, place)
kennenlernen to get acquainted, meet
Kerl,-e m. fellow
Kind,-er n. child
Kindheit,-en f. childhood
Kino,-s n. movies
Kirche,-n f. church
klagen complain
klappen to go well
klar clear
Klasse,-n f. class
Klavier,-e n. piano
kleben to stick, paste
Kleid,-er n. dress
Kleiderschrank,-"e m. wardrobe
Kleidung,-en f. clothes
klein small, little
Kleingeld n. small change
Kleinigkeit,-en f. little matter
Kleinkunstbühne,-n f. cabaret
klingen st.v. to ring
klopfen to knock
Knabe,-n m. boy
Knopf,-"e m. button
Koffer,- m. trunk
Kofferraum,-"e m. baggage
  compartment
kommen st.v. to come
Kommode,-n f. dresser
komponieren to compose
Komponist,-en m. composer
Kompott,-e n. stewed fruit
können to be able, can
Kontor,-e n. office
Kopf,-"e m. head
Kopfschmerz,-es,-en m. headache
kopfschüttelnd shaking one's head
Kopf,-"e waschen m. to shampoo
Korb,-"e m. basket
Korrespondenz,-en f.
  correspondence
Korridor,-e m. hall, floor

Korsett,-s *n.* girdle, corset
kosten to cost
Kraft,-ˮe *f.* strength, power
Kraftwagen,- *m.* automobile
Kragen,- *m.* collar
krank sick
Krankenhaus,-ˮer *n.* hospital
Krankenwagen,- *m.* ambulance
Krempe,-n *f.* brim
kreuzen to cross
Krieg,-e *m.* war
Krug,-ˮe *m.* pitcher
krumm winding; crooked
Küche,-n *f.* kitchen
Kuchen,- *m.* cake
Kuh,-ˮe *f.* cow
Kühler,- *m.* radiator
Kultur,-en *f.* culture
Kunst,-ˮe *f.* art
Künstler,- *m.* artist
künstlerisch artistic
Kunstwerk,-e *n.* work of art
Kupferstecher,- *m.* engraver
Kupplung,-en *f.* clutch
Kurs,-e *m.* rate of exchange
kurz short
Kusin,-s *m.* cousin
Kusine,-n *f.* cousin
Kuss,-ˮe *m.* kiss
küssen to kiss
Kuvert,-s *m.* envelope

L

lächeln to smile
lachen to laugh
Laden,-ˮ *m.* store
Lage,-n *f.* site, situation
Lampe,-n *f.* lamp
Land,-ˮer *n.* country, land
landen to land
Landschaft,-en *f.* landscape
Landkarte,-n *f.* map
lang long
Länge,-n *f.* length
lassen *st.v.* to let
laufen *st.v.* to run
leben to live
Leben,- *n.* life
Leber,- *f.* liver
lebhaft lively
Lederwaren *f. pl.* leather goods

ledig unmarried
legen to lay, put
Lehrer,- *m.* teacher
lehrreich instructive
leicht easy, light
leichtlebig happy-go-lucky
Leiden,- *n.* suffering
leider unfortunately, alas
Leitung,-en *f.* connection, line, management
lernen to learn
lesen *st.v.* to read
letzt last
leuchtend shining
Leute *pl.* people
Licht,-e *n.* light
    elektrisches ... electric light
Lichtmaschine,-n *f.* generator
Liebe *f.* love
liebenswürdig charming, kind
lieber rather, to prefer
lieblich lovely
Lieblingslied,-er *n.* favorite song
Lied,-er *n.* song, carol
liegen *st.v.* to lie
Liegestuhl,-ˮe *m.* deck chair
Likör,-e *m.* cordial
links left
loben to praise
Loch,-ˮer *n.* hole
Löffel,- *m.* spoon
Loge,-n *f.* box (in theater)
Löschblatt,-ˮer *n.* blotter
losfahren *st.v.* to start (on vehicle)
losgehen *st.v.* to get started, come off
loswerden *st.v.* to get rid off
Löwe,-n *m.* lion
Luft *f.* air
Luftpostbrief,-e *m.* air mail letter
Luftpostkarte,-n *f.* air mail postal card
Luftpostleichtbrief,-e *m.* air mail letter
Lunge,-n *f.* lung
Lust *f.* desire
lustig gay, jolly
Lyriker,- *m.* lyric poet

M

machen to make, do

Macht.-"e f. power
mächtig mighty, powerful
Mädchen,- n. girl, servant girl
Magen,- m. stomach
Mahlzeit,-en f. meal
Mai m. May
Maler,- m. painter
Malerei,-en f. painting
malnehmen st.v. to multiply
mancher many a
Mandel,-n f. tonsil; almond
Maniküre,-n f. manicure
maniküren to manicure
Mann,-"er m. man
männlich masculine
Manschette,-n f. cuff
Mantel,-" m. coat, topcoat
Mappe,-n f. brief case
Märchenwelt f. world of romance
Mark f. mark
Marmelade,-n f. marmalade, jam
März m. March
Mauer,-n f. wall (outside)
Maus,-"e f. mouse
Mechaniker,- m. mechanic
Medizin,-en f. medicine
mehr more
mehr als more than
Meile,-n f. mile
meinen to mean
meistens mostly
Meisterwerk,-e n. masterpiece
Mensch,-en m. human being
merken to notice
    sich . . . to remember
messen to measure
Messer,- n. knife
mieten to rent
Mietshaus,-"er n. apartment house
Milch f. milk
Minute,-n f. minute
Missverständnis,-se n. misunder-
    standing
mit with
mitbringen irr.w.v. to bring
    (with one)
Mitleid, n. compassion
miteinander with each other
Mittag,-e m. noon, midday
Mittagessen n. dinner, lunch
mittags at noon

Mitte,-n f. middle
Mittel,- n. means
Mittelalter n. Middle Ages
Mitteldeutschland n. Central
    Germany
Mittelpunkt,-e m. center
Mitternacht,-"e f. midnight
Mittlerin,-nen f. middleman
Mittwoch m. Wednesday
mitwirken to contribute to
Möbel pl. furniture
möblieren to furnish
mögen to like, may
möglich possible
Möglichkeit,-en f. possibility
möglichst if possible
Monat,-e m. month
Montag,-e m. Monday
Morgen,- m. morning
morgen tomorrow
morgens in the morning
Mostrich m. mustard
Motorboot,-e motor boat
Motorrad,-"er n. motorcycle
müde tired
multiplizieren to multiply
Mund,-"er m. mouth
Mundwasser,- n. mouth wash
munter lively, brisk
Musik f. music
Muskel,-n f. muscle
müssen must
Mutter,-" f. mother

N

nach after, to (place), according to
nachdem conj. after
nachgehen st.v. to be slow (watch);
    to follow
nachher afterwards
nachholen to catch up on
Nachmittag,-e m. afternoon
    Spätnachmittag,-e m. late
    afternoon
nachmittags in the afternoon
Nachmittagszug,-"e m. afternoon
    train
nachsehen st.v. to check;
    to look after
nächst next
Nacht,-"e f. night

Nachtisch,-e *m.* dessert
nachts at night
Nachttisch,-e *m.* night table
Nacken,- *m.* neck
Nagel,- *m.* nail
nageln to nail
Nagelpolitur,-en *f.* nail polish
Nagelschere,-n *f.* nail scissors
Nähe *f.* nearness
   in der . . . near, in the
   neighborhood
nahekommen *st.v.* to come close to
nähen to sew, stitch
näherkommen *st.v.* to come closer
nähern *refl. v.* to approach
Naht,-"e *f.* (s) seam
Name,-n *m.* name
Nase,-n *f.* nose
Natur *f.* nature
natürlich naturally
neben next to, near
nebenan next door
Nebenfluss,-"e *m.* tributary
necken to tease
Neffe,-n *m.* nephew
nehmen *st.v.* to take
neigen to be inclined
nein no
nennen *irr.w.v.* to call, name
Nerv,-en *m.* nerve
nett nice, pretty, lovely
neu new
Neubau,-s,-ten *m.* rebuilding
Neuste *n.* the latest thing
Neuzeit *f.* modern times
nicht not
nicht mehr anymore
Nichte,-n *f.* niece
nicken to nod
niedlich cute
niemand nobody
Niederlage,-n *f.* defeat
noch yet, still
noch ein(e) another one
nochmals once again
Norden *m.* north
Norwegen *n.* Norway
Norweger,- *m.* Norwegian
Not *f.* need, distress
nötig necessary
Nötige *n.* the necessary thing

November *m.* November
Nummer,- *f.* number
numerieren to number
nun now
nur only

O

ob whether, if
oben above, upstairs
   nach . . . (to go) upstairs
   von . . . from the top
Oberhemd,-s,-en *n.* shirt
obgleich although
Obst *n.* fruit
oder or
öffentlich public
oft often
ohne without
Ohr,-s,-en *n.* ear
Oktober *m.* October
Öl *n.* oil
ölen to oil, grease
Omnibus,-se *m.* bus
Onkel,- *m.* uncle
Oper,-n *f.* opera
Opfer,- *n.* sacrifice, victim
Orange,-n *f.* orange
Orangensaft,-"e *m.* orange juice
Ordnung,-en *f.* order
Originalwerk,-e *n.* original work
Ort,-e *m.* spot
Osten *m.* east
Österreich *n.* Austria
Österreicher,- *m.* Austrian
Ozeandampfer,- *m.* ocean liner

P

Paar,-e *n.* pair, couple
   ein paar a few
paarmal, ein several times
Panne,-n *f.* flat tire
Papier,-e *n.* paper
Park,-e *m.* park
Pass,-"e *m.* passport
passen to fit, suit
passieren to pass, go on, happen
Passionsspiel,-e *n.* Passion Play
Passkontrolle,-n *f.* passport control
patent smart

Personenzug,-"e *m.* local train
persönlich personal
Pest *f.* pestilence
Pflasterstein,-e *m.* cobble stone
Pfeffer *m.* pepper
Pfeife,-n *f.* whistle, pipe
Pfennig,-e *m.* penny
Pferd,-e *n.* horse
Pfirsich,-e *m.* peach
Pflaume,-n *f.* plum
Pflaumenkompott,-e *n.* stewed
plums (prunes)
Piano,-s *n.* piano
planen to plan
Platz,-"e *m.* seat, square
Platzkarte,-n *f.* ticket for a reserved
seat
plaudern to chat
Plombe,-n *f.* filling (tooth)
plombieren to fill (tooth)
plötzlich suddenly
Pole,-n *m.* Pole
Polen *n.* Poland
Polizei *f.* Police
Pompelmus,-e *f.* grapefruit
Portwein,-e *m.* port wine
Porzellan,-e *n.* china, porcelain
Postamt,-"er *n.* post-office
Postkarte,-n *f.* postal card
Preis,-e *m.* price
preiswert worth the money, cheap
Privatkontor,-e *n.* private office
Prosit (Prost) your health
Prozent,-e *n.* percent
Publikum *n.* people, public
spectators
Punkt,-e *m.* point, dot
putzen to shine; to clean

Q

Qualität,-en *f.* quality

R

Rad,-"er *n.* bicycle, wheel
Rasierklinge,-n *f.* razor blade
Rasierpinsel,- *m.* shaving brush
Rasierseife,-n *f.* shaving soap
raten *st.v.* to advise, guess
Rathaus,-"er *n.* city hall

Ratte,-n *f.* rat
rauchen to smoke
Raucherabteil,-e *n.* smoking
compartment
Rauchsalon,-s smoking room
Raum,-"e *m.* room, space
rechnen to figure, calculate
Rechnung,-en *f.* bill
Rechnungsbetrag,-"e amount of bill
recht very, right
rechts right (direction)
Regen *m.* rain
Regenmantel,-" raincoat
Regenschirm,-e *m.* umbrella
regnen to rain
reich rich
reichen to reach
Reichsversammlung *f.* congress of
the empire
Reichtum,-"er *m.* wealth
Reifen,- *m.* tire
reihen an *refl. v.* to put in a row
rein clean, pure
reinigen to clean
Reis *m.* rice
Reise,-n *f.* trip, voyage
Reiseamt,"er *n.* official .travel
bureau
Reisebüro,-s *n.* travel bureau
Reiseerlebnis,-se *n.* traveling
experience
Reisegefährte,-n *m.* traveling
companion
reisen to travel
Reisecheck,-s *m.* travelers' check
Reisetasche,-n *f.* traveling bag
Reiz,-e *m.* charm
reizend charming
Reparatur,-en *f.* repairs
reparieren to repair
reservieren to reserve
Rest,-e *m.* rest, remainder
Rettung,-en *f.* salvation
Rezept,-e *n.* prescription
Rheinwein,-e *m.* Rhine wine
richtig gehen *st.v.* to be right
(watch)
Riese,-n *m.* giant
Riesenrad,-"er *n.* ferris wheel
riesig enormous
Ring,-e *m.* ring

riskieren to risk
Ritter,- *m.* knight
Rock,-"e *m.* skirt
Roggenbrot,-e *n.* rye bread
Röntgenaufnahme,-n *f.* X-ray
photograph
rosa pink
rot red
Rotkohl *m.* red cabbage
Rotwein,-e *m.* red wine
Rücken,- *m.* back
Rückenlicht,-e *n.* tail light
Rückkehr *f.* return
Rucksack,-"e *m.* knapsack
Rückweg,-e *m.* way back
Ruderboot,-e *n.* rowboat
Ruf *m.* reputation
rufen *st.v.* to call, shout
ruhen to rest
ruhig calm, quiet
Rührei,-er *n.* scrambled egg
rührend touching
rund round
Russe,-n *m.* Russian
Russland *n.* Russia

S

Saal (*pl.* Säle) *m.* hall, large room
Sache,-n *f.* thing, matter
getragene ... *pl.* worn clothes
(used)
Saft,-"e *m.* juice
sagen to say
Sahne *f.* cream
Salat,-e *m.* salad, lettuce
Salz,-e *n.* salt
Salzkartoffeln *pl.* boiled potatoes
sammeln to gather
Samstag,-e *m.* Saturday
Saum,-"e *m.* hem, seam
sausen to whiz along
schaffen *st.v.* to make, create
schallend roaring
Schalter,- *m.* switch; ticket window
Schatten,- *m.* shade
schattig shady
Schauspieler,- *m.* actor
Schauspielerin,-nen *f.* actress
Schauspielkunst *f.* art of acting
Scheck,-s *m.* check
Scheibe,-n *f.* slice

Schein,-e *m.* bill
scheinbar seemingly
scheinen *st.v.* to seem, appear
Scheitel,- *m.* part (of hair), crown
of head
schelten *st.v.* to scold
scherzen to joke
Scheu *f.* awe
Schicksal,-e *n.* fate
schiefgetreten worn down
(on one side)
Schiff,-e *n.* ship
Schiffsfahrkarte,-n *f.* steamer ticket
Schild,-er *n.* sign
Schimmer,- *m.* glamour
Schinken *m.* ham
Schlaf *m.* sleep
Schläfe,-n *f.* temple
schlafen *st.v.* to sleep
Schlafzimmer,- *n.* bedroom
schlagen *st.v.* to strike, beat
Schlange,-n *f.* snake
schlapp low; limp
schlecht bad, badly
schliesslich finally
schlimm bad
Schlips,-e *m.* necktie
Schloss,-"er *n.* castle
Schlüssel,- *m.* key
schmecken to taste
Schmerz,-es,-en *m.* pain
schmutzig dirty, soiled
Schnee,- snow
schneebedeckt snow covered
schneiden *st.v.* to cut
schnell fast, quick
Schnelldampfer,- *m.* fast steamer
Schnellzug,-"e *m.* express train
Schnitte,-n *f.* slice
eine ... (Scheibe) Brot a slice of
bread
Schnürsenkel,- *m.* shoelace
Schokolade *f.* chocolate
schon already
schön beautiful
Schönheit,-en *f.* beauty
Schornstein,-e *m.* chimney
Schrank,-"e *m.* closet
schreiben *st.v.* to write
Schreibmaschine,-n *f.* typewriter
Schreibpult,-e *n.* writing desk

Schritt,-e *m.* step, pace
Schublade,-n *f.* drawer
Schuh,-e *m.* shoe
Schuhmacher,- *m.* shoemaker
Schule,-n *f.* school
Schüler,- *m.* pupil
Schutzmann (*pl.* **Schutzleute**) *m.*
  policeman
Schwager,- *m.* brother-in-law
Schwägerin,-en *f.* sister-in-law
schwarz black
Schwarzbrot,-e *n.* pumpernickel
Schwede,-n *m.* Swede
Schweden *n.* Sweden
schweigen to be silent
Schweigen,- *n.* silence
Schweinebraten,- *m.* roast pork
Schweiz *f.* Switzerland
Schweizer,- *m.* Swiss
schwellen *st.v.* to swell
schwer heavy, difficult
Schwester,-n *f.* sister
Schwiegermutter,- *f.* mother-in-law
Schwiegervater,- *m.* father-in-law
Schwierigkeit,-en *f.* difficulty
schwitzen to sweat, perspire
See,-s,-n *m.* lake
See,- *f.* sea
Seefahrt,-en *f.* sea voyage
Seehund,-e *m.* sea lion
seekrank seasick
Seekrankheit *f.* seasickness
Seele,-n *f.* soul
Seeluft *f.* sea air
Seereise,-n *f.* sea trip
Segelboot,-e *n.* sail boat
Segen,- *m.* blessing
sehen *st.v.* to see
sehenswert remarkable
Sehenswürdigkeiten *pl.* sights
sehr very
Seife,-n *f.* soap
sein *irr. st.v.* to be
seit since (time)
seitdem since (time)
Seite,-n *f.* side, page
Selbstbildnis,-se *n.* self-portrait
selbstverständlich of course,
  naturally
Seligkeit *f.* supreme happiness,
  salvation
senden *irr. w.v.* to send

Sendung,-en *f.* shipment
Senf,-e *m.* mustard
September *m.* September
servieren to serve
Serviette,-n *f.* napkin
Sessel,- *m.* easy chair
setzen to set, put
  sich . . . to sit down
sicher sure, surely
sie she, they; her, them
Sie you (pol. pl.)
Siedlung,-en *f.* settlement
singen *st.v.* to sing
Sitz,-e *m.* seat
sitzen *st.v.* to sit, fit
so so, thus
sobald as soon as
Socke,-n *f.* sock
sofort immediately, right away
Sohle,-n *f.* sole
Sohlenleder *n.* leather for soles
sogar even
Sohn,-e *m.* son
solange as long as
solch such, such a
solide substantial, conservative,
  sound
sollen ought to, shall
Sommer,- *m.* summer
sondern but (on the contrary)
Sonnabend,-e *m.* Saturday
Sonne,-n *f.* sun
Sonntag,-e *m.* Sunday
sonst otherwise, formerly
sorgen *refl. v.* to worry
sorglos carefree
soviel als as much as
soweit so far, that far
sowie as well as; as soon as
Spanien *n.* Spain
Spanier,- *m.* Spaniard
spät late
Spätnachmittag,-e *m.* late afternoon
Speck *m.* bacon
Speisehaus,-er *n.* restaurant
Speisekarte,-n *f.* menu
Speisesaal,-säle *m.* dining hall
Speisezimmer,- *n.* dining room
Speisewagen,- *m.* diner, dining car
Spiegel,- *m.* mirror
Spiegelei,-er *n.* fried egg
Spiel,-e *n.* game, play

spielen to play
Spinat,-e *m.* spinach
Sprache,-n *f.* language
sprechen *st.v.* to speak
Sprechstunde,-n *f.* office hour
Sprichwort,-"er *n.* proverb
sprichwörtlich proverbial
Spur,-en *f.* trace
Staat,-s,-en *m.* state
Staatsbürger,- *m.* citizen
Stadt,-"e *f.* city
städtisch municipal
stammen aus to originate from
Standuhr,-en *f.* grandfather's clock
stark strong
starten to take off, start
stattfinden *st.v.* to take place
stecken to put
stehen *st.v.* to stand, stop (watch)
stehlen *st.v.* to steal
steif stiff
Stein,-e *m.* stone
Stelle,-n *f.* place
stellen to set, put, place
Stenogramm,-e *n.* shorthand note
Stenographie,-n *f.* shorthand
stenographieren to write shorthand
Stenotypistin,-nen *f.* stenographer
sterben *st.v.* to die
stetig perpetual; steady
Steuer,- *n.* steering wheel
Stich,-e *m.* trick (card game); stitch,
   puncture
Stil,-e *m.* style
still quiet, still
stimmen to tally, be correct
   das stimmt that's correct
Stimmung,-en *f.* atmosphere, mood
Stirn,-en *f.* forehead
Stock,-"e *m.* flight, floor
Stockwerk,-e *n.* flight, floor
stören to disturb
stramm solid
Strasse,-n *f.* street
Strassenbahn,-en *f.* streetcar
Strecke,-n *f.* distance
strecken to stretch
Streichholz,-"er match
streiken to strike
strömen to stream
Strumpf,-"e *m.* hose, stocking

Stück,-e *n.* piece, play
studieren to study
Stuhl,-"e *m.* chair
Stunde,-n *f.* hour, lesson
Sturm,-"e *m.* storm
stürmen to rush
subtrahieren to subtract
suchen to look for, seek, search
Südamerika South America
Süddeutschland *n.* South Germany
Süden *m.* south
Summe,-n *f.* sum
sündigen to sin
Suppe,-n *f.* soup
Suppenlöffel,- *m.* table spoon
süss sweet
Sweater,- *m.* sweater

T

Tabak,-e *m.* tobacco
Tafel,-n *f.* banquet table
Tag,-e *m.* day
tagelang for days
Taille,-n *f.* waist, waistline
Tal,-"er *n.* valley
Tankstelle,-n *f.* gas station
Tante,-n *f.* aunt
Tanz,-"e *m.* dance
tanzen to dance
Tanzkunst *f.* art of dancing
Tasche,-n *f.* pocket
Taschenuhr,-en *f.* pocket watch
Tasse,-n *f.* cup
taub deaf
Taube,-n *f.* dove, pigeon
Taubheit *f.* deafness
Taxi,-s *f.* taxi
technisch technical
Tee *m.* tea
Teelöffel,- *m.* teaspoon
Teil,-e *m.* part
Teilhaber,- *m.* partner
teilnehmen *st.v.* to participate
teilweise partly
Telefon,-e *n.* telephone
telefonieren to telephone
Telefonnummer,- *f.* telephone
   number
telegrafieren to telegraph
telegrafisch by wire

Telegramm,-e *n.* telegram
Teller,- *m.* plate
Teppich,-e *m.* rug
teuer dear, expensive
Teufel,- *m.* devil
tief deep
Tiefe,-n *f.* depth
Tiger,- *m.* tiger
Tinte,-n *f.* ink
Tisch,-e *m.* table
Tischtuch,-"er *n.* tablecloth
Tochter,-" *f.* daughter
Tod,-e *m.* death
Tomate,-n *f.* tomato
Tor,-e *n.* gate
Tor,-s,-en *m.* fool
töten to kill
Tracht,-en *f.* costume
tragen *st.v.* to wear, carry
Träne,-n *f.* tear
träumen to dream
treffen *st.v.* to meet
treiben *st.v.* to drive
trennen *refl.v.* to separate, part
Treppe,-n *f.* stairs, staircase
treten *st.v.* to step
Trieb,-e *m.* impulse, drive
trinken *st.v.* to drink
Trinkgeld,-er *n.* tip
trotz in spite of
Trumpf,-"e *m.* trump
tüchtig efficient, vigorous
tun *st.v.* to do, make
Turm,-"e *m.* tower
Turmuhr,-en *f.* tower clock

U

über over, above
überall everywhere
überallher from all over
Überbinger,- *m.* bearer
überhängen *st.v.* to hang over
überhaupt at all
überlassen *st.v.* to leave to
Übermensch,-en *m.* superman
übermorgen day after tomorrow
übermüden to overtire
übernachten to stay overnight
übernehmen *st.v.* to take over
überraschen surprise

Überraschung,-en *f.* surprise
übersetzen to translate
übertragen *st.v.* to transcribe,
  carry over
überwältigend overpowering
Uhr,-en *f.* watch, clock
Uhrfeder,-n *f.* watch spring
Uhrmacher,- *m.* watchmaker
Uhrmacherwerkstatt,-"en *f.*
  watchmaker's workshop
Uhrwerk,-e *n.* the works of a watch
um around, about
um . . . zu in order to
umdrehen *refl. v.* to turn
umgeben *st.v.* surround
Umgebung,-en *f.* vicinity
umsehen *refl. st.v.* to look around,
  look back
umsonst for nothing, in vain
umstritten controversial
umwechseln to change, exchange
unangenehm unpleasant
unbedingt by all means
und and
ungefähr about, approximately
ungefährlich harmless
ungemütlich uncomfortable
ungern reluctantly, unwillingly,
  not like
Unglück,- *n.* misfortune, bad luck
unglücklich unhappy
Unkraut *n.* weeds
unmöglich impossible
unruhig restless
unschuldig innocent
unstillbar unappeasable
unten down, downstairs
unter under, below, among
unterbrechen *st.v.* interrupt
untergehen *st.v.* to perish
Untergrundbahn,-en *f.* subway
Unterhemd,-en *n.* undershirt
Unterhose,-n *f.* underpants
Unterkunft,-"e *f.* shelter
unternehmen *st.v.* to undertake
Unterrock,-"e *m.* slip
untersuchen to examine, investigate
Untersuchung,-en *f.* examination
Untertasse,-n *f.* saucer
unterwegs on the road
unvergesslich unforgettable

unvollendet unfinished
unzufrieden dissatisfied
Uraufführung,-en *f.* première
Urheimat *f.* original home

V

Vater,-" *m.* father
Verabredung,-en *f.* appointment
Veränderung,-en alteration, change
verbergen *refl. st.v.* to hide
verbinden *refl. st.v.* combine, connect
Verbindung,-en *f.* connection, fraternity
verbieten *st.v.* to forbid
verboten forbidden
verbringen *irr. w.v.* to spend
verbunden sein to be obliged
verdächtig suspicious
vereinen to unite
vereinigen to combine, unite
Vereinigten Staaten *pl.* United States
Vereinigung,-en *f.* combination
verfassen to draft
Verfassung,-en *f.* constitution
vergeblich in vain
vergehen *st.v.* to perish
vergessen *st.v.* to forget
vergesslich forgetful, careless
vergiessen *st.v.* to shed, spill
Vergnügen,- *n.* pleasure
Vergnügungspark,-e *m.* amusement park
verhaftet werden *st.v.* to be arrested
verheiraten to marry
Verherrlichung,-en *f.* glorification
verkaufen to sell
Verkehr *m.* traffic
verkehrt wrong
verlängern to lengthen
verlassen *st.v.* to leave
verlässlich dependable
verlieren *st.v.* to lose
verlockend tempting
verneinen to negate
verschmelzen *st.v.* to fuse
verschont bleiben to be spared
verschreiben *st.v.* to prescribe
verschweigen *st.v.* to keep a secret
verschwenden to waste, squander

Versprechen,- *n.* promise
verstauen to pack
verstehen *st.v.* to understand
Versuch,-e *m.* attempt
versuchen to try, attempt
vertonen to compose
Vertonung,-en *f.* composition
vertragen *refl. st.v.* to get along
Verwandte,-n *f. & m.* relative
verwenden *irr. w.v.* to use
verwirklichen to realize
verzeihen *st.v.* to forgive, excuse
verzollen to pay duty
Vetter,-s,-n *m.* cousin *(masc.)*
viel much
vielleicht perhaps
Viertel,- fourth
Vogel,-" *m.* bird
Volk,-"er *n.* people, nation
Volkslied,-er *n.* folk song
volkstümlich popular
voll full
vollenden to complete
vollkommen completely
von of, from, by
vor before, in front of, ago
voraus in advance
vorbeihuschen to whiz by, fly by
vorbeikommen *st.v.* to pass
vorbereiten *refl. w.v.* to prepare
Vorbereitung,-en *f.* preparation
Vorderzimmer,- *n.* front room
vorgehen *st.v.* to be fast (watch), to go on
vorgestern day before yesterday
Vorhang,-"e *m.* drape, curtain
vorher first, previously, in advance
vorkommen *st.v.* to seem so, to be found
vorläufig for the present
Vormittag,e- *m.* forenoon
vormittags in the forenoon
vorn(e) in front
Vorname,-ns,-n *m.* first name
Vorort,-e *m.* suburb
vorschlagen *st.v.* to suggest
vorstellen *refl.v.* to introduce oneself, to imagine
Vorstellung,-en *f.* performance
Vortrag,-"e *m.* lecture
vorübergehend passing

W

Wagen,- *m.* car
wählen to elect, choose
wahr true
während while *(conj.)*
    during *(prep.)*
wahrscheinlich probably
Wahrzeichen,- *n.* distinctive mark
Wald,-¨er *m.* forest, woods
Walzer,- *m.* waltz
Wanderlied,-er *n.* hiking song
wandern to hike, wander
Wanderung,-en *f.* hike
wann? when?
Ware,-en *f.* goods, commodity
Warenhaus,-¨er *n.* department
    store
warten to wait
Wartesaal,-säle *m.* waiting-room
    (railroad)
Wartezimmer,- *n.* waiting room
warum? why?
was what, which, that
Wäsche *pl.* underwear
waschen *st.v.* to wash
Wasser,- *n.* water
Wechselgebühr,-en *f.* discount on
    bills
wechseln to change
Wecker,- *m.* alarm clock
weder . . . noch neither . . . nor
Weg,-e *m.* way, road, path
wegen on account of, because of
weich soft
Weihnachtszeit *f.* Christmas time
weil because
Weile,-n *f.* while
Wein,-e *m.* wine
Weisheit *f.* wisdom
weiss white
Weissbrot,-e white bread
Weisswein,-e *m.* white wine
weit far, wide
weiter further
weiterfahren *st.v.* to go on
weitergehen *st.v.* to continue, go on
Welt,-en *f.* world
Weltkrieg,-e *m.* world war
Weltstadt,-¨e *f.* metropolis
wenig little
weniger less

wenigstens at least
wenn when, if
wer who, whoever
werden *irr. v.* to get, become
Werk,-e *n.* works
Werkstatt,-¨en *f.* workshop
Wert,-e *m.* value, worth
Wertbrief,-e insured letter
Wertsachen *pl.* valuables
Wesen *n.* character
weshalb why
Weste,-n *f.* vest
Westen *m.* west
Wetter,- *n.* weather
wichtig important
wider against
wie how, as
wieder again
Wiederentdeckung,-en *f.*
    rediscovery
wiederholen to repeat
wiederkommen *st.v.* to return
wiedersehen *st.v.* to see again
wie viele? how many?
Wien Vienna
Wiener Wald *m.* Vienna Woods
wieso how, why
wieviel how much
. . . Uhr ist es? what time is it?
Wille,-ns,-n *m.* will
willkommen welcome
Wind,-e *m.* wind
winken to wave
Winter,- *m.* winter
wirklich real, really
Wirklichkeit *f.* reality
Wissen *n.* knowledge
wissen *irr. v.* to know (a fact)
wo where
Woche,-n *f.* weak
woher whence, how
wohin where to
wohl well, probably
wohnen to live, to reside
Wohnhaus,-¨er *n.* apartment
    house, house
Wohnung,-en *f.* apartment
Wohnzimmer,- *n.* living room
Wolke,-n *f.* cloud
wollen to want, wish
woraufhin whereupon

Wort,-ˮer *n.* word
Wörterbuch,-ˮer *n.* dictionary
worüber what of
Wunder,- *n.* wonder
wunderbar wonderful
wünschen to wish
Wurst,-ˮe *f.* sausage, cold cuts
Würstchen,- *n.* sausage, frankfurter
Wurzel,-n *f.* root

Z

Zahl,-en *f.* number
zahlen to pay
zählen to count
Zahlmeister,- *m.* paymaster, purser
Zahn,-ˮe *m.* tooth
Zahnarzt,-ˮe *m.* dentist
Zahnbürste,-n *f.* toothbrush
Zahnpaste,-n *f.* toothpaste
Zahnpulver,- *n.* tooth powder
Zahnwurzel,-n *f.* root of a tooth
Zeh,-(e)s,-en *m.* toe
zeigen to show
Zeile,-n *f.* line
Zeit,-en *f.* time
Zentrum, Zentren *m.* center
zerstören to destroy
Zettel,- *m.* slip, label
Ziegel,- *m.* brick
ziehen *st.v.* to draw
ziemlich rather
Zigarette,-n *f.* cigaret
Zimmer,- *n.* room
Zitrone,-n *f.* lemon
Zitronenlimonade,-n *f.* lemonade
Zoll,-ˮe *m.* custom, duty

Zollamt,-ˮer *n.* custom-house
Zollbeamte,-n *m.* revenue officer
custom
Zolldeklaration,-en *f.* customs
declaration
Zollerklärung,-en *f.* customs
declaration
zollfrei free of duty
zollpflichtig subject to duty
Zollrevision,-en *f.* customs
examination
Zollstelle,-n *f.* custom-house
zu to (the house of)
Zucker *f.* sugar
zuerst first, at first
Zufall,-ˮe *m.* coincidence, chance
zufrieden satisfied, happy
Zug,-ˮe *m.* train
zugeben *st.v.* to admit
Zukunftsplan,-ˮe *m.* plan for the
future
Zünder,- *m.* spark plug
Zunge,-n *f.* tongue
zurück back
zurückkehren to return
zurücksehen *st.v.* to look back
zurückziehen *st.v.* to retire
zusammen together
Zusammenbruch,-ˮe *m.* collapse
zwar to be sure
zweieinhalb two and a half
zweimal twice
zweitens secondly
Zwerg,-e *m.* dwarf
Zwiespalt,-ˮe *m.* conflict
zwingen *st.v.* to force
zwischen between

English-German
Dictionary

A

a ein
able, to be können
about ungefähr, um
above über, oben
  ... it darüber
accept, to annehmen *st.v.*
accompany, to begleiten
according to nach
acquaintance Bekanntschaft,-en *f.*
act, to fungieren
actor Schauspieler,- *m.*
actress Schauspielerin,-nen *f.*
add, to aufschlagen *st.v.*; addieren,
  zusammenzählen
add to, to beilegen
address Adresse,-n *f.*
adjust, to ausgleichen *st.v.*
admire, to bewundern
admission ticket Eintrittskarte,-n *f.*
admit, to zugeben *st.v.*
adventure Erlebnis,-se *n.*
advise, to raten *st.v.*
affair Angelegenheit,-en *f.*
after nach, *prep.;* nachdem, *conj.*
  ... that danach
afternoon Nachmittag,-e *m.*
  in the ... nachmittags,
  am Nachmittag
afterwards nachher
again wieder
against gegen, wider
age *n.* Alter,- *n.*
agree, to einverstanden sein
air Luft *f.*
airfield Flugplatz,-¨e
airmail Luftpost *f.*
airplane Flugzeug,-e *n.*

airport Flughafen,- *m.*
alarm clock Wecker,- *m.*
alas leider
all all, alle; ganz
  ... kinds of things allerlei
alley Gässchen,- *n.*
almost beinah (e), fast
alone allein
along entlang
Alps Alpen *f.*
already bereits, schon
also auch, ebenfalls
alteration Veränderung,-en *f.*
although obgleich
always immer
ambulance Krankenwagen,- *m.*
America Amerika *n.*
American Amerikaner,- *m.;*
  amerikanisch *adj.*
amount Betrag,-¨e *m.*
amuse oneself, to sich amüsieren
amusement park
  Vergnügungspark,-e *m.*
and und
angel Engel,- *m.*
angry, to be böse sein
another (one) noch ein(e)
antagonism Gegensatz,-¨e *m.*
any etwas
any time jederzeit
anymore nicht mehr
apartment Wohnung,-en *f.*
apartment house Wohnhaus,-¨er *n.*,
  Mietshaus,-¨er *n.*
apothecary Apotheke,-n *f.*
apparatus Apparat,-e *m.*
appear, to scheinen, *st.v.*,
  erscheinen, *st.v.*, aussehen, *st.v.*
apple Apfel,-¨ *m.*

apple cake Apfelkuchen,- *m.*
applesauce Apfelmus, *n.*
appointment Verabredung,-en *f.* `
approach, to nähern *refl. v.*
approximately ungefähr
April April,-e *m.*
architecture Bauart,-en *f.*,
    Baukunst *f.*
arm Arm,-e *m.*
around um
arrested, to be verhaftet werden
    st.v.
arrival Ankunft,-ˉe *f.*
arrive, to anlangen
art Kunst,-ˉe *f.*
article Artikel,- *m.*
artist Künstler,- *m.*
artistic Künstlerisch
as wie
ask, to fragen
ask for, to bitten um, *st.v.*
asleep, to fall einschlafen *st.v.*
assume, to annehmen *st.v.*
at an, um (time)
attempt Versuch,-e *m.*
attend, to beiwohnen
attend to, to besorgen
August August *m.*
aunt Tante,-n *f.*
Austria Österreich *n.*
Austrian Österreicher,- *m.*
au revoir auf Wiedersehen
automobile Automobil,-e *n.;*
    Auto,-s *n.*; Kraftwagen,- *m.*
auto trip Autotour,-en *f.*
avenue Allee,-n *f.*
awe Scheu *f.*

B

back Rücken,- *m.*,
    zurück, *adv.*
    at the . . . hinten
bacon Speck *m.*
bad schlimm, schlecht
bad luck Unglück *n.*
baggage Gepäck,-e *n.*
baggage compartment
    Kofferraum,-ˉe *m.*
baggage label Gepäckzettel,- *m.*
balcony Balkon,-e, *or*, -s *m.*

band (of musicians)
    Kapelle,-n *f.*
bank Bank,-en *f.*
banquet table Tafel,-n *f.*
barber Barbier,-e *m.*
barber shop Barbiergeschäft,-e *n.;*
    Barbierladen,- *m.*
basket Korb,-ˉe *m.*
bath towel Badetuch,-ˉer *n.*
bathroom Badezimmer,- *n.*
Bavaria Bayern
Bavarian bayrisch
be, to sein, *irr.v.;* befinden
    refl. st.v.
bean Bohne,-n *f.*
bear Bär,-en *m.*
bearer Überbringer,- *m.*
beat, to schlagen
beautiful schön
beauty Schönheit,-en *f.*
because weil, denn
because of wegen
become, to werden *irr. v.*
bed Bett,-en *n.*
bedroom Schlafzimmer,- *n.*
beer Bier,-e *n.*
before bevor *conj.;* vor *prep.*
beg, to bitten *st.v.*
begin, to anfangen *st.v.;*
    beginnen *st.v.*
beginning Anfang,-ˉe *m.*
behind hinten, hinter
believe, to glauben
below unter
beside(s) ausser, ausserdem
better besser
between zwischen
beverage Getränk,-e *n.*
bill Rechnung,-en *f.;* Schein,-e *m.*
    (money)
bird Vogel,-ˉ *m.*
birth Geburt,-en *f.*
bitter bitter
black schwarz
blank Formular,-e *n.*
bleach, to bleichen *st.v.*
bleak kahl
blessing Segen,- *m.*
blotter Löschblatt,-ˉer *n.*
blouse Bluse,-n *f.*

blue blau
board Brett,-er *n.*
boil, to kochen
border Grenze,-n *f.*
born geboren
both beide
bottle Flasche,-n *f.*
bottom Boden *m.*; Grund *m.*
    from the ... von unten
box (theater) Loge,-n *f.*
boy Junge,-n *m.*; Knabe,-n *m.*
brake Bremse,-n *f.*
branch Geschäftszweig,-e *m.*;
    Branche,-n *f.*
brassiere Büstenhalter,- *m.*
bread Brot.-e *n.*
    ... and butter Butterbrot,-e *n.*
breakfast Frühstück,-e *n.*
breathe, to atmen
brick Ziegel,- *m.*
bridge Brücke,-en *f.*
briefcase Aktentasche,-n *f.;*
    Mappe,-n *f.*
bright hell
brim Krempe,-n *f.*
bring, to bringen *irr. w.v.*
bring (with one), to mitbringen *st.v.*
broad breit
broken gebrochen, verbrochen
brother Bruder,-¨ *m.*
brother-in-law Schwager,-¨ *m.*
brown braun
brush Bürste,-n *f.*
buckle on, to festschnallen, *refl.v.*
build, to bauen
build up, to aufbauen
building Gebäude,- *n.*;
    Bau,-s,-ten *m.*; Bauwerk,-e *n.*
bulb Birne,-n *f.*
burned out ausgebrannt
bus Autobus,-se *m.*; Bus,-se *m.*
business Geschäft,-e *n.*
business trip Geschäftsreise,-n *f.*
busy besetzt
but aber, sondern
butter Butter *f.*
button Knopf,-¨ *m.*
buy, to kaufen
by von, bei, durch, zu
by all means unbedingt

C

cabaret Kleinkunstbühne,-n *f.,*
    Kabarett,-s *n.*
cabbage Kohl,- *m.*
cabin Kajüte,-n *f.*, Kabine,-n *f.*
    ... number Kabinennummer,-n *f.*
    outside ... Aussenkabine,-n *f.*
cage Käfig,-e *m.*
cake Kuchen,- *m.*
calamity Jammer *m.*
call, to rufen *st.v.*, nennen *irr.w.v.*
    to ... for abholen
    to ... up anrufen *st.v.*
called, to be heissen *st.v.*
calm ruhig
camel Kamel,-e *n.*
can können
capital Haupstadt,-¨e *f.*
car Wagen,- *m.*
card Karte,-n *f.*
carefree sorglos
careful, to be hüten *refl. v.*
careless vergesslich
carp Karpfen,- *m.*
carrot Karotte,-n *f.*
carry, to tragen *st.v.*, führen
    (a store)
carry over, to übertragen *st.v.*
carton of cigarets Karton
    Zigaretten
case Fall,-¨e *m.*
    in any ... jedenfalls
    in ... falls
castle Schloss,-¨er *n.*
cat Katze,-n *f.*
catch up on, to nachholen
cauliflower Blumenkohl,-e *m.*
cause, to bereiten, versuchen
center, Mittelpunkt,-e *m.*;
    Zentrum, Zentren *n.*
Central Germany Mitteldeutsch-
    land *n.*
century Jahrhundert,-e *n.*
certain gewiss
chair Stuhl,-¨e *m.*
    deck ... Liegestuhl,-¨ *m.*
    easy ... Sessel,- *m.*
chance Zufall,-¨e *m.*
change Veränderung,-en *f.*
change, to wechseln
change for, to umwechseln

character Wesen,-n, Charakter,- m.
charm Reiz,-e m.
charming liebenswürdig, reizend
chat, to plaudern
cheap billig, preiswert
check Scheck,-s m.,
check, to nachsehen, st.v.
... the luggage, to das Gepäck
aufgeben
... in, to absteigen st.v. (hotel)
cheek Backe,-n f.
cheerful fröhlich
cheerfulness Fröhlichkeit f.
cheese Käse,- m.
chicken Huhn,-ʺer n.
... fricassee Frikassee von
Huhn n.
... soup Hühnersuppe,-n f.
roast ... gebratene Huhn,-ʺer n.
child Kind,-er n.
childhood Kindheit,-en f.
chimney Schornstein,-e m.
china Porzellan,-e n.
chocolate Schokolade f.
choose, to wählen
Christmas time Weihnachtszeit f.
church Kirche,-n f.
cigaret Zigarette,-n f.
citizen Staatsbürger,- m.
city Stadt,-ʺe f.
commercial ... Handelsstadt,-ʺe f.
city hall Rathaus,-ʺer n.
class Klasse,-n f.
clean rein
clean, to reinigen
clock Uhr,-en f.
tower ... Turmuhr,-en f.
closet Schrank,-ʺ m.
clothes Kleidung,-en f.
used ... getragene Sachen
cloud Wolke,-n f.
be cloudy, to bewölkt sein
clutch Kupplung,-en f.
coarse derb
coat Mantel,-ʺ m.
cobblestone Pflasterstein,-e m.
coffee Kaffee m.
coincidence Zufall,-ʺe m.
cold cuts Wurst,-ʺe f.
collapse Zusammenbruch,-ʺe m.
collar Kragen,- m.
color Farbe,-n f.

comb Kamm,-ʺe m.
comb, to kämmen
combination Vereinigung,-en f.
combine, to verbinden st.v.
come, to kommen st.v.
... close, to nahekommen st.v.
... off, to losgehen st.v.
... out, to herauskommen st.v.
come in! herein!
comfort Bequemlichkeit,-en f.
comfortable bequem, gemütlich
commodity Artikel,- m.
common, in gemeinsam
company (commercial)
Gesellschaft,-en f.
compassion Mitleid n.
compartment Abteil,-e n.
complain, to klagen
complete ganz
complete, to vollenden
completely vollkommen
compose, to vertonen, komponieren
composer Komponist,-en m.
composition Vertonung,-en f.
confess, to gestehen st.v.
conflict Zwiespalt,-ʺe m.
congratulate, to gratulieren
connect, to verbinden st.v.
connection Verbindung,-en f.,
Leitung,-en f. (telephone)
conquer, to erobern
conservative solide
construct, to anlegen
content zufrieden
to be ... with begnügen mit
refl. v.
continue, to weitergehen st.v.,
fortfahren st.v.
contribute, to beitragen st.v.,
mitwirken
controversial umstritten
cook, to kochen
cookie Keks,-e m.
cordial herzlich
cordial Likör,-e m.
corner Ecke,-n f.
correct richtig
correct, to be stimmen
correspondence Korrespondenz f.
cost, to kosten
costume Tracht,-en f.
country Land,-ʺer n.

couple Paar,-e *n.*
course Gang,-"e *m.*
cousin Kusin,-s *m.*, Kusine,-n *f.*
   Vetter,-s,-n *m.*
cover, to bedecken
cow Kuh,-"e *f.*
cozy gemütlich
cream Sahne *f.*
create, to schaffen *st.v.*
cross, to kreuzen
crowded besetzt, voll
crown (of head) Scheitel,- *m.*
cuff Manschette,-n *f.*
culture Kultur,-en *f.*
cup Tasse,-n *f.*
curse Fluch,-"e *m.*
curtain Gardine,-n *f.*
custom (usage) Gebrauch,-"e *m.*
custom-house Zollamt,-"er *n.*,
   Zollstelle,-n *f.*
customs Zoll,-"e *m.*
   ... declaration Zolldeklara-
      tion,-en *f.*
   ... examination Zollrevision,-en *f.*
cut, to schneiden *st.v.*
cute niedlich

D

dance *n.* Tanz,-"e *m.*
dance, to tanzen
danger Gefahr,-en *f.*
dark dunkel
date Datum, Daten *n.*
daughter Tochter,-" *f.*
day Tag,-e *m.*
   days, for tagelang
deaf taub
deafness Taubheit *f.*
dealer Händler,- *m.*
dear teuer
death Tod *m.*
December Dezember *m.*
deck Deck,-e *m.*
deduction Abzug,-"e *m.*
deep tief
defeat Niederlage,-n *f.*
definite bestimmt
deliverance Erlösung *f.*
den (room) Herrenzimmer,- *n.*
dentist Zahnarzt,-"e *m.*
depart, to abfahren *st.v.*

department Abteilung,-en *f.*
department store Warenhaus,-"er *n.*
departure Abfahrt,-en *f.*
dependable verlässlich, zuverlässig
deposit Handgeld,-er *n.*
depth Tiefe,-n *f.*
desire Lust,-"e *f.*
desk Schreibpult,-e *n.*
dessert Nachtische,-e *m.*
destroy, to zerstören
develop, to entwickeln
devil Teufel,- *m.*
dictate, to diktieren
dictionary Wörterbuch,-"er *n.*
die, to sterben *st.v.*
different anders
difficult schwer
difficulty Schwierigkeit,-en *f.*
dig, to graben *st.v.*
diner (car) Speisewagen,- *m.*
dining hall Speisesaal,-säle *m.*
dining room Speisezimmer,- *n.*,
   Esszimmer,- *n.*
dinner Mittagessen *n.*
directly gleich
dirty schmutzig
discount Abzug,-" *m.*
   ... on bills Wechselgebühr,-en *f.*
dish Gang,-"e *m.*
dissatisfied unzufrieden
dissolve, to auflösen
distance Strecke,-n *f.*, Ferne,-n *f.*
distress Not *f.*
disturb, to stören
ditch Graben,-" *m.*
divine göttlich
do, to machen, tun *st.v.*
dog Hund,-e *m.*
dot Punkt,-e *m.*
dove Taube,-n *f.*
down unten
downstairs unten
   to go ... nach unten (gehen)
downward hinunter
drape Vorhang,-"e *m.*
draw, to ziehen *st.v.*
drawer Schublade,-n *f.*
dream Traum,-"e *m.*
dream, to träumen
dress Kleid,-er *n.*
dress, to anziehen *st.v.*

dresser Kommode,-n *f.*
dressing table Frisiertoilette,-n *f.*
drink, to trinken *st.v.*
drive, to treiben *st.v.*
driver Fahrer,- *m.*
druggist Drogist,-en *m.*
drugstore Apotheke,-n *f.*
during während
dwarf Zwerg,-e *m.*
dye, to färben

E

each (one) jeder
eagle Adler,- *m.*
ear Ohr,-s,-en *n.*
early früh
earnest ernst
east Osten *m.*
easy leicht
eat, to essen *st.v.*
eating Essen *n.*
eating house Speisehaus,-¨er
efficient tüchtig
egg Ei,-er *n.*
  fried . . . Spiegelei,-er *n.*
  scrambled . . . Rührei,-er *n.*
either . . . or entweder . . . oder
elect, to wählen
electric light elektrisches Licht
elephant Elefant,-en *m.*
elevated railroad Hochbahn,-en *f.*
elevator Fahrstuhl,-¨ *m.*
emigrant Auswanderer,- *m.*
emperor Kaiser,- *m.*
empire Reich,-e *n.*
enchant, to bezaubern
enclose, to beilegen
encourage, to ermuntern
end Ende,-s,-n *n.*
end, to enden
England England *n.*
Englishman Engländer,- *m.*
engraver Kupferstecher,- *m.*
enjoy, to geniessen *st.v.*
enormous riesig
enough genug
enter, to eintreten *st.v.*
entire ganz
entrance Eingang,-¨e *m.*,
  Eintritt,-e *m.*

entrust oneself, to anvertrauen
  refl. v.
envelope Kuvert,-s *n.*, Briefumschlag,-¨e *m.*
equality Gleichberechtigung *f.*
especially besonders
Europe Europa *n.*
even sogar
evening Abend,-e *m.*
  in the . . . abends, am Abend
everywhere überall
everything alles
evil Böse *n.*
exactly gerade
examine, to untersuchen
examination Examen,- *n.*,
  Untersuchung,-en *f.* (medical)
excellent ausgezeichnet
except ausser
exchange, to austauschen
excited aufgeregt
excuse, to entschuldigen,
  verzeihen *st.v.*
exert, to ausüben
exhausted erschöpft
exist, to bestehen *st.v.*, existieren
exit Ausgang,-¨ *m.*
expect, to erwarten
expensive teuer
experience, to erfahren *st.v.*,
  erleben
experienced erfahren
explain, to erklären
explanation Erklärung,-en *f.*
export Ausfuhr,-en *f.*
export, to exportieren
express train Schnellzug,-¨e *m.*,
  D-Zug,-¨e (Durchgangszug) *m.*
expression Ausdruck,-¨e *m.*
extraordinary ausserordentlich
eye Auge,-s,-n *n.*
eyebrow Augenbraue,-n *f.*

F

face Gesicht,-e *n.*
fall (season) Herbst,-e *m.*
fall, to fallen
  to . . . apart auseinanderfallen
  st.v.
  to . . . out herausfallen

false falsch
familiar bekannt
famous berühmt
far weit, fern
farmer Bauer,-s,-n *m.*
fast schnell
  to be . . . (watch) vorgehen
fasten, to festschnallen, *refl. v.*
fate Schicksal,-e *n.*
father Vater,-" *m.*
father-in-law Schwiegervater,-" *m.*
fear Angst,-"e *f.*
fear, to fürchten
feather Feder,-n *f.*
feature Gepräge,- *n.*
February Februar,-e *m.*
fee Gebühr,-en *f.*, Honorar,-e *n.*
  (physician's)
feel, to fühlen, empfinden *st.v.*,
  sich fühlen
fellow Kerl,-e *m.*
ferris wheel Riesenrad,-"er *n.*
festival Festspiel,-e *n.*
fever Fieber *n.*
few, a few einige, ein paar
fight, to kämpfen
figure Figur,-en *f.*, Zahl,-en *f.*,
  Gestalt,-en *f.*
figure, to rechnen
fill, to füllen
fill (tooth), to plombieren,
  füllen, erfüllen
fill out, to ausfüllen
fill up, to auffüllen
filling (tooth) Plombe,-n *f.*
film Film,-e *m.*
finally endlich, schliesslich
find, to finden *st.v.*
finger Finger,- *m.*
finished fertig
fire Feuer *n.*
firm Firma, Firmen *f.*
  commercial . . . Geschäftshaus,
  -"er *n.*
first, at first zuerst, erst, vorher
firstly erstens
first name Vorname,-ns,-n *m.*
fish Fisch,-e *m.*
fishing village Fischerdorf,-"er *n.*
fit, to passen, sitzen, *st.v.*
flat tire Panne,-n *f.*

flee, to fliehen *st.v.*
flesh Fleisch *n.*
flight (stairs) Stock,-" *m.*,
  Stockwerk,-e *n.*
flight ticket Flugkarten,- *f.*
floor Stock,-" *m.*, Stockwerk,-e *n.*,
  Korridor,-e *m.*
flounder Flunder,-n *f.*
flower Blume,-n *f.*
folk song Volkslied,-er *n.*
follow, to folgen
food Essen *n.*
fool Narr,-en *m.*, Tor,-en *m.*
foot Fuss,-"e *m.*
for für *prep.*, denn *conj.*
forbid, to verbieten *st.v.*
forbidden verboten
force, to zwingen *st.v.*
forehead Stirn,-en *f.*
foreign language Fremdsprache,-n
  f.
foreigner Ausländer,- *m.*,
  Ausländerin,-nen *f.*
forenoon Vormittag *m.*
  in the . . . vormittags, am Vormittag
forest Wald,-"er *m.*
forget, to vergessen *st.v.*
forgetful vergesslich
forgive, to verzeihen *st.v.*
fork Gabel,-n *f.*
forks and spoons Bestecke *pl.*
form Form,-en *f.*, Formular,-e *n.*
formal förmlich
formerly sonst, früher
fortification Befestigung,-en *f.*
fortified befestigt
fortress Festung,-en *f.*
fortunate glücklich
fortunately glücklicherweise
founder Gründer,- *m.*
fountain Brunnen,- *m.*
fountain pen Füllfeder,- *f.*
fourth, a ein Viertel
France Frankreich *n.*
fraternity Verbindung,-en *f.*,
  Brüderlichkeit *f.*
free frei
free of charge gratis
free of customs duty zollfrei
freight Fracht,-en *f.*

freighter Frachtdampfer,- *m.*,
   Frachtschiff,-e *n.*
Frenchman Franzose,-n *m.*
fresh frisch
Friday Freitag,-e *m.*
friend Freund,-e *m.*,
   Freundin,-nen *f.*
friendly freundlich
friendship Freundschaft,-en *f.*
frightened, to be erschrecken *st.v.*
from von, aus
from all over überallher
from it davon
front, in vorn(e)
front of, in vor
fruit Obst *n.*
   stewed . . . Kompott,-e *n.*
fulfill, to erfüllen
full voll
function, to funktionieren
furnish, to möblieren
furnished möbliert
furniture Möbel *pl.*
further weiter
fuse, to verschmelzen *st.v.*
future Zukunft,- *f.*

G

gable Giebel,- *m.*
game Spiel,-e *n.*
garden Garten,-" *m.*
gasoline Benzin *n.*
   . . . tank Benzintank,-e *m.*
gas station Tankstelle,-n *f.*
gate Tor,-e *n.*
gather, to sammeln
gay lustig
gear Gang,-"e
gender Geschlecht,-er *n.*
general allgemein
generator Lichtmaschine,-n *f.*
gentleman Herr,-en *m.*
German Deutsche *m. & f.*
Germany Deutschland *n.*
get, to besorgen, werden, *irr.v.*,
   bekommen *st.v.*
get along, to vertragen *refl. st.v.*
get dressed, to sich anziehen
get in, to hereinbekommen *st.v.*,
   einsteigen *st.v.*

get off, to aussteigen *st.v.*
get rid of, to loswerden *st.v.*
get up, to aufstehen *st.v.*
giant Riese,-n *m.*
girdle Korsett,-e *n.*
girl Mädchen,- *n.*
give, to geben *st.v.*
give advice, to beraten *st.v.*
give change, to herausgeben
give in exchange, to einwechseln
give up, to herausgeben
give a message, to bestellen
glad froh
glad, to be sich freuen
gladly gern
glamour Schimmer,- *m.*
glass Glas,-"er *n.*
glassware Glaswaren *pl.*
glorification Verherrlichung,-en *f.*
glove Handschuh,-e *m.*
go, to gehen *st.v.*
   to . . . down hinuntergehen *st.v.*
   to . . . on passieren, vorgehen,
     st.v., weitergehen, *st.v.*,
     weiterfahren, *st.v.*
good gut
good fellowship Brüderschaft,-en *f.*
goods Ware,-en *f.*
gradually allmählich
grand grossartig
grandfather Grossvater,-" *m.*
grandfather's clock Standuhr,-en *f.*
grandmother Grossmutter,-" *f.*
grandson Enkel,- *m.*
grapefruit Pompelmus,-e *f.*
grateful dankbar
gray grau
grease, to ölen
great gross
greed Gier *f.*
green grün
greet, to grüssen
ground floor Erdgeschoss,-e *n.*
grown-up erwachsen
guess, to raten *st.v.*
guest Gast,-" *m.*
guest room Fremdenzimmer,- *n.*
guidance Führung,-en *f.*
gum Gaumen,- *m.*

H

hair Haar,-e *n.*
hair oil Haaröl,-e *n.*
hair tonic Haarwasser,- *n.*
hairdresser Friseur,-e *m.*,
    Friseuse,-n *f.*
hairdressing salon Frisiersalon,-s *m.*
half halb
    a . . . ein Halbes
    the . . . die Hälfte
hall Saal, Säle *m.*, Korridor,-e *m.*
ham Schinken *m.*
hang over, to überhängen *st.v.*
hang up, to aufhängen *st.v.*
happen, to passieren, geschehen *st.v.*
happiness Glück *n.*
happy glücklich, zufrieden,
    froh, fröhlich
happy-go-lucky leichtlebig
harbor Hafen,-ˮ *m.*
hard hart
hardly kaum
harmless ungefährlich
hat Hut,-ˮe *m.*
    felt . . . Filzhut,-ˮ *m.*
have, to haben *irr.v.*
he er
head Kopf,-ˮe *m.*
headache Kopfschmerz,-es,-en *m.*
hear, to hören
heart Herz,-ens, en *n.*
heartily herzlich
heaven Himmel,- *m.*
heavy schwer, derb
height Höhe,-n *f.*
help Hilfe,-n *f.*
help, to helfen *st.v.*
hem Saum,-ˮe *m.*
here hier
    . . . (direction to place) hierher
hide, to verbergen *refl., st.v.*
high hoch
highway Autobahn,-ˮen *f.*
hike Wanderung,-en *f.*
hike, to wandern
historical geschichtlich
history Geschichte *f.*
hold, to halten *st.v.*
hole Loch,-ˮer *n.*
holy heilig
homesickness Heimweh *n.*

hope, to hoffen
hope, I (it is to be hoped)
    hoffentlich
horrified entsetzt
horse Pferd,-e *n.*
hose Strumpf,-ˮe *m.*
hospital Krankenhaus,-ˮer *n.*
hotel Hotel,-s,-s *n.*
    . . . lobby Hotelhalle,-n *f.*
hour Stunde,-n *f.*
house Haus,-ˮer *n.*
    at the . . . of bei
    one-family . . .
    Einfamilienhaus,-ˮer *n.*
housewife Hausfrau,-en *f.*
how wie, wieso, woher
how many? wie viele?
human being Mensch,-en *m.*
hunger Hunger *m.*
hungry hungrig
hunt, to jagen
hurry, to beeilen *refl. v.*
husband Gatte,-n *m.*

I

ice cream Gefrorenes *n.*
ice water Eiswasser *n.*
idea Idee,-n *f.*
identification paper
    Ausweispapier,-e *n.*
if wenn, ob
imagine, to vorstellen *refl. v.*
immediately gleich, sofort
immigrant Einwanderer,- *m.*
import Einfuhr,-en *f.*
import, to einführen
importance Bedeutung,-en *f.*
important wichtig
impossible unmöglich
impress, to beeindrucken
impression Eindruck,-ˮe *m.*
impressive eindrucksvoll
impulse Trieb,-e *m.*
in in
in advance im voraus
inasmuch da
incline, to neigen
increase, to erhöhen
indulge, to hingeben *refl. st.v.*
inflammation Entzündung,-en *f.*
inflame, to entzünden

influence Einfluss,-"e *m.*
inform, to benachrichtigen
information Auskunft,-"e *f.*
information desk
   Auskunftsstelle,-n *f.*
inhabitant Einwohner,- *m.*
ink Tinte,-n *f.*
innocent unschuldig
insane geisteskrank
inspire, to einflössen *st.v.*
instead of anstatt
instill, to einflössen *st.v.*
instructive lehrreich
intellectual geistig
interesting interessant
interlock, to einhaken
interrupt, to unterbrechen *st.v.*
into in, hinein
introduce, to bekanntmachen,
   vorstellen, einführen
introduce oneself, to sich vorstellen
in vain vergeblich, umsonst
investigate, to untersuchen
invitation Einladung,-en *f.*
invite, to einladen *st.v.*
it es
Italian Italiener,- *m.*
Italy Italien *n.*

J

jacket Jacke,-n *f.*
jam Marmelade,-n *f.*
January Januar *m.*
jelly Gelee,-s *n.*
join, to anschliessen *refl., st.v.*
joint gemeinsam
joke, to scherzen
joy Freude,-n *f.*
jubilation Jubel *m.*
juice Saft,-"e *m.*
July Juli,- *m.*
June Juni,- *m.*
just ebenso
just now gerade
just so ebenso
just across gerade über

K

keep, to halten *st.v.*
   to ... a secret verschweigen *st.v.*
key Schlüssel,- *m.*

kill, to töten
kind freundlich
kiss Kuss,-"e *m.*
kiss, to küssen
kitchen Küche,-n *f.*
knapsack Rucksack,-"e *m.*
knife Messer,- *n.*
knight Ritter,- *m.*
knives, forks, and spoons
   Bestecke,- *pl.*
knock, to klopfen
know, to erkennen *irr. w. v.*
   to ... (a fact) wissen *irr. v.*
   to ... (a person, place)
   kennen, *irr. w. v.*
knowledge Wissen *n.*
known bekannt

L

label Zettel,- *m.*
lace, to einziehen *st.v.*
lady Dame,-n *f.*
lady's coat Damenmantel,-"
lake See,-n *m.*
lamb chop Hammelkotelett,-s *n.*
lamb, leg of Hammelkeule,-n *f.*
lamp Lampe,-n *f.*
land, to landen
landscape Landschaft,-en *f.*
language Sprache,-n *f.*
large gross
last letzt
   ... at endlich
last, to dauern
late spät
latest thing Neuste *n.*
laugh, to lachen
laughter Gelächter,- *n.*
lay, to legen
lead, to führen
learn, to lernen
least, at wenigstens
leather Leder *n.*
leather goods Lederwaren *pl.*
leave, to verlassen *st.v.*,
   überlassen *st.v.*
lecture Vortrag,-"e *m.*
left links
leg Bein,-e *n.*
lemon Zitrone,-n *f.*
lemonade Zitronen Limonade,-n *f.*

length Länge,-n *f.*
lengthen, to verlängern
less weniger
lesson Stunde,-n *f.*
let lassen *st.v.*
letter Brief,-e *m.*
    insured ... Wertbrief,-e *m.*
    air mail ... Luftpostbrief,-e *m.*
    registered ...
        Einschreibebrief,-e *m.*
    ... of recommendation
        Empfehlungsbrief,-e *m.*
lettuce grüner Salat
lie, to liegen *st.v.*
light hell, leicht
light Licht,-e *n.*
light, to leuchten
lighten, to blitzen
lighter (cigarette) Feuerzeug,-e *n.*
lightning Blitz *m.*
like wie (*prep.*)
like gern
like, to gefallen, *st.v.*, mögen
limb Glied,-er *n.*
limited begrenzt
line Leitung,-en *f.*, Zeile,-n *f.*
liner, ocean Ozeandampfer,- *m.*
lion Löwe,-n *m.*
listen, to hören
little klein, gering
little, a etwas, ein bisschen, wenig
little matter Kleinigkeit,-en *f.*
live, to leben (exist); wohnen
    (reside)
lively lebhaft, munter
    calf's ... Kalbsleber *f.*
living room Wohnzimmer,- *n.*
local train Personenzug,-"e *m.*
long lang
    as ... as solange
look, to aussehen *st.v.*
look after, to aufpassen
look around, to sich umsehen *st.v.*
look back, to zurücksehen *st.v.*
look up, to aufsuchen
lose, to verlieren *st.v.*
love Liebe *f.*
love, to lieben
lovely nett, lieblich
low (tire) schlapp
luggage Gepäck,-e *n.*

... office Gepäckannahme,-n *f.*
... rack Gepäcknetz,-e *n.*
lung Lunge,-n *f.*

M

main road Hauptverkehrsstrasse,-n *f.*
main street Hauptstrasse,-n *f.*
make, to machen, schaffen *st.v.*,
    tun, *st.v.*
man Mann,-"er *m.*
management Leitung,-en *f.*
manicure Maniküre,-n *f.*
many viel
many a mancher
map Landkarte,-n *f.*
March März,-e *m.*
mark Mark *f.*
marmalade Marmelade,-n *f.*
marry, to heiraten, verheiraten
    refl.v.
masculine männlich
master Herr,-en *m.*
masterpiece Meisterwerk,-e *n.*
match Streichholz,-"er *m.*
matter Angelegenheit,-en *f.*
    ... of taste Geschmacksache,-n *f.*
may mögen, dürfen
May Mai,-e *m.*
meal Essen,- *n.*, Mahlzeit,-en *f.*
means Mittel,-n *n.*
    by all ... jedenfalls
mean, to meinen, bedeuten
meantime, in the inzwischen
measure, to messen
meat Fleisch *n.*
meat broth Fleischbrühe,-n *f.*
mechanic Mechaniker,- *m.*
medicine Medizin,-en *f.*
meet, to kennenlernen, treffen
menu Speisekarte,-n *f.*
merry fröhlich
metropolis Grosstadt,-"e *f.*,
    Weltstadt,-"e *f.*
midday Mittag,-e *m.*
middle Mitte,- *n.*
Middle Ages Mittelalter *n.*
middleman Mittler,- *m.*,
    Mittlerin,-nen *f.*
midnight Mitternacht,-"e *f.*
mighty mächtig
mile Meile,-n *f.*

milk Milch *f.*
minute Minute,-n *f.*
mirror Spiegel,- *m.*
misfortune Unglück,- *m.*
miss, to fehlen
Mister Herr,-en *m.*
misunderstanding
  Missverständnis,-se *n.*
modern times Neuzeit *f.*
moment Augenblick,-e *m.,*
  Moment,-e *m.*
Monday Montag,-e *m.*
money Geld *n.*
monkey Affe,-n *m.*
month Monat,-e *m.*
monument Denkmal,-¨er *n.*
mood Stimmung,-en *f.*
more mehr
  ... than mehr als
morning Morgen,- *m.*
  in the ... morgens, am Morgen
mostly meistens
mother Mutter,-¨ *f.*
mother-in-law Schwiegermutter,-¨ *f.*
motion Bewegung,-en *f.*
motorboat Motorboot,-e
motorcycle Motorrad,-¨er *n.*
mountain Berg,-e *n.*
mountain lake Bergsee,-n *m.*
mountain top Gipfel,- *m.*
mouse Maus,-¨e *f.*
mouth Mund,-¨er *m.*
mouth wash Mundwasser,- *n.*
movies Kino,-s *n.*
Mrs. Frau,-en *f.*
much viel
  as ... as soviel als
  how ... wieviel
multiply, to multiplizieren
municipal städtisch
muscle Muskel,-n *f.*
music Musik *f.*
must müssen
mustard Mostrich *m.,* Senf *m.*
mutual gegenseitig

N

nail Nagel,-¨ *m.*
  ... polish Nagelpolitur,-en *f.*
  ... scissors Nagelschere,-n *f.*
name Name,-ns,-n *m.*

named, to be heissen *st.v.*
napkin Serviette,-n *f.*
narrow eng
nation Volk,-¨er *n.,* Nation,-en *f.*
native country Heimat,-en *f.*
naturally selbstverständlich,
  natürlich
nature Natur *f.*
near neben, in der Nähe
nearness Nähe *f.*
necessary nötig
necessary things(s) Nötige *n.*
neck Hals,-¨e *m.,* Nacken,- *m.*
necktie Schlips,-e *m.*
need, to brauchen
negate, to verneinen
neither ... nor weder ... noch
nephew Neffe,-n *m.*
nerve Nerv,-en *m.*
new neu
next nächst
next to neben
next door nebenan
nice nett
niece Nichte,-n *f.*
night Nacht,-¨e *f.*
  at ... nachts, in der Nacht
night table Nachttisch,-e *m.*
no nein
nobody niemand
nod, to nicken
noise Geräusch,-e *n.*
noon Mittag,-e *m.*
  at ... mittags, in der Mittag
north Norden
Norway Norwegen *n.*
Norwegian Norweger,- *m.*
nose Nase,-n *f.*
not nicht
notice, to bemerken, merken
notify, to benachrichtigen
November November *m.*
now jetzt, nun
number Nummer,-n *f.,* Zahl,-en *f.*
number, to numerieren

O

oatmeal Hafergrütze *f.*
occupy, to beschäftigen
occur, to einfallen *st.v.*
October Oktober *m.*

odd eigenartig
of von
...it davon
offer, to darbieten *st.v.*,
   anbieten *st.v.*
office Büro,-s *n.*, Kontor,-e *n.*
office building Geschäftshaus,-"er *n.*
office hour Sprechstunde,-n *f.*
office room Büroraum,-"e *m.*
often oft
oil Öl,-e *n.*
old alt
on an, auf
once einmal
once again nochmals
one ein, eins
one and a half anderthalb,
   eineinhalb
only einzig, nur
open, to aufmachen
opera Oper,-n *f.*
opportunity Gelegenheit,-en *f.*
opposite geradeüber, gegenüber
or oder
orange Orange,-n *f.*
orange juice Orangensaft,-"e *m.*
order Ordnung,-en *f.*
   ...to be in in Ordnung sein
order, to bestellen
order to, in um ... zu
originate from, to stammen aus
other ander
otherwise sonst
ought to sollen
out aus, hinaus
   ...into hinaus
outside aussen
   ...of ausserhalb
over über
   ...it darüber
over there drüben
overpowering überwältigend
own eigen
owner Inhaber,- *m.*

P

pace Schritt,-e *m.*
pack, to verstauen
pack (in), to einpacken
page Seite,-n *f.*

pain Schmerz,-es,-en *m.*
paint, to malen
painter Maler *m.*
painting Gemälde,- *n.*
   Malerei,-en *f.*
paintings, collection of
   Gemäldesammlung,-en *f.*
pair Paar,-e *n.*
pants Hose,-n *f.*
paper Papier,-e *n.*
parents Eltern *pl.*
park Park,-e *m.*
part Teil,-e *m.*
part, to sich trennen
participate teilnehmen *st.v.*
partly teilweise
partner Teilhaber,- *m.*
party Gesellschaft,-en *f.*
   Partei,-en *f.*
pass, to passieren, vorbeikommen
   st.v.
   ...an examination ein Examen
   bestehen
passageway Gang,-"e *m.*
passing vorübergehend
Passion Play Passionsspiel,-e *n.*
passport Pass,-" *m.*
paste, to kleben
path Weg,-e *m.*
pay, to zahlen, bezahlen
pay attention, to aufpassen
pay duty, to verzollen
paymaster Zahlmeister,- *m.*
peach Pfirsich,-e *m.*
pear Birne,-n *f.*
pea Erbse,-n *f.*
pencil Bleistift,-e *m.*
penetrate, to eindringen *st.v.*
penny Pfennig,- *m.*
people Leute, *pl.*, Volk,-"er *n.*,
   Publikum *n.*
pepper Pfeffer *m.*
perceive, to erkennen *irr. w.v.*
per cent Prozent,-e *n.*
perform, to aufführen
performance Vorstellung,-en *f.*
   Aufführung,-en *f.*
perhaps vielleicht
permanent wave Dauerwelle,-n *f.*
permission Erlaubnis,-se *f.*

permitted, to be dürfen
perpetual stetig
personal persönlich
perspire, to schwitzen
physician Arzt,-¨e *m.*
piano Klavier,-e *n.*
pick, to aussuchen
pick up, to aufnehmen *st.v.,*
  aufheben *st.v.*
picture Bild,-er *n.*
piece Stück,-e *n.*
pigeon Taube,-n *f.*
pinch, to drücken
pink rosa
pitcher Krug,-¨ *m.*
place Stelle,-n *f.*
  Ort,-e *m.,* Amt,-¨er *n.*
  Platz,-¨e *m.*
  ...of birth Geburtsstätte,-n
place, to stellen
place oneself, to versetzen *refl. v.*
plague Pest,-en *f.*
plain einfach
perish, to vergehen *st.v.,*
  untergehen *st.v.*
plan, to planen
plate Teller,- *m.*
platform Bahnsteig,-e *m.*
play Stück,-e *n.,* Spiel,-e *n.*
play, to spielen
pleasant angenehm
please bitte
pleased, to be gefallen
pleasure Vergnügen,- *n.*
plum Pflaume,-n *f.*
pocket Tasche,-n *f.*
pocket watch Taschenuhr,-en *f.*
poet Dichter,- *m.*
point Punkt,-e *m.*
Poland Polen *n.*
Pole Pole,-n *m.*
police Polizei *f.*
policeman Schutzmann (*pl.*
  Schutzleute) *m.*
poor arm
popular volkstümlich
porcelain Porzellan,-e *n.*
pork Schweinefleisch *n.*
porter Gepäckträger,- *m.*
possession Besitz,-e *m.*
possibility Möglichkeit,-en *f.*

possible möglich
  if ... möglichst
post card Postkarte,-n *f.*
post office Postamt,-¨er *n.*
potato Kartoffel,-n *f.*
  ...dumpling Kartoffelkloss,
  -¨e *m.*
  boiled ... Salzkartoffeln *pl.*
  fried ... Bratkartoffeln *pl.*
  mashed ... Kartoffelbrei *m.*
power Macht,-¨e *f.*
powerful gewaltig
praise, to loben
pray, to beten
prefer, to lieber haben, vorziehen
  st.v.
première Uraufführung,-en *f.*
premonition Ahnung,-en *f.*
preparation Vorbereitung,-en *f.*
prepare, to vorbereiten *refl.v.*
prepared bereit
prescribe, to verschreiben *st.v.*
prescription Rezept,-e *n.*
present Gegenwart
  for the ... vorläufig
presently bald
preserve, to erhalten *st.v.*
press, to drücken
pretty hübsch, nett
prevail, to herrschen
previously vorher
price Preis,-e *m.*
  raise the ... aufschlagen *st.v.*
private office Privatkontor,-e *n.*
probably wahrscheinlich, wohl
proceed, to abspielen *refl.v.*
promenade deck Promenaden-
  deck,-e *n.*
promise Versprechen,- *n.*
proverb Sprichwort,-¨er *n.*
proverbial sprichwörtlich
prune Backpflaume,-n *f.*
public öffentlich
pull in, to einziehen *st.v.*
pump up, to aufpumpen
pumpernickel Schwarzbrot,-¨e
pupil Schüler,- *m.*
purchase Einkauf,-¨e *m.*
pure rein
purser Zahlmeister,- *m.*
put, to legen, stecken, setzen, stellen

put on, to aufsetzen, anziehen *st..v*
put soles on, to besohlen

Q

quality Qualität,-en *f.*
quick schnell
quiet ruhig, still

R

radiator (car) Kühler,- *m.*
railroad Eisenbahn,-en *f.*
rain Regen,- *m.*
rain, to regnen
raincoat Regenmantel,-‥
raise, to heben *st.v.*
rampart Festungswall,-‥e *m.*
raspberry Himbeere,-n *f.*
rat Ratte,-n
rate of exchange Kurs,-e *m.*
rather lieber, eher, ziemlich
razor Rasiermesser,- *n.*
razor blade Rasierklinge,-n *f.*
reach, to erreichen, reichen
reach into, to hineinreichen
read, to lesen *st.v.*
ready bereit, fertig
real wirklich, echt
reality Wirklichkeit *f.*
realize, to verwirklichen
rear, in the hinten
rebuild, to aufbauen
rebuilding Neubau,-s,-ten *m.*
receive, to bekommen *st.v.*
recognize, to erkennen *irr. w.v.,*
   anerkennen *irr. w.v.*
recommend, to empfehlen *st.v.*
recommendation Empfehlung,-en *f.*
recreation Erholung,-en *f.*
red rot
redeem, to einlösen
rediscovery Wiederentdeckung,-en *f.*
refer to, to beziehen auf *refl.v.*
refreshing erfrischend
register, to einschreiben *st.v.*
rejoice, to freuen *refl.v.*
relate, to erzählen
relative Verwandte,-n *f. & m.*
reluctantly ungern
remain, to bleiben *st.v.*

remainder Rest,-e *m.*
remarkable sehenswert
remember, to merken *refl.v.*
remind one, to erinnern *refl.v.*
remote entfernt
rent, to mieten
repair, to reparieren
repairs Reparatur,-en *f.*
repeat, to wiederholen
report, to berichten
reputation Ruf *m.*
reserve, to reservieren
reside, to wohnen
respectfully hochachtungsvoll
rest Rast *m.*
rest, to ruhen, ausruhen
restaurant Speisehaus,-‥er *n.,*
   Gasthaus,-‥er *n.*
restless unruhig
retire, to zurückziehen   *refl. st.v.*
return Rückkehr *f.*
return, to zurückkehren
revenue officer Zollbeamte,-n *m.*
rice Reis *m.*
rich reich
ride, to fahren *st.v.*
ride around, to herumfahren
right recht, rechts
right away gleich, sofort
ring Ringe,-e *m.*
ring, to klingen *st.v.*
rip, to aufreissen *st.v.*
rise, to aufstehen *st.v.*
rise up, to hinaufsteigen *st.v.*
risk, to riskieren
river Fluss,-‥e *m.*
road Weg,-e *m.*
road map Autobahnkarte,-en *f.*
roaring schallend
robust drall
roll Brötchen,- *n.*
roller coaster Berg-und
   Talbahn,-en *f.*
roof Dach,-‥er *n.*
room Zimmer,- *n.*, Raum,-‥e *m.*
   single . . . Einzelzimmer,- *n.*
   back . . . Hinterzimmer,- *n.*
   front . . . Vorderzimmer,- *n.*
root Wurzel,-n *f.*
round rund
rowboat Ruderboot,-e *n.*

rubber Gummischuh,-e *m.*
rug Teppich,-e *m.*
run, to laufen *st.v.*
... around herumlaufen *st.v.*
rush, to stürmen
Russia Russland *n.*
Russian Russe,-n *m.*
rye bread Roggenbrot,-e *n.*

S

sailboat Segelboot,-e *n.*
salad Salat,-e *m.*
sale Ausverkauf,-"e *m.*
salt Salz,-e *n.*
salvation Rettung,-en *f.*
same, the ebenso, dasselbe
satisfied zufrieden
satisfy, to befriedigen
Saturday Sonnabend,-e *m.*
saucer Untertasse,-n *f.*
sausage Wurst,-"e *f.*
save, to erlösen
save for, to aufsparen
say, to sagen
school Schule,-n *f.*
scold, to schelten *st.v.*
sea See,-n *f.*
sea lion Seehund,-e *m.*
seam Naht,-"e *f.*, Saum,-"e *m.*
seaport Hafenstadt,-"e *f.*
search, to suchen
seasick seekrank
seasickness Seekrankheit *f.*
seat Platz,-"e *m.*, Sitz,-e *m.*
second zweite
secondly zweitens
secret Geheimnis,-se *n.*
see, to sehen *st.v.*
see again, to wiedersehen
seek, to suchen
seek for, to aufsuchen
seem, to scheinen *st.v.*
seem to, to vorkommen *st.v.*
seemingly scheinbar
self-portrait Selbstbildnis,-se *n.*
sell, to verkaufen
send, to senden *irr.w.v.*
send regards, to grüssen
separate, to trennen *refl.v.*
September September *m.*
serious ernst

serve, to dienen, servieren
service Bedienung,-en *f.*
Dienst,-e *m.*
set, to stellen, setzen
set upon, to aufsetzen
settlement Siedlung,-en *f.*
several verschieden, mehrere
several times ein paarmal
sew, to nähen
sex Geschlecht,-er *n.*
shade Schatten,- *m.*
shady schattig
shake off, to abschütteln
shall sollen
shape Form,-en *f.*
shaving brush Rasierpinsel,- *m.*
shaving soap Rasierseife,-n *f.*
she sie
shed, to vergiessen *st.v.*
shelter Unterkunft,-"e *f.*
site Lage,-n *f.*
shining leuchtend
ship Schiff,-e *n.*
shipment Sendung,-en *f.*
shirt Oberhemd,-en *n.*
shoe Schuh,-e *m.*
shine, to putzen
shoelace Schnürsenkel,- *m.*
shoemaker Schuhmacher,- *m.*
short kurz
shorthand Stenographie,-n *f.*
shorthand note Stenogramm,-e *n.*
shorts Unterhose,-n *f.*
shout, to rufen *st.v.*
show, to zeigen
shuffle (cards), to mischen
shutter Fensterladen,-" *m.*
sick krank
side Seite,-n *f.*
sight Anblick,-e *m.*
sights Sehenswürdigkeiten *pl.*
sign Schild,-er *n.*
significant bedeutend
silence Schweigen,- *n.*
silverware Bestecke *pl.*
similar ähnlich
simple einfach
simplicity Einfachheit *f.*
sin, to sündigen
since da (reason) *conj.*; seitdem
(time)

sing, to singen *st.v.*
sister-in-law Schwägerin,-nen *f.*
sit, to sitzen *st.v.*
sit down, to setzen *refl.v.*
size Grösse,-n *f.*
skirt Rock,-"e *m.*
sky Himmel,- *m.*
sleep Schlaf *m.*
sleep, to schlafen *st.v.*
sleeve Ärmel,- *m.*
slice Scheibe,-n *f.*, Schnitte,-n *f.*
slip (paper) Zettel,-*m.*
    . . . (clothing) Unterrock,-"e *m.*
slow (watch), to be nachgehen
small klein
small change Kleingeld *n.*
smile, to lächeln
smoke, to rauchen
smoking room Rauchsalon,-s *m.*,
    Rauchzimmer,- *n.*
snake Schlange,-n *f.*
snow Schnee,- *m.*
so so
so far soweit
so that damit
soap Seife,-n *f.*
sock Socke,-n *f.*
soft weich
soiled schmutzig
sold out ausverkauft
sole Sohle,-n *f.*
some ein bisschen, etwas
son Sohn,"e *m.*
song Lied,-er *n.*
soon bald
    as . . . as sobald
soul Seele,-n *f.*
soup Suppe,-n *f.*
south Süden *m.*
South America Südamerika
South Germany Süddeutschland
space Raum,-" *m.*
Spain Spanien *n.*
Spaniard Spanier,- *m.*
spare, to verschonen
spark plug Zünder,- *m.*
speak, to sprechen *st.v.*
specialty Branche,-n *f.*, Geschäfts-
    zweig,-e *m.*
specialty Geschäftszweig,-e *m.*
spectators Publikum *n.*

spell Bann,- *m.*
spend (time), to verbringen *irr. w.v.*
spill, to vergiessen *st.v.*
spinach Spinat,-e *m.*
spirit Geist *m.*
spite of, in trotz
splendid herrlich
spoon Löffel,- *m.*
spot Ort,-e *m.*
spring Frühling,-e *m.*
spring Feder,-n *f.*
square Platz,-"e *m.*
staircase Treppe,-n *f.*
stairs Treppe,-n *f.*
stamp Briefmarke,-n *f.*
stand, to stehen *st.v.*
start, to abfahren *st.v.*, starten,
    losfahren *st.v.*
state Staat,-s,-en *m.*
stateroom Kabine,-n *f.*, Kajüte,-n *f.*
station (railroad) Bahnhof,-"e *m.*
stay, to bleiben *st.v.*
steal, to stehlen *st.v.*
steamer Dampfer,- *m.*
steam ticket Schiffsfahrkarte,-n *f.*
steering wheel Steuer,- *n.*
stenographer Stenotypistin,-nen *f.*
step Schritt,-e *m.*
step, to treten *st.v.*
step up to, to herantreten an *st.v.*
stick, to kleben
stiff steif
still (yet) noch, doch
stimulate, to anregen
stimulation Anregung,-en *f.*
stitch, to nähen
stocking Strumpf,-"e *m.*
stomach Magen,- *m.*
stone Stein,-e *m.*
stop, to halten *st.v.*, haltmachen
store Laden,-" *m.*
storm Sturm,-"e *m.*
story Geschichte,-n *f.*
straight ahead geradeaus
strawberry Erdbeere,-n *f.*
stream, to strömen
streetcar Strassenbahn,-en *f.*
strength Kraft,-"e *f.*
strenuous anstrengend
street Strasse,-n *f.*
stretch, to strecken

strike, to schlagen *st.v.*, streiken
strive for, to streben nach
strong stark
stronghold Burg-en *f.*
struggle Kampf,-"e *m.*
study, to studieren
style Bauart,-en *f.*, Stil,-e *m.*
substantial solide
subtract, to abziehen *st.v.*,
  subtrahieren
suburb Vorort,-e *m.*
subway Untergrundbahn,-en *f.*
such solch
suddenly plötzlich
suffering Leiden,- *n.*
sugar Zucker *f.*
suggest, to vorschlagen *st.v.*
suit Anzug,-"e *m.*
suit, to passen
suitcase Handkoffer,- *m.*
sum Betrag,-"e *m.*, Summe,-n *f.*
summer Sommer,- *m.*
sun Sonne,-n *f.*
Sunday Sonntag,-e *m.*
supper Abendmahl,-e *n.*,
  Abendessen *n.*
sure sicher
surprise Überraschung,-en *f.*
surpise, to überraschen
surround, to umgeben *st.v.*
suspicious verdächtig
sweat, to schwitzen
sweater Sweater,- *m.*
Swede Schwede,-n *m.*
Sweden Schweden *n.*
sweet süss
swell, to schwellen *st.v.*
switch Schalter,- *m.*
switch on, to einschalten
switch off, to ausschalten
Swiss Schweizer,- *m.*
Switzerland Schweiz *f.*
synchronize, to synchronisieren

T

table Tisch,-e *m.*
tablecloth Tischtuch,-"er *n.*
tablespoon Suppenlöffel,- *m.*
tail light Rückenlicht,-er *n.*
take, to nehmen *st.*
take care of, to erledigen

take a rest, to sich ausruhen
take in, to aufnehmen *st.v.*
take off, to abziehen *st.v.*, starten
take out, to herausnehmen *st.v.*
take over, to übernehmen *st.v.*
take place, to stattfinden *st.v.*
tally, to stimmen
taste Geschmack,-"e *m.*
taste, to schmecken
taxi Autodroschke,-n *f.*, Taxi,-s *f.*
tea Tee *m.*
teacher Lehrer,- *m.*
tear Träne,-n *f.*
tear, to reissen *st.v.*
tear open, to aufreissen *st.v.*
tease, to necken
teaspoon Teelöffel,- *m.*
technical technisch
telegram Telegramm,-e *n.*
telegraph, to telegrafieren
telephone Telefon,-e *n.*
  Fernsprecher,- *m.*
telephone book Telefonbuch,-"er *n.*
telephone number
  Telefonnummer,- *n.*
telephone, to telefonieren,
  anrufen *st.v.*
tell, to erzählen, sagen
temple Schläfe,-n *f.*
tempting verlockend
than als
thank, to danken
thanks, thank you danke
that das *dem. or rel. pron.;* das *conj.*
that is das heisst(d.h.)
that much so viel
that one jener
the der, die, das
the . . .the je . . . desto
then dann
there da, dort
therefore darum
thing Sache,-n *f.*, Ding,-en *n.*
think, to denken *irr.w.v.*, glauben
third dritte
third, a ein Drittel
this dies
this one dieser
thorough gründlich
three drei
three times dreimal

throat Hals,-"e *m.*
through durch
thunder Donner,- *m.*
thunderstorm Gewitter,- *n.*
Thursday Donnerstag,-e *m.*
ticket Karte,-n *f.*, Eintrittskarte,-n *f.*,
    Fahrkarte,-n *f.*
ticket window Schalter,- *m.*
tiger Tiger,- *m.*
tight eng
tighten (a screw), to anziehen *st.v.*
till bis
time Zeit,-en *f.*, Mal,-e *n.*
  at that ... damals
  for the ... being vorläufig
timetable Fahrplan,-"e *m.*
tip Trinkgeld,-er *n.*
tire Reifen,- *m.*
tired müde
to zu, nach, bis, an
tobacco Tabak,-e *m.*
today heute
today's heutig
toe Zeh,-es,-en *m.*
together zusammen
tomato Tomate,-n *f.*
tomorrow morgen
  day after ... übermorgen
tongue Zunge,-n *f.*
too auch
tooth Zahn,-"e *m.*
toothbrush Zahnbürste,-n *f.*
toothpaste Zahnpaste,-n *f.*
tooth powder Zahnpulver,- *n.*
touching rührend
tourism Fremdenverkehr, *m.*
tourist trade Fremdenverkehr, *m.*
toward gegen
towel (hand) Handtuch,-"er *n.*
tower Turm,-"e *m.*
trace Spur,-en *f.*
traffic Verkehr *m.*
train Zug,-"e *m.*
  express ... Schnellzug,-"e *m.*
training Ausbildung *f.*
transcribe, to übertragen *st.v.*
travel, to reisen, fahren *st.v.*
travel bureau Reisebüro,-s *n.*
travelers' check Reisescheck,-s *m.*
traveling bag Reisetasche,-n *f.*
traveling companion
  Reisegefährte,-n *m.*

traveling experience
  Reiseerlebnis,-se *n.*
tree Baum,-"e *m.*
tributary Nebenfluss,-"e *m.*
trick (card game) Stich,-e *m.*
trip Reise,-n *f.*, Fahrt,-en *f.*
trousers Hose,-n *f.*
trout Forelle,-n *f.*
true wahr
truly yours hochachtungsvoll
trump Trumpf,-"e *m.*
trunk Koffer,- *m.*
try, to versuchen
try out, to ausprobieren
Tuesday Dienstag,-e *m.*
turn (road) Biegung,-en *f.*
turn, to umdrehen *refl.v.*
turn into, to einbiegen *st.v.*
turn off, to ausschalten
turn on, to einschalten
twice zweimal
two zwei
two and a half zweieinhalb
type Art,-en *f.*
typewriter Schreibmaschine,-n *f.*

U

ugly hässlich
umbrella Regenschirm,-e *m.*
uncle Onkel,- *m.*
uncomfortable ungemütlich
under unter
undershirt Unterhemd,-en *n.*
understand, to erkennen *irr.w.v.*,
  verstehen, *st.v.*
undertake, to unternehmen *st.v.*
understanding Erkenntnis,-se *f.*
underwear Wäsche, Unterwäsche *pl.*
uneven holprig
unfinished unvollendet
unforgettable unvergesslich
unfortunately leider
unhappy unglücklich
unique einzigartig
unit Einheit,-en *f.*
unite, to vereinen
United States Vereinigten
  Staaten *pl.*
unlock, to aufschliessen *st.v.*
unmarried ledig
unpack, to auspacken

unpleasant unangenehm
until bis
unwillingly ungern
up oben,auf
up to now bisher
upon auf
upstairs oben
upstairs, to go nach oben (gehen)
upward hinauf
use Gebrauch *m.*
use, to gebrauchen, benutzen,
    verwenden *irr. w.*

V

valley Tal,-̈er *n.*
valuables Wertsachen *pl.*
value Wert,-e *m.*
veal Kalbfleisch *n.*
very sehr, recht, ganz
vest Weste,-n *f.*
vicinity Umgebung,-en *f.*
victim Opfer,- *n.*
view Anblick,-e *m.*
vigorous tüchtig
village Dorf,-̈er *n.*
vinegar Essig *m.*
visit Besuch,-e *m.*
visit, to besuchen
vow Gelübde,- *n.*
vow, to geloben
voyage Reise,-n *f.*

W

waist Taille,-n *f.*
wait, to warten
waiter Kellner,- *m.*
waiting room Wartesaal,-säle, *m.,*
    Wartezimmer,- *n.*
waitress Kellnerin,-nen *f.*
wake up, to aufwachen
walk, to gehen *st.v.,* zu Fuss gehen
wall (outside) Mauer,-n *f.*
waltz Walzer,- *m.*
want, to wollen
war Krieg,-e *m.*
    world ... Weltkrieg,-e *m.*
wardrobe Garderobe,-n *f.,*
    Kleiderschrank,-̈e *m.*
wash, to waschen *st.v.*
watch, to beobachten, aufpassen

watch Uhr,-en *f.*
watchmaker Uhrmacher,- *m.*
watch spring Uhrfeder,-n *f.*
water Wasser *n.*
wave, to winken
way Weg,-e *m.*
way back Rückweg,-e *m.*
way through Durchgang,-̈e *m.*
wealth Reichtum,-̈er *m.*
wear, to tragen *st.v.*
wear out, to abnützen
weather Wetter,- *n.*
wedding trip Hochzeitsreise,-n *f.*
Wednesday Mittwoch,-e *m.*
weed Unkraut,- *n.*
week Woche,-n *f.*
welcome willkommen
welcome, you are bitte (*after* danke)
well gut, wohl
    as ... as sowie
west Westen *m.*
what was
    of ... worüber
when wann, *int.,* als *conj.,*
    wenn *conj.*
whence woher
where wo
    ... to wohin
whereupon woraufhin
whether ob
which das, welch
while während *conj.,* indem
while Weile,-n *f.*
whisper, to flüstern
whistle Pfeife,-n *f.*
white weiss
who wer *int.,* der *rel.pro.*
whoever wer
why wieso, warum, weshalb
wide breit, weit
wife Frau,-en *f.* Gemahlin,-nen *f.*
will Wille,-ns,-n *m.*
wind (watch), to aufziehen
wind Wind,-e *m.*
winding krumm
window Fenster,- *n.*
wine Wein,-e *m.*
winged beschwingt
winter Winter,- *m.*
wisdom Weisheit *f.*
wish, to wünschen, wollen

with mit
within innerhalb
without ohne
woman Frau,-en *f.*
wonder Wunder,- *n.*
wonderful wunderbar
word Wort,-"er *n.*
work Arbeit,-en *f.*
work, to arbeiten
work of art Kunstwerk,-e *n.*
works Werk,-e *n.*
  ... of a watch Uhrwerk,-e *n.*
workshop Werkstatt,-"en *f.*
world Welt,-en *f.*
worn down schiefgetreten
worry, to sorgen
worth Wert,-e *m.*
worth the money preiswert
wrist watch Armbanduhr,-en *f.*
write to schreiben *st.v.*

write down, to aufschreiben *st.v.*
write shorthand, to stenographieren
wrong verkehrt
  to be ... (watch) falsch gehen

X Y Z

X-ray photograph
  Röntgenaufnahme,-n *f.*
year Jahr,-e *n.*
yes ja
yesterday gestern
  day before ... vorgestern
yet noch, doch
yonder drüben
young jung
youth (period of life) Jugend,- *f.*
youth (person) Junge,-n *m.*
your health! Prosit (Prost)!
zoo Zoo,- *m.*